DEBATING THE HUNDRED YEARS WAR: *POUR CE QUE PLUSIEURS (LA LOY SALICQUE)* AND *A DECLARACION OF THE TREW AND DEWE TITLE OF HENRY VIII*

DEBATING THE HUNDRED YEARS WAR: *POUR CE QUE PLUSIEURS (LA LOY SALICQUE)* AND *A DECLARACION OF THE TREW AND DEWE TITLE OF HENRY VIII*

edited by
CRAIG TAYLOR

CAMDEN FIFTH SERIES
Volume 29

CAMBRIDGE
UNIVERSITY PRESS

FOR THE ROYAL HISTORICAL SOCIETY
University College London, Gower Street, London WC1 6BT
2006

Published by the Press Syndicate of the University of Cambridge
The Edinburgh Building, Cambridge CB2 8RU, United Kingdom
32 Avenue of the Americas, New York, NY 10013-2473, USA
477 Williamstown Road, Port Melbourne, VIC 3207, Australia
Ruiz de Alarcón 13, 28014 Madrid, Spain
Dock House, The Waterfront, Cape Town 8001, South Africa

First published 2006

A catalogue record for this book is available from the British Library
Library of Congress Cataloging-in-Publication Data applied for

ISBN 0 521 87390 8 hardback

SUBSCRIPTIONS. The serial publications of the Royal Historical Society, *Royal Historical Society Transactions* (ISSN 0080–4401) and Camden Fifth Series (ISSN 0960–1163) volumes, may be purchased together on annual subscription. The 2006 subscription price, which includes print and electronic access (but not VAT), is £84 (US $136 in the USA, Canada and Mexico) and includes Camden Fifth Series, volumes 28 and 29 (published in July and December) and Transactions Sixth Series, volume 16 (published in December). Japanese prices are available from Kinokuniya Company Ltd, P.O. Box 55, Chitose, Tokyo 156, Japan. EU subscribers (outside the UK) who are not registered for VAT should add VAT at their country's rate. VAT registered subscribers should provide their VAT registration number. Prices include delivery by air.

Subscription orders, which must be accompanied by payment, may be sent to a bookseller, subscription agent or direct to the publisher: Cambridge University Press, The Edinburgh Building, Shaftesbury Road, Cambridge CB2 2RU, UK; or in the USA, Canada and Mexico: Cambridge University Press, Journals Fulfillment Department, 100 Brook Hill Drive, West Nyack, New York, 10994–2133, USA.

SINGLE VOLUMES AND BACK VOLUMES. A list of Royal Historical Society volumes available from Cambridge University Press may be obtained from the Humanities Marketing Department at the address above.

Printed and bound in the United Kingdom at the University Press, Cambridge

CONTENTS

LIST OF ILLUSTRATIONS

ACKNOWLEDGEMENTS

This book offers the first scholarly edition of *Pour ce que plusieurs*, a French treatise on the legal debates that underpinned the Hundred Years War. It was written in 1464, perhaps by Guillaume Cousinot II, and survives in twenty manuscripts; it was also printed at least eleven times by 1558, most commonly under the title *La Loy Salicque, première loy des françois*. One of those books fell into the hands of an anonymous English customs official, perhaps from Ipswich, who composed an extremely detailed reply which he called *A declaracion of the trew and dewe title of Henry VIII*. This work did not enjoy the same success, surviving in just two autograph manuscripts, together with a seventeenth-century transcription of the presentation copy. As a result, this unique and important treatise has received no attention from historians.

The research for this book was completed in two stages. I originally prepared an edition of *Pour ce que plusieurs* as an appendix to my DPhil at Oxford University ("'La querelle Anglaise'": diplomatic and legal debate during the Hundred Years War'), funded by a British Academy research studentship, the A.M.P. Reid studentship awarded by the Modern History Faculty, and a grant from the Richard III Society. During the course of that research, I looked at a range of manuscripts containing English discussions of the legal issues of the Hundred Years War and came across the manuscripts containing *A declaracion of the trew and dewe title of Henry VIII* in the British Library and the College of Arms. Thanks to my detailed knowledge of *Pour ce que plusieurs*, I instantly realized that the English treatise was directly quoting from, and responding to, the French text. A number of years later, I was able to return to this puzzle thanks to the research leave granted to me by the University of York in the form of an Anniversary Lectureship. In addition, the British Academy provided me with a Small Research Grant from the Neil Ker fund to enable me to complete my work on the manuscripts in London, Paris, Brussels, and Lille.

My doctoral research was supervised by Peter S. Lewis who gave me tremendous advice and support throughout this project. I might never have discovered the Tudor treatise but for Pierre Chaplais who provided me with a number of manuscript references to chase up, drawing upon research originally carried out by the late John Ferguson. I would also like to thank Ian Archer, Françoise Autrand, James Binns, James Campbell, Antonio de Castro Henriques, Gabriella Corona, Gregory

Clark, Kathleen Daly, Cliff Davies, Jean Dunbabin, Steven Gunn, Ralph Hanna, Richard Helmholz, Michael C.E. Jones, Michael K. Jones, Maryanne Kowaleski, Linne Mooney, Richard Mortimer, Catherine Nall, Suzie Nash, Marigold Anne Norbye, Christopher Norton, Mark Ormrod, David Palliser, Andrew Pettegree, Nicole Pons, Daniel Power, Gareth Prosser, Peter Rycraft, Richard Sharpe, Emmitt Smith, Elizabeth Tyler, and Jocelyn Wogan-Browne for their advice and assistance at various stages of this research. I would particularly like to thank Peggy Brown for checking some information in the Bibliothèque Nationale de France at the very last stage of this project.

Images are reproduced by permission of the Bibliothèque Nationale de France and the Bibliothèque Royale de Belgique. I am extremely grateful for the assistance and cooperation of the staff of those libraries as well as the College of Arms, the British Library, the Bodleian Library, the Codrington Library, the Brotherton Library, the Bibliothèque Municipale of Lille, the Österreichische Nationalbibliothek, and the Biblioteca Apostolica Vaticana. Unfortunately I have not been able to gain entrance to the Biblioteca Reale di Torino in time for the completion of this book, though I would like to thank my fiancée, Gabriella Corona, and our Italian family and friends for their assistance in that challenging enterprise.

I would like to dedicate this book to the memories of my mother, Maxine Taylor, and of Lorenzo Corona.

York, 15 November 2005 Craig Taylor

ABBREVIATIONS

BL	British Library
BNF	Bibliothèque Nationale de France
BR	Bibliothèque Royale de Belgique
Beaucourt	Gaston Du Fresne de Beaucourt, *Histoire de Charles VII* (6 vols, Paris, 1881–1891)
Berners, *Froissart*	John Bourchier, Lord Berners, trans., *The Cronicle of Sir John Froissart translated out of the French by Sir John Bourchier, Lord Berners, annis 1523–25* (6 vols, London, 1901–1903)
Chronica Hovedene	Roger of Howden, *Chronica magistri Rogeri de Hovedene*, ed. William Stubbs (4 vols, London, Rolls Series, 1868–1871)
Chronicles of Monstrelet	Thomas Johnes (trans.), *The Chronicles of Enguerrand de Monstrelet* (2 vols, London, 1845)
Chronique d'Escouchy	Mathieu d'Escouchy, *Chronique de Mathieu d'Escouchy*, ed. Gaston du Fresne de Beaucourt (3 vols, Paris, 1863–1864)
Chronique de la Pucelle	Auguste Vallet de Viriville (ed.), *Chronique de la Pucelle, ou Chronique de Cousinot, suivie de la Chronique Normande de P. Cochon, relatives aux règnes de Charles VI et de Charles VII* (Paris, 1859)
Chronique de Monstrelet	Louis Douët d'Arcq (ed.), *La Chronique d'Enguerran de Monstrelet en deux livres avec pièces justicatives (1400–44)* (6 vols, Paris, 1857–1862)
Dudo of Saint Quentin	Dudo of Saint Quentin, *History of the Normans*, ed. and trans. Eric Christiansen (Woodbridge, 1998)
EHR	*English Historical Review*
EMDP	Pierre Chaplais (ed.), *English Medieval Diplomatic Practice, Part I: Documents and interpretations* (2 vols, London, 1982)
Flores historiarum	Henry Richards Luard (ed.), *Flores historiarum* (3 vols, London, Rolls Series, 1890)
Foedera	Thomas Rymer (ed.), *Foedera, conventiones, literae, et cujuscunque generis acta publica inter reges Angliae et alios . . . ab anno 1101, ad nostra usque tempora [1654], habita aut tractata* (2nd edition, 20 vols, 1727–1735)

Fortescue, *The Works*   John Fortescue, *The Works of Sir John Fortescue,*
                            Knight, Chief Justice of England and Lord Chancellor to
                            King Henry the Sixth, ed. Thomas [Fortescue]
                            Lord Clermont (2 vols, London, 1869)
Gesta Normannorum ducum   Elisabeth van Houts (ed.), *Gesta Normannorum*
                            ducum of William of Jumièges, Orderic Vitalis and
                            Robert of Torigni (2 vols, Oxford, 1992)
Grandes chroniques   Jules Viard (ed.), *Les Grandes chroniques de France*
                            (10 vols, Paris, 1920–1953)
GTGCA   Eugène Cosneau (ed.), *Les Grands traités de la*
                            Guerre de Cent Ans (Paris, 1889)
Jean Juvénal   Jean Juvénal des Ursins, *Les écrits politiques de Jean*
                            Juvénal des Ursins, ed. Peter S. Lewis (3 vols,
                            Paris, 1978–1992)
L&P   Joseph Stevenson (ed.), *Letters and Papers Illustra-*
                            tive of the Wars of the English in France during the Reign
                            of Henry VI (2 vols in 3, London, 1861–1864)
L&P, HVIII   John S. Brewer et al. (eds), *Letters and Papers,*
                            Foreign and Domestic, of the Reign of Henry VIII
                            (23 vols, London, 1864–1932)
Lettenhove, *Froissart*   Joseph M.B.C. Kervyn de Lettenhove (ed.),
                            Oeuvres de [Jean] Froissart publiées avec les variantes
                            des divers manuscrits (26 vols, Brussels, 1867–1877)
Lettres de Louis XI   Joseph Vaesen and Etienne Charavay (eds),
                            Lettres de Louis XI, roi de France (11 vols, Paris,
                            1883–1909)
Montreuil   Jean de Montreuil, *Opera,* ed. Nicole
                            Grévy-Pons, Ezio Ornato, and Gilbert Ouy
                            (4 vols, Turin and Paris, 1963–1986)
Morice   Dom Hyacinthe Morice (ed.), *Mémoires pour servir*
                            de preuves à l'histoire ecclesiastique et civile de Bretagne
                            (3 vols, Paris, 1742)
Narratives   Joseph Stevenson (ed.), *Narratives of the English*
                            Expulsion from Normandy, 1449–1450 (London,
                            1863)
Somnium viridarii   Marion Schnerb-Lièvre (ed.), *Somnium viridarii*
                            (2 vols, Paris, 1993–1995)
Le songe du vergier   Marion Schnerb-Lièvre (ed.), *Le Songe du vergier,*
                            édité d'après le manuscrit Royal 19 C IV de la British
                            Library (2 vols, Paris, 1982)
STC   A.W. Pollard, G.R. Redgrave et al. (eds), *A Short-*
                            title Catalogue of . . . English Books . . . 1475–1640
                            (London, 1926); 2nd edition ed. W.A. Jackson,
                            F.S. Ferguson, and K.F. Pantzer (3 vols, London,
                            1976–1991)

SIGLA

A	Paris, BNF MS français 5056
B	Paris, BNF MS français 5058
C	Paris, BNF MS français 12788
D	Paris, BNF MS français 15490
F	Paris, BNF MS nouvelle acquisition française 6214
H	Paris, BNF MS nouvelle acquisition française 20962
I	Turin, Biblioteca Reale di Torino MS L II 36
J	Paris, Bibliothèque de l'Arsenal MS 3434
K	Brussels, BR MS 9469–9470
L	Brussels, BR MS 12192–12194
M	Lille, Bibliothèque Municipale MS 322
N	Vienna, Österreichische Nationalbibliothek MS 3392
O	Città del Vaticano, Biblioteca Apostolica Vaticana MS Reginensi Latini 1933
P	Paris, Bibliothèque Mazarine MS 2031
Q	London, BL MS Additional 36541
T	London, College of Arms MS Arundel 39
W	London, BL MS Additional 48005

INTRODUCTION

Pour ce que plusieurs

During the fifteenth century, a series of French administrators and officials prepared polemical treatises defending the Valois monarchy against the rival claims of the kings of England.[1] The *notaire et secrétaire du roi*, Jean de Montreuil, composed two major works, *Regali ex progenie* (1406–1413) and the *Traité contre les Anglais* (1413–1416), that served as models for a series of texts that developed a coherent historical and legal defence of the Valois succession, prerogatives, and rights.[2] Jean Juvénal des Ursins drew heavily upon Montreuil's work for *Audite celi* (1435); he further developed his arguments in *Tres crestien, tres hault, tres puissant roy* (1446), written in response to a royal request that 'je me transportasse en vos Chambres des comptes, du Tresor de vos chartres, et ailleurs, pour veoir les lettres et chartres' and thereby compose a treatise for 'la convention que devés avoir avec tres hault et puissant Prince Henry vostre nepveu et adversaire, soy disant roy d'Angleterre'.[3] Another *notaire et secrétaire*, Noël de Fribois, prepared two chronicles, the *Mirouer historial* (1451) and the *Abregé des chroniques* (1453–1461), while his colleague, Louis Le Blanc, was almost certainly the author of a short treatise, *Pour vraye congnoissance avoir* (1471).[4]

Yet the most successful and widely circulated French polemical treatise of the late middle ages was *Pour ce que plusieurs*, which survives in twenty manuscripts and was printed at least eleven times between the 1480s and 1558, most frequently under the title *La Loy Salicque, première loy des françois*.[5] This treatise must have been completed between 1461

---

[1] Peter S. Lewis, 'War, propaganda and historiography in fifteenth-century France and England', in *Essays in Later Medieval History* (London, 1985), pp. 193–213, and Craig Taylor, 'War, propaganda and diplomacy in fifteenth-century France and England', in Christopher T. Allmand (ed.), *War, Government and Power in Late Medieval France* (Liverpool, 2000), pp. 70–91.

[2] Montreuil, II.

[3] Jean Juvénal, II, pp. 13–14 and, in general, I, pp. 145–281 and II, pp. 1–177.

[4] Noël de Fribois, *Abregé des croniques de France*, ed. Kathleen Daly (Paris, 2006), and Kathleen Daly, '*Pour vraye congnoissance avoir*: historical culture and polemic in the French royal *Chambre des comptes* in Paris in the fifteenth century', *Nottingham Medieval Studies*, 49 (2005), pp. 142–189.

[5] It has also been published under the titles *Discussion des differendz entre les roys de France & d'Angleterre* and *Pretensions des Anglois à la couronne de France*, while the copies in post-medieval

and 1467 because manuscript K is listed in a 1467 inventory of the library of Philippe le Bon, duke of Burgundy, while Louis XI (1461–1483) and Edward IV (1461–1483) are frequently cited in the text as being the reigning kings of France and England.[6] Two references in the first section of *Pour ce que plusieurs* may provide a more accurate date for the completion of the treatise. The author declared that the papacy, the church, and all the Christian princes had accepted Philippe VI and his five successors as the true kings of France for 134 years, suggesting that the current date was 1462 or 1463. A few pages later, the author reported that Philippe VI and his heirs up to 'le Roy Loys qui a present est ou V^e degré', had possessed the crown 'l'espace de VI^{XX} et XVI ans, c'estassavoir depuis l'an mil III^C XXVIII jusques a l'heure presente que l'en comte mil IIII^C LXIIII'.[7] Thus it is almost certain that *Pour ce que plusieurs* was written in 1464, that is to say between Easter 1464 and Easter 1465 according to the new style of dating.

The author explained that he was composing the treatise in order to ensure that 'chascun clerement et sans aucune ambiguité ou doubte puisse congnoistre et estre deuement informé du droit que les parties en chascune desdictez matieres puet avoir et reclamer l'une a l'encontre de l'autre et les solutions aussi et justifications dont elles se puent deffendre'.[8] Such statements were common in the polemical treatises written by royal officials, even though such works were primarily intended for a more closed audience of fellow diplomats and administrators.[9] Indeed it seems most likely that *Pour ce que plusieurs* was written to provide information for French diplomats attending negotiations at Saint-Omer in 1464. On 8 October 1463,

---

manuscripts have been catalogued as the *Traicté des différends entre les roys de France et d'Angeleterre, dédié au roy Louis XI* and the *Traité contre les prétentions des Anglais à la couronne de France* (see pp. 289–290). Colette Beaune has referred to the treatise as both *La grand traité sur la Loi Salique* and *La grand traité de 1450*, in *The Birth of an Ideology: myths and symbols of nationhood in later medieval France* (Berkeley, 1992), pp. 254–264 and 349–350.

[6] See pp. 73, 78, 83, 111, 132, and 282 below. When citing the descendants of Edward III, the author referred to the 'conte de Staffort derrainement mort lequel avoit esté fait duc de Boguinquam', that is to say Humphrey, duke of Buckingham, who had died in 1460 (see page 75). Also see Appendix III, pp. 291–292.

[7] See pp. 78 and 83. The date 1464 has been accepted by most scholars: Georges Doutrepont, *La Littérature française à la cour des ducs de Bourgogne* (Paris, 1909), pp. 411–412; Joseph Calmette and Georges Périnelle, *Louis XI et Angleterre, 1461–1483* (Paris, 1930), p. 59; Lewis, 'War, propaganda and historiography', p. 204; Kathleen Daly, 'The *Vraie cronicque d'Escoce* and Franco-Scottish diplomacy: an historical work by John Ireland?', *Nottingham Medieval Studies*, 35 (1991), p. 122. Colette Beaune has confusingly stated that the treatise was written both in 1450 and between 1450 and 1464, without citing any supporting evidence, in *The Birth of an Ideology*, pp. 255–256 and 349.

[8] See p. 53.

[9] Taylor, 'War, propaganda and diplomacy', pp. 73–79.

Louis XI had signed the truce of Hesdin with Edward IV, and a second meeting was scheduled to be held at Saint-Omer in April 1464 in order to arrange a marriage between the English king and a French princess. That summit was subsequently delayed until 1 July and then 1 October, because domestic problems made it impossible for Edward IV to keep the appointment, at least according to the English ambassadors.[10] *Pour ce que plusieurs* may have served as a briefing paper for the French diplomats, or possibly even Louis XI himself; the king had certainly taken an active role in the previous negotiations at Saint-Omer in autumn 1463, as well as in July 1464.[11] The value of such detailed information was clear given the continued debate over English claims in France. The Yorkist Edward IV may have been keen to ensure that Louis XI did not support the Lancastrians, but that did not mean that he was willing to renounce ancient English claims. John Wenlock and the embassy sent to the continent in 1462 had been instructed to cite the rights of the kings of England to the crown of France, and to seek the return of the duchies of Normandy and Guyenne, together with the counties of Maine and Anjou.[12] Faced by such demands, French diplomats might have turned to Jean Juvénal's *Tres crestien, tres hault, tres puissant roy*, but that treatise had implicitly supported the Yorkist claim to the French throne and, more relevantly, said nothing about the French reconquest of Normandy and Guyenne between 1449 and 1453. Indeed, Charles VII had written to Jean Juvénal himself, in the aftermath of the English attack on Fougères in 1449, calling for a written justification for the renewal of the war against the English.[13] Thus *Pour ce que plusieurs* updated and replaced *Tres crestien, tres hault, tres puissant roy*, providing a unique counter to Edward IV's title to not only the French but also the English crown, as well as a lengthy discussion of the breach of the Anglo-French truce in 1449.

There was another reason why an official French account of the events leading up to the recovery of Normandy would have been useful in 1464, namely the debate about French sovereignty over the duchy of Brittany. At that time, Louis XI's strategy was to circumscribe the duke's freedom to conduct an independent foreign policy by asserting that Brittany was part of the French kingdom and hence automatically subject to any alliance or treaty contracted by the king. Thus Duke François II was not explicitly named in the truce of Hesdin in 1463 and,

---

[10] Calmette and Périnelle, *Louis XI et Angleterre*, pp. 50–63, and also see Cora L. Scofield, *The Life and Reign of Edward the Fourth* (2 vols, London, 1923), I, pp. 305–307, 321–326 and 344–347.

[11] Scofield, *Edward the Fourth*, I, pp. 305–307 and 344–347.

[12] Calmette and Périnelle, *Louis XI et Angleterre*, pp. 14–15.

[13] Jean Juvénal, III, p. 79.

despite the protests of the duke, there was again no direct mention of
Brittany or its duke when the truce was extended to maritime affairs
on 12 April 1464.[14] There were clear echoes of the debates surrounding the allegiance of Brittany during the final years of the English
possession of Normandy. The new account of these events presented
in *Pour ce que plusieurs* argued that Brittany had rightly been included
on the French side in the prorogations of the truce of Tours from
1444 and 1449, despite the devious efforts of the English to claim the
overlordship of the duchy for their king. This dramatic story served to
emphasise the 'natural' loyalty owed by Brittany to the French crown.[15]
Of course, in practice Louis XI's strategy failed when Edward IV
negotiated an alliance with both François II of Brittany and Charles,
count of Charolais, son of Philippe of Burgundy. Moreover, Edward's
secret marriage to Elizabeth Woodville pre-empted any chance of a
French marriage to cement an alliance with Louis.[16]

There is additional evidence to connect *Pour ce que plusieurs* with
the diplomatic sphere. Firstly, the text appears in three manuscripts
with another work that was almost certainly written for diplomats, the
Vraie cronicque d'Escoce. This was a short treatise in French recounting
the history of the Scots from their legendary origins up to December
1463. It was almost certainly written by John Ireland, a Scotsman who
served as 'counsaloure, oratoire and familiaire' to Louis XI. It outlined
the history of Anglo-Scottish relations, highlighting the main points
of dissension, and thus provided French diplomats with background
knowledge and material to use when negotiating with either side.[17]
Secondly, two of the surviving manuscripts of *Pour ce que plusieurs* were
almost certainly commissioned by Louis de Bruges, who presented one
to Philippe le Bon before 1467, when it first appeared in the inventory
of the ducal library, and kept one for himself.[18] The lord of Gruthuyse
was a councillor and chamberlain to the duke of Burgundy and had
been closely involved in the complex diplomacy of the early 1460s. This
may explain how he managed to acquire *Pour ce que plusieurs*. Certainly
the world of the diplomat appears to have been imagined in the
miniatures prepared by the workshop of Guillaume Vrelant in Bruges

[14] Barthélemy-Admée Pocquet du Haut-Jussé, *François II duc de Bretagne et l'Angleterre (1458–1488)* (Paris, 1929), p. 84 and *idem*, 'Une idée politique de Louis XI: la sujétion éclipse la vassalité', *Revue historique*, 226 (1961), pp. 386–389.

[15] See pp. 116–134.

[16] Scofield, *Edward the Fourth*, I, pp. 350–353 and Mark H.A. Ballard, 'Anglo-Burgundian relations 1464–1472' (DPhil thesis, Oxford, 1992), pp. 26–27.

[17] Daly, 'The *Vraie cronicque d'Escoce*', pp. 130–133 and see pp. 23–24 below. *Pour ce que plusieurs* and the *Vraie cronicque d'Escoce* appear together in three manuscripts: F, H, and K.

[18] Manuscripts B and K, and see Joseph Basile Bernard van Praet, *Recherches sur Louis de Bruges, seigneur de la Gruthuyse* (Paris, 1831), pp. 5–10 and 252–253.

that decorate the frontispieces of these two sumptuous manuscripts. These images depict two officials engaged in debate while courtiers look on. There is no indication that this is a representation of the fictional debate between Edward III and Philippe VI described in the text, or even that the two sides are French and English. Rather this appears to be an acknowledgement of the connection between *Pour ce que plusieurs* and the world of diplomacy.[19]

The author of *Pour ce que plusieurs* was not identified in any of the surviving manuscripts.[20] Nevertheless, a strong circumstantial case may be made for Guillaume Cousinot II de Montreuil (*c*.1400–1484).[21] On 16 August 1464, Louis XI wrote to Charles de Melun, his lieutenant in Paris, authorizing Cousinot and Jean Dauvet to carry out archival research in the *Trésor des chartes*, the *Chambre des Comptes*, the Parlement of Paris, and the abbey of Saint-Denis:

> Nostre amé et feal, pour ce que nous desirons que à la journée qui se doit tenir entre nous et nostre trés cher neveu le duc de Bretagne, ou noz commis et depputez d'une part et d'autre, les droiz que nous pretendons audit pays de Bretagne soient clerement monstrez de nostre part, à ce que chascun puisse connoistre le bon droit que avons en ceste partie, pour ces causes nous vous avons ordonné faire voir et visiter en plusieurs lieux de nostre royaume tout ce qui se pourra trouver touchant ladicte matiere. Et entre autres avons ordonné que en nostre ville de Paris, tant ès registres de nostre cour de Parlement que au Tresor et en la Chambre des comptes, semblablement en l'abbaye de Saint Denis et partout ailleurs ès marches de par delà soit veu et regardé tout ce qui nous pourra servir touchant lesdictes matieres; et à ceste cause envoyons de present par delà nostre amé et feal Guillaume Cousinot, chevalier, lequel avons chargé avec vous de besogner et vaquer esdictes matieres. Si voulons et vous mandons bien expressement que vous et lui ensemble besognez esdictes

---

[19] It is possible that manuscript F also contained a miniature on the missing first folio; certainly the text is very close to that offered in manuscript B. A fourth manuscript, H, has a miniature which does represent a meeting between the kings and was probably prepared by Jean Roland III in the Loire valley. See figures 1–3, together with p. 282, n. 27 below.

[20] The treatise has been variously attributed to Claude de Seyssel, Jean Juvénal des Ursins, Jean Rogier of Rouen, and John Ireland, generally because of its association with their writings in manuscripts or printed editions. See, for example, Jacques Lelong, *Bibliothèque historique de la France, contenant le catalogue de tous les ouvrages, tant imprimez que manuscrits, qui traitent de l'histoire de ce roiaume* (Paris, 1719), numbers 7426* and 11760–11762; Pocquet du Haut-Jussé, 'Une idée politique de Louis XI', p. 388; Bernard Bousmanne, *Item a Guillaume Wyelant aussi enlumineur. William Vrelant, un aspect de l'enluminure dans les Pays-Bas méridionaux sous le mécenat des ducs de Bourgogne Philippe le Bon et Charles le Téméraire* (Turnhout, 1997), p. 230.

[21] Cousinot was created lord of Montreuil, near Vincennes, in around 1450. He should not be confused with his uncle, Guillaume Cousinot I, chancellor of the duke of Orléans from 1416 to 1438, who died shortly after 1442; see Auguste Vallet de Viriville, 'Essais critiques sur les historiens originaux du règne de Charles VII', *Bibliothèque de l'Ecole des Chartes*, 3 (1857), pp. 1–20 and 105–126, reprinted in *Chronique de la Pucelle*, pp. 15–33.

matieres en la plus grande diligence qu'il sera possible; et tout ce que vous trouverez faictes le mettre en forme deue et authentique, telle qu'on y puisse adjouster foi quand temps et lieu sera.[22]

This request echoed the instructions given to Jean Juvénal des Ursins in 1446, when he was asked by the king to go to the 'Chambres des comptes, du Tresor de vos Chartres, et ailleurs, pour veoir les lettres et chartres' in order to research and write *Tres crestien, tres hault, tres puissant roy* for the meeting with Henry VI.[23] The immediate context for Cousinot's research in 1464 was a dispute over regalian rights in Brittany, and the meeting referred to in the letter was probably the conference with the ambassadors of Duke François II, originally scheduled to take place at Chinon on 8 September 1464 and then put off until 15 October.[24] Nevertheless, research into 'les droits que pretendons au dit pays de Bretagne' would also have supported the impending negotiations with the English at the Diet of Saint-Omer, and provided Cousinot with the information necessary to write the crucial new section of *Pour ce que plusieurs* regarding the events between 1444 and 1449.[25]

There were few men with greater experience and understanding of the events and diplomatic negotiations that had preceded the recapture of Normandy. Cousinot had been 'l'agent principal des relations diplomatiques qui eurent lieu, pendant le cours des trêves, entra la France et l'Angleterre'.[26] He had travelled to England with two embassies in 1445, and represented Charles VII in the negotiations leading up to the handover of Maine and the subsequent discussions of infractions of truce, including the seizure of Fougères.[27] Indeed, Cousinot frequently acted as spokesman for Charles VII, including at the negotiations at Louviers in August 1448 and the conferences at Saint-Ouen and Vaudreuil three months later.[28] The extent of

[22] *Lettres de Louis XI*, X, pp. 218–219. On 29 September 1464, Louis XI issued a similar letter of credence for Cousinot, addressed to Dreux Budé, keeper of the *Trésor des chartes*. The king stated that Cousinot was carrying out 'aucuns matieres qui fort nous touchent, et pour lesquelles puet estre sera besoing de veoir au Tresor de noz chartres', and therefore asked Budé to provide him with all necessary assistance (*ibid.*, II, p. 219).

[23] Jean Juvénal, II, pp. 13–14.

[24] Philippe Contamine, 'Méthodes et instruments de travail de la diplomatie française. Louis XI et la régale des évêchés bretons (1462–5)', in *Des pouvoirs en France, 1300–1500* (Paris, 1992), pp. 147–167; *Lettres de Louis XI*, X, pp. 204–206.

[25] See pp. 116–134.

[26] *Chronique de la Pucelle*, p. 25. Cousinot also took part in missions to Scotland, Mantua, Savoy, Milan, and Rome. See *ibid.*, pp. 25, 29, 31, and 76–80; *Lettres de Louis XI*, III, pp. 116–118, IV, pp. 22–23, 100–101, and 155–156, X, pp. 288–289; Calmette and Périnelle, *Louis XI et Angleterre*, pp. 306–308; Beaucourt, VI, pp. 254–256 and 299.

[27] Beaucourt, IV, pp. 103, 163–165, 285, and 290.

[28] Morice, II, col. 1430 and BNF MS français 4054, fos 101r–110v.

his personal involvement in these events is amply illustrated by a manuscript that was completed after 1531, but which contains a remarkable number of documents relating to Cousinot and may represent a dossier that he himself had collected.[29] Included in this manuscript are documents concerning the embassy sent to London in June 1445 and the conferences at Evreux and Louviers in April and May 1446, all of which were attended by Cousinot, as well as two documents relating to the meeting of 31 July 1449 when Charles VII informed the English that the truce was at an end.[30] Even more significantly, the manuscript also included thirteen documents relating to François de Surienne, which may well be the 'deposicion' cited in *Pour ce que plusieurs*.[31] Although a direct connection between Cousinot and the dossier contained in the manuscript cannot be proved for certain, his personal involvement in these complex diplomatic relations, and his deep familiarity with the thorny debates, would have made him a natural choice to write a polemical treatise like *Pour ce que plusieurs*. After all, he had written a letter to the count of Foix on 25 September 1449, foreshadowing the material in the treatise.[32]

At the same time, Cousinot certainly had the detailed knowledge of English and Scottish affairs demonstrated by the author of *Pour ce que plusieurs*.[33] He had visited London in person in 1445, and spent another three years in captivity in England after being taken prisoner while returning from an embassy to Scotland in 1451.[34] In 1457, Cousinot was a member of an expedition led by Pierre de Brézé that raided Sandwich on 28 August.[35] Soon after March 1463, he was dispatched as an emissary to the exiled Lancastrian court in Scotland by Louis XI and returned to France via the Hanse, appealing for support for Henry VI against Edward IV, with whom the merchants had recently

[29] BNF MS français 4054, and see p. 17 below.

[30] BNF MS français 4054, fos 39r–v, 86r–91v, and 153r–157r. The record of the official inquiry into the attack on Fougères appears in Thomas Basin, *Histoire des règnes de Charles VII et de Louis XI*, ed. Jules Quicherat (4 vols, Paris, 1855–1859), IV, pp. 290–347.

[31] BNF MS français 4054, fos 111r–131r. *Pour ce que plusieurs* referred to the 'deposicion de Messire François de Surienne dit l'Arragonnois, executeur de laditte enterprise et de pluiseurs autres qui aidierent a icelle conduire', as well as the records of the negotiations of June and July 1449, which were prepared by apostolic and imperial notaries. See pp. 119 and 130 below.

[32] Beaucourt, V, pp. 437–444.

[33] See pp. 23–27.

[34] *Chronique de la Pucelle*, pp. 27–28 and 76–80, and Beaucourt, VI, pp. 132–133. On 7 April 1464, the cathedral chapter of Rouen recorded the thanks offered by Cousinot for prayers in support of him during his captivity in England. It seems most likely that this was a reference to the events a decade earlier, though Scofield has suggested that Cousinot was pretending to have been a prisoner at Bamburgh in order to protect Louis XI, who had promised in the truce of Hesdin not to support the Lancastrians: Scofield, *Edward the Fourth*, I, p. 324.

[35] Beaucourt, VI, pp. 145–146.

quarrelled. The next year, Cousinot rejoined Henry VI at Bamburgh, returning to France in February carrying detailed instructions from the Lancastrian king to his wife.[36] Indeed, Cousinot was certainly partial to the Lancastrian cause, as a member of the circle of René of Anjou and Pierre de Brézé, who led and organized most of the direct French support for Henry VI and Margaret of Anjou during the 1460s. This would certainly accord with the use in *Pour ce que plusieurs* of anti-Yorkist arguments similar to those employed by Sir John Fortescue, not to mention the strong assertion of the Lancastrian claim to the English throne and the silence regarding the murder of Richard II, a crime that had been strongly denounced by all previous polemical writers.[37]

Cousinot also had the appropriate skills to compose a defence of the rights of the French crown. Though little is known of his education, he had been appointed as a *notaire et secrétaire du roi* by 1438 and shortly afterwards became a *maître des requêtes*, the first president of the *Conseil delphinal* (later to become the *Parlement* of the Dauphiné at Grenoble), and, in May 1445, a member of the royal council.[38] Though it does not now seem likely that he was the author of the *Chronique de la Pucelle*, he did write the *Réponse à Robertet sur le départ de la belle Etiennette* (1469), a work in verse and prose that survives in one of the manuscripts of *Pour ce que plusieurs*, alongside a short history of the conquest of Normandy by Henry V. If the manuscript was prepared for Cousinot, as seems likely, then it is possible that he was not only the author of the *Réponse*, but also *Pour ce que plusieurs*.[39]

Cousinot was without doubt one of the most prominent figures in a remarkable effort by Valois administrators and diplomats to define and extend the prerogatives and rights of the crown under Louis XI.[40] He had certainly played an important role in the efforts regarding Brittany

---

[36] Scofield, *Edward the Fourth*, I, pp. 291 and 315–318, together with the instructions given to Cousinot in Jean de Wavrin, *Anchiennes chroniques d'Engleterre*, ed. Emilie Dupont (3 vols, Paris, 1858–1863), III, pp. 178–181.

[37] On the use of arguments from Fortescue, see pp. 24–26. The story of the murder of Richard II was widely known in fifteenth-century France: Craig Taylor, ' "Weep thou for me in France": French views of the deposition of Richard II', in W. Mark Ormrod (ed.), *Fourteenth-century England*, III (Woodbridge, 2004), pp. 207–222.

[38] *Chronique de la Pucelle*, pp. 23–24 and Beaucourt, IV, p. 411. There is no evidence that Cousinot continued to serve as a royal secretary during the reign of Louis XI: André Lapeyre and Rémy Scheurer, *Les Notaires et secrétaires du roi sous les règnes de Louis XI, Charles VIII et Louis XII (1461–1515): notices personelles et généalogiques* (Paris, 1978), p. 104.

[39] René Planchenault, 'La Chronique de la Pucelle', *Bibliothèque de l'Ecole des Chartes*, 93 (1932), pp. 55–104, and Jean Robertet, *Oeuvres*, ed. Margaret Zsuppán (Geneva, 1970), p. 33. The manuscript in question is C.

[40] I intend to examine this in a forthcoming monograph but see, for example, Contamine, 'Méthodes et instruments de travail', and *idem*, 'La mémoire de l'état: les archives de la

in 1464.[41] He subsequently spoke alongside other royal councillors at the Estates General at Tours in 1468, attacking the duke of Brittany and Charles of France, and also setting out the legal issues surrounding the status of Normandy, which Louis XI had been forced to cede to his brother during the War of the Public Weal.[42] Cousinot was also a key figure in the defence of Louis XI against the treasonous actions of certain of his subjects in the late 1460s and early 1470s. He served as one of the commissioners who condemned Charles d'Albret to death on 7 April 1473 for his involvement in the uprising led by Jean V d'Armagnac, and was one of the interrogators of Jean d'Alençon later that year, following the duke's arrest for plotting with Edward IV and the duke of Brittany.[43] In addition, in 1469, Cousinot served on the commission for the prosecution of Cardinal Jean Balue of Angers, who was charged with conspiring to form a league against the king. Because Louis XI wanted Pope Paul II to condemn Balue and Guillaume de Haraucourt, bishop of Verdun, Cousinot appeared before the curia in Rome in December 1469, where he successfully argued the case with the support of Pierre Gruel, president of the Parlement of Grenoble, and Guillaume Lefranc, doctor of laws.[44] An anonymous memoir presented the evidence for Balue and Haraucourt's guilt and also argued for royal authority over all traitors, even if they were clerics, supposedly subject only to the authority of their true sovereign, the pope. It certainly seems possible that Cousinot had had a hand in the writing of this important briefing memoir.[45]

Remarkably, Cousinot was still involved in the defence of the French crown as he approached his eightieth birthday. His expertise in the legal debates of the Hundred Years War was highlighted when Louis XI wrote to him in 1478. The king asked him to join Bishop

---

Chambre des Comptes du roi de France à Paris au XVe siècle', in *Des pouvoirs en France, 1300–1500* (Paris, 1992), pp. 147–167 and 237–250.

[41] See pp. 3–4.

[42] Summaries of the speeches survive in Archives Communales, Rodez, BB 3, fos 61v–66r; Archives Communales, Poitiers, carton 98, reg. 5, fos 115r–119r.

[43] In 1456, Cousinot went to Charles VII with news that Jean II, duke of Alençon, was conspiring with the English, and was then sent by the royal council to comission Dunois to arrest Alençon at Paris on 27 May, during the Nullification trial of Joan of Arc. He also attended the *lit de justice* convened to try Alençon in August 1458: *Chronique de la Pucelle*, pp. 83–86; Beaucourt, VI, pp. 59–61 and 188; and Simon Cuttler, *The Law of Treason and Treason Trials in Later Medieval France* (Cambridge, 1981), pp. 210 and 222–223.

[44] Henri Forgeot, *Jean Balue, cardinal d'Angers, 1421?–1491* (Paris, 1895), pp. 66–84 and 185–188, and Cuttler, *The Law of Treason*, pp. 64 and 74–77. For Cousinot's arguments before the pope on 15 December 1469, see BNF MS 10237, fos 126ff, MS français 10238, fos 202ff, and MS français 10971, fos 295r and 315r–345r.

[45] BNF MS nouvelle acquisition française 1001, fos 76r–82r.

Louis Raguier of Troyes, Bishop Pierre de Ranchicourt of Arras, Guillame de Corbie, Jean de Popaincourt, and Jean Havart in drafting materials very much in the vein of *Pour ce que plusieurs* for the impending negotiations with the English:

> Par quoy est besoing de faire dresser beaux, notables, grans et emples memoires et instructions pour bien fonder mes drois, mais respondre a tout ce que les Anglois vouldront pretendre, tant en la couronne de France, comme es pays et duchiez de Normandie et de Guyenne, et generalement a toutes les autres choses qu'ilz pourroient demander et alleguer, et commectre notables et grans personnaiges saiges, preudens et cognoissans en telles matieres, seurs et feables pour besoigner. Et pour ce que entre autres vous estes l'un de ceuls qui plus en avez veu, jay vous y ay espicialement ordonné et commis. Aussi y ay commis [the other five men]. Et a semblé le myeulx de vous faire tous assembler a Paris, que pour ce des choses qu'il sera besoing de veoir, tant en la court de Parlement, comme ou Tresor des Chartres, en la Chambre des comptes et croniques de Saint Denis et aillieurs, l'ou on pourra illecq plus aisement servir que autre part. S'y vous pry, Monseigneur de Monstereul, que le plus tost que vous pourrez, vous rendiez a Paris pour besoigner avecques les dessusdiz, pour besoigner en ladicte matiere le myeulx et plus meurement que faire se poura, et en maniere que se soit au bien et honneur de moy, du royaume, de la couronne, et me y servez comme je en ay vers la conscience.[46]

Shortly afterwards, Cousinot was called upon to assist in an even more pressing matter. Following the death of Duke Charles of Burgundy at the battle of Nancy in January 1477, Louis XI had tried to seize the duchy by force, despite the claim of Charles's daughter, Marie. The failure of these military efforts led to the opening of diplomatic negotiations in the summer of 1477. On 13 July, Louis XI informed the Parlement of Paris that he was commissioning agents to examine the archives in the *Chambre des Comptes*, the *Trésor des chartes*, and the Parlement itself in order to investigate the legal aspects of the case.[47] A month later, Cousinot responded to a request by the royal council for advice on the legal status of the Burgundian territories in a rushed letter written on 12 August 1478.[48] Later that winter, Cousinot led a group of royal officials in the preparation of a memorandum supporting Louis XI's pretensions to Burgundy and the county of Mâcon, responding to the defence of Marie's claim prepared by Jean

---

[46] The letter was written at Arras on 22 April 1478: BNF MS français 4054, fo. 240r, edited in *Lettres de Louis XI*, VII, pp. 31–33.

[47] *Lettres de Louis XI*, VII, pp. 112–114.

[48] BNF MS français 5041, fos 78r–79v, in Philippe de Commynes, *Mémoires de Philippe de Commynes*, ed. M. Dupont (3 vols, Paris, 1840–1847), III, pp. 315–320.

d'Auffay.[49] His contribution was acknowledged in a note at the end of one of the drafts: 'Intendit fait par feu M^c G^e de Cusinot'.[50]

Given his advanced years, Cousinot must inevitably have depended upon the assistance of his colleagues, though his involvement in the project is surely indicative of his expertise and knowledge. In this regard, it is significant that the memorandum itself is markedly similar to *Pour ce que plusieurs*, both in terms of rhetorical style and structure, and in the treatment of the central issue of female succession. Arguing that Burgundy could not be inherited by Marie because it was an apanage and hence subject to the same rules as the French crown itself, the memorandum rehearsed many of the points made in *Pour ce que plusieurs*:

> Nous voyons plusieurs royaulmez la ou les fillez succedent quant il n'y a enfans malez. Et toutesfoiz au royaulme de France elles n'y succedent jamaiz des le temps de la Loy Salique qui fut la premiere loy des Françoys. Et depuis a ceste gardé et observé sans infraction nulle. Et quant il y a en aucune contradiction ou question sur ce, il a aest tousjours dit que les fillez ne succederoient point, et que la couronne et le royaume vindroient au plus prouchain hoir male comme plus aplain il a esté dessus desclaré, en cas qui advint aprés le trespas du Roy Louys Hutin et de son filz qui ne vesquit que X jours, quant le royaume et la couronne vindrent a Philippe conte de Poitiers, qui depuis fut appellé le Roy Philippe le Long, et non pas a la contesse d'Esvreux, fille dudit Roy Louys Hutin. Et pareillement aprés le trespas du Roy Charles le Bel, pour ce qu'il n'avoit que une fille, entre Philippe conte de Valloys d'une part qui depuis fut appellé le roy Philippe de Valloys, et Edouart le Tiers le roy d'Engleterre, appellé le roy Edouart de Wynderose.[51]

---

[49] This attribution was originally proposed by Marguerite Milliez, 'La succession de Charles le Téméraire d'après deux mémoires contemporains' (2 vols, PhD thesis, Paris, 1941), I, pp. 94–99 and *idem*, 'La succession de Charles le Téméraire d'après deux mémoires contemporains', *Positions des thèses de l'Ecole des Chartes* (Paris, 1941), pp. 87–92. This has been supported by Kathleen Daly, 'French pretensions to Valois Burgundy: history and polemic in the fifteenth and early sixteenth centuries', *Marguerite d'York et son temps. Rencontres des Malines (25 au 27 septembre 2003). Publication du Centre Européen d'Etudes Bourguignonnes (XIVe–XVIe siècles)*, 44 (2004), pp. 13–14. Paul Saenger attributed the treatise to Michel de Pons but was unaware of Milliez's work: 'Burgundy and the inalienability of apanages in the reign of Louis XI', *French Historical Studies*, 10 (1977), pp. 13–26. Kathleen Daly is currently preparing a critical edition of these texts.

[50] Elizabeth A.R. Brown has advised me that the unusual term 'intendit' may echo the usage of the Parlement of Paris. The note appears at the end of two working drafts of the treatise in BNF MS français 5042, fos 105r–166v; Daly has suggested that there are autograph corrections to this copy, in 'French pretensions to Valois Burgundy', p. 14n.

[51] BNF MS français 5042, fos 131v–132r, and compare with pp. 56 and 63 below. The memorandum also denied the relevance of the *Libri feudorum*, both to the royal succession and to apanages, fo. 132v. The impact of these arguments upon Louis XI is demonstrated by his remark in 1480 that if women were permitted to succeed to Flanders and Burgundy, then Charles of Navarre or the king of England would have been ruler of France: *Lettres de Louis XI*, VIII, pp. 275–277.

The similarities between this memorandum and *Pour ce que plusieurs* 'reinforce the case that both were composed by Cousinot'.[52]

The extent of the challenge that Cousinot and his colleagues faced in defending the Valois monarchy was set out in a memoir written between 1478 and 1480 that was included in the manuscript associated with Cousinot.[33] It called for the preparation of 'beaulx livres a perpetuel memoire pour estre mis tant en la Chambre des comptes que ou Tresor des chartes'. The subject of these books would be 'les matieres qui touchent plus grandement le fait du roy et de la couronne de France' and which needed to be justified and defended in negotiations with England, Flanders, Brabant, Hainault, Brittany, Aragon, Castile, Scotland, and the papacy. First on the list was:

La querelle du roy al'encontre du roy d'Angleterre touchain troys poins.

La premier pour monstrer la justifficacion de la querelle du roy contre le roy d'Angleterre touchain la duchié de Normandie, la duchié de Guienne, la conté d'Anjou, la conté du Maine, la conté de Touraine, la conté de Poictou et la conté de Ponthieu qui souloient appartenir au roy d'Angleterre et par forfaicture et appoinctemens fais entre lesdits roys sont advenus au roy ou a ses predecesseurs dont il a la cause. Car les Anglois tous les jours auroit un question qui ne leur respondroit a cest article.

Le second est pour monstrer que le roy d'Angleterre n'a aucun droit au royaume n'y a la couronne de France et qui a bon et juste tiltre elle appartient au roy nostre souverain seigneur et non a aultre.

Item le tiers point de la rompure des treves l'an mil CCCCXLIX dont le roy d'Angleterre demande reparacion luy en estre faite actendu qu'elles avoient esté jurés sollemnellement par lesdits roys de France et d'Angleterre ou leurs ambastadeurs et depuis par lesdits roys confermées, approuvés, promisés et a accordées estre loyaument entretenues et gardées entre lesdittes parties. Et que a ceste cause le roy rende ausdiz Anglois la duchié de Normandie et la duchié de Guienne dont il estoit pocesseurs en temps tresves furent prinses entre lesdits deux roys. Sur quoy est bien besoing que la querelle du roy soit bien justiffiée car plusieurs en parlent hors du royaume en pluseurs manieres a la charge du roy.

These themes had been addressed in *Pour ce que plusieurs*, a work that had carefully outlined the response to English claims regarding the royal succession, territories within France, and the responsibility for

[52] Daly, 'French pretensions to Valois Burgundy', p. 15.
[53] BNF MS français 4054, fo. 241r–243v. Lewis suggested that this document was written in 1491 (Jean Juvénal, III, pp. 193–194), but Pons prefers the date of 1479 on the grounds that the materials in the manuscript are organized in a chronological fashion: Nicole Pons, 'A l'origine des dossiers polemiques: une initiative publique ou une demarche privée?', in *Pratiques de la culture écrite en France au XVe siècle: Actes du colloque internationale du CNRS* (Louvain, 1995), p. 364, and also see Daly, 'French pretensions to Valois Burgundy', p. 16n.

the breach of the truce in 1449.[54] Yet Cousinot's expertise in the other important areas was also apparent; he was more than qualified to address 'la querelle du roy touchant ce que le duc d'Autriche et le conte de Flandres pretendent avoir este fait par le Roy Loys al'encontre du traictie d'Arras, du traictie de Conflans, du traictie de Paris et du traictie de Peronne' as well as debates with Brittany.

The rewards for Cousinot's long service to Charles VII and Louis XI were great. Following his role in the recovery of Normandy, Cousinot was knighted after the recapture of Rouen and made bailly (until 1461), and the following year created lord of Montreuil, near to Vincennes.[55] Because of his close association with Dunois and Brézé, Cousinot was briefly imprisoned at the start of the reign of Louis XI, but soon recovered royal favour and was restored to the office of chamberlain in 1463, serving a useful role during the War of the Public Weal as well as in the negotiations with Brittany. As a result, on 20 November 1465, his pension of 600 livres tournois was increased to 3,000 livres per annum; on 2 June, he was appointed as *concierge* of the *conciergerie du Palais* at Paris, with a stipend of 1,200 livres tournois; between 1465 and 1468, he became captain of Cabrières in Languedoc, *châtelain* of Lates-lès-Montpellier, captain of Salses near to Perpignan, and, finally, governor of Montpellier and of the barony of Omellas.[56] These were fitting rewards for a lifetime of royal service. It seems extremely likely that *Pour ce que plusieurs* was the most enduring example of Cousinot's work.

Given that *Pour ce que plusieurs* was intended as an update to previous polemical works including *Tres crestien, tres hault, tres puissant roy*, it is not surprising that Cousinot built upon a core of arguments developed in those texts. Yet, like his predecessors, Cousinot rarely identified his sources, merely declaring that he was drawing upon:

anciennes cronicquez et histoires tant de France comme d'Angleterre, es lettres aussi auctentiquez et enseignemens vaillables fais esdittez matieres,

[54] The lack of reference to *Pour ce que plusieurs* in this document does beg the question of how far the treatise was in practical use by royal officials at the end of the 1470s. It is possible that the writer(s) were aware that the treatise could serve as the model for the 'beaulx livres a perpetuel memoire'. In this regard, it is important to note that, even though no official copy of *Pour ce que plusieurs* survives from the French royal archives, a seventeeth-century manuscript may be a copy of just such a text. See p. 28, n. 131 below.

[55] Along with Dunois, Brézé, Culant, and Floquet, Cousinot received 'soixante-treize muids de sel' from Mantes and Vernon for his service on the campaign to recover Normandy. He also received 600 livres tournois when he became bailly of Rouen in August 1449. See *Chronique de la Pucelle*, pp. 25–26, and Beaucourt, V, pp. 420–421.

[56] On 4 August 1469, Louis exempted him from the need to carry out all of these offices in person: *Chronique de la Pucelle*, pp. 29–31 and 81–82, and, for correspondence relating to his pension, see *Lettres de Louis XI*, III, pp. 135–136 and 178–179.

subjoingnant aux choses dessusdittez ce qu'il treuve conformé en raison
naturele et escripte, tant des drois civilez comme canons. Pareillement de
la Loy Salicque qui est la vraie loy des François, des usages aussy et coustumes
dont les François et les Anglois ont usé et usent tant en France comme en
Angleterre.[57]

As the instructions issued to Cousinot in 1464 and 1479 demonstrate,
the most important repository of historical knowledge in fifteenth-
century France was the abbey of Saint-Denis.[58] Renowned as a centre
for royal historiography, the abbey's connection with the crown was
reaffirmed by Charles VII in 1437, by the appointment of the monk
Jean Chartier as royal historiographer, responsible for composing a
history of his reign and acting as custodian of a library that contained
as many as 16,000 volumes by 1465. The most important chronicles
were the Latin texts from which the *Grandes chroniques* derived, such
as the *Historia Francorum* of Aimoin de Fleury, the *Gesta Dagoberti*,
the *Annales royales*, the *Vita Karoli* of Einhard, the *Pseudo-Turpin*, the
Vita Ludovici Pii of the Astronomus, the *Historia Francorum Seonensis*,
the *Annales Bertiniani*, and the life of Louis VI by Suger, together
with continuations of the chronicle of Géraud de Frachet produced
by individuals including Richard Lescot and Michel Pintoin, the
Religieux de Saint-Denis. The French tradition of the *Grandes chroniques*
was based upon Primat's *Roman des rois* (1274) that ended in 1223,
together with a continuation by Richard Lescot and the *Chronique des
regnes de Jean II et Charles V*, written at the behest of Charles V; thereafter
there was a complex group of chronicles including a history of the reign
of Charles VI attributed to Jean Juvénal des Ursins and others works
by Gilles le Bouvier, the Berry Herald, and Jean Chartier.[59] Thus the
library at Saint-Denis would have provided an invaluable resource for
royal officials.

Unfortunately Cousinot never did name the historical sources
that he was using, and the problem of identification is magni-
fied by the fact that royal officials enjoyed a remarkable knowledge
of French history, without necessarily having to draw upon famous

---

[57] He later reported that his arguments about English territorial claims were
confirmed 'par lettres auctenticques comme par cronicquez, histoires anciennes et autres
enseignemens, et en soy conformant aux drois canons, civilz et a l'usage et coustume du
royaume de France'. See pp. 53–54 and 111.

[58] See pp. 5–6 and 10.

[59] Gabrielle M. Spiegel, *The Chronicle Tradition of Saint-Denis: a survey* (Brookline, MA, 1978);
Bernard Guenée, 'Les Grandes chroniques de France: le roman aux rois (1274–1518)', in Pierre
Nora (ed.), *La Nation. I,2: Les lieux de mémoire* (Paris, 1986), pp. 189–214; Peter S. Lewis, 'Some
provisional remarks upon the chronicles of Saint-Denis and upon the *(Grandes) Chroniques de
France* in the fifteenth century', *Nottingham Medieval Studies*, 39 (1995), pp. 146–181.

chronicles and histories.[60] In *Pour ce que plusieurs*, just as in other writings including the memorandum on the Burgundian succession, Cousinot preferred to invoke the vague authority of 'les cronicquez de France', such as when he declared that no cognates had ever succeeded to the French throne, described the tensions between Richard I and Philippe Augustus, claimed that Eleanor of Aquitaine had plotted the death of her husband Louis VII, or reported the invasion of England by Prince Louis in 1216.[61] In many of these cases, Cousinot clearly exaggerated and developed upon the historical record, particularly when fabricating speeches to illustrate his arguments and add drama to his treatise: there is no evidence that Philippe VI gave the lengthy monologue attributed to him in *Pour ce que plusieurs*, setting out the case for his succession to the French throne and citing the Salic Law.[62] Similarly, the speech attributed to Charles IV when addressing his nephew Edward in 1325 was just as dramatized as the debate between the English and French ambassadors following the capture of Fougères.[63] On two occasions, Cousinot claimed to be using English chronicles, though it is far from certain that this was true. He had travelled to England and therefore could easily have secured access to such sources, but the references are suspicious. For example, when discussing the fates of Arthur and Eleanor, the nephew and niece of King John, the French writer said:

> a ceste cause sa cronique d'Angleterre dit de lui en substance telles paroles: *Iste Johannes propter feloniam commissam in personis Arturii nepotis sui quem proditorie occidere fecit, et Elyenoris nepotis sue quam mancipatam ducit apud Winctonias, rex Francorum abstulit ei omnes terras omniaque dominia que et quas possidebat in regno Francie.*[64]

This statement does not appear in any of the obvious English chronicles. None of those sources linked Eleanor with Winchester, principally because she was never held there, though confusions about such details would have been possible, given that she was moved so often during the final thirty-nine years of her life. More importantly, it is extremely unlikely that any English chronicler would have accepted at face value the argument that Philippe Augustus confiscated the French lands of King John because of the treatment of Arthur and

---

[60] To cite just one example, in the early years of the reign of Louis XI, genealogies of kings, with a short account of their reigns, were incorporated into a chancellery formula, probably prepared for a *notaire et secrétaire*: BNF MS français 14371, fo. 325r.

[61] See pp. 62, 88, 100, and 113–114.

[62] See pp. 58–67.

[63] See pp. 104 and 120–127.

[64] See p. 88.

Eleanor. Cousinot also cited a chronicle of England as a source for the invasion of England by Prince Louis, though he did not attempt to claim that it supported his contention that Henry III promised to pay homage to the French crown in 1216, in order to persuade Louis to leave.[65]

Throughout *Pour ce que plusieurs*, Cousinot referred to 'authentic' documents and, on three separate occasions, he went further in citing items that were stored in the *Trésor des chartes*. This was the primary archive for the chancellery, near to the Sainte-Chapelle in Paris, and was administered by a royal *notaire et secrétaire* who was also *audiencier* in the chancellery. Ambassadors or commissioners would often accompany the archivist in the search for particular documents: for example, in 1457, the *Trésorier* Dreux Budé was accompanied by Jean Dauvet, Jean Symon, and Raoul I de Refuge in the search for past treaties in preparation for negotiations between Charles VII and Ladislas, king of Bohemia.[66] Cousinot would certainly have had access to these archives, not only because of his royal commission to conduct research for the negotiations in 1464, but also because of his normal function within the royal administration. It is therefore possible that he had seen the documents which he claimed were in the *Trésor*, such as: the letter patent issued by Edward III in 1329, acknowledging Philippe VI as king of France;[67] a document supposedly proving that Blanche of Castile was the sole heiress to the throne of Castile after the death of her older brother, Enrique I, in 1217;[68] and the treaty of Paris agreed in 1259.[69] Cousinot also cited letters patent issued by Henry V before the signing of the treaty of Troyes in 1420,

[65] See p. 114.

[66] BNF MS français 2811, fos 35r–36r, and also see Jean L. Dessalles, *Le Trésor des chartes: sa création, ses gardes et leurs travaux, depuis l'origine jusqu'en 1582* (Paris, 1844) and Olivier Guyotjeannin, 'Super omnes thesauros rerum temporalium: les fonctions du *Trésor des Chartes* du roi de France (XIVe–XVe siècles)', in Kouky Fianu and DeLloyd J. Guth (eds), *Ecrit et pouvoir dans les chancelleries médiévales: espace Français, espace Anglais. Actes du colloque international de Montréal, 7–9 septembre 1995* (Louvain, 1997), pp. 109–131.

[67] See pp. 68–69 and 72. Interestingly, Cousinot indicated that the 1331 letter should also have been in the *Trésor*, suggesting that he had not seen that document in person. Both documents were transcribed, for example, in Jean Juvénal, II, pp. 171 and 173.

[68] See p. 87. This is a curious reference because the notion that Blanche was the sole heir to the Castilian throne following the death of her brother ignored the superior claim of her elder sister, Berenguela, and her son, Fernando. It is therefore possible that Cousinot was invoking the authority of the *Trésor des chartes* to reinforce an argument that he knew to be unreliable.

[69] See p. 92. Even if Cousinot did have access to the treaty of Paris (which was also transcribed in Jean Juvénal, II, pp. 170 and 173), there were still errors in his account. Note that Cousinot did not claim to have seen an official copy of the treaty of Troyes (see pp. 78–79).

and by Henry VI during the negotiations in the 1440s, including a letter patent confirming previous promises to hand over Maine in documents issued under the royal signature and secret seal.[70] He may also have seen other documents, such as the official letters patent summoning the Black Prince to attend Parlement in 1369, authentic letters relating to the status of the duchy of Brittany in the truce of Tours of 1444, and English attempts to justify the capture of Fougères in 1449.[71]

Indeed, the best evidence for Cousinot's knowledge of official records appears in the account of the events surrounding the capture of Fougères. He claimed to have detailed knowledge of 'pluiseurs procés, informations, depositions et tesmoingz et autres evidences notables en forme deue et auctentique touchant la prise dudit Fougieres et dont elle proceda'; he also cited the 'deslyen des treves', the notarized accounts of the conferences with the English in June and July 1449.[72] There is no doubt that the French diplomats involved in those events had ensured that there was sufficient written evidence to justify the final decision to break the truce and invade Normandy.[73] Cousinot himself had played a central role in these events, and it is therefore not surprising that he placed so much emphasis upon the authentic nature of the notarized French records in *Pour ce que plusieurs*.[74] Indeed, he may well have owned copies of many of the items, including thirteen documents relating to François de Surienne and an account of the meeting on 31 July 1449, which included a statement of the English breaches of the truce.[75] He certainly had detailed information about the personnel employed by both sides for embassies during the negotiations surrounding Fougères: only Jean Chartier and *Pour ce que plusieurs* correctly identified Cousinot

---

[70] See pp. 80–81 and 125–126.

[71] See pp. 106–107, 121, and 123.

[72] See pp. 128–130. Intriguingly, Cousinot also claimed to be privy to information acquired from English prisoners (p. 159).

[73] The best example of the use of notaries to authenticate such documents was the record of the inquiry into the action by François de Surienne, led by the chancellor, Guillaume Juvénal des Ursins. See Thomas Basin, *Histoire des règnes de Charles VII et de Louis XI*, IV, pp. 290–347.

[74] The French efforts to acquire authenticated records of the negotiations with the English was paralleled by Charles VII's commission of Guillaume Bouillé on 15 February 1450 to locate documents relating to the trial of Joan of Arc in 1431: Paul Doncoeur and Yvonne Lanhers (eds), *La Réhabilitation de Jeanne la Pucelle. L'enquête ordonnée par Charles VII en 1450 et le codicille de Guillaume Bouillé* (Melun, 1956), pp. 33–35.

[75] BNF MS français 4054. Cousinot spoke of 'nostre relation, instruite et justifiee par loyaux instrumens appliques' in his letter to the count of Foix on 25 September 1449 (Beaucourt, V, p. 439).

and Pierre Fontenil as the ambassadors who had met with Somerset in April 1449.[76]

The title assigned to *Pour ce que plusieurs* in its earliest printed editions, *La Loy Salicque, première loy des françois*, highlights the central importance of this authority in the treatise.[77] This ancient law code was almost certainly compiled by Clovis between 507 and 511, and offered a creative synthesis of Frankish custom, Roman law, and the new law that Clovis had himself brought into being. It was subsequently modified and enlarged under later Merovingians and Carolingians but slowly became archaic and irrelevant to new needs and so was forgotten until it was rediscovered in the middle of the fourteenth century by scholars associated with the abbey of Saint-Denis.[78] There is no reliable evidence that it was invoked during the complex debates surrounding the French royal succession following the deaths of the last three Capetian kings between 1316 and 1328. Rather, its first use by an official Valois writer occurred between 1409 and 1414, most likely in 1413, when Jean Montreuil cited the Salic Law in a brief note towards the end of his treatise *A toute la chevalerie*. His attention was drawn by the chapter *De alode* of the *Pactus legis Salicae* which included a clause designed to safeguard the family patrimony: men should receive the allodial land (the 'terra salica' or land of the family and ancestors) and women just the personal property. In order to make this statement apply to the French royal succession, Montreuil inserted the words 'in regno' into an inaccurate transcription of this clause.[79] Yet Montreuil was clearly troubled by this deception; in later works he quoted the Salic Law as stating that 'Nulla portio hereditatis mulieri veniat, sed ad virilem sexum tota terre hereditas

---

[76] See p. 120, together with Jean Chartier, *Chronique de Charles VII, roi de France*, ed. Auguste Valet de Viriville (3 vols, Paris, 1858), II, pp. 62–63. Both texts reported that this embassy was dispatched when Charles VII heard about the capture of Fougères when, in reality, they were already at Rouen to discuss recent violations of the truce. This would appear to be an attempt to massage the facts in order to shift even more blame onto Somerset.

[77] Craig Taylor, 'The Salic Law and the Valois succession to the French crown', *French History*, 15 (2001), pp. 358–377.

[78] Katherine Fischer Drew (trans.), *The Laws of the Salian Franks* (Philadelphia, 1991), pp. 28–55, and William H. Daly, 'Clovis: how barbaric, how pagan?' *Speculum*, 69 (1994), pp. 647–655.

[79] Montreuil, II, pp. 7–17 and 132, together with Nicole Pons and Ezio Ornato, 'Qui est l'auteur de la chronique latine de Charles VI, dite du religieux de Saint-Denis?', *Bibliothèque de l'Ecole des Chartes*, 134 (1976), pp. 91–93 and plate 1. Montreuil was using a text whose formulation matched redaction K, chapter 62, § 6, in which the *De alode* article appears as 'De terra vero salica nulla portio hereditatis mulieri veniat, sed ad virilem sexum tota terrae hereditatis perveniat': Karl A. Eckhardt (ed.), *Pactus legis salicae. Monumenta Germaniae historica, legum sectio I, leges nationum Germanicarum, IV, part I* (Hanover, 1962), p. 223.

perveniat', adding a gloss 'qui exclut et forclot femmes de tout en tout de povoir succeder a la couronne de France, comme icelle loy et decret die absolument que femme n'ait quelconque portion ou royaume'.[80]

Thereafter, Valois writers continued to cite the Salic Law in connection with the French royal succession, albeit with some trepidation, given that no manuscript could be found which included the words 'in regno' in the *De alode* clause. For example, Jean Juvénal des Ursins repeated Montreuil's original formulation of the Salic Law in 1435, but then admitted in 1446 that he had not found a copy of the text with that version, and so was forced to quote the clause that did appear in the ancient manuscripts: 'De terra vero sallica, nulla portio hereditatis mulieri veniat sed ad virilem sexum tota terre hereditas perveniat'. His explanation of the inability to find a 'correct' manuscript of the text was that the words 'in regno' had been omitted out of 'mauvais esperit' or by copy error, and he declared that Montreuil's formulation would be found in an exemplary copy of the Salic Law in an abbey near to Poitiers.[81] Meanwhile, royal officials were engaged in an active hunt for just such a manuscript. In 1451, Noël de Fribois gave an account of a meeting that had taken place between 1435 and 1444, during which Geoffroy Vassal claimed to have seen the Salic Law at Savigny in Poitou; Fribois implied that this manuscript was found not to have contained the 'in regno' version of *De alode*, but also reported that Gérard Machet believed there to be another copy at the abbey of Saint-Rémy of Reims.[82] These searches were presumably fruitless because Fribois preferred not to cite the 'in regno' clause in either the *Mirouer historial* or the *Abregé des chroniques*, which he completed ten years later.[83]

Yet while other Valois writers and officials were becoming increasingly nervous about the authenticity of the Salic Law, Guillaume Cousinot brazenly assigned it the central role in his discussion of the royal succession in *Pour ce que plusieurs*. Though he only cited the authentic version of the *De alode* clause, minus the 'in regno' clause, Cousinot also built on the argument of Jean Juvénal that the French kingdom was synonymous with Salian lands and therefore governed

[80] Montreuil, II, p. 168, and also pp. 167, 269, 272–273, 320, and 326.

[81] Jean Juvénal, I, p. 156 and II, pp. 20–22.

[82] Kathleen Daly and Ralph E. Giesey, 'Noël de Fribois et la Loi Salique', *Bibliothèque de l'Ecole des Chartes*, 151 (1993), pp. 13–14, and see also Colette Beaune, 'Histoire et politique: la recherche du texte de la Loi Salique de 1350 à 1450', in *Congrès des Sociétés Savantes, Bordeaux 1979. Section de philologie et d'histoire* (Paris, 1981), 31–32, and *idem*, *The Birth of an Ideology*, pp. 345–347.

[83] Daly and Giesey, 'Noël de Fribois et la Loi Salique', pp. 17–36.

by the Salic Law.[84] Cousinot embedded this argument in the clause itself, by means of a Latin gloss that would have deceived all but the most well-informed reader into believing that it was part of the original text: 'Nulla portio hereditatis de terra salicqua *qui est interpretandum de regali dominio quod a nullo deppendet nec alicui subicitur, ad differenciam aliarum terrarum que in alodio conceduntur* mulieri veniat, sed ad virilem sexum tota hereditas perveniat'. He then asserted that 'Lex Salica est constitutio regia' and observed that 'terra autem salica dicitur que adheret corone'.[85] At the same time, he explored the etymology of the term 'Salic'.[86] The first explanation offered for the word 'Salic' was that it derived 'a civitate Sylechayni ultra Renum', that is to say, Salaheim in Germany, where those who created it had first lived. But then the author offered a far more interesting notion, arguing that the term 'Salic' came from 'sal' meaning salt, a simple pun from the notion that the law would conserve the kingdom for all time to come.[87]

More remarkably, Cousinot rewrote history in order to clarify the role of the Salic Law in the French royal succession. Jean Juvénal had simply stated that the custom 'que fille ne succedoit point' had determined the royal succession in 1316 and 1322, following the deaths of Louis X and Philippe V.[88] Yet *Pour ce que plusieurs* went much further, offering an entirely fictitious account of the way that the Salic Law was employed in the debate over the succession after the death of Charles IV in 1328. This narrative appeared to demonstrate that Edward III's claim to the French throne had been defeated in 1328, thereby removing any justification for the subsequent wars of the English. At the same time, the claim that the Salic Law had been used in 1328, to defeat the title of Edward III, whose claim came through his mother, Isabella, also reinforced Cousinot's argument that the authority barred both females and their cognate sons from the royal succession: 'les femmes estoient forclosez de laditte succession et disoit point qu'elle venist aux plus prochains masles, mais au plus prochain sexe masculin. Or n'estoit point le Roy Edouart du sexe masculin'.[89] This was the most direct link between the Salic Law

---

[84] Jean Juvénal, II, p. 22.

[85] See pp. 59–61.

[86] Guillebert de Metz had argued that the term Salic was used because 'les gens du pays estoient nobles peuple': Adrien Leroux de Lincy and Lazare M. Tisserand (eds), *Paris et ses historiens aux XIVe et XVe siècles* (Paris, 1867), p. 135.

[87] See pp. 59–60. For a discussion of the etymologies, see Beaune, *The Birth of an Ideology*, p. 260, and also Donald R. Kelley, *Foundations of Modern Historical Scholarship: language, law and history in the French renaissance* (New York, NY, 1970), p. 293.

[88] Jean Juvénal, II, pp. 21–22.

[89] See pp. 61 and 77.

and the exclusion of cognates that any French polemical writer had offered.[90] But, typically, the author of *Pour ce que plusieurs* showed no concerns about extending the prohibition of the Salic Law to cognates, even though they were not mentioned in the authority.

It is impossible to know precisely how Cousinot developed his unique and influential account of the Salic Law, especially given his clear willingness to embellish and even fabricate arguments. It has been suggested that he had access to a manuscript of the *Lex Salica* that contained the authentic version of the *De alode* clause together with a prologue speaking of King Pharamond and the four 'dictators', Usogast, Visogast, Salagast, and Wisogast.[91] These particular details were also available in a range of sources, including the chronicle of Fredegar, the *Gesta regum Francorum*, and the *Chronographia* of Sigebert of Gembloux, as well as more recent writings.[92] Yet, even though many of these histories did connect the origins of the Salic Law with Salaheim, this was just one of many cities mentioned and none associated it with the origins of the *term* 'Salic'; moreover, most reported that Pharamond had reigned for eleven years, rather than the twelve claimed by Cousinot.[93]

Ultimately, it is impossible to be certain whether Cousinot really had sources for these small details, or simply fabricated them. Either way, it is clear that he completely changed the position of the Salic Law in the debate over the French royal succession. *Pour ce que plusieurs* was the first Valois treatise to claim that, since its first enactment by Pharamond, the Salic Law had regulated every succession to the throne, including not only the problematic events of 1316, 1322, and 1328, but even Merovech's succession to Clodio. Cousinot simply asserted that 'il ne sera par trouvé que oncquez fille succedast a la couronne de France ne autre masle au moyen de fille' and even went on to suggest that it supported the king's right to confiscate lands in France from the

[90] See, for example, Jean Juvénal, I, 156–157 and II, 20–22 and 26, and Daly and Giesey, 'Noël de Fribois et la Loi Salique', pp. 31–32.

[91] Ralph E. Giesey, 'The juristic basis of dynastic right to the French throne', *Transactions of the American Philosophical Society*, new series, 51 (1961), p. 18.

[92] The chronicle of Fredegar in Bruno Krusch (ed.), *Scriptores rerum Merovingicarum, II. Fredegarii et aliorum chronica vitae sanctorum.* (Hanover, 1888), p. 244, and the *Gesta regum Francorum* and the *Chronographia* of Sigebert of Gembloux in Jacques-Paul Migne (ed.), *Patrologiae Cursus Completus, sive bibliotheca universalis . . . omnium S.S. Patrum, Doctorum, Scriptorumque ecclesiasticorum . . . Series secunda* (221 vols, Paris, 1844–1864), XCVI, col. 1424a–b and CLX, col. 77b–78a. For late medieval French uses of the story of Pharamond and the dictators of the Salic Law, see, for example, Leroux de Lincy and Tisserand, *Paris et ses historiens*, pp. 105–106 and Jean Juvénal, I, p. 345.

[93] See p. 58, n. 35.

English.[94] Such a brazen approach to the Salic Law was crucial in its elevation to the status of a fundamental law of France.[95]

The new-found confidence in the Salic Law meant that *Pour ce que plusieurs* did not need to make as much use of other legal authorities as previous polemical writers.[96] Thus, when outlining the case supposedly presented by Philippe VI in 1328, Cousinot argued that Roman law, in the form of the *Libri feudorum*, was not relevant to that debate because 'le royaume de France n'est point subget a l'empire'.[97] Nevertheless, Cousinot did follow Jean Juvénal in citing God's judgment against Eve (Genesis 3: 16) and also supported the exclusion of cognates from the royal succession by two citations from the Roman law: 'Nemo plus juris ad alium transferre potest, quam ipse haberet' (*Digest*, 50.17.54) and 'In rusticis autem praediis impedit servitutem medium praedium, quod non servit' (*Digest*, 8.3.7.1).[98] These authorities were effectively treated as legal maxims and accorded similar status to other sayings such as 'nemo dat quod non habet', a common proverb probably derived originally from Seneca.[99] Indeed, Cousinot demonstrated a great fondness for Latin proverbs and sayings, invoking them on a number of occasions to lend authority to his arguments.[100]

Canon law was less problematic and so Cousinot was happy to defend the well-known principle that the French king was emperor in his own kingdom by reference to the *Liber extra*, particularly the

---

[94] See pp. 63 and 90.

[95] In this regard, it is important to note that the unofficial genealogies of the first half of the fifteenth century were almost entirely silent about the Salic Law, emphasizing the danger of overstating its importance in the contemporary understanding of the French royal succession before the advent of printing. See Marigold Anne Norbye, 'The king's blood: royal genealogies, dynastic rivalries and historical culture in the Hundred Years War. A case study of *A tous nobles qui aiment beaux faits et bonnes histoires*' (2 vols, PhD thesis, London, 2004), together with Sanford Zale, 'Unofficial histories of France in the late middle ages' (PhD thesis, Columbus, OH, 1994).

[96] This contrasts sharply with Jean Juvénal, II, pp. 22–23 and 48–50. Cousinot also shunned the detailed discussion of legal authorities that had marked previous debates of the treaty of Troyes, perhaps because the death of Charles VII made this a less significant issue. Compare pp. 81–82 below with Nicole Pons (ed.), *L'Honneur de la couronne de France: quatre libelles contre les Anglais (vers 1418–vers 1429)* (Paris, 1990), pp. 120, 123–124, and 130–131; Jean Juvénal, I, pp. 186–188 and II, pp. 55–56; and Robert Blondel, *Oeuvres de Robert Blondel*, ed. A. Héron (2 vols, Rouen, 1891–1893), I, pp. 273–274 and 458–460. Cousinot also avoided a discussion of inalienability when discussing the treaty of Brétigny, in contrast to Jean Juvénal, II, pp. 132–133.

[97] See pp. 57–58.

[98] See pp. 61 and 78.

[99] See p. 61.

[100] See pp. 63, 65, 73, and 113.

famous papal bull of Innocent III, *Per venerabilem*.[101] More controversial would have been a remarkably liberal reading of the principle of self-defence in a gloss to Gratian's *Decretum*, interpreted as 'qui injustement fait guerre, justement on lui puet faire, non pas seulement en soy deffendant, mais en lui ostant tout le sien propre jusquez il ait deuement reparé l'offence qu'il a faitte'.[102] Cousinot cited both Gratian's *Decretum* and English common law in support of his argument that William Longsword was illegitimate and thus could not have inherited the duchy of Normandy, even if he conveniently ignored the fact that canon law did allow for children to be legitimized by the subsequent marriage of their parents.[103] Similarly, he cited both the *Liber extra* and Gratian's *Decretum* to support the principle of confiscation that underpinned his entire argument in favour of the French crown's recovery of English-held territories, later stating that this was justified not only by canon and civil law but also by the Salic Law and the general custom of the realms of both France and England.[104]

Indeed, even though Cousinot repeatedly declared that the only relevant authorities were the laws, customs, and usages of the place where a particular debate arose, he was not averse to making use of English law in support of his own cause.[105] Yet this raises the difficult question of whether Cousinot simply drew upon knowledge that he had acquired in his travels in the British Isles, or was relying upon indirect sources. When Cousinot challenged the English title to lands north of the river Humber, he asserted that 'les roys d'Escoce soloyent tenir la conté de Hontiton, Nothombelland, [Westmelland], Tindal et pluiseurs grans terres et seignouries en Angleterre, lesquelles les Anglois par semblable leur ont osteez et les en ont privez et deboutés'.[106] This brief reference echoed a more substantial discussion in the *Vraie cronicque d'Escoce*, which reported that the earldoms of Huntingdon, Northumberland, Cumberland, and Tynedale were granted to the Scottish crown by King Henry I in return for the renunciation of any claim to the English throne, and that these lands were subsequently returned to Henry II in 1157 by Malcolm IV.[107] In addition, the author of the *Vraie cronicque d'Escoce*, John Ireland, echoed Cousinot

---

[101] *Liber Extra*, 4.17.13, and see pp. 65–66 below.
[102] See pp. 110–111.
[103] See pp. 95–96.
[104] See pp. 69 and 90.
[105] See pp. 112–113, as well as p. 96.
[106] See pp. 90 and 112–113.
[107] BNF MS nouvelle acqustion française 20962, fos 58v–59v and Daly, 'The *Vraie cronicque d'Escoce*', pp. 116 and 121–122.

in citing an unusual proverb, ultimately derived from an anonymous fourteenth-century diatribe known as the *Proprietates Anglicorum*: '*Anglicus angelus est cui nunquam credere fas est. Dum tibi dicit ave tanquam ab hoste cave*'.[108] Walter Bower had quoted this in his *Scotichronicon*, in the course of a lengthy diatribe against Edward III and the English for misleading King David with their innocent faces, while striking him with a scorpion's sting.[109] Variations on the same proverb also appeared in Bower's *The chronycle of Scotland in a part*, written during the reign of James II, as well as an epilogue to the *Polychronicon*.[110] Ireland was clearly knowledgeable of the work of Bower and so it is possible that he served as the intermediary through which Cousinot learned of the proverb. There are, though, some contrasts between their accounts. In the *Vraie cronicque d'Escoce*, the saying was cited in the context of an etymological discussion, immediately after the claim that the word Angleterre came '*ab angulo quia veritas non querit angulos*'; like Bower, Cousinot used it as an illustration of the argument that the English were a double-dealing race, and also attributed it to Bede. In short, either the *Vraie cronicque d'Escoce* or its author may have served as a source for *Pour ce que plusieurs*, though it is impossible to be certain of the precise relationship between the two texts.

A similar question is raised by the extensive parallels between *Pour ce que plusieurs* and the Lancastrian pamphlets of Sir John Fortescue.[111] For example, both Fortescue and Cousinot denied that the Yorkist Edward IV had inherited any claim to the throne through his ancestor, Philippa, because she was not the true daughter of Lionel, duke of Clarence, and hence granddaughter of King Edward III. Fortescue defended this fiction by suggesting that Philippa might have been the product of an affair between her mother and Sir James Audeley, who was subsequently executed for treason, and by claiming that Lionel's heirs acknowledged their dubious status by failing to adopt his arms, and instead taking up those of March and Ulster.[112] The same arguments were made in *Pour ce que plusieurs*,

[108] See p. 73 and BNF MS nouvelle acquisition française 20962, fo. 57r.

[109] Walter Bower, *Scotichronicon*, ed. A. Brian Scott and Donald E.R. Watt (9 vols, Aberdeen, 1987–1998), VII, pp. 84–86.

[110] David Laing, Walter Scott, and Thomas Thomson (eds), *The Bannatyne Miscellany* (Edinburgh, 1855), p. 41, and Lambeth Palace MS 99, fo. 186r.

[111] This relationship was first examined by Veikko Litzen, 'A war of roses and lilies: the theme of succession in Sir John Fortescue's works', *Suomalaisen tiedeakatemian tomituksia Annales Academiae Scientiarum Fennicae*, 173 (1971), pp. 57–61. Also see Margaret L. Kekewich, ' "Thou shalt be under the power of the man": Sir John Fortescue and the Yorkist succession', *Nottingham Medieval Studies*, 43 (1998), pp. 205–206, and Craig Taylor, 'Sir John Fortescue and the French polemical treatises of the Hundred Years War', *EHR*, 114 (1999), pp. 112–129.

[112] Fortescue, *The Works*, pp. 67*–68*, 499, and 517–518, and *idem, The Governance of England*, ed. Charles Plummer (Oxford, 1885), p. 354. Also see Kekewich, 'Fortescue and the Yorkist succession', p. 227.

albeit with some minor variations. Unlike Fortescue, the French writer identified Philippa's mother as Elizabeth de Burgh, countess of Ulster, but then erroneously claimed that Philippa had a sister and that the two girls had married the count of Northumberland and the count of March, Roger Mortimer.[113] He later used this genealogical fiction that Philippa was a younger sister to further undermine the Yorkist claim to the English throne.[114] Another parallel between the writings of Fortescue and *Pour ce que plusieurs* is the discussion of the English entail. Guillaume Cousinot defended the claim that a son could not inherit the French throne through his mother by raising a parallel case in English law: in an entail where a daughter was prevented from succeeding her father, her son was also excluded from the inheritance.[115] Cousinot did not argue that such an entail barred the Yorkists from inheriting the English throne, as Sir John Fortescue had tried to argue.[116] Nevertheless, the parallel use of the argument is striking, especially when Sir John Fortescue made the same limited argument as Cousinot in the *Opusculum de natura legis naturae*.[117]

It is extremely difficult to be precise about the nature of the relationship between Fortescue's writings and *Pour ce que plusieurs*. Ideas and arguments appear to have flowed in both directions and, to complicate matters further, many points had been made by previous French polemical treatises, including the key argument that women could not rule because God had placed them under the power of men in Genesis 3: 16. It is certainly conceivable that Cousinot saw one of Fortescue's pamphlets, or that both were drawing upon a shared source. Yet it is equally possible that the similarities between the texts were the result of informal communication between the two men in Scotland

---

[113] In reality, Philippa was an only child and Roger was her son; she also had a daughter named Elizabeth who married Henry Percy, son of the first earl of Northumberland. The error was compounded when the French author presented Anne Mortimer, daughter of Roger Mortimer and mother of Richard, duke of York, as the daughter of Philippa and Roger Mortimer together. See pp. 74 and 76–77, together with the commentary of the Tudor author on pp. 158–159 and 163.

[114] See pp. 76–77.

[115] See p. 77. As Lyttleton argued in the *Tenures*, if the heir to lands held in tail-male dies with only a daughter, '[il] est mort sauns issue male en la ley, entaunt que lissue de la fille ne puit conveyer a luy mesme le discent per heire male, &c': Thomas Lyttleton, *Lyttleton, his Treatise of Tenures*, ed. T.E. Tomlins (London, 1841), I, chapter II, § 24, and also see John H. Baker, *Introduction to English Legal History* (3rd edition, London, 1990), pp. 303–307, and Kenneth Bruce McFarlane, *The Nobility of Later Medieval England* (Oxford, 1973), p. 270.

[116] Michael Bennett, 'Edward III's entail and the succession to the crown, 1376–1471', *EHR*, 113 (1998), pp. 580–609.

[117] Fortescue, *The Works*, pp. 124–125, 506, and 517–518, and also see *idem*, *The Governance of England*, pp. 353–354.

or in France.[118] Either way, Guillaume Cousinot certainly had strong connections with Henry VI and the Lancastrian court. Moreover, even though *Pour ce que plusieurs* steadfastedly rejected the English king's claim to the French crown, it remained unusually supportive of the Lancastrian claim to the throne of England.[119]

Indeed, the author of *Pour ce que plusieurs* showed far greater knowledge of the British Isles than any previous French polemical writer. He was able to talk with confidence and authority about the English common law, the royal succession from William the Conqueror onwards, and the history of both Scotland and Wales.[120] The most striking piece of information that he provided was a transcription of an epitaph for Henry V, written 'en son palais de Westmonstre que par tout ailleurs ou royaume'.[121] Henry's tomb at Westminster Abbey was completed by 1431, and included a silver effigy on a deeply recessed tomb-chest set in a chapel. Underneath the effigy was a wooden block with 'plain chamfered edges six inches broad, probably for a long rhyming inscription like that on the tomb of Edward Prince of Wales at Canterbury'.[122] No trace of the epitaph survives today because both the effigy and the woodwork were originally covered with silver plates, stolen piece by piece before the middle of the sixteenth century. In 1631, Weever reported that the epitaph painted on the tomb read:

> *Dux Normannorum, verus conquestor eorum*
> *Heres Francorum; decessit et Hector eorum*
> Here Normans duke, so stil'd by conquest just,
> True heire of France; Great Hector, lies in dust.
> *Gallorum mastix jacet hic Henricus in urna*
> *Domat omnia virtus.*[123]

This is extremely close to the version reported in *Pour ce que plusieurs* in 1464, albeit with an alternative reading of '*Rector*' which seems far more plausible than '*Hector*'; the confusion might possibly be explained by

---

[118] Kekewich argues that a common source for the two accounts is more likely, emphasizing the small variations in the points that they make: 'Fortescue and the Yorkist succession', pp. 205–206.

[119] On two separate occasions, Cousinot expressly declared that the Lancastrian claim was superior to the Yorkist title, using arguments that also appeared in Fortescue's writings: see pp. 76 and 90. In contrast, see Jean Juvénal, II, pp. 39, 135–136, and 149–159.

[120] For the discussion of Wales, see p. 112.

[121] See p. 80.

[122] William H. St. John Hope, 'The funeral, monument and chantry chapel of King Henry the Fifth', *Archaeologia*, 65 (1913–1914), p. 150 and in general pp. 129–186.

[123] John Weever, *Ancient Funerall Monuments* (London, 1631), p. 474. The earliest guidebook, by William Camden, *Reges, Reginae, nobiles et alii in ecclesia collegiata B. Petri Westmonasterii sepulti* (London, 1600), sig. B3, p. 4, gives the inscription as '*Gallorum mastix jacet hic Henricus in urna. / Domat omnia virtus. / Pulchra virumque suum sociat tandem Katherina*', followed by a long poem in English.

the similiarity between the Gothic majuscule R and H.[124] Thus there is
every reason to suppose that the transcription in *Pour ce que plusieurs* was
authentic, the earliest surviving witness to the epitaph to Henry V.[125]
If so, it is another piece of evidence to demonstrate that the author of
Pour ce que plusieurs had remarkable personal knowledge and experience
of the British Isles.

There are fifteen surviving manuscripts of *Pour ce que plusieurs* written
before the end of the fifteenth century, together with another five post-
medieval copies.[126] It would therefore appear that *Pour ce que plusieurs*
was extremely successful, especially in comparison with an equivalent
work such as *Tres crestien, tres hault, tres puissant roy* by Jean Juvénal des
Ursins, of which there are just two contemporary copies, and two
more dating from the end of the century.[127]

In the absence of an autograph manuscript, the earliest dateable
example is K, which was cited in an inventory of the library
of Duke Philippe le Bon of Burgundy in 1467. This manuscript
was almost certainly commissioned by Louis de Bruges, lord of
Gruthuyse, who himself owned a companion manuscript, B, which
was presumably prepared at the same time as manuscript K.[128]
Manuscripts A, C, and possibly D were prepared around 1470 and
1471, at a time when the treatise might have attracted additional
attention in the context of the Lancastrian and Yorkist struggles
for the English throne, and Louis XI's role in such events.[129]
Manuscript A carries a colophon indicating that it was completed
on 7 February 1469 (that is to say, 1470), for Jeanne de France,
sister of Louis XI and the wife of Jean duke of Bourbon, count
of Clermont. Manuscript C offers a compilation of texts, and the
colophon to *Pour ce que plusieurs* suggests that this particular transcription was completed on 17 July 1471. Finally, manuscript O was owned

[124] I am extremely grateful to Richard Mortimer, Christopher Norton, and David Palliser
for their advice on this matter.

[125] This is one of the rare occasions when Cousinot used the adverb 'expressement'
to describe a quotation, rather than his usual qualifier, 'en substance'. See, for example,
p. 103.

[126] For detailed discussions of the manuscripts, see Appendices II and III below.

[127] His earlier work, *Audite celi*, survives in ten manuscripts produced between 1435 and
1475, together with another five from the end of the fifteenth century: Jean Juvénal, I,
pp. 93–142 and II, pp. 1–11.

[128] There are a number of minor differences between the text offered in manuscripts B
and K, and the nearest analogue to B is manuscript F; it seems likely that the missing first
folio of F presented a similar illumination from the workshop of Guillaume Vrelant. See
pp. 4–5, and Appendix II, p. 272.

[129] The same point is noted with regard to *Pour vraye congnoissance avoir* by Kathleen Daly,
'*Pour vraye congnoissance avoir* ', p. 152.

by the *notaire et secrétaire du roi* Jean Budé, whose autograph note on the final folio indicates that the transcription was completed on 21 December 1486. Unfortunately, it is difficult to date other manuscripts or to identify their contemporary owners, except for Jacques d'Armagnac, duke of Nemours (manuscript H).[130]

Manuscripts A, C, and O, together with the incomplete texts in D and M, may well form a discrete group, judging by the evidence of homoeoteleutic errors and amendments to *Pour ce que plusieurs*. Intriguingly, three of these five manuscripts were directly connected with the French royal administration. Manuscript C contains a collection of material associated with Guillaume Cousinot, who was both an important administrator and diplomat and probably the author of *Pour ce que plusieurs* itself. Manuscript D presents not only the initial portion of *Pour ce que plusieurs* but also the *Memoire abregée grossement* and *Pour vraye congnoissance avoir*, two treatises that were closely associated with the *Trésor des chartes*; it is possible that this manuscript was owned by Louis le Blanc, the probable author of *Pour vraye congnoissance avoir*. Manuscript O was prepared in 1486 by Jean Budé, *notaire et secrétaire du roi* and *Trésorier et garde des chartes* like his father, Dreux Budé. It may well be that the unusual level of correction and adaptation of the text in these manuscripts is testimony to the continued use and circulation of the treatise in such circles. Indeed, though no 'official' copy of *Pour ce que plusieurs* survives, Nicole Pons has made the interesting suggestion that a seventeenth-century manuscript containing both Cousinot's treatise and Jean Juvénal's *Tres crestien, tres hault, tres puissant roy* may have been a transcription of a dossier originally held in the *Trésor des chartes*.[131]

In nearly half of the contemporary manuscripts, *Pour ce que plusieurs* either appeared on its own (B, J, O, P) or in conjunction with the *Vraie cronicque d'Escoce* by John Ireland (F, H, K), a treatise that was almost certainly written at around the same time and for the same purpose, that is to say, the instruction of French diplomats. Nicole Pons has drawn attention to the fact that *Pour ce que plusieurs* appears in a number of other manuscripts alongside texts that shared an antipathy towards the English, namely the *Abregé des chroniques* by Noël de Fribois (M), *Audite celi* by Jean Juvénal des Ursins (A, M), and the *Chronique de la traïson et mort de Richart II* (L, N, Q). These manuscripts formed anti-English dossiers, for Pons, and demonstrate

---

[130] See Appendices II and III below.

[131] BNF MS nouvelle acquisition française 7006, was previously MS 35 of the Brienne collection, prepared under Antoine de Loménie, lord of Ville-aux-Clercs, secretary of state under Henry IV and Louis XIII. See Pons, 'A l'origine des dossiers polemiques', p. 362n.

'la diffusion d'une véritable conscience nationale'.[132] As she observes, the variety of combinations shows that this was not merely mechanical copying, though, in the case of *Pour ce que plusieurs*, the choice to include the work alongside the *Vraie cronicque d'Escoce* or *Audite celi* by Jean Juvénal des Ursins may have been the product of the natural, existing relationship between the texts. Moreover, those manuscripts where *Pour ce que plusieurs* was presented alongside other texts were either directly associated with the milieu of the royal administrators and diplomats, or included texts not normally associated with the polemical debates of the Hundred Years War, such as *L'instruction d'un jeune prince* by Ghillebert de Lannoy (A), the *Chronique du Pseudo-Turpin* (L), and the *Débat de honneur* and *Controversie de noblesse* translated by Jean Miélot (N).[133] As a result, the only example that would really support the argument is M, an extremely wide-ranging collection of polemical and anti-English materials, produced after 1488.

The real success of *Pour ce que plusieurs* occurred following the advent of printing. The first edition was possibly published in Rouen as early as 1488 by Jacques Le Forestier, under the title *La Loy Salicque qui est la première loy des Françoys faicte par le Roy Pharamon, première roy de France*.[134] This, and subsequent versions, accidentally repeated a brief discussion of the judgement against King John in 1202, in the context of the invasions of England by Prince Louis of France in the following decade.[135] This curious error is only found in one surviving manuscript, O, owned by Jean Budé and apparently completed on 21 December 1486. The fact that the published text only repeated nineteen of the thirty-three significant and unique variants in Budé's copy means that it is unlikely that the book was prepared directly from this manuscript. Nevertheless, it does seem likely that the printed editions were based upon a manuscript closely related to that of Budé, perhaps owned by a fellow royal administrator.

---

[132] Pons, *L'Honneur de la couronne de France*, pp. 33–36, and *idem*, 'A l'origine des dossiers polemiques', p. 377, together with Peter S. Lewis, 'Jeu de cubes: reflexions sur quelques textes et manuscrits', in *Pratiques de la culture écrite en France au XVe siècle: Actes du colloque internationale du CNRS* (Louvain, 1995), pp. 313–330.

[133] Even the manuscript associated with Guillaume Cousinot included works of a more literary character, particularly with regard to his exchange with Jean Robertet. See pp. 274–275.

[134] In 1839, the librarian Jules Pautet published a brief prospectus describing a copy held at Beaune, which he said was published in 1488. It is unclear why he offered this date given that the Bibliothèque Municipale Gaspard Monge at Beaune still holds an edition printed by Jacques Le Forestier at Rouen which exactly matches the description offered by Pautet but is not dated and may have been printed as late as 1500. Additional copies survive in Rouen and Autun.

[135] See pp. 113 and 244–245.

A second undated edition of *La Loy Salicque* was published in Rouen by Michel Angier and included a speech delivered at Easter 1522 by the rector of the university of Caen, Jean Rogier, before King François I and the Dauphin. Angier was responsible for two further printings in Caen, one of which contained both of the texts from his Rouen edition and was printed in 1532;[136] there are also a number of surviving copies of an undated and unattributed version which reproduce Angier's Rouen edition minus the speech of Jean Rogier.[137] Undated copies of *La Loy Salicque* were printed in Paris by Pierre Le Caron, on behalf of Guillaume Nyuerd, and by Thomas Du Guernier; Michel Le Noir issued a third version on 12 June 1507, which also included an anonymous poem on peace that had appeared in Le Forestier's edition.[138] Finally, the treatise was appended to two separate editions of Claude de Seyssel's *La Grande monarchie de France*, first in 1540 by Denys Janot, on behalf of Galliot du Pré, and then again in late 1557 and early 1558 by Galliot du Pré and Vincent Sertenas.[139] In short, *Pour ce que plusieurs* enjoyed a remarkable diffusion in up to eleven different editions, or at least reprints, between the 1480s and 1558.[140] This demand for *Pour ce que plusieurs* was presumably driven by its crucial role in the evolution of the Salic Law into a Fundamental Law

---

[136] This version is 120 pages long and has a woodcut at the opening, showing the king chairing a meeting of eight people, seven of them seated, together with a royal coat of arms. There are two copies in the BNF.

[137] The first of these was printed by Michel Angier at Caen and Jehan Macé at Rennes, at an unidentified date. See Léopold Delisle (ed.), *Catalogue des livres imprimés ou publiés à Caen avant le milieu du XVIe siècle* (2 vols, Caen, 1903), I, pp. 218 and 244; Alain R. Girard and Anne Le Bouteiller (eds), *Catalogue collectif des livres imprimés jusqu'à 1600 conservés dans les bibliothèques publiques de Basse-Normandie* (3 vols, Baden-Baden, 1987–1993), III, p. 210; Pierre Aquilon (ed.), *Repertoire bibliographique des livres imprimés en France au seizième siècle. 27e livraison. 27 Caen* [suite] (Baden-Baden, 1978), p. 73.

[138] Le Caron printed books until 1502, including works published in conjunction with Du Guernier; Le Noir's edition was reprinted in 1510. Brigitte Moreau (ed.), *Inventaire chronologique des éditions parisiennes du XVI siècle d'après les manuscrits de Philippe Renouard* (5 vols, Paris, 1972–2004), I, pp. 82, 86, and 245. Two copies of the Le Caron edition survive in the BL and a further copy in Yale. There is a copy of the Du Guernier edition in the Bibliothèque Municipale of Orléans and copies of the Le Noir edition in the BNF, the Bibliothèque Mazarine, and at George Washington University.

[139] In the first version, the text of *La Loy Salicque* is dated 1 December 1540, but Seyssel's text is said to have been published in 1541. There are copies in the BL and BNF, as well as the Bibliothèques Municipales at Caen and Lunel. The second version survives in multiple copies in the BNF, the Bibliothèque de l'Arsenal, the Bibliothèques Municipales at Dijon and Lyon, the Université Paul Cezanne, and the National Library of Scotland.

[140] I am extremely grateful to Andrew Pettegree and the French Vernacular Book Project at the University of St Andrews for confirming my findings on early printed books containing *Pour ce que plusieurs*. They have drawn my attention to what may be an additional edition without date or place of publication in the Biblioteca Colombina in Seville.

of France, an issuing of mounting importance during the continuing debates over royal succession during the sixteenth century.[141]

In 1700, the treatise was published under the title of the *Discussion des differendz entre les roys de France & d'Angleterre* by Gottfried Leibnitz, using a manuscript that appears to have been close to A. In 1847, the Roxburghe Club published an edition prepared by Robert Anstruther under the title *Pretensions des Anglois à la couronne de France*, along with the *Vraie cronicque d'Escoce*, from manuscript K.[142]

A declaracion of the trew and dewe title of Henry VIII

The long history of the wars between the kings of England and France loomed large during the reign of King Henry VIII. The adventurous campaigns of Edward III, the Black Prince, and particularly Henry V served as a model for a king who was keen to secure his new dynasty, to unite the nation by an aggressive foreign policy, and to establish his personal reputation in front of an international audience.[143] Even though there was no shortage of justifications for war with France, the ancient Plantagenet claims remained an important and constant factor. One of Henry VIII's ambassadors argued that diplomatic relations with Burgundy and Castile were 'devoid of all quarrels and demands, for none of them hath against the other any titles', in stark contrast with the history of disputes between the French and English crowns.[144] Throughout his reign, Henry VIII styled himself 'roy d'Angleterre, et de France, et seigneur d'Irlande' or 'rex Franciae et Angliae ac dominus Hiberniae'.[145] In 1513, Henry led an army

[141] See, for example, the essays in Kelley, *Foundations of Modern Historical Scholarship*, and Ralph E. Giesey, *Rulership in France, 15th–17th Centuries* (Aldershot, 2004), together with *idem*, 'The juristic basis of dynastic right to the French throne'.

[142] Gottfried Leibnitz (ed.), *Mantissa codicis juris gentium* (Hanover, 1700), pp. 63–97 and Robert Anstruther (ed.), *La Vraie cronicque d'Escoce; Pretensions des Anglois à la couronne de France; Diplome de Jacques VI, roi de la Grande Bretagne* (London, 1847), pp. 1–117.

[143] Steven J. Gunn, 'The French wars of Henry VIII', in Jeremy Black (ed.), *The Origins of War in Early Modern Europe* (Edinburgh, 1987), pp. 28–51 and *idem*, 'Chivalry and the politics of the early Tudor court', in Sydney Anglo (ed.), *Chivalry in the Renaissance* (Woodbridge, 1990), pp. 107–128; Glenn Richardson, 'Eternal peace, occasional war: Anglo-French relations under Henry VIII', in Susan Doran and Glenn Richardson (eds), *Tudor England and its Neighbours* (Basingstoke, 2005), pp. 45–46.

[144] Steven J. Gunn, 'Henry VIII's foreign policy and the Tudor cult of chivalry', in Charles Giry-Deloison (ed.), *François Ier et Henri VIII: deux princes de la renaissance (1515–1547)* (Paris, 1995), p. 33.

[145] Clifford S.L. Davies, '"Roy de France et roy d'Angleterre": the English claims to France, 1453–1558', in *Publications du Centre Européen d'Etudes Bourguignonnes (XIVe–XVIe siècle)*, 35 (1995), pp. 123–132. In 1523, the duke of Suffolk led an expedition across the Somme, during the course of which he forced captured towns to swear allegiance to Henry VIII as

of 30,000 men on an expedition from Calais alongside the emperor Maximilian. After their forces won the battle of the Spurs and captured Thérouanne, the city of Tournai surrendered to 'le roy très chrestien Henry, par la grace de Dieu roy de France et d'Angleterre huitiesme de ce nom'.[146] Following the capture of François I at Pavia in March 1525, Henry again pressed his claim to the kingdom of France, or at least to the duchy of Normandy.[147] Eleven years later, the English king was still demanding that his title to Normandy and Aquitaine should be recognised by the Emperor Charles V.[148]

Henry VIII's aggressive foreign policy towards France and the importance of the history of the ancient quarrel were inevitably reflected in contemporary writings. The most famous instance was the translation of the chronicles of Jean Froissart by John Bourchier, lord Berners, printed in two volumes by Richard Pynson in 1523 and 1525. The translation enabled a wide audience to read about the glorious, chivalric deeds of fourteenth-century heroes, such as Edward III and the Black Prince, who had inspired Henry VIII.[149] Even before this, Pynson had played an even more direct role in promoting the war with France. In 1512, at the instigation of Cardinal Wolsey, Pynson had published a papal bull of Pope Julius II which declared the French king to be an enemy of the church, together with a scholarly commentary by James Whytstons arguing that Henry was the rightful king of France and therefore could legitimately remove the tyrant and schismatic Louis XII.[150] The following year, Pynson published a new edition of John Lydgate's *Troy Book*, whose preface, praising Henry V as a paragon of chivalry, would have resonated for a contemporary audience.[151] Around the same time, a translation and amplification of Tito Livio Frulovisi's *Vita Henrici Quinti* was prepared for Henry VIII. It not only celebrated the chivalric deeds of Henry V, but also recounted the famous story of how the English king persuaded St Vincent Ferrer to acknowledge the justice of his war in France; this was dramatically re-enacted when John Colet's objections to war were

---

king of France: Steven J. Gunn, 'The duke of Suffolk's march on Paris in 1523', *EHR*, 101 (1986), pp. 616 and 619.

[146] Clifford S.L. Davies, 'Tournai and the English crown, 1513–1519', *Historical Journal*, 41 (1998), pp. 4–6.

[147] George W. Bernard, *War, Taxation and Rebellion in Early Tudor England: Henry VIII, Wolsey and the Amicable Grant of 1525* (Brighton, 1986), pp. 31–40, and Peter Gwyn, *The King's Cardinal: the rise and fall of Thomas Wolsey* (London, 1990), pp. 389–410.

[148] *L&P, HVIII*, XI, no. 285.

[149] *STC*, 11396 and 11397, and Berners, *Froissart*.

[150] *De iusticia & s[an]ctitate belli per Iuliu[m] pontifice[m] secu[n]du[m] in scismaticos [et] tira[n]nos p[at]rimoniu[m] Petri inuade[n]tes indicti allegatio[n]es* (*STC*, 25585), and P.A. Neville, 'Richard Pynson, king's printer (1506–1529): printing and propaganda in early Tudor England' (PhD thesis, London, 1990), pp. 108–109.

[151] *STC*, 5579.

overcome by Henry VIII, who successfully persuaded the preacher of the justification for the war.[152] A more populist work was *The Gardyners Passetaunce Touchyng the Outrage of Fraunce*, which represented the conflict between the crowns of France and England through a metaphorical battle between their symbolic flowers, contrasting the fresh red rose with the unpleasant odour of the lily.[153]

Though many of these books dealt in passing with the English claims in France, there was no real English equivalent to *La Loi Salique*, the printed version of *Pour ce que plusieurs*, which was enjoying such success in France at the beginning of the sixteenth century. The problem, of course, was that it would have been difficult to find a medieval English text to match *Pour ce que plusieurs*. Where fifteenth-century French writers like Jean de Montreuil, Jean Juvénal, Noël de Fribois, and Guillaume Cousinot had drafted vernacular, prose treatises setting out the legal arguments, Lancastrian and Yorkist officials preferred to collect together documents relating to the ancient claims in France. As a result, medieval English discussions of the legal issues of the war were not only few in number, but also less sophisticated, as they were not written for administrative and diplomatic audiences. These included, for example, a host of genealogies setting out Lancastrian and Yorkist claims to both the English and French thrones,[154] Thomas Walsingham's *Ypodigma neustriae*,[155] William of Worcester's *Boke of Noblesse*,[156] and a series of Latin texts which briefly discussed the English title to Wales, Aquitaine, Normandy, Ireland, and Scotland, written by Andrew Aston, hosteller at Bury St Edmunds.[157] None of these works were printed during the reigns of Henry VII or Henry VIII.

This lack of English writing on the legal and historical issues framing the Hundred Years War underlines the uniqueness and importance

---

[152] Charles Lethbridge Kingsford (ed.), *The First English Life of King Henry the Fifth, written in 1513 by an anonymous author known commonly as the Translator of Livius* (Oxford, 1911), together with John J. Scarisbrick, *Henry VIII* (London, 1968), pp. 54–55, and Clifford S.L. Davies, 'Henry VIII and Henry V: the wars in France', in John L. Watts (ed.), *The End of the Middle Ages? England in the fifteenth and sixteenth centuries* (Stroud, 1998), p. 237n.

[153] *STC*, 11562.5 and 11562.7; Franklin B. Williams Jr. (ed.), *The Gardyners Passetaunce (c.1512)* (London, 1985), p. 27.

[154] See, for example, B.J.H. Rowe, 'King Henry's claims to France in picture and poetry', *The Library*, 4th series, 12 (1932–1933), pp. 77–88; Raluca Radulescu, 'Yorkist propaganda and The Chronicle from Rollo to Edward IV', *Studies in Philology*, 100 (2003), pp. 401–424; Olivier de Laborderie, ' "Ligne de reis": culture historique, représentation du pouvoir royal et construction de la mémoire nationale en Angleterre à travers les généalogies royales en rouleau du milieu du XIIIe siècle au début du XVe siècle' (PhD thesis, Paris, 2002).

[155] Thomas Walsingham, *Ypodigma neustrie a Thoma Walsingham, quondam monacho monasterii S. Albani, conscriptum*, ed. H.T. Riley (London, 1876). This chronicle was first published in 1574: *STC*, 25005.

[156] William Worcester, *The Boke of Noblesse*, ed. John G. Nichols (London, 1860).

[157] BL MS Cotton Claudius A xii, fos 145v–155v.

of *A declaracion of the trew and dewe title of Henry VIII.* This anonymous work was prepared as a direct response to *Pour ce que plusieurs*, but was never published and now survives in just two autograph manuscripts.[158] The first (T) is a heavily corrected and damaged copy that was undoubtedly a working draft. The author was constantly changing the text as he wrote, from minor alterations of specific words within sentences to the deletion of entire pages of writing. At least four folios are now inexplicably missing from the manuscript and one entire folio has been sown into the book at a ninety-degree angle, as a replacement for a deleted block of text. The second manuscript (W) is a polished, presentation version of the same text. The autobiographical introduction that had appeared in the draft copy,[159] was replaced by a brief prologue and a table of contents, while the text itself was clearly divided into twenty-five chapters. This version was almost twice as long as the draft, partly because of the missing folios from the first manuscript, but also because the author became more consistent about including translations from *Pour ce que plusieurs* and generally offered a much fuller discussion of the issues raised by the French treatise.

The reference to the reigning monarch in the title, *A declaracion of the trew and dewe title of Henry VIII*, indicates that the treatise must have been written between 1509 and 1547. The anonymous author probably completed the first draft of his treatise at the very beginning of the reign, perhaps by 1513. A marginal note refers to 'Loys the XIth king of Ffraunce, ffather to Charles which last died king of Ffraunce', indicating that this version was written after the death of King Charles VIII in 1498, and perhaps before the death of his successor, Louis XII, in 1515.[160] The author also mentioned 'Edmond de la Pole now prisoner', suggesting that he was writing before 4 May 1513 when the grandson of William de la Pole, first duke of Suffolk, was executed.[161] There is no direct evidence as to when the author revised this material for the presentation copy, though it is unlikely to have been too long afterwards. The author's handwriting is more commonly associated with the 1480s or 1490s, suggesting that he was at least middle-aged when he first drafted the treatise; it is therefore improbable that he wrote the presentation copy late in the reign of

---

[158] That is to say, London, College of Arms MS Arundel 39, fos 1r–52v (T) and BL MS Additional 48005, fos 6r–97r (W). There is also a seventeenth-century transcription of the treatise in BL MS Additional 48079, fos 30r–125r. See pp. 287–290 below.

[159] See pp. 265–268.

[160] See p. 267.

[161] See p. 265. Moreover, the conclusion expresses opposition to warfare that would have been out of place in the immediate aftermath of Henry VIII's expedition to Calais in 1513: see pp. 269–270.

Henry VIII. The author also suggested in a number of marginal notes that he was using the library of the abbey of Bury St Edmunds, which was closed in 1539.[162] The treatise would have served little purpose after the treaty of perpetual peace was signed at Westminster in April 1527, when attention inevitably shifted away from the ancient claims in France, at least until 1544.[163] Finally, *A declaracion of the trew and dewe title of Henry VIII* does not bear the mark of the extreme religious changes of the second half of the reign. The English author consistently ignored mentions in *Pour ce que plusieurs* of papal support for the Valois monarchy during the Hundred Years War.[164] He did hotly contest the claim that the papacy had authorized a crusade against King John, but tactfully neglected to mention that the tables were only turned when the English king surrendered the kingdom to Pope Innocent III, who then excommunicated Philippe II for threatening to invade England.[165] Similarly, the Tudor author largely ignored the discussion of the special heavenly gifts granted to the 'très chrétien roi de France', except for a brief statement in the conclusion to the draft in manuscript T that the French aimed 'to color that their arrogant and covetous myndes and to come to atteyne to such soverainte they calle ther king the most christen prince'.[166] The only real outburst came when the author angrily denied that Clovis was the first Christian king in the world when, in fact, *Pour ce que plusieurs* had actually been talking about France.[167] This may suggest that the treatise was finished before the break with Rome, which in turn might help to explain its

[162] See pp. 45–46.

[163] In the words of Clifford S.L. Davies, 'The whole tenor of the Reformation was to stress English separateness; the concept of a "dual monarchy" had become an irrelevant memory' (Davies, 'Roy de France et roy d'Angleterre', p. 130). Also see Charles Giry-Deloison, 'A diplomatic revolution? Anglo-French relations and the treaties of 1527', in David Starkey (ed.), *Henry VIII: a European court in England* (London, 1991) pp. 77–86, and *idem*, 'Une alliance contre nature? La paix Franco-Anglaise du 1525–1544', in Charles Giry-Deloison (ed.), *François Ier et Henry VIII*, pp. 53–62.

[164] See pp. 68, 78, and 109, together with the translations on pp. 148–149, 163, and 228.

[165] See pp. 246 and 249–250, together with p. 191. This contrasts strongly with the more heated reaction in Coke's *Debate Between the Heralds*, written in 1549, in Léopold Pannier and Paul Meyer (eds), *Le Débat des hérauts d'armes de France et d'Angleterre, suivi de 'The debate between the heralds of England and France' by John Coke* (Paris, 1887), pp. 15–16 and 61.

[166] See pp. 65–67, 145–146, and 269. The Tudor author made no mention of the temporary transfer of the title of 'most Christian king' to Henry VIII in 1512 for the war against the 'schismatic' Louis XII: David S. Chambers, *Cardinal Bainbridge in the Court of Rome, 1509 to 1514* (Oxford, 1965), pp. 38–41, and Gunn, 'The French wars of Henry VIII', p. 36. Again, the lack of interest in such matters contrasts markedly with the *Débat des hérauts*, pp. 12–16 and 64–66.

[167] See p. 146. The translator also ignored the statement that the French recovery of Anjou, Maine, and Touraine demonstrated God's judgement that these lands did not rightfully belong to the English: see pp. 100 and 215.

subsequent lack of success, a work out of step with a rapidly changing world.

According to the autobiographical preface in the draft (Appendix I), the anonymous author sought to avoid 'slouthe & idelnesse' by writing about Henry VIII's ancient claims in France. In the course of his research, he came upon 'a litil boke or pamphlet imprinted conteynyng false, untrew and dampnable matier, divided into III principall partes', that is to say, *Pour ce que plusieurs*. Outraged at what he saw as a French attempt to undermine Henry VIII's claims in both France and England, the anonymous Englishman prepared a genealogical roll presenting 'the lyne or descent of the kinges of Englond as of the regions of Ffraunce, Castell & Leons, Arragon and Navarre, and also of the dukes of Normandie and Guyan, and of Angeo, Toreyn and Mayne, and of other seignories'.[168] He then decided to write 'this litil boke to impugne the allegacions and fals surmyses made, the premisses rehersing the same their surmyses and in that directly as nere as my symple witte wol serve me'.[169] There is a clear parallel here with John Coke's decision to write the *Debate between the heralds* in 1549 as a reponse to the publication of the anonymous French treatise known as *Le Débat des hérauts d'armes de France et d'Angleterre*.[170]

In the conclusion to the draft version of *A declaracion of the trew and dewe title of Henry VIII*, the English author claimed that *Pour ce que plusieurs* was part of a devious French plot to rewrite history. He argued that Louis XI

> ded to be brought afore him all bookes of cronikes which were within his regalie and dominion and for that they were somoche declaring against him to defeat his title aswel of the coroune and reame of Ffraunce as of the duches of Normandie and Guyan [. . .], the said Loys the Ffrenssh king caused all the said bookes of cronikes to be brent through out his dominions and caused the said boke conteynyng the fals imaginacions as is aforesaid divided into III principall partes and from thens hetherto cause in effect every yere to have new bookes to be made of cronikes of the reame of Ffraunce as by severall auctores to have ther fals and fayned imaginacions by processe of tyme to be of the more auctorite. Which newly compiled bookes of cronikes be emprinted by them and conveyed in to this reame of Englond and undir so fals pretence that the reders therof not have knowlege to the contrary may lightly be seducted

[168] *Non inveni*. For a survey of examples in London, Cambridge, Oxford, and Manchester, see Sydney Anglo, 'The British history in early Tudor propaganda', *Bulletin of the John Rylands Library*, 44 (1961–1962), pp. 17–48.

[169] See p. 267.

[170] See p. 35, n. 165.

and geve credens therunto, which in theffect of the causes conteyned in this boke be falsly imagined.[171]

This remarkable story aimed to undermine the credibility of any evidence offered by the French, and also served as the ultimate example of the deceit that was said to have marked both their actions and those of their allies, the Scots.[172] Given that the history of English claims in France was framed by the failed treaties of Paris (1259), Brétigny (1360), and Troyes (1420), it was inevitable that the Tudor author echoed other polemical writers in condemning the enemies of his king for their consistent failure to live up to the obligations of such peace accords.[173] He repeatedly attacked their breaches of treaties and agreements, culminating with his heated complaint that the French were guilty of violating the truce of Tours in 1444: 'for the Frensshmen never helde hetherto eny treatie or peax hough fermely so ever it were made by othes upon the consecrat body of Crist, the holy evangelies, by censures of the churche, by hostages or otherwise, lenger than they may espie ther singuler avauntage. And ther principall stodie is by cautelles, histories and recordes to witnesse'.[174] His own sources must have demonstrated the problems in sustaining some of his examples, but such charges of deceit were a standard rhetorical weapon in the legal debates between the two monarchies. Indeed, French writers, including both Cousinot and Jean Juvénal des Ursins, had repeatedly levelled the exact same charge against the English.[175]

The Tudor writer was also extremely concerned about internal division within England, which he regarded as the key to all past French successes. He attacked *Pour ce que plusieurs* for its account of the rival Lancastrian and Yorkist claims to the English throne, charging the French treatise with attempting 'to conveye false titles to the corone of Englond, to have and stere division amonges the Englisshmen, to thentent that by suche division, rebellions and werres might growe'.[176] He painted such attempts to play upon tensions in England as a common thread running through the history of Anglo-French relations. A lengthy narrative of the relationship between Richard I

---

[171] See p. 269.

[172] For the attack on the Scots, see pp. 156 and 191.

[173] See pp. 156, 220, 238, and 251–252. Similar claims were made in *The Boke of Noblesse* by William Worcester, while Sir William Paget famously described the French as 'these false dogs' while finalizing the terms of a treaty in June 1546: Worcester, *The Boke of Noblesse*, pp. 4–5 and 22, and Martin A.S. Hume (ed.), *Chronicle of King Henry VIII of England* (London, 1889), p. 120.

[174] See p. 257.

[175] See, for example, Jean Juvénal, II, pp. 164–165, and pp. 72–73 and 125–126 below.

[176] See p. 158. According to the Tudor author, the French also took advantage of internal divisions in England in 1449: see pp. 257–258 and 262–263.

and Philippe Augustus served not only to defend the English king against charges of dishonourable behaviour, but also revealed the Machiavellian actions of the French king as he tried to turn Richard's allies against him; even John emerged from this story with credit, as he resisted the blandishments of the French king and ultimately demonstrated his loyalty towards his elder brother.[177] Internal distractions were said to have prevented King John from responding to Philippe Augustus's invasion of Normandy, while Henry III's failure to act in France was blamed on the actions of rebels like Simon de Montfort, who were actively encouraged and funded by the French crown.[178] Clearly such arguments were logically and rhetorically necessary as explanations for the great disasters of medieval history, from the low point of the reign of King John to the loss of Normandy and Aquitaine at the end of the Hundred Years War. Yet they must also have carried genuine resonance at the beginning of the sixteenth century, especially in the aftermath of the Wars of the Roses and Henry VII's attempts to ensure the stability of the Tudor regime.

Nevertheless, the author of *A declaracion of the trew and dewe title of Henry VIII* did not seem to encourage war with France, either to repay the wrongs committed by the Valois kings and their ancestors, or to bring the English together and unite the realm. He concluded the draft version by stating that

> this werk which is not made to move or stere the king my soverayn lord to invade the reame of Ffraunce therin to move or mak werre for the premisses which if he ded shuld not be other but therby shuld be moche confusion of humayn blode and theend therof at the first begynnyng not knowen. But is writen oonly to enduce his grace to take knowlege not oonly of his right to the contentes in this same but also of the subtil and cautellous imaginacions of his ennemyes the Ffrenshmen and also to consider the losses which his noble progenitoures have susteyned by reason of the dyvysions amonges the noble persones of this regne and to eschue lyk dangeres. *Quia omne regnum in se ipsum divisum desolabitur & domus supra* &c.[179]

This statement was removed from the final, presentation copy, perhaps because it was completed after Henry VIII had already led the successful expedition of 1513. Yet on just one occasion in the presentation copy did the author declare that

> I trust that God wold geve to Englisshmen soche coragious hertes not oonly to defende ther paternell cuntre of Englond, thir heritage and ther wiefes and children against the Frensshmen that they shuld be confused of his

---

[177] See pp. 176–184.
[178] See pp. 191 and 195–197.
[179] See pp. 269–270. The Latin quotation is from Luke 11: 17.

presumpcion, but also to reclayme, entir and recover ther dewe hereditamentes aswel of the corone and totalite of the reame of Ffraunce as the particler londes and seignories.[180]

In general, then, *A declaracion of the trew and dewe title of Henry VIII* did not elevate the history of the Anglo-French wars into a call to arms.

Indeed, to all intents and purposes, *A declaracion of the trew and dewe title of Henry VIII* was a commentary or gloss upon *Pour ce que plusieurs*. In the draft version, the English author often offered a brief précis of Cousinot's treatise before each section but in the presentation copy he was much more consistent, beginning all but one of the chapters with an extended translation of a section of the French treatise, which was then analysed and carefully refuted.[181] By and large these were faithful translations, though the Englishman did occasionally make important mistakes, such as when he thought that the French author was arguing that Gaunt's father-in-law, Henry of Lancaster, should have been the king of England when, in fact, the French treatise was actually speaking about Gaunt's son, Henry IV.[182] On occasion, the Tudor writer did shorten passages that were, perhaps, unnecessarily repetitive, including much of the third section of *Pour ce que plusieurs* concerning the aftermath of the English capture of Fougères.[183] Yet other editorial decisions were more devious. The translations often omitted the more embarrassing points raised by the French treatise, including the murders of Thomas Becket, Edward II, and Thomas of Woodstock, as well as two statements that Henry VI had a better claim to the English throne than his rival, Edward IV.[184] The Tudor author also passed over in silence the vast majority of legal arguments used by the French author in *Pour ce que plusieurs*, particularly relating to the key themes of female and cognate inheritance, and the confiscation of lands from the English kings. With regard to royal succession,

[180] See pp. 252.

[181] The sole exception was chapter nine, pp. 170–171 below.

[182] See p. 157, n. 58, together with pp. 159–161 below. Other errors in the translation include a reference to Jacques van Artevelde rather than his son Philippe, and the attribution of an anti-English slogan to Philippe VI rather than to Bede: see pp. 153 and 154 below.

[183] See pp. 255–256, notes 399, 401, 402, and 405. The Tudor author also omitted a lengthy summary of why Henry I had forfeited the duchy of Normandy (pp. 98–99 and p. 211, n. 260), as well as a fictional speech attributed to Charles IV (pp. 104 and 219).

[184] See p. 172, n. 111, p. 219, n. 291, p. 158, n. 60, p. 161, n. 80, and p. 192, n. 187. It is true that the claim in *Pour ce que plusieurs* that Thomas Becket had been murdered by Prince Henry the Young was dubious, as were his references to English chronicles' accounts of the fates of Arthur and Eleanor of Brittany and of the treaty agreed between Henry III and Prince Louis, which the Tudor author also ignored. See pp. 88 and 114, together with the translations on pp. 175 and 244–245.

the Tudor author completely ignored almost all of the Latin glosses upon the Salic Law in *Pour ce que plusieurs*, which supported the contention that the Salian land was synonymous with the kingdom of France.[185] In chapter three, the Englishman condensed Cousinot's extensive justification of the exclusion of women from the French royal succession into a very short paragraph that omitted a host of important arguments, including God's judgement against Eve, the claim that a woman lacked the judgement to rule and could only hold positions of power under the supervision of a sovereign, and the concern that a queen might marry a commoner.[186] Similarly, the English translation ignored a host of arguments used by Cousinot to defend the principle that cognates like Edward III could not inherit the French throne, including citations from Roman law.[187] The French treatise had not only presented arguments on royal succession but also defended the confiscation of the lands of Henry VIII's ancestors. As well as arguing the historical case for the forfeiture of these territories by Henry I, John, Edward III, and Henry VI, *Pour ce que plusieurs* defended the practice of confiscation by reference to canon law and also claimed that the English crown had taken certain lands from Welsh and Scottish rulers.[188] The Tudor author largely ignored or edited most of this material when he was preparing the translation and, at the same time, turned the tables by offering a case for resistance against an oppressive ruler, particularly through the repeated maxim that '*injuriam armis irrogatam armorum propulsare remedia leges & jura permittunt*'.[189] To a certain degree, this reluctance to acknowledge the legal authorities cited by the French treatise may reflect an English concern over the relevance of Roman and canon law, though the consistent removal of the intellectual framework underpinning the French case did inevitably make it easier to respond to the arguments.[190]

The Tudor writer clearly did not have access to the same kinds of resources as Guillaume Cousinot, who had used both official archives and earlier polemical treatises by writers such as Jean de Montreuil and

---

[185] See pp. 140 and 145, which were based upon pp. 59–60.

[186] See pp. 63–67 and the translations on pp. 148–149.

[187] Compare pp. 61–62 and 77–78 with the translations on pp. 141 and 161–162.

[188] See p. 69 and the translation on p. 151, along with the presentation of cases justifying confiscation by a series of French kings on pp. 99, 105, 110–111, and 114. For Wales and Scotland, compare pp. 90 and 112–113 with pp. 194 and 242.

[189] See pp. 190, 222, 225, and 251–252.

[190] Another example of the editing of legal arguments is the failure to translate the discussion of canon law on bastardy in relation to the inheritance of the duchy of Normandy by William Longsword (pp. 95 and 203).

Jean Juvénal des Ursins.[191] Instead the Englishman had to rely almost entirely upon chronicles. Throughout the treatise, he referred in vague terms to 'the croniques and histories of diverse famous historiens aswel of Ffrenshmen as of other which make mencion of the accidentes and dedes of suche cases'.[192] More directly, he claimed in the preface to the working draft that he 'had in my keping diverse other books of croniks aswel in Ffrenssh and Latyn as in Englissh and Duche'.[193] This is certainly plausible given the clear evidence that he was using a printed copy of *Pour ce que plusieurs*.[194] Unfortunately, however, it is difficult to identify all of the chronicles used in composing *A declaracion of the trew and dewe title of Henry VIII*.[195]

The author did identify three French sources – the famous chronicles of Jean Froissart and Enguerrand de Monstrelet, and *Les Chroniques d'Espagne ou de Burgos* translated from Latin between 1370 and 1373 by Jean Golein. Taken together, Froissart and Monstrelet offered a chivalric history of the Hundred Years War. Although a number of manuscripts containing these works were in circulation in England at the start of the sixteenth century, it seems more likely that the Tudor writer had access to one of the printed editions published by Antoine Vérard and Michel le Noir.[196] The importance of these chronicles for *A declaracion of the trew and dewe title of Henry VIII* is clear. For example,

---

[191] Though there were no official English polemical treatises, there were dossiers and compilations of documents, most notably the collections prepared by Thomas Bekynton that included memoranda relating to Edward III's claim to the French throne, the treaties of Brétigny and Troyes, and even an *Extractum ab originali libri antiqui cronicarum Sancti Severini Burdegalensis*, setting out the ancient boundaries of Gascony and Guyenne: Taylor, 'War, propaganda and diplomacy', pp. 84–88.

[192] See p. 136, together with, for example, pp. 220, 224, and 263.

[193] P. 266. For the use of 'Duche' in the region of Calais, see P.T.J. Morgan, 'The government of Calais 1485–1558' (DPhil thesis, Oxford, 1966), p. 56, and David Grummitt, ' "One of the mooste pryncipall treasours belongyng to his Realme of Englande": Calais and the Crown, c.1450–1558', in David Grummitt (ed.), *The English Experience in France, c.1450–1558: war, diplomacy and cultural exchange* (Aldershot, 2002), p. 56.

[194] The most important piece of evidence in this regard is his translation of an anomalous paragraph which appeared in the printed versions of *Pour ce que plusieurs* and in one manuscript (see pp. 244–245).

[195] Writing in 1549, John Coke claimed to have used chronicles in English, French, and Flemish ('Douche'), and specifically identified writings by Colman, Bede, Gildas, Orosius, and Lucan, as well as the *Cronica cronicarum*, the chronicles of Petit Bretagne, the chronicles of Brabant, the *Mer des histoires*, and texts by Froissart, Monstrelet, Gaguin, Hardyng, and Fabyan: *Débat des hérauts*, pp. xxv, 65, and 74.

[196] Michel le Noir published a four-volume edition of Froissart's chronicles in Paris in 1505, along with a three-volume edition of Monstrelet seven years later. Vérard printed a two-volume edition of Monstrelet at the start of the sixteenth century. There are similarities between the translation of passages from Froissart offered in *A declaracion of the trew and dewe title of Henry VIII* and the later, more famous version effected by John Bourchier, Lord Berners, at the express command of Henry VIII between 1522 and 1525.

the author did not have access to official documentation concerning the treaty of Brétigny but instead relied upon the account in Froissart: 'the said treatie and also the renonciacions ar to be shewed in writing under ther sealles, I doubt not undir the seale of the said King John, in the receipt at Westminster and the tenour therof be conteyned in diverse histories, and in especiall in the croniques of Maistre John Ffroisart'. He then proceeded to draw upon the famous chronicle for a long and detailed account of the treaty of Brétigny and the events leading up to the resumption of the war in 1369.[197] As a result, the Tudor author was not completely sure what had happened in 1360: where *Pour ce que plusieurs* had argued that Edward III failed to complete the renunciations agreed in the treaty, the Englishman responded by inaccurately asserting that they were exchanged but later voided by the actions of the French.[198] *A declaracion of the trew and dewe title of Henry VIII* also drew upon Froissart's chronicle for events following the death of Charles IV of France, including the accession of Philippe VI, the homage paid by Edward III to the new French king, and the flight of Robert of Artois to England.[199]

The *Chronique* of Enguerrand de Monstrelet was the chief source for the discussion of the treaty of Troyes, which concluded with the statement that 'by the tenur of the same treatie in the first volume of the croniques of Enguerain Monstrellet appierith more at large'.[200] The Tudor author returned to the same source for his discussion of the truce signed at Tours in 1444, 'the tenores of the same treatie to witnes which be expressed in the croniques of Enguaran', without realising that this was the last original material in the chronicle; the subsequent account of the events from 1444 to the reconquest of Normandy was, in fact, an anonymous continuation of Monstrelet's *Chronique*.[201] The final chapter of *A declaracion of the trew and dewe title of Henry VIII* also demonstrated that the Tudor author was very poorly informed about the diplomatic negotiations and had no real knowledge of the surviving records, beyond the account in the continuation of the chronicle of Monstrelet: he failed to understand the complicated and anomalous position of the duchy of Brittany in the extensions of the truce of Tours,

---

[197] P. 228, and in general pp. 228–240.

[198] Pp. 232–234 and 238, together with the statements in *Pour ce que plusieurs*, pp. 105–106.

[199] Pp. 143–144 and 151–152. The Tudor author conveniently ignored Froissart's transcription of the letter patent issued by Edward III on 30 March 1331, which declared that the homage paid to Philippe VI was liege (see p. 152, n. 46).

[200] See pp. 168–170.

[201] See pp. 257–262.

and was forced to ignore arguments in *Pour ce que plusieurs* relating to the authority of the Parlement of Paris over the duchy.[202]

The third French chronicle used by the Tudor writer was *Les Chroniques d'Espagne ou de Burgos*. In the preface to the draft copy of *A declaracion of the trew and dewe title of Henry VIII*, the author cited 'a book of cronikes in Frenssh compiled by the bisshop of Burges, and translated into Frenssh tonge by oon Ffrere John Golein of the order of Carmelites at the commaundement of Charles le Beale'.[203] Later he repeated the information, declaring

> And for the trouth herof I shal principally grounde me a great part by the cronikes compiled by the somtyme bisshop of Burges in Latyn tonge and translated out of Latyn in to the Frenssh tonge by oon Maister John Golyn by the commaundement of Charles somtyme king of Ffraunce and Navarre, yonger sone of King Philip le Beale . . .[204]

This was the *Chronica ab initio mundi ad Alfonsum XI, regem Castellae*, a universal chronicle ending in 1327, which was written by Bishop Gonzales d'Hinojosa, bishop of Burgos from 1313 to 1327.[205] The chronicle was translated into French as *Les Chroniques d'Espagne ou de Burgos* between 1370 and 1373 by the Carmelite friar Jean Golein, as part of the extraordinary programme of translation carried out during the reign of King Charles V.[206] For the Tudor writer, the main value of this enormous historical encyclopedia must have been to provide genealogical information, not only for *A declaracion of the trew and dewe title of Henry VIII* but also for the pedigree that he claimed to have written beforehand. There are six marginal notes in the presentation copy that refer the reader to *Les Chroniques d'Espagne ou de Burgos*, and all indicate that the chronicle was used for basic information regarding

---

[202] See pp. 256–263, together with the discussion of Brittany and the Parlement on pp. 122–124, omitted in the préçis on pp. 255–256.

[203] Pp. 265–266.

[204] P. 268.

[205] Auguste Castan, 'Les chroniques de Burgos traduites pour le roi de France Charles V en partie retrouvées à la bibliothèque de Besançon', *Bibliothèque de l'Ecole des Chartes*, 44 (1883), pp. 265–283; Cesáreo Fernández Duro, 'La crónica general de Gonzalo de la Finojosa', *Boletín de la Real Academia de la Historia*, 10 (1887), pp. 438–443; and Peter Linehan, *History and the Historians of Medieval Spain* (Oxford, 1993), p. 479. The bishop had consulted historical materials belonging to King Sancho IV of Castile at either Burgos or Leon between 1306 and 1315.

[206] Jean Golein also translated other historical works by Bernard Gui, the *Rational divinorum officiorum* of Guillaume Durand, and the *De informacione principum*. The Tudor author of *A declaracion of the trew and dewe title of Henry VIII* assumed that the work had been translated for King Charles IV, presumably because the chronicle ended during the reign of that monarch.

the earliest kings of France and the children of King Philippe IV.[207] It is impossible to be certain whether this source was responsible for the genealogical errors in *A declaracion of the trew and dewe title of Henry VIII*, though it is intriguing, for example, that *Les Chroniques d'Espagne ou de Burgos* also failed to recognise the existence of Louis X's daughter, Jeanne.[208] A more difficult problem is how the Tudor writer was able to find such an extremely rare text. Golein's translation has never been published, though there was certainly at least one manuscript in England during the reign of Henry VIII, in the royal library at Richmond, an elaborately illuminated copy that had been purchased by the duke of Berry on 29 October 1407.[209] Unfortunately, there is no evidence to suggest that the author of *A declaracion of the trew and dewe title of Henry VIII* either had access to the royal library or travelled in such exalted circles. One possible solution may lie in the fact that the translator of the chronicle, Jean Golein, was a Carmelite; there may have been a copy of the text in a Carmelite convent, perhaps at Ipswich or at Norwich.[210]

For events pre-dating the Hundred Years War and, in particular, for the reigns of Richard I, John, and Henry III, the anonymous author relied heavily upon two Latin chronicles written in England. For the extremely detailed discussion of the reign of Richard I, he translated and summarized large sections of the *Chronica* of Roger of Howden, as four marginal notes indicated.[211] The same source was used for a briefer discussion of the war between Stephen and Henry II between 1148 and 1153, as two further marginal notes attested.[212] The *Chronica*

---

[207] See pp. 141 and 145–149. Other passages that may derive from this source include, for example, the discussion of the children of Alfonso VIII of Castile and Eleanor, pp. 173–174.

[208] See pp. 141–142 and 165. Needless to say, the author might have drawn his genealogical information from a range of sources; Roger of Howden, for example, included pedigrees of the kings of France and the dukes of Normandy in *Chronica Hovedene*, I, pp. 183 and 239–241.

[209] BL MS Royal 19 E vi, cited in the 1535 inventory of books at Richmond Palace, in James P. Carley (ed.), *The Libraries of King Henry VIII* (London, 2000), p. 7. Also see Léopold Delisle, *Recherches sur la librarie de Charles V* (2 vols, Paris, 1907), II, p. 264.

[210] For the author's connection with Suffolk, and Ipswich in particular, see pp. 46–49. There is no surviving trace of *Les Chroniques d'Espagne ou de Burgos* in the inventories of John Bale, who was himself educated at the Carmelite convent in Norwich and briefly served as prior of the convent in Ipswich between 1533 and 1534.

[211] See pp. 177–187.

[212] See pp. 192–193. In addition, fos 1r–3v, immediately preceding *A declaracion of the trew and dewe title of Henry VIII* in manuscript W, contain a number of passages both in Latin and in translation from Howden's *Chronica*, relating to the passage of certain lands in France into English hands and Richard I's visit to Messina in 1191, during the crusade that was described in chapter eleven of the treatise. The marginal notes confirm that this material was taken from Roger of Howden, and the materials clearly represented the working notes of the author.

offered a history of England from the time of Bede up to 1201, and were written between 1192 or 1193 and Roger's death in 1201 or 1202. They are a particularly useful source for the final years of the reign of Henry II and for the reign of Richard I, when Roger was serving Hugh du Puiset, bishop of Durham, and took part in the crusade of 1190 to 1191.[213]

This source was supplemented by the *Flores historiarum*, which provided historical material ranging from 1153 to 1324, that is to say, from the reign of Henry II to that of Edward II, and was identified in seven marginal notes in the presentation copy.[214] This chronicle was once ascribed to a single author, Matthew of Westminster, but is now regarded as the work of a number of individuals. The material up to at least 1249 was written by Matthew Paris between 1250 and 1255, selectively abridging his own *Chronica maiora*.[215] Following Paris's death in 1259, the *Flores historiarum* was one of his only works to enjoy popularity outside St Albans. It passed to other religious centres, including, most famously, Westminster Abbey, and served as the basis for further continuations up to 1306 and to 1326 by a number of annalists.[216]

It would appear that the Tudor writer gained access to both the *Chronica* of Roger of Howden and the *Flores historiarum* in the library of the abbey of St Edmund at Bury, one of the largest monastic collections in England at the start of the sixteenth century.[217] In the presentation copy, a reference to the adultery committed by the first wife of Louis

---

[213] The *Chronica* were in part a revision of the author's own *Gesta Henrici II Benedicti abbatis*, which covered the years 1169 to 1192: David Corner, 'The *Gesta regis Henrici secundi* and *Chronica* of Roger, parson of Howden', *Bulletin of the Institute of Historical Research*, 56 (1983), pp. 126–144, and also see Michelle R. Warren, 'Roger of Howden strikes back: investing Arthur of Brittany with the Anglo-Norman future', *Anglo-Norman Studies*, 21 (1998), pp. 261–272.

[214] See pp. 142, 180, 196, and 198–199.

[215] V.H. Galbraith, *Roger Wendover and Matthew Paris* (Glasgow, 1944), pp. 25, 31–32, and 45–46; Richard Vaughan, *Matthew Paris* (Cambridge, 1979), pp. 35–41; Thomas Walsingham, *The St Albans Chronicle, 1376–1394: the Chronica Maiora of Thomas Walsingham*, ed. John Taylor and Wendy Childs (Oxford, 2003), pp. xv–xviii.

[216] Richard Vaughan, *Matthew Paris*, pp. 92–109; Antonia Gransden, *Historical Writing in England, c.550 to c.1307* (London, 1974), pp. 378–379, and 'The continuations of the *Flores historiarum* from 1265 to 1327', in *idem, Legends, Traditions and History in Medieval England* (London, 1992), pp. 245–265. It is difficult to identify the particular recension of the *Flores historiarum* used by the author of *A declaracion of the trew and dewe title of Henry VIII*, though he was clearly looking at a copy that ran through to the reign of Edward II.

[217] Montague Rhodes James, *On the Abbey of S. Edmund at Bury: I, the library; II, the church* (Cambridge, 1895); Neil R. Ker (ed.), *Medieval Libraries of Great Britain: a list of surviving books* (2nd edn, London, 1964), pp. 16–22; and Richard Sharpe, James P. Carley, Rodney M. Thomson, and Andrew G. Watson (eds), *English Benedictine Libraries: the shorter catalogues* (London, 1996), pp. 43–98.

X was supported by a marginal note citing the '*fflores historiarum apud Saint Edmundes Bury*'.[218] There are two similar references in the margins of the working draft, both citing an unidentified '*chronica*' of Bury St Edmunds in support of stories relating to the treaty of Louviers agreed by Richard I and Philippe Augustus in January 1196, mistakenly attributed to 1197 in the text. In both cases, the Tudor text closely follows the *Chronica magistri* of Roger of Howden, though one passage might come from the *Flores historiarum*.[219] The abbey was closed on 4 November 1539, shortly after John Leland had visited and prepared an inventory listing twenty-two books, none of which came to the royal library. Included in this list was a work entitled *Hovedeni historia incipiens a Beda*, which may be a reference to the *Chronica* of Roger of Howden.[220] Unfortunately, there is no surviving record of a copy of the *Flores historiarum* at Bury St Edmunds, though there are references to a number of unidentified chronicles that might fit the bill.[221]

The fact that the Tudor author had access to the library of the abbey of Bury St Edmunds when composing both the draft and presentation copies of the treatise does suggest that he lived somewhere nearby. Moreover, the preface to the first manuscript highlighted the author's direct interest in the first duke of Suffolk, William de la Pole:

> by common report that William de La Pole first duke of Suffolk [...] havying the governaunce of the most part of the premisses under and for the most vertuous prince of famous memorie king Henry the VIth, shuld have bargained and sold and so delivered the same to the Frenssh king for certain mony which the said duke shuld have taken to his owne use, which comon report gave not perfite knowlege to me therof, nor is not but seldom to be beleved.[222]

Most interesting of all, though, is the local knowledge that the author demonstrated in his unusual comment on the burial site of a key figure in his narrative: 'Elizabeth wief of duc Leonell [of Clarence] died in the yere MCCCLXIII and lieth buried at Brusyard in Suffolk'.[223] Elizabeth de Burgh did indeed die in 1363, but she was buried in the family mausoleum at Clare Priory. Nevertheless, both Elizabeth and Clare

---

[218] See p. 142.

[219] See p. 182.

[220] B16, no. 22, in *English Benedictine Libraries*, p. 96.

[221] Ker (ed.), *Medieval Libraries of Great Britain*, pp. 16, 20, and 22, and Andrew G. Watson, *Supplement to the Second Edition of Medieval Libraries of Great Britain: a list of surviving books. Edited by N.R. Ker* (London, 1987), p. 6.

[222] See p. 265.

[223] See p. 159.

Priory were intimately linked with Bruisyard parish, just twenty-five miles away. Bruisyard was the site of a Franciscan nunnery founded by Elizabeth's husband, Lionel, together with a secular college and chantry offering prayers for the souls of her father and the second husband of her mother, Matilda of Lancaster, which had been moved from Campsey Ash in 1354. Moreover, Matilda was living at Bruisyard by 1369 and was buried there after her death in 1377, while the secular college was surrendered for the use of the Nuns Minoresses or Sisters of St Clare.[224] In other words, the statement that Elizabeth de Burgh was buried at Bruisyard may be the result of a confusion with her mother, Matilda, or of the fact that the parish was connected with Clare Priory, where Elizabeth was actually interred. Either way, the reference to Bruisyard does seem to suggest genuine local knowledge on the part of the Tudor writer. Ironically, the link between *A declaracion of the trew and dewe title of Henry VIII* and Bruisyard was maintained when the draft copy fell into the hands of Robert Hare in 1563. His father, Sir Nicholas Hare, had purchased the former nunnery at Bruisyard in 1539, following the dissolution of St Augustine's, Canterbury.[225]

According to the preface in the working draft, the anonymous writer was composing the book as a means to fill his time, having found that 'the charge of an office for to levye, gather and answer unto [...] my most dredde soverayn lord Henry the VIIIth [...] the customes and subsidies of merchaundises of oon of his poorts of Englond' did not fill his days, since he was prevented from trading himself.[226] If this description was true and the author was indeed from Suffolk, then it would suggest that his home was in the head port of Ipswich.[227] The author claimed that there was little work for him to do as a customs collector, which certainly echoes the reality that, by the first decade of the sixteenth century, exports of cloth through Ipswich had fallen by over half, not least because of the rising importance of London.[228] By the reign of Henry VIII, each customs head port usually had two

---

[224] William Page (ed.), *The Victoria History of the County of Suffolk* (2 vols, London, 1907–1911), II, pp. 131–132, and Roberta Gilchrist and Marilyn Oliva, *Religious Women in Medieval East Anglia: history and archaeology c.1100–1540* (Norwich, 1993), pp. 57–60.

[225] See p. 228. Robert died there on 2 November 1611: May McKisack, *Medieval History in the Tudor Age* (1971), pp. 60–61, and Diarmaid MacCulloch, *Suffolk and the Tudors: politics and religion in an English county, 1500–1600* (Oxford, 1986), p. 71.

[226] See p. 265.

[227] Maryanne Kowaleski, 'Port towns: England and Wales, 1300–1540', in David M. Palliser (ed.), *Cambridge Urban History of Britain. I, c.600–c.1540* (Cambridge, 2000), pp. 472–473.

[228] Eleanora M. Carus-Wilson and Olive Coleman (eds), *England's Export Trade, 1275–1540* (Oxford, 1963), pp. 93–95 and 112–113. The Tudor author did not demonstrate any great love for Londoners when reporting the assistance that they gave to Prince Louis during the invasion of England and his war with Henry III (see p. 251).

collectors and one, or rarely two, controllers, primarily drawn from the merchants of the town, together with a controller whose function was to check the accounts of the collectors.[229]

Given that the evidence for even suggesting that the author came from Ipswich is so thin, it is clearly impossible to identify the author of *A declaracion of the trew and dewe title of Henry VIII*. Nevertheless, there are some possibilities. Thomas Hall (d. between 1511 and 1519) was appointed as a collector of customs and subsidies on 8 December 1507 and his patent as comptroller of customs for the port of Ipswich was registered on 20 October 1509. Almost certainly the younger son of an Essex mercer who may have had some legal training, Hall also served as common clerk, clerk of peace, member of the Twenty-Four of Ipswich, and Member of Parliament in 1510. He was disenfranchised in November 1510 'for diverse disobediences and contempts' and, two months later, he was sent to the Fleet prison for claiming that Katherine of Aragon was 'delivered of a knave child', and this may explain his effective disappearance from public records in Ipswich from this point until his death by 1519.[230] Such public declarations do not seem in keeping with the attitudes of the author of *A declaracion of the trew and dewe title of Henry VIII*. A more appropriate candidate might be William Spencer (d. *c.*1529). He was appointed as a collector of customs and subsidies in Ipswich on 1 June 1498, and became comptroller of customs for the port from 1501 to 1506 and a Member of Parliament for the borough in 1510. Intriguingly, he was living in Bury St Edmunds when he first became a freeman of Ipswich on 6 January 1494.[231]

Whatever the true identity of the author of *A declaracion of the trew and dewe title of Henry VIII*, there is no evidence to suggest that this unofficial treatise on the king's claims in France was ever read by Henry VIII himself or any of his immediate circle. Nevertheless, the work was far from a private project, as demonstrated by the effort put into preparing the presentation copy, which conveniently organized the material into chapters and included a table of contents that would have made it

[229] Some customs collectors may have been physically based at one of the sub-ports, though it is more likely that the collectors were based at the head port and then appointed deputies to report on customs collection in the member ports.

[230] *Calendar of the Fine Rolls Preserved in the Public Record Office, XXII, Henry VII, 1485–1509* (London, 1962), p. 396, and *L&P, HVIII*, I, part I, document 218, p. 112, together with the biographical account by John Pound in *The History of Parliament on CD-ROM* (Cambridge, 1998).

[231] *Calendar of the Fine Rolls, XXII*, pp. 265–266, and the brief biographical account by Pound in *The History of Parliament on CD-ROM*. Richard Percyvale was appointed as a collector of customs and subsidies for the port of Ipswich on 3 July 1502, with effect from the following Easter (*Calendar of the Fine Rolls, XXII*, p. 336), but he was described as the late collector of customs in 1512, in *L&P, HVIII*, I, part I, document 1512, p. 705.

simple to use. Moreover, the treatise clearly did circulate, because the draft copy came into the hands of a local man, Robert Hare, in 1563 and, more relevantly, because the presentation copy of the treatise was later bound under the title *Titulum ad Franciam* alongside Nicholas Upton's Latin paraphrase of Henry V's ordinances of Mantes, issued in 1419, and a number of medieval lists of summonses to Parliament, council, and war. This manuscript became part of the Yelverton collection, together with a seventeenth-century transcription of *A declaracion of the trew and dewe title of Henry VIII* in a miscellany of diplomatic and political papers that also included the same text by Upton and letters relating to Edward III's original claim to the French throne (London, BL MS Additional 48079). In the absence of further evidence, the most likely explanation is that the treatise was originally intended for, or to attract the attention of, an important local patron, perhaps an administrator or diplomat with local connections such as Sir Nicholas Harvey, or Sir Richard and Sir Robert Wingfield. Indeed, in this regard, it is striking that Sir Robert was recorded as reciting the claims of kings John, Edward III, and Henry V to the French throne – themes central to *A declaracion of the trew and dewe title of Henry VIII* – when speaking before the emperor in 1515.[232]

---

[232] *L&P, HVIII*, II, i, document 1165. The treatise would clearly have been useful for the expanding class of diplomats: Luke MacMahon, 'Courtesy and conflict: the experience of English diplomatic personnel at the court of Francis I', in David Grummitt (ed.), *The English Experience in France*, pp. 182–183.

EDITORIAL PRINCIPLES

For each of the texts, my goal is to offer a semi-diplomatic edition of one manuscript: that is to say, manuscript B for *Pour ce que plusieurs* and the autograph manuscript W for *A declaracion of the trew and dewe title of Henry VIII*. Limitations of space mean that it is not possible to record all of the variants from the numerous medieval manuscripts of *Pour ce que plusieurs*, though significant examples are identified in the footnotes. In the case of *A declaracion of the trew and dewe title of Henry VIII*, there are significant variations between the draft version (T) and the presentation copy (W), and I have recorded these in the footnotes and have also provided a transcription of the introduction and conclusion to the draft in Appendix I.

In preparing the documents for publication, every effort has been made to produce clear and accurate texts. I have avoided emending manuscript readings and scribal morphology unless necessary, but have lightly edited the texts to aid reading comprehension, using conventions of diplomatic editing: that is to say, adding modern punctuation and capitalization, apostrophes, the cedilla, and restricted use of acute accents. Doubtful or missing words or passages have been enclosed in square brackets. Abbreviations have been expanded in the usual manner, according to the form in which they are most often written out in full in the manuscript. J and V have been used for consonantal I and U. I am grateful to Jocelyn Wogan-Browne and Thelma Fenster for their expert advice and assistance.

POUR CE QUE PLUSIEURS

|**1r**| Pour ce que plusieurs[1] a la relation d'autrui,[2] sans avoir certaine congnoissance de la verité des matieres ou a l'appetit des[3] parties ausquellez ilz sont plus affectionez, parlent des questions et debas qui ja par longz temps ont esté et ainçoires durent entre les roys et royaumes de France et d'Angleterre[4] tant a cause des drois pretendus, et que chascune desdictez parties querele et maintient avoir a la couronne et totalité dudit royaume de France en aucunes terres et seignouries aussi particulieres dicellui; et pareillement au fait de la roupture des tre- |**1v**| ves qui fut l'an mil quatrecens quarante neuf, soubz umbre et confiance desquelles les Anglois se dient avoir perdu et leur avoir esté osté par le feu Roy Charles le VIIe les duchez de Normandie et de Guyenne avecquez autres terres et seignouries qu'ilz tenoyent et possidoient en diverses parties du royaume de France; et par ce que la verité desdictez matieres n'est pas a tous congneue, ne le fondement dicelles, ne les incidences qui sont entrevenues, maintes gens en ce deffault errent, et cuident les choses estre autres que a la verité elles ne sont. Pour oster la dicte erreur et affin que chascun clerement et sans aucune ambiguité ou doubte puisse congnoistre et estre deuement informé du droit que les parties en chascune desdictez matieres puet avoir et reclamer l'une a l'encontre de l'autre, et les solutions aussi et justifications dont elles se puent deffendre, l'aucteur de ce present traittié a volu cy dessoubz escripre et inferer tout ce qu'il a peu veoir, congnoistre et entendre veritablement des choses dessusdittez,[5] soy fondant es anciennes cronicquez et histoires tant de France comme d'Angleterre, es lettres aussi auctentiquez et enseignemens vaillables fais esdittez matieres, subjoingnant aux choses dessusdittez ce qu'il treuve conformé en raison[6] naturele et escripte,

---

[1] The manuscript B actually reads 'pluiseurs' but on this one occasion I have corrected the reading to accord with the standard incipit of the text.

[2] D adds 'parlent des questions et debatz qui sont entre et Engleterre'. M replaces 'd'autrui' with 'ou a l'appetit des parties'.

[3] O omits 'matieres ou a l'appetit des'.

[4] D omits 'ou a l'appetit des parties [. . .] royaumes de France et d'Angleterre'.

[5] N adds 'ce qu'il treuve conservir en raison'.

[6] N repeats 'soy fondant es anciennes cronicquez et histoires tant de France comme d'Angleterre selon raison'.

tant des drois civilez comme canons. Pareillement de la Loy Salicque qui est la vraie loy des François, des usages aussy |**2r**| et coustumes dont les François et les Anglois ont usé et usent tant en France comme en Angleterre quant les cas particuliers si sont offers, et semblablement des inconveniens qui s'en pourroient ensuyr se autrement se faisoit. Priant et requerant a tous ceulx qui ce present traittié liront ou lire orront que s'ilz y voient chose trop dilatee ou moins declaree ou qu'il leur semble qu'il y ait contrarieté en aucunes choses, ambiguité, obscurité ou quelque erreur, vice d'escripvain ou autre deffault, leur plaisir soit avant donner aucun blasme[7] a ce present euvre eulx bien informer de la verité desdittez matieres.[8] Et se faulte aucune y est trouvee, les ygnorances suppleer et les deffaulz benignement supporter et amender.[9]

Et pour entrer[10] esdittes matieres affin que mieulx et plus clerement elles puissent estre entendues semble estre neccessaire declairier premierement[11] les drois tiltres et reclaims que lesdiz Anglois pretendent et font es choses dessusdittez, et les diviser chascun a part soy; et après mettre les solutions et responses qui y sont; avisé le tout que la verité est et que clerement se puet monstrer et prouver par aux moiens et par les facons enseignemens et evidences dont dessus est faitte mention.[12]

En ensuivant lequel train et pour mieulx et |**2v**| plus clerement entendre ceste matiere semble estre besoing icelle diviser en trois parties principales.[13]

La premiere es drois que lesdis Anglois pretendent a la couronne et a la totalité du royaume de France,[14] et les moyens par lesquelz ilz dient qu'ilz leur competent et appartiennent.

La seconde partie si est es singulieres terres et seignouries du royaume que a tiltre heredital lesdis Anglois pretendent a eulx appartenir et estre leur vray et droit heritage.

---

[7] A repeats the phrase 'avant donner aucuns blasme'.

[8] C omits: 'leur plaisir soit avant donner aucun blasme a ce present euvre eulx bien informer de la verité desdittez matieres'.

[9] N adds 'a leur pouvoir et bon entendement'.

[10] F begins the transcription at this point, presumably because of the missing first folio that may have contained an illumination (see p. 277).

[11] H begins the transcription of the text here, following an exceptionally long rubric (see pp. 277–278).

[12] H: 'Et aprés mettre les solutions et responses ainsi que la verité est et que au plaisir de dieu il sera clerement monstré et prouvé quant le cas y escherra et la matiere le requera'.

[13] ACDMO: 'En [A: 'et'] ensuivant lequel train l'aucteur a divisé [A: 'mise'] ladicte matiere en trois parties principalles'.

[14] L adds 'et a la totalité de la couronne de France'.

La tierce partie est touchant le fait des treves aux moyens dessus declariez et que icy dessoubz seront ainçoires plus amplement specifiez.[15]

Au regard de la premiere partie faisant mencion de la couronne et des drois que les Anglois y pretendent et a la totalité du royaume, est vray pour fonder ceste matiere[16] que le Roy Phelippe filz Sainct Loys eut deux filz:[17] un nommé Phelippe le Bel lequel fut roy; et l'autre Charles qui fut[18] conte de Valois, de Beaumont, de Chartres, d'Alençon et du Perche et depuis d'Anjou et du Maine au moyen de l'appointement fait par le Pape Innocent le Quart entre ledit Roy Phelippe le Bel, le Roy Charles Second de Cecile, duquel ledit |3r| conte de Valois espousa sa fille, [et] du Roy Pietre aussi d'Arragon querelant le royaume de Cecile, contre lequel avoit esté donnee la croisee par les Papes Clement et Innocent pour ce qu'il troubloit l'eglise et les vassaulx dicelle et ledit Charles conte de Valois.[19]

Ledit Roy Phelippe le Bel roy de France et de Navarre regna XXIX ans, c'estassavoir depuis l'an mil deuxcens IIII^{XX} et VI jusquez en l'an mil III^{C} et XV,[20] et eut trois filz et trois fillez; c'estassavoir Loys Hutin lequel regna environ ung an et fut l'aisné des filz; Phelippe le Long qui fut le second [lequel] regna environ V ans; et Charles le Bel qui fut le tiers lequel regna sept ans.[21] Et au regard des filles l'une eut nom Margarite qui fut femme de Ferrant aisné filz de Sanxe roy de Castelle. La seconde fut Ysabel femme du Roy Edouart le Second,

---

[15] ACMO replace this paragraph with 'La tierce partie [A omits 'partie'] est touchant le fait des treves rompues l'an mil CCCCXLIX et ces [C: 'aux'] choses qui en sont ensuyvies aux moyens et par la façon que cy [A omits 'cy'] dessoubz [O adds 'aprez'] sera plus amplement [O adds 'parlé'] declairé et specifié' [M: 'specifié et declairé'; C adds: 'si venons a la premiere partie'].

[16] ACO replace 'est vray pour fonder ceste matiere' with 'pour mieulx fonder et entendre ceste matiere, il est vrai'.

[17] King Philippe III (d. 1285) was the son of Louis IX (d. 1270). In reality, he had four sons: Louis (d. 1276), King Philippe IV le Bel (d. 1314), and Charles, count of Valois (d. 1325), together with Louis, count of Evreux (d. 1319), by a second marriage.

[18] The transcription in manuscript D ends here.

[19] Charles was given the county of Valois as an apanage in 1285. He later received the counties of Anjou and Maine because of his marriage to Marguerite, daughter of Charles II of Anjou, king of Sicily (d. 1309), his ally in the crusade against the Aragonese following an invasion of Sicily in 1282 by King Pedro III (d. 1285).

[20] Philippe IV ruled from 1285 to 1314, in modern dating. O gives the length of Philippe IV's reign as 'XIX' years, that is to say, from 'mil II^{C} IIII^{XX} et XVI jusques en l'an mil III^{C} et XV'.

[21] Philippe IV was actually the father of four sons: King Louis X le Hutin (d. 1316), King Philippe V le Long (d. 1322), King Charles IV le Bel (d. 1328), and their brother Robert (d. 1308).

surnommé de Carnarinam, duquel mariage issy Edouart le Tiers[22] que on appelloit de Windezore, qui depuis querela le royaume de France. Et la tierce fut Katherine qui mourut sans estre mariee.[23]

Ledit Loys Hutin fut roy aprés son pere et eut ung filz nommé Jehan qui morut en alant Rains pour le faire sacrer, et pource n'est il point mis ou nombre des roys de France.[24] Et si eut une fille qui fut mariee au conte d'Evreux dont descendit |3v| le mauvais roy de Navarre qui fist tant de mal en France, pere du Roy Charles de Navarre qui a esté le derrenier hoir masle dudit royaume.[25] Et pour ce que lesdis Loys Hutin et Jehan son filz n'eurent aucuns enfans masles, Phelippe le Long son frere succeda ausdis royaumes de France et de Navarre, lequel semblablement n'eut que une fille laquelle fut mariee au conte d'Artois.[26] Et par samblable moyen aprés sa mort Charles le Bel son frere recueilly la succession desdis royaumes de France et de Navarre.

Ledit conte de Valois Charles eut deux filz, c'estassavoir Phelippe qui depuis fut roy et Charles conte d'Alençon qui morut a la bataille de Crecy, duquel sont descendus les autres contes et ducs d'Alençon jusques a cellui qui est a jourdhuy.[27]

---

[22] C omits 'le Second surnommé de Carnarinam duquel mariage issy Edouart', thereby skipping from Edward II to his son Edward III. A marginal note in J, in a different hand, reads 'qui fut le premiere qui querella droit au royaume de France'.

[23] The three daughters of Philip IV were Marguerite (d. 1300), Blanche (d. 1294), and Isabella (d. 1358), wife of King Edward II (d. 1327) and mother of King Edward III (d. 1377): see p. 000 n. 259. Blanche and Marguerite died at the ages of four and twelve, thereby preventing a proposed marriage between Marguerite and Fernando IV of Castile (d. 1312): see p. 62.

[24] Louis X's posthumous son, Jean, died in 1316, and was not numbered amongst the kings of France in many late medieval chronicles and genealogies: see, for example, Jean Juvénal, II, pp. 17–18, and Sanford Zale, 'Unofficial histories of France in the late middle ages', (PhD thesis, Columbus, OH, 1994), pp. 400–422 and 482–487. In this account, Guillaume Cousinot implies that the crucial issue was that Jean was never crowned, no doubt because of the importance of royal coronation in the debate over female succession to the throne, as well as his later argument that the Englishman, Henry VI, was never properly crowned as king of France. See pp. 63, 65–67, and 79 below, as well as Jacques Krynen, *L'Empire du roi: idées et croyances politiques en France XIIIe–XVe siècle* (Paris, 1993), especially pp. 135–153.

[25] P omits 'qui fist tant de mal en France pere du Roy Charles de Navarre', perhaps because of a homoeoteleutic error, jumping from 'Navarre' to 'Navarre'. Though Louis X's daughter Jeanne (d. 1349) was passed over for the royal succession, she did inherit the kingdom of Navarre in April 1328 following the death of her uncle, Charles IV. She married Philippe, count of Evreux (d. 1343), and her son was King Charles II of Navarre (d. 1387), father of King Charles III of Navarre (d. 1425).

[26] In reality, Philippe V had a son named Louis, who died before him in 1317, together with four daughters by his wife Jeanne of Burgundy: Jeanne, wife of Eudes, duke of Burgundy, and mother of Philippe, count of Artois; Marguerite; Isabelle; and Blanche.

[27] The two sons of Charles, count of Valois, were King Philippe VI of France (d. 1350) and Charles, count of Alençon, great-grandfather of Jean II, duke of Alençon.

Si avint que ledit Roy Charles le Bel morut sans aucuns enfans. Mais il laissa sa femme grosse d'une fille qui eut nom Blanche, laquelle depuis fut mariee au duc Phelippe d'Orleans frere du Roy Jehan.[28] A l'occasion duquel deffault d'avoir lignee se meut grant trouble et question ou royaume de France tant durant la grossesse de la royne Jehanne de Bourgoingne vesve dudit feu Roy Charles le Bel pour savoir qui auroit |**4r**| le gouvernement du ventre comme le plus prochain hoir, comme depuis que laditte fille fut nee, pour savoir a qui le royaume devoit appartenir. Et furent mandez les trois estas generaulx du royaume ensemble tous les notables clers, docteurs et autres gens d'estat expers et congnoissans en telz matieres.

Ausquelz trois estas se presenta d'un costé Phelippe conte de Valois, filz et heritier dudit Conte Charles, frere dudit Roy Phelippe le Bel, lequel Phelippe conte de Valois comme cousin germain en ligne masculine desdis trois roys freres, c'est assavoir Loys Hutin, Phelippe le Long et Charles le Bel, par ce qu'ilz n'eurent aucuns enfans masles ne autres heritiers descendans d'eulx en ligne masculine si prochain comme lui, disoit et maintenoit le royaume et la couronne lui devoit appartenir.

L'autre part se comparut esdiz trois estas Edouart le Tiers roy d'Angleterre, filz de Edouart le Second autrement dit de Carnarinam et de Madame Ysabel, suer desdiz trois roys freres, lequel pretendoit au contraire le royaume et la couronne lui devoit appartenir par ce qu'il disoit qu'il estoit masle et le plus prochain hoir masle[29] desdiz trois roys dessus nommez, car il estoit leur |**4v**| nepveu, filz de leur seule suer germaine Madame Ysabel ainsi comme dit est, et par consequent plus prochains diceulx trois roys. Et a ceste cause voloit maintenir que lesdis royame et couronne lui competoient et appartenoient.[30]

Pour la justification du droit desquelles parties pluiseurs grans raisons furent allegueez d'unepart et d'autre tant de la loy et coustume du royaume de France en telles matieres comme de l'usage qui avoit esté gardé quant telz cas estoyent avenus. Pareillement aussi de l'ordonnance de la Loy Salicque ou cas dessudit et de la constitucion

---

[28] When Charles IV died in 1328, he was survived by a daughter named Marie from his third marriage, to Jeanne of Evreux, together with another girl, Blanche, who was born posthumously and died in 1358. Blanche married Philippe, duke of Orléans, brother of King Jean II (d. 1364). Jean Juvénal had also referred to just one surviving daughter of Charles IV, in Jean Juvénal, I, p. 159 and II, p. 19.

[29] O omits 'et le plus prochain hoir masle'.

[30] Charles IV died on 31 January 1328, and his daughter Blanche was born shortly afterwards, on 1 April. The fifteen-year-old Edward III of England did not play any role in the subsequent debate over the French royal succession, though he was represented by the bishops of Worcester, Coventry, and Lichfield.

des empereurs es matieres de fiefz selon les chappitres de la dixieme collation.[31]

Et aprés lesdittes allegations les parties assistans d'un commun consentement se departirent de la constitution imperial, pource que le royaume de France n'est point subget a l'empire[32] et pareillement de la loy et coustume du royame en ce cas, pour ce que on n'y savoit trouver fondement si cler comme en si grans matieres estoit bien requis. Et se resolurent sur les autres deux poins, c'estassavoir sur la Loy Salicque qui fut la premiere loy dont les François ussassent oncques et commença du temps de Pharamon premier roy de France, estant pour lors Pape Boniface le Premier,[33] et Empereur |5r| Honorius Primus,[34] et ou XIIe an de son regne, dont les dictateurs premiers furent Usogast, Bosogast,[35] Salagast et Wisogast, lesquelz estoient commis par le dit roy Pharamon a la nomination et election des grans princes et seigneurs qu'il avoit avecques lui des le temps que les François habitoient ainçoires sur la riviere du Rin, a respondre de toutes les questions doubteuses que on leur faisoit. Et leur response estoit mise par escript et aprés gardee pour loy et fut le droit commencement de la Loy Salicque, laquelle depuis a esté accreue et augmentee par les autres roys successeurs dudit Phara[m]on, tant sarrasins que crestiens, jusquez au temps de Charlemaigne.[36] Depuis lequel tamps n'y fut aucune chose adjousté pource que la science positive commença lors

---

[31] A: 'de la premiere collation'. There is no evidence to confirm this report that the Salic Law was cited in the debates of 1328. It is more plausible that the lawyers would have cited the 'Tenth Collation' or *Libri feudorum*, a collection of feudal laws from Italy that were added to Justinian's *Corpus juris civilis* in the mid-twelfth century, and which was used, for example, by Jean Juvénal to justify the exclusion of females and cognates from the French royal succession: Jean Juvénal, II, pp. 22–24 and 44. Also see Craig Taylor, 'The Salic Law and the Valois succession to the French crown', *French History*, 15 (2001), pp. 358–377, and *idem*, 'Edward III and the Plantagenet claim to the French throne', in James Bothwell (ed.), *The Age of Edward III* (Woodbridge, 2001), pp. 155–169.

[32] M presents 'pource que le royaume de France n'est point subget a l'empire' as a marginal note in the same hand.

[33] M: 'estant pour lors pape Innocent [underlined with a series of dots] Boniface'.

[34] Boniface I was pope from 418 to 422 and Emperor Honorius reigned from 395 to 423. These references establish a historical context for the mythical Frankish King Pharamond, who had been commonly associated with the Salic Law according to a tradition established by Fredegar around 660. See p. 21, n. 92.

[35] CO omit 'Bosogast'. Most medieval sources, including Sigebert of Gembloux and Raoul de Presles, reported that Pharamond only reigned for eleven years: Jacques-Paul Migne (ed.), *Patrologiae Cursus Completus, sive bibliotheca universalis. . .omnium S.S. Patrum, Doctorum, Scriptorumque ecclesiasticorum. . .Series secunda* (221 vols, Paris, 1844–1864), CLX, col. 77b–78a, and Adrien Leroux de Lincy and Lazare M. Tisserand (eds), *Paris et ses historiens aux XIVe et XVe siècles* (Paris, 1867), pp. 105–106. According to the *Grandes chroniques de France*, Pharamond was king for twenty years: *Grandes chroniques*, I, pp. 19–20.

[36] The connection between Charlemagne and the Salic Law was a common topos in fifteenth-century polemical treatises: Montreuil, II, pp. 164, 168, 209, 226, 274, and 326;

a venir en France a la promotion de Alcuynus et des deux disciples de Bede.[37] Et aussi que ledit Charlemaigne fut fait empereur de Romme et eut congnoissance des drois, lesquelz il fist apporter en France parquoy on eut eut autre maniere de faire que on avoit eu auparavant,[38] non pas pour riens deroguer a laditte Loy Salicque, mais aussi depuis on n'y adjousta ne y accreut l'en aucune chose. Et pour ce que laditte Loy Salicque estoit la vraye loy des François chascune des parties et aussi les assistans se fonderent principalement sur icelle Loy Salicque.

Aussi lesdittez parties et assistans se arresterent |5v| fort sur l'usage notoirement gardé quant telz cas estoient avenus car ce la estoit une grande evidence et clere demonstrance du droit des parties.

Et sur ces deux poins disoit Phelippe de Valois en tant qu'il touchoit la Loy Salicque que *in titulo De alode LXVII° capitulo primi libri in fine,*[39] elle disoit telz motz en substance: *Nulla portio hereditatis de terra salicqua, qui est interpretandum de regali dominio quod a nullo deppendet nec alicui subicitur, ad differenciam aliarum terrarum que in alodio conceduntur, mulieri veniat;*[40] *sed ad virilem sexum tota hereditas perveniat.*[41] Lesquelles parolles donnoient clerement a entendre que en matiere de couronne et regalité le royaume et la couronne devoient venir au plus prochain hoir masle descendu de hoyr masle du roy derrain trespassé.[42] Or disoit il qu'il estoit hoir masle et le plus prochain descendant en ligne masculine du Roy Charles le Bel qui avoit esté le derrenier des trois roys et par ce moyen le royame lui devoit appartenir.

Et affin de mieulx entendre ceste matiere et que est *Lex Salica*, pourquoy elle est appellee *salica*, et aussi que est *de terra salica*, il est vray que *Lex Salica est constitutio regia ex responsis sapientum iniciata a*

Jean Juvénal, I, pp. 156 and 159, and II, pp. 20 and 41; Kathleen Daly and Ralph E. Giesey, 'Noël de Fribois et la Loi Salique', *Bibliothèque de l'Ecole des Chartes*, 151 (1993), pp. 31–32.

[37] The notion that a transfer of culture and learning, or 'translatio studii', had occurred during the reign of Charlemagne was a commonplace in late medieval France: Serge Lusignan, 'L'université de Paris comme composante de l'identité du royaume de France: étude sur le thème de la translatio studii', in Rainer Babel and Jean-Marie Moeglin (eds), *Identité régionale et conscience nationale en France et en Allemagne du moyen âge à l'époque moderne* (Sigmaringen, 1997), pp. 59–72, and *idem, Vérité garde le roy: la construction d'une identité universitaire en France (XIIIe–XVe siècle)* (Paris, 1999), pp. 225–291.

[38] N changes 'parquoy on eut eut autre maniere de faire que on avoit eu auparavant' to 'par quoy ilz ont eu de la en avant toute autre maniere de faire dont par avant on n'avoit riens fait'.

[39] ACHMO: '*alode LXII°*'.

[40] ACMO place '*mulieri veniat*' earlier in the quotation, immediately after '*terra salicqua*'.

[41] This transcription accords with redaction K in Karl A. Eckhardt (ed.), *Pactus legis salicae: monumenta Germaniae historica, legum sectio I, leges nationum Germanicarum, IV, part I* (Hanover, 1962), chapter 62, § 6, though Cousinot has incorporated a Latin gloss into the quotation: see pp. 18–20 above and 61 below.

[42] C omits: 'descendu de hoyr masle'.

prudentibus, subsequentu emologata, et demum secundum diversitatem temporum per varios reges emen- |**6r**| *data et augmentata.*[43]

Et est *dicte salica secundum aliquos a civitate Sylechayni ultra Renum, eo que in dicta civitate primi auctores eam iniciaverunt verum verior interpretatio viget que a sale quod interpretatur condimentum et licito dirivatur quasi licitum condimentum vel lex licite condita.*[44]

Terra autem salica dicitur que adheret corone quia auctores dum loquebantur De Alode semper intelligebant de terra sine hereditate subditorum[45] *que datur et recipitur in allodium. Et ideo ad differenciam terre allodialis nuncupabant terram regiam, terram salicam. Quia Lex Salica a principibus constituta primo formam succedendi et modum regendi in terra regia docuit. Quod secus ante ea fiebat quia sine lege vivebant et fortior obtinebat.* Et cecy est en tant qu'il touche la Loy Salicque et ce que ledit Phelippe de Valois pretendoit ou royaume et en la couronne de France a cause dicelle.

Et quant a l'usage notoirement gardé en tel cas disoit ledit Roy Phelippe que la chose estoit toute clere pour lui, car par ce que le Roy Loys Hutin et Jehan son filz n'eurent aucuns enfans masles, la succession estoit venue a Phelippe le Long, frere dudit Loys Hutin, et en semblable de Phelippe le Long au |**6v**| Roy Charles le Bel. Et se ainsi eust esté que filles eussent peu succeder au royaume et a la couronne, la fille de Loys Hutin eust esté preferee a Phelippe le Long, et la fille de Phelippe le Long a Charles le Bel, et la fille de Charles le Bel audit Roy Edouart,[46] voulant conclure ledit Phelippe de Valois par lesdits deux moyens que sans aucune difficulté le royame et la couronne lui devoit competer et appartenir.

Au contraire disoit le Roy Edouart nonobstant toutes les raisons alleguees par ledit Phelippe de Valois que le royaume et la couronne lui devoient appartenir tant par la Loy Salicque que autrement.[47]

Premierement par la Loy Salicque pour ce qu'elle mettoit que le plus prochain hoir masle devoit succeder a la couronne. Or disoit il qu'il estoit masle et estoit le plus prochain du Roy Charles car il estoit son nepveu, et ledit Phelippe de Valois n'estoit que son cousin

---

[43] O omits '*et demum secundum diversitatem temporum per varios reges emendata*'. M has a marginal note, '*Quid sit Lex Saliqua*'; Q offers a marginal note, '*Saliqua*'.

[44] JP change this to '*verum verior interpretatio condimentum et licito* [J adds '*dirivatur quasi*'] *condimentum vel lex licite condita*'. M presents a marginal note, '*unde dicatur*'.

[45] JKLNPQ omit '*subditorum*'; M offers a marginal note, '*Que sit terra saliqua*'.

[46] This complex list of names caused confusions for the scribes of J and P, but C altered the argument by reporting that 'la fille de Louys Hutin eust esté preferee a Phelippe le Long, et la fille Phelippe le Long a la fille Charles le Bel, et dudit Charles le Bel a la fille femme dudit Philippe d'Orleans, avant que Edouart de par sa mere y eust peu succeder'.

[47] C omits this paragraph. Though no record survives of any case made for the succession of Edward III in 1328, his lawyers did develop a legal position in preparation for the negotiations in 1340 and 1344. See Taylor, 'Edward III and the Plantagenet claim', pp. 155–169.

germain, et par consequant qu'il devoit estre preferé audit Phelippe de Valois.

Et se on vouloit dire qu'il venoit par fille si disoit il que ce la ne servoit de riens au cas car la Loy Salicque ne declaire point dont on doivent descendre les hoirs masles, mais seulement dit que le plus prochain hoir masle habile a succeder |**7r**| doit venir a la succession. Or disoit il qu'il estoit le plus prochain hoir masle, *quare* &c.

Touchant l'usage disoit ledit Roy Edouart que ce qui avoit esté alleguié des trois roys dessusnommez ne faisoit riens a la matiere. Car bien estoit vray que les filles ne succedoyent point[48] et a ceste cause estoit venue la succession ausdis freres l'un aprés l'autre, par ce que au temps du trespas de chascun d'eulx leurs filles n'avoient aucuns enfans maslez. Mais lui il estoit masle, et combien que sa mere n'eust peu succeder a la couronne, lui comme masle et plus prochain dudit Roy Charles le Bel au temps de son trespas disoit que le royame et la couronne lui devoient appartenir.

Le Roy Phelippe de Valois replicquoit que ledit Roy Edouart n'y povoit avoir droit si non par la main de sa mere. Et puis que ainsi estoit qu'il confessoit que sa mere n'estoit pas habille a succeder, il faloit clerement conclurre qu'elle ne lui povoit riens transporter, *quia nemo plus juris* &c,[49] *item nemo dat quod non habet* &c,[50] *item medium predium quod non servit* &c.[51] *Item* y eut pluiseurs autres drois canons et civilz qui furent alleguiez avecquez beaucop de grandes raisons moralez et naturellez lesquellez pour cause de briefté sont icy obmisez.

|**7v**| Et oultre plus disoit ledit Roy Phelippe que les motz de laditte Loy Salicque estoient biens clers pour lui en ladicte matiere car elle disoit en ceste maniere, *nulla portio hereditatis mulieri veniet ad virilem sexum tota hereditas pertineat.*[52] Laquelle chose clerement concluoit que les femmes estoient forclosez de laditte succession et disoit point qu'elle venist aux plus prochains masles, mais au plus prochain sexe masculin. Or n'estoit point le Roy Edouart du sexe masculin, *quare* &c.[53]

---

[48] ACO add 'a la couronne de France'.

[49] '*Nemo plus juris ad alium transferre potest, quam ipse haberet*' (*Digest.* 50.17.54). This well-known legal maxim was cited, for example, in the *Somnium viridarii*, II, p. 24; *Le Songe du vergier*, II, p. 33; and John Fortescue, *The Works*, pp. 66* and 506. See p. 78 below.

[50] O omits '*item nemo dat quod non habet* &c'. This was a common proverb, probably derived from Seneca. It was used, for example, in Dante Alighieri, *Dante's Monarchia*, ed. and trans. Richard Kay (Toronto, 1998), pp. 244–245 and 298–299.

[51] '*In rusticis autem praediis impedit servitutem medium praedium, quod non servit*' (*Digest.* 8.3.7.1). This law was cited, for example, in the *Somnium viridarii*, I, p. 283 and *Le Songe du vergier*, I, p. 249.

[52] ACHMO insert the words '*de terra salicqua*' after '*nulla portio hereditatis*', and present the final word as '*perveniat*'. LNQ abbreviate the citation to '*nulla portio hereditatis pertineat*'. See p. 59 above.

[53] JKLNPQ omit 'Or n'estoit point le Roy Edouart du sexe masculin *quare* &c'.

Disoit aussi ledit Phelippe de Valois touchant le fait de l'usage que les raisons alleguiez par ledit Edouart ne lui povoient de riens servir tant par les moiens dessus touchies comme par ung fait qui trop clerement abat ses raisons. Car jasoit ce que ou temps que le Roy Loys Hutin et Jehan son filz morurent, il ne demourist que une fille suer dudit Jehan et fille dudit Loys laquelle pour lors n'avoit point de suyte. Toutesfoiz ou temps que le Roy Charles le Bel morut qui fut le derrenier desdis trois roys, laditte fille de Loys Hutin mariee au conte d'Evreux avoit ung filz lequel fut depuis roy de Navarre. Et se ainsi eust esté que les filles eussent peut transporter leurs drois de la couronne a leurs enfans maslez ledit roy de Navarre filz de la fille Loys Hutin eust esté beaucop plustost roy que le Roy Edouart. |**8r**| Et toutesfoiz icellui roy de Navarre ne sa mere n'en firent oncquez querele ne poursuite sachans que ce eust esté atort et contre raison. Et pour ce disoit le dit Phelippe de Valois qu'il apparoit clerement que c'estoit a tort et contre raison de[54] ce que ledit Edouart demandoit ne contendoit a la couronne ne au royaume de France.[55]

Disoit par semblable que Margarite qui estoit l'aisnee fille dudit Phelippe le Bel, et femme de Ferrant aisné filz du roy d'Espaigne, ainsi qu'il appert par lettres dudit mariage dudit Ferrant et de laditte Margarite dattés de l'an mil II^C IIII^{XX} et XIIII, y fust plustost venue que laditte Ysabel qui n'estoit que la seconde.[56] Et toutesfoiz elle ne son mari ne leur suyte n'y demanderent oncquez riens, sachans que ce eust esté a tort et contre raison, *quare* &c.[57]

Disoit en oultre ledit Phelippe de Valois qu'il estoit quasi impossible que ledit Edouart peust venir a laditte couronne attendu qu'il ne vient que par moyen de fille, car soient veues toutez les cronicquez de France depuis le temps de Pharamon qui fut premier roy de France et n'estoit point crestien jusques au temps dudit Charles le Bel, quelque deffaulte de lignie masculine qui ait esté, soit des le temps de Clodio le |**8v**| Chevelu qui morut sans hoir masle. Et vint a ceste cause la succession

---

[54] C omits 'Et pour ce disoit le dit Phelippe de Valois qu'il apparoit clerement que c'estoit a tort et contre raison de'.

[55] In reality, none of these grandsons were even alive in 1328: Charles II of Navarre, grandson of Louis X, was not born until 1332, while Louis II of Mâle, count of Flanders and grandson of Philippe V, was born in 1330. Nevertheless, Charles of Navarre did subsequently lay claim to the French throne; in the negotiations for an alliance with the English between December 1354 and January 1355, he promised to cede his title to Edward III: Roland Delachenal, 'Premières négociations de Charles le Mauvais avec les Anglais (1354–1355)', *Bibliothèque de l'Ecole des Chartes*, 61 (1900), pp. 253–282. This explains why Jean Juvénal offered a response to potential English claims based upon such a transferral of Navarre's claim to the English king, in Jean Juvénal, II, pp. 51–52.

[56] CJP give the date as 'mil III^C IIII^{XX} et XIIII', while K offers 'mil II^C IIII^{XX} et VIIII'. See p. 56, n. 23 above.

[57] M omits this paragraph.

a Merouvee, pere de Chilperic et grant pere du roy Clovis premier crestien, comme plus prochain hoir masle dudit Clodio, le jugant ainsi la Loy Salicque.[58] Soit de tous les descendans de Charlemaigne et de Hue Capet il ne sera par trouvé que oncquez fille succedast a la couronne de France ne autre masle au moyen de fille. Car bien fut practiquié cest article aprés la mort de Loys Hutin, car Jehan son filz lui succeda, qui morut sans hoir masle en alant au sacre du roy, et estoit sa suer fille de Loys sa plus prochaine heritiere. Et toutesfois la couronne remonta a Phelippe le Long son oncle, et de Phelippe le Long[59] qui avoit fille, elle vint a Charles le Bel son frere. Par quoy estoit bien grant demonstrance qu'elle devoit venir au plus prochain hoir masle et non pas aux femelles ne aux descendans d'elles. Car se elle eust peut venir le roy de Navarre, filz de la fille Loys Hutin, et le conte de Flandres, filz de la fille Phelippe le Long, y fussent plustost venus que le Roy Edouart lesquelz toutesfois n'y demanderent oncques riens,[60] *quare* &c.

Item et la raison y est bien grande, *quia omnis Christi actio nostra est instructio.*[61] Or dit Dieu en l'euvangile que l'arbre portera fruit de tele qualité soit doulz ou amer que fait cellui dont |9r| il procede.[62] Se doncquez la mere dudit Roy Edouart estoit inhabile a succeder a la couronne de France, il convient doncques que le fruit issant de elle, c'estassavoir ledit Roy Edouart, parcillement soit inhabile.[63]

En oultre Dieu ordonna toutes femmes estre subgetez a homme et avoir souverain sur elles en disant ces parolles: *A modo eris sub potestate viri et ipse dominabitur tui, Genes III°.*[64] Et en signe meismes de ce les roynes, quant elles sont enoinctez en la teste, elles doivent estre enoinctez plus bas que les roys en demonstrant que elles ont souverain. Et se ainsi

---

[58] Late medieval French chroniclers almost universally accepted that the first five kings of France were Pharamond, Clodio the Hairy, Merovech, Childeric, and Clovis. Many admitted that Merovech was not the son of Clodio but rather 'de son lignage', as, for example, in *Grandes chroniques*, I, p. 26. *Pour ce que plusieurs* appears to be the first text to claim that Merovech inherited because of the Salic Law, perhaps reacting to the suggestion that Merovech had inherited through a daughter of Clodio. This claim had been made forty years earlier by an anonymous Anglo-Burgundian chronicler: BNF MS français 1623, fo. 89v, as discussed in Zale, 'Unofficial histories of France', p. 213n.

[59] P omits 'son oncle et de Phelippe le Long', perhaps because of a homoeoteleutic error, jumping from 'Long' to 'Long'.

[60] ACMO add 'comme dessus est dit'.

[61] C omits '*quia omnis Christi actio nostra est instructio*'. This was a common theological axiom, almost certainly derived from Cassiodorus.

[62] Matthew 7: 18: 'A good tree cannot produce evil fruit and a corrupt tree cannot produce good fruit'.

[63] C adds 'a succeder a la couronne de France'.

[64] Genesis 3: 16. The same argument was made in Jean Juvénal, II, p. 48, and Fortescue, *The Works*, pp. 66*–67*, 497–498, and 507–508, and *idem, De laudibus legum Anglie*, ed. Stanley B. Chrimes (Cambridge, 1949), p. 104.

estoit que les femmes fussent roynes de France de leur heritage, elles ne recongnoistroient aucun souverain et ne seroient subgettez a nul, ainsi la loy de Dieu seroit illusoire.[65]

D'autrepart ce seroit bien grant inconvenient que une femme fust juge en causes criminelez pour condempner une personne a morir, car leurs penseez et leurs jugemens pourroient estre ung pou trop soudains. Or est ainsi que se une femme povoit estre royne de France elle seroit juge souverain du royaume, *quare* &c.

Item femmes prendent aucunesfois maris |**9v**| a leurs volontéz. Or est vray que se la couronne de France povoit tumber en femme il seroit possible que la royne prenderoit ung homme de vil estat et de tres mauvaises condicions, lequel il convendroit qu'il dominast sur tout le royame dont murmures, debas, questions, rihotez et guerres pourroient ensuivir et puet estre la totale destruction du royaume. Ou par adventure la ditte dame prendoit a mari l'ennemy capital dudit royaume lequel pour se vengier ou pour destruire le royaume vouldroit persecuter tous les princes, prelas, nobles et gens notables dudit royaume et icellui mettre a totale destruction et perdicion ou la subgettir a l'empereur ou a quelconquez autre prince espirituel ou temporel, ce qu'il ne fut oncquez et en pourroyent avenir inconveniens irreparablez qui ne sont a souffrir ne a tollerer.[66]

Avec ce en pourroit ensuivir en France d'autres inconveniens bien dangereux et de perilleuse consequence. Car il est possible que ung roy de France puet avoir beaucop de fillez et selon la coustume de France, c'estassavoir de Paris et de l'Isle de France ou[67] le principal siege du roy est institué et assiz autant, et en la succession du pere et de la mere l'une fille comme l'autre. Se le royaume doncques povoit tumber en fille et qu'il y eust XII ou XV filles il convendroit que le royame fust |**10r**| divisé en XII ou en XV parties.[68]

---

[65] ACMO omit the final sentence of this paragraph. For the coronation of the French queen, see Craig Taylor, 'The Salic Law, French queenship and the defence of women in the late middle ages', *French Historical Studies*, 29 (2006), pp. 543–564.

[66] P omits 'Ou par adventure la ditte dame prendoit a mari l'ennemy capital dudit royaume lequel pour se vengier ou pour destruire le royaume', perhaps because of a homoeoteleutic error, jumping from 'royaume' to 'royaume'. Jean Juvénal des Ursins had cited the danger of a commoner marrying an heiress, but did not mention the parallel problem of a potential marriage to a foreigner: Jean Juvénal, II, p. 45.

[67] O omits 'c'estassavoir de Paris et de l'Isle de France ou'.

[68] In many French provinces, including, most notably, Paris, a noble inheritance was divided equally between sisters in the absence of a direct male heir: Eusèbe Laurière, *Texte des coutumes de la prévôté et vicomté de Paris* (3 vols, Paris, 1777), I, p. 55, and Paul Viollet, *Les Etablissements de Saint Louis accompagnés des textes primitifs et de textes dérivés* (4 vols, Paris, 1881–1886), III, pp. 4–5. When making this argument in the context of a discussion of the exclusion of daughters in collateral lines from the royal succession, Jean Juvénal had cited the custom of the vicomté of Paris: Jean Juvénal, II, p. 44.

Et que en advendroit il s'il estoient toutes a marier il y auroit XII ou XV roynes ou royaume et autant de roys quant elles seroient mariees. Et fauldroit demander laquelle porteroit l'auriflamble a la bataille, laquelle diroit l'euvangille du Noel quant le pape y seroit, ainsi que doivent et sont tenus de faire les trescrestiens roys de France,[69] et laquelle d'elle s'appelleroit trescrestienne, ou se chascune d'elles le seroit, et en effect ne seroit que toute confusion, guerres, divisions et maulz infinis comme Nostre Seigneur meismez en l'euvangille quant il dit, *Omnis potestas videlicet suprema impaciens consortis erit.*[70] Et ne fauldroit plus que nul se appellast roy de France, mais roy en France. Ainsi le nom de trescrestien roy de France qui par si grans dons de graces envoie des cieulx et par tant excellens services dignes de memoire fais a Dieu, a son eglise et a la loy et a la foy crestienne, a esté par si long temps continué, fust de present inutile et du tout mis au neant.[71]

Nous trouverons bien es drois *quod ab Augusto nominatur Augusta*, mais nous ne trouvons point *quod ab Augusta ullus umquam cognominatus fuit Augustus.*[72] Bien y'a eut de vaillantez emperris et de vaillantes roynes de France et qui ont fait |**10v**| de grandes et notables choses, mais c'estoit comme femmes, vesues ou meres de roys ou d'empereurs, et non que de leur heritaige elles fussent roynes de France ou emperris. Et la raison y est grande. Car le roy de France est roy et empereur en son royame et ne recongnoit nul souverain.[73] Ainsi le tesmoingne l'eglise en ce chappitre, *Per venerabilem qui filii sunt legitimi*, et en ceste decretale, *Novit ille qui nichil ygnorat in antiquis.*[74] Et pareillement ledit

---

[69] The phrase 'ainsi que doibvent et sont tenus de faire les trescrestiens roys de France' appears in the margin in M, written in the same hand.

[70] This well-known proverb derives from Lucan, *Pharsalia*, I, 92: '*Nulla fides regni sociis, omnisque potestas inpatiens consortis erit*'. The fact that Cousinot included the word '*suprema*' may mean that he regarded it as a gloss on Matthew 28: 18: 'All authority in heaven and on earth has been given to me'.

[71] For the title 'roi très créstien', see Jacques Krynen, '*Rex Christianissimus*: a medieval theme at the roots of French absolutism', *History and Anthropology*, 4 (1989), pp. 79–96.

[72] A: 'Nous trouvons bien aux droiz que *ab Augusto nominateur umquam Augustua cognominatus fuit Augustus*'; C omits 'mais nous ne trouvons point *quod ab Augusta ullus*'. For the notion that the name Augustus derived from the Latin verb '*augeo*', and hence implied that a ruler should increase rather than alienate the property of the crown, see *Le Songe du vergier*, I, p. 285, together with Peter N. Riesenberg, *Inalienability of Sovereignty in Medieval Political Thought* (New York, NY, 1956), pp. 28–29, and André Bossuat, 'La formule "Le roi est empereur dans son royaume"', *Revue historique de droit français et étranger*, 4th series, 39 (1961), p. 378, translated as 'The maxim "The king is emperor in his kingdom": its use in the fifteenth century before the Parlement of Paris', in Peter S. Lewis (ed.), *The Recovery of France in the Fifteenth Century* (London, 1971), p. 192.

[73] For the maxim *Rex in regno suo imperator est*, see Bossuat, 'The maxim "The king is emperor in his kingdom"', pp. 185–195. The argument that women could not act as sovereigns was raised in Jean Juvénal, II, p. 26.

[74] ACJKLMNOQ add: '*De Judicis in antiquis*'; P adds: '*in idem in antiquis*'. These famous letters of Innocent III, *Liber extra*, 4.17.13 (*Qui filii sint legitimi*, c. *Per venerabilem*) and 2.1.13 (*De*

empereur est ou doit estre roy et souverain par tout le monde excepté ou royaume de France et se lesdittes deux dignités d'empereur et de roy de France pouoient tumber en main de femme, il convendroit que tout le monde fust subget aux femmes. Et qu'elles n'eussent point de souverain ce que oncquez ne fut, *quare*, &c.

Et ainçoires en especial, depuis que les roys de France furent crestiens, la raison est bien que le royaume de France ne puet tumber en fille car les roys de France ont trois dons singuliers envoyés des cieulx que nul autre roy n'a, c'estassavoir les trois fleurs de lis, la saincte ampule et l'auriflambe, dont les deux en especial ne puent tumber en femme, c'estassavoir la sainte ampule[75] dont les roys de France sont enoingz et sacrés, a cause de quoy le roy de France n'est point pur lay mais participe *in divinis* en |11r| pluiseurs choses, et a ceste occasion donne et confere en regale *pleno jure* sans nomination ne presentacion a nul quelconque. Ce que ne pourroit pas faire une femme.[76]

L'autre si est l'auriflambe laquelle semblablement n'y puet,[77] car c'est *intersignium virile* pour aler en bataille pour la deffence de la foy qui n'est la vocation ne l'usage des femmes, et si seroit aussi la chose bien estrange de veoir une femme porter une espee nue en sa main la pointe dessus, ce que doivent faire tous roys pour deux causes, l'une pour faire justice, l'autre pour deffendre le royaume et les subgetz desquelz il a la garde, seignourie et gouvernement. Et a ceste cause sont ilz enoingz pars les mains et les femmes ne le sont point ne pourroient touchier a nulles chosez sacrees ce que font bien les roys de France, lesquelz en oultre garissent des escroelles qui est miracle evident, ce qui ne fut oncques veu que femme feist.[78] Et aussi les roys de France s'appellent sacrez et couronnez et les roynes de France, posé qu'elles

judicis, c. *Novit*) recognized the independence of the kingdom of France, and were extensively cited by defenders of the French crown in the late middle ages, appearing, for example, over thirty times in the *Somnium viridarii* and *Le Songe du vergier*.

[75] A omits 'dont les deux en especial ne puent tumber en femme, c'estassavoir la sainte ampule'.

[76] For the importance of the quasi-sacerdotal status of the French monarchy in the debate over female succession, see Richard Jackson, 'The *Traité du Sacre* of Jean Golein', *Proceedings of the American Philosophical Society*, 113 (1969), pp. 323–324 and William M. Hinkle, *The Fleurs de Lis of the Kings of France, 1285–1488* (Carbondale, 1991), pp. 162–165, together with Taylor, 'The Salic Law, French queenship and the defence of women', pp. 552–554.

[77] ACMO replace these eight words with 'Secondement l'oriflamme ne puet tumber en femme'. For the oriflamme, see Anne Lombard-Jourdan, *Fleur de lis et oriflamme: signes célestes du royaume de France* (Paris, 1991), and Franck Collard, 'Ranimer l'oriflamme: les relations des rois de France avec l'abbaye de Saint-Denis à la fin du XVe siècle', in Françoise Autrand, Claude Gauvard, and Jean-Marie Moeglin (eds), *Saint-Denis et la royauté: études offertes à Bernard Guenée* (Paris, 1999), pp. 563–581.

[78] C omits 'ce qui ne fut oncques veu que femme feist'. See Marc Bloch, *The Royal Touch: sacred monarchy and scrofula in England and France* (London, 1973), and Georges Peyronnet, 'Un

soient aucunement enoingtez, si ne s'appellent elles que couronneez, ne aussi ne garde l'en pas les solemnitez a leur couronnement que l'en fait au sacré des roys.[79] Parquoy fault selon raison que la couronne tumbe tousjours en hoir masle.[80]

|11v| Se doncquez les femmes sont inhabiles a y succeder par la Loy Salicque ainsi comme dessus est dit, qui est la vraye loy des François, par la commune observance aussi en tel cas depuis qu'il eut premier roy en France jusques au temps dessusdit; par les prerogatives pareillement venues des cieulx aux roys de France aux moyens dessus touchiez et par l'usage especial qui a esté practiquié esdittes matieres quant les cas y sont escheuz et autres raisons dessus toucheez,[81] concluoit ledit Phelippe de Valois avec les autres raisons dessus alleguiez qu'il estoit impossible que lesdictez filles peussent baillier droit a autre lequel elles n'avoyent point. Et par consequent que au moyen d'elles ledit Roy Edouart ne autre que lui ne povoit demander ne clamer aucun droit a la couronne ne au royaume de France.

Amablement parties oyés en tout ce qu'ilz vouldrent alleguier d'unepart et d'autre, les princes, prelas, nobles, gens des bonnes villes et autres notables clers, faisans et representans les trois estas generaulx du royaume assemblez pour ladicte matiere, dirent et declarerent que selon Dieu, raison et justice a leur adviz le droit dudit Phelippe de Valois estoit le plus apparant pour parvenir a la couronne et au royaume et qu'il leur sembloit qu'il estoit et devoit |12r| estre vray roy de France. Et a ceste cause et par ce qu'ilz avoyent peu veoir, savoir et congnoistre desdictes matieres, ilz le reputoient et tenoient pour tel. Et se deliberent tous et conclurent icellui recevoir comme vray roy de France et leur droit souverain seigneur et non autre, et a lui obeir et le servir envers et contre tous comme leur vray droiturier et souverain seigneur.

Et fut ledit Roy Phelippe enoingt, sacré et couronné paisiblement comme vray roy de France au veu et sceu de tous ceulx qui le vouldrent

problème de légitimité: Charles VII et le toucher des écrouelles', in *Jeanne d'Arc: une époque, un rayonnement. Colloque d'histoire médiévale, Orléans, Octobre, 1979* (Paris, 1982), pp. 197–202.

[79] Only manuscripts B and H cite the miraculous cure of scrofula before the discussion of the terminology used to describe the kings and queens of France; ACFJKLMNOPQ reverse the order of these two points. F omits 'lesquelz en oultre garissent des escroelles [. . .] a leur couronnement que l'en fait au sacré des roys', but this material appears as a marginal note in the same hand.

[80] B repeats 'tumbe', with the second instance appearing at the beginning of a new line. The error is repeated by F.

[81] AC omit 'par l'usage especial qui a esté practiquié esdittes matieres quant les cas y sont escheuz et autres raisons dessus toucheez'. P omits 'quant les cas y sont escheuz et autres raisons'. O omits 'toucheez, concluoit ledit Phelippe de Valois avec les autres raisons dessus', perhaps because of a homoeoteleutic error, jumping from 'dessus' to 'dessus'.

veoir et savoir, et mesmement dudit Roy Edouart sans aucun contredit ou empeschement.

Item et comme tel fut par le pape et l'eglise de Romme et les concilles generaulx qui depuis ont esté receu, clamé et reputé, et a lui et a ses successeurs baillié le lieu et la place en l'eglise de roy de France au veu et sceu des Anglois et de tous ceulx qui l'ont volu veoir et savoir *usque in hodiernum diem.*[82]

Item et qui plus est, pour monstrer cas plus especial que ledit Roy Edouart acquiessa a la declaracion qui fut faitte es estas de France touchant Phelippe de Valois et qui se departi totalement de la poursuite qu'il faisoit de la |**12v**| couronne et du royaume de France[83] et est vray que ladicte declaration fut faitte esdiz trois estas l'an mil trois cens vingthuit, aprés laquelle declaration et le couronnement dudit Phelippe de Valois: ledit Roy Edouart le Tiers envoyé devers ledit Roy Phelippe affin de prendre jour et lieu ou il peust venir devers lui pour lui faire l'ommage de la duchié de Guienne.[84]

Et l'an mil troiscens vingtneuf ensuivant, icellui Roy Edouart vint devers ledit Phelippe en la ville d'Amiens et lui fist la l'ommage de ladicte duchié de Guienne comme per de France recongnoissant ledit Roy Phelippe son naturel et souverain seigneur[85] a cause de ladicte duchié de Guienne, et deslors en bailla ses lettres de recongnoissance telles que au cas appartient lesquellez sont ou Tresor de Chartres.[86]

Et pour ce qu'il y eut aucune difficulté sur la forme de l'ommage, pource que le Roy Phelippe voloit avoir hommage lige, et ledit Roy Edouart, duc de Guienne, disoit qu'il ne devoit pas hommage lige,[87] et que sans le consentement du Parlement d'Angleterre il ne le vouldroit faire en ceste maniere, il fut enconvenancié entre ledit Roy Phelippe et lui que sur cest incident ledit Roy Phelippe envoieroit ambassade en Ang- |**13r**| leterre pour remonstrer amiablement[88] la ou il appartendroit les droitures du roy, et que les Anglois feroient de leur part le semblable affin de conduire ceste matiere en bonne amour et union, et eschever toutes causes de guerres et discors.

---

[82] Jean Juvénal had also emphasized that the Valois succession was approved by the church, citing the Council of Basel, in Jean Juvénal, II, pp. 40 and 55–56. Also see p. 83, n. 166 below.

[83] P omits 'qu'il faisoit de la couronne et du royaume'.

[84] P omits 'Edouart le Tiers envoyé devers ledit Roy', perhaps because of a homoeoteleutic error, jumping from 'Roy' to 'Roy'.

[85] N adds 'comme a son naturel et souverain, et per de France'.

[86] On 6 June 1329, Edward III paid simple homage to Philippe VI for the duchy of Aquitaine in the cathedral of Amiens; this was neither liege nor unconditional because the formula did not include an oath of fidelity.

[87] A omits 'et ledit Roy Edouart, duc de Guienne, disoit qu'il ne devoit pas hommage lige', perhaps because of a homoeoteleutic error, jumping from 'lige' to 'lige'.

[88] A omits 'ambassade en Angleterre pour remonstrer'.

En fournissant ausquellez choses l'an mil III^C XXXI ensuivant, ledit Roy Phelippe envoya son ambassade en Angleterre, la ou les matieres furent debatues bien au long. Et rapporterent lesdiz ambassadeurs lettres dudit Roy Edouart passeez en son Parlement et de l'auctorité et consentement dicelluy, confirmatoires de celles qu'il avoit bailliés au Roy Phelippe touchant la duchié de Guienne, et par lesquellez il recongnoissoit le Roy Phelippe roy de France et son souverain seigneur a cause de ladicte duchié de Guyenne et a ceste cause estre son homme et vassal lige, lesquellez lettres doivent samblablement estre ou Tresor des Chartres.[89] Au moien desquelles choses appert clerement que ledit Roy Edouart a confessé solemnelement et en telle auctorité qu'il n'est point revocable, ne contre quoy il ne puet licitement ne raisonnablement venir ne ses successeurs a cause de lui. Car le Roy Phelippe de Valois estoit vray et droit roy de France, et par consequent n'est pas recevable icellui Edouart ne ses successeurs a venir demander reclamer aucun droit ne tiltre a la couronne ne au royaume de France. Car non |**13v**| mie seulement cellui qui par parolles expressez confesse aucun estre seigneur ou roy d'aucun pays ne puet licitement venir a l'encontre de ce qu'il a unefoiz confessé. *Juxta juris civilis disposicionem ubi dicit quod quisque sua voce dilucide protestatus est sive professus in contrarium venire et proprio resistere testimonio nullatenus permittitur.*[90] Mais meis[m]e se aucun en adheresant a la commune oppinion salue ou fait reverence a autre comme a roy ou seigneur, il ne puet plus venir a l'encontre et est reputé comme exprés fauteur et consentant avec ledit roy ou seigneur [pour prendre et recevoir tel parti comme le dit seigneur][91] en ceste qualité, ainsi le note expressement la glose du decret *Cum Adrianus Secundus, LXIII di*, et pareillement le decret *Omnis XXIIII q. 1*,[92] la ou il dit *Qui dicit enim illi ave communicat operibus suis.*[93]

Et supposé que depuis messire Robert d'Artois qui avoit esté al'assemblee des trois estas de France dont dessus est faitte mention,

---

[89] H omits 'et par lesquellez il recongnoissoit le roy [. . .] Guyenne', perhaps because of a homoeoteleutic error, jumping from 'Guienne' to 'Guyenne'. Under pressure from Philippe, who was threatening to confiscate Saintes, Edward III acknowledged by letters patent issued at Eltham on 30 March 1331 that the homage was liege before making a secret journey to France, disguised as a merchant, to swear the oath in person. Documents relating to these actions circulated amongst the fifteenth-century French polemical writers, and were cited, for example, in Montreuil, II, pp. 106–108, 175–177, 232–234, and 279–281, and Jean Juvénal, I, pp. 170–173 and II, pp. 29–30 and 171.

[90] *Liber extra*, 2.19.10. N omits the Latin quotation; Q omits '*juris civilis deposicionem*'.

[91] This material from K does not appear in B but is also found in ACFHJLMNOPQ.

[92] JP omit '*di*, et pareillement le decret *Omnis XXIIII q. 1*'; C omits 'et pareillement le decret *Omnis XXIIII q. 1*'.

[93] The gloss to *Decretum Gratiani*, D. 63 c. 29 and C. 24 q. 1, though '*Qui enim dicit illi ave communicat operibus illius malignis*' appears in 2 John 1: 11.

l'un des principaulx qui avoit donné son oppinion au prouffit et a l'intencion dudit Roy Phelippe,[94] pour la hayne qu'il concut contre ledit Roy Phelippe[95] et qu'il estoit banny du royaume de France, desirant porter dommage et prejudice audit roy son souverain et naturel seigneur, eust donné a entendre audit Roy Edouart que le [*sic*] couronne et le royaume de France lui appartenoit.[96] Si |**14r**| ne lui povoit ledit donner a entendre[97] baillier plus grant droit en la dicte matiere que cellui qu'il avoit au paravant ne depuis, ne lui survint chose qui accreust ne augmentast sondit droit.

Et a parler a la verité de ceste matiere, la chose surquoy les Anglois se fonderent plus pour quereler le royaume de France aprés ce que ledit messire Robert d'Artois eut esté en Angleterre, et fut quant il leur offry l'aliance du conte de Henau et de Messire Jehan de Haynau, celle aussi des ducs de Brabant et de Gueldres, contes de Cleves et de Julliers, et des archevesques de Coulongne, Trevez et de Strabourg, ensemble des Gantois et préz que de toutes les bassez Allomaignez.[98]

Pour laquelle cause ledit Roy Edouart, avant commencer ladicte querele en forme de guerre, vint a Bruxelles la ou tous les seigneurs dessusdiz furent tous assemblez.[99] Et illec tous jurez, alliez et confederez ensemble a l'encontre dudit Roy Phelippe et a la conqueste dudit royaume de France au prouffit dudit Roy Edouart. Et en icellui temps ne se nommoit point ainçoires ledit Edouart roy de France ne

[94] In C, the name of 'Phelippe' has been crossed out and replaced with 'Edouart'.

[95] O omits 'pour la hayne qu'il concut contre ledit Roy Phelippe', perhaps because of a homoeoteleutic error, jumping from 'Phelippe' to 'Phelippe'.

[96] According to a number of fourteenth-century chroniclers, including Jean le Bel, Geoffrey le Baker, and Jean de Venette, Edward III was encouraged to pursue his claim to the French throne by Robert d'Artois (d. 1343), who was taking refuge from Philippe VI at the English court. The story may have originated in a contemporary poem: J.L. Grigsby and N.J. Lacy (eds), *The Vows of the Heron (Les Voeux du héron): a Middle French vowing poem* (New York, NY, 1992). The account in *Pour ce que plusieurs* closely follows Jean Juvénal des Ursins, though the same argument had also been used in Montreuil, II, pp. 211–212, 249–250, and 299: Jean Juvénal, II, pp. 33–36.

[97] O omits 'audit Roy Edouart que le couronne et le royaume de France lui appartenoit. Si ne lui povoit ledit donner a entendre', perhaps because of a homoeoteleutic error, jumping from 'entendre' to 'entendre'.

[98] Edward III's coalition initially included his father-in-law, Guillaume, count of Hainault; the count's brothers, Jean of Hainault, lord of Beaumont, and Reginald, count (and subsequently duke) of Guelders; Guillaume's son and heir, Guillaume II, count of Hainault; Jean, duke of Brabant; Dietrich, count of Cleves; Guillaume, margrave (and subsequently count) of Juliers; Walram von Jülich, archbishop of Cologne; Baldwyn of Luxembourg, archbishop of Trier [Trèves]; and Berthold II of Bucheck, archbishop of Strasburg.

[99] The initial negotiations were carried out by ambassadors led by Henry Burghersh, bishop of Lincoln, and took place mainly at Valenciennes, before the English went to meet the duke of Brabant at his court in Brussels.

ne portoit point les armes escarteleez de France et d'Angleterre, ains seulement portoit les trois lieppars.[100]

|14v| Si avint que les Flamens dirent audit Roy Edouart que se il ne se intituloit roy de France et qu'il prist les armes de France, ilz ne l'oseroient servir.[101] Car par les guerres qui avoyent esté auparavant entre les roys de France et lesdiz Flamens aprés une bataille qu'ilz eurent contre eulx,[102] se soubzmirent et obligerent soubz les censures de l'eglise et sur paine de excommuniement et de la somme de XII^C mille escus de la monnoye qui couroit pour le temps de lors, de ne faire jamais guerre aux roys de France ne eulx rebeller contre eulx. Et en cas qu'ilz le feroient *ipso facto* ilz encouroient en sentence d'excommuniement et demouroit le pays en interdit sans jamais povoir estre osté, ne eulx absoubz sans le consentement du roy de France.[103] Pour lesquelles causes Jacquez d'Artevelde Gantois, pere de Phelippe d'Artevelde qui fut tué a la bataille de Rosebecke l'an mil III^C IIII^{XX} et deux,[104] lequel Jacquez de Arthevelde estoit chief des Gantois,[105] dist en publicque devant tous les seigneurs, princes et prelas dessus nommés qu'il convenoit que ledit Roy Edouart fist ce que dit est, c'estassavoir

---

[100] Both Edward III and his mother, Isabella, quartered the leopards of England with the fleurs-de-lis of France before 1340, though he did change the order of precedence following his public declaration of a claim to the French throne in that year: Adrian Ailes, 'Heraldry in medieval England: symbols of politics and propaganda', in Peter Coss and Maurice Keen (eds), *Heraldry, Pageantry and Social Display in Medieval England* (Woodbridge, 2002), pp. 88–89.

[101] N omits 'et qu'il prist les armes de France', perhaps because of a homoeoteleutic error, jumping from 'France' to 'France'. Manuscript A presents a marginal note in a later hand: 'Armoyrie et nom de roy de France pris par le roy d'Angleterre'.

[102] ACMO add 'a moins en peine [C omits 'en peine'] au temps du Roy Phelippe le Bel'. This was the battle of Mons-en-Pévèle, near Lille, on 18 August 1304.

[103] By the terms of the treaty of Athis-sur-Orge in 1305, confirmed by the treaty of Pontoise in 1312, the Flemings were liable to a papal interdict if they rebelled against their French overlord; the original treaty also called for the Flemings to give significant financial compensation to the French king, though this remained largely unpaid. The connection between this indemnity and Flemish support for Edward III's claim to the French throne had previously been noted in the treatise *Fluxo biennale spacio* (1422–1429), in Nicole Pons (ed.), *L'Honneur de la couronne de France: quatre libelles contre les Anglais (vers 1418–vers 1429)* (Paris, 1990), pp. 186–187, though it is unlikely that this served as a direct source for *Pour ce que plusieurs* given that the anonymous author argued that financial indemnity was set at two millions florins.

[104] C omits 'Gantois pere de Phelippe d'Artevelde'. Jacques van Artevelde (d. 1345) became the captain of Ghent in 1338. He was the father of Philippe, captured by the French at the battle of Roosebeke and then executed in 1382.

[105] LNQ replace 'Jacquez d'Artevelde Gantois, pere de Phelippe d'Artevelde qui fut tué a la bataille de Rosebecke l'an mil III^C IIII^{XX} et deux, lequel Jacquez de Arthevelde estoit' with 'Jacques d'Arthevelde qui estoit [N adds 'lors']'; M replaces 'lequel Jacquez de Arthevelde estoit chief des Gantois' with 'pour lesquelles causes Jacques d'Artevelle Gantois'; P omits 'Jacquez de Arthevelde estoit chief des'.

soy intituler roy de France et prendre les armes de France,[106] ou autrement que les Gantois ne leurs adherens ne le serviroient point ne ne se allieroyent point avec lui.

A l'occasion desquelles chosez et aussi par l'en- |**15r**| hortement desdiz seigneurs dessusnommez qui voloyent a toutesfins avoir les Flamens avecquez eulx et de leur alliance, ledit Roy Edouart prist le nom et les armes de France, que depuis il a continué sans quelque autre fondement en la matiere fors cellui que dessus est dit, et vela le droit fondement[107] originel et la cause, forme et maniere comment le Roy Edouart prinst le titre, nom et les armes de France, en quoy chascun puet congnoistre comment la matiere est bien fondee.[108]

Et est bien a noter en ceste matiere que c'est que de la condicion des Anglois et quele seureté il y'a avecques eulx ne en chose qu'ilz promettent. Car ledit Roy Edouart comme dit est dessus avoit avoé et recongneu le dit Roy Phelippe vray roy de France, et repris de luy comme tel la duchié de Guienne, lui avoit le serement de feaulté et baillie ses lettres patentes depuis confermees en son Parlement touchant ceste matiere. Et lui avoit ledit Roy Phelippe de grace especial fait rendre pluiseurs terres et seignouries en laditte duchié de Guienne qui avoyent esté prisez par ses predecesseurs roys de France et l'auctorité de justice et mis en leur main les aucunes par fault dommage et les autres par rebellions et desobeissances.

Et non obstant toutes ces choses, si tost que |**15v**| ledit Roy Edouart vit qu'il eut pie deça la mer et alliance pour invader le royaume de France, non ayant regart a droit raison et justice et en venant directement contre ses foy, seremens et promesses s'efforça de invader ledit royaume et son souverain seigneur a cause de ladicte duchié de Guyenne, ledit Roy Phelippe,[109] entra dedens ledit royaume et y fist les maulz dont la voix et renommee durent ainçoires. Et non pas seulement des gens ne de l'armee qui vint d'Angleterre ne des Allemaignez, ainçois des terres et subgez de la dicte duchié de Guienne et mesmez de celles que ledit Roy Phelippe lui avoit rendues quant il lui fist l'ommage. Au fort il ne s'en fault point merveillier, car Bede

---

[106] ACHMO omit 'et prendre les armes de France'.

[107] ACH omit 'en la matiere fors cellui que dessus est dit, et vela le droit fondement'. This was perhaps because of a homoeoteleutic error, jumping from 'fondement' to 'fondement', though A gives the preceding phrase as 'sans quelque autre commencement'.

[108] On 26 January 1340, Edward III publicly assumed the title and arms of king of France in Ghent. The account offered here is more detailed than that given by Jean Juvénal des Ursins, drawing upon the chronicle of Jean de Venette and another unidentified source: Jean Juvénal, II, pp. 36–37.

[109] ACMO replace 'Phelippe' with 'Edouart' and in N the scribe has crossed out 'Philippe' and replaced it with 'Edouart'. This alteration was presumably introduced because the 'Roy' was understood to be the subject of the verb 'entra'.

qui fut ung des notables hommes de son temps et si estoit du pays de pardela dist en disnant desigant la proprieté et condicion des Anglois,[110] *Anglicus [angelus] est cui nunquam credere fas est. Dum tibi dicit ave tanquam ab hoste cave.*[111] Et d'autrepart les Anglois dient qu'ilz ont esté prerogative, et ce droit et usage que toutez et quantesfois qu'il voient leur evident prouffit, ilz ne sont point subgetz a seremens ne a promesses qu'ilz ayent fais, et pour ce plantez y vigne.

En revenant a nostre premiere matiere touchant le fait de la couronne et du royame |16r| de France par les moyens dessus touchiez, il est cler et manifeste que ledit Roy Edouart le Tiers n'avoit ne ne povoit juridicquement ne raisonnablement demander, requerir ne reclamer droit ne tiltre a la couronne ne au royame de France. Ainçois ledit Roy Phelippe de Valois qui estoit le plus prochain hoir masle[112] descendu d'hoir masle de Sainct Loys, lequel Sainct Loys fut grant ayeul en ligne masculine dudit Roy Phelippe de Valois, estoit vray roy et heritier de la couronne de France, et a lui par droit et par raison competoit et appartenoit et non a autre.

Et quant au droit que y pretent le Roy Edouart le IIIIe qui a present est, il est cler sans voloir nullui injurier qu'il n'y a ne puet avoir ne pretendre aucun droit.

Et pour entendre ceste matiere, est vray que le Roy Edouart le Tiers, dont meut la question, eut V filz qui tous vindrent en eage de perfection et furent chascun mariéz.[113]

L'aisné fut Edouart prince de Gallez qui espousa la contesse de Salsebery et de Hontiton, dont descendy le Roi Richart qui n'a point eu de sieute.[114]

[110] N adds 'ce vers qui cy aprés sensuit'.
[111] The beginning of the quotation in B is cited as '*Anglicus angelus est*'. Manuscript A omits '*Dum tibi dicit ave tanquam ab hoste cave*' and a marginal note reads '*Nota bene ce auctorite*'; a marginal note by the scribe in C reads 'vers Bede'; in M there is a picture of a hand with a finger pointing towards the section with this anti-English slogan. A similar verse also appeared in the *Vraie cronicque d'Escoce* of John Ireland, and may have derived from Walter Bower's *Scotichronicon*: BNF MS nouvelle acquisition française 20962 fo. 57r, and Walter Bower, *Scotichronicon*, ed. A. Brian Scott and Donald E.R. Watt (9 vols, Aberdeen, 1987–1998), VII, pp. 84–86. See p. 24 above. The ultimate source may have been the *Proprietates Anglicorum*, written during the reign of Philippe IV by a clerk from the University of Paris: BNF MS latin 2477 fos 85r–87r, discussed by Charles Victor Langlois in 'Les Anglais du moyen âge d'après les sources françaises', *Revue historique*, 52 (1893), pp. 304n and 314.
[112] H omits 'descendu d'hoir masle'; N offers 'descendu d'hoir en hoir masle'.
[113] The five sons of Edward III were Edward of Woodstock, prince of Wales (d. 1376), later known as the Black Prince; Lionel of Antwerp, duke of Clarence (d. 1368); John of Gaunt, duke of Lancaster (d. 1399); Edmund of Langley, duke of York (d. 1402); and Thomas of Woodstock, duke of Gloucester (d. 1397).
[114] C adds 'et fut fait mourir ainsi que dessus est notoire'. The Black Prince actually had two sons, Edward (d. 1371) and Richard II (d. 1399). His wife was Joan of Kent, who had previously been married to Thomas Holland and then wed William Montagu, earl of

Le second fut Messire Leonnel duc de Clarence |**16v**| qui espousa la contesse de Woulstre en Irlande, de laquelle issi deux filles, lesquelles pluiseurs Anglois dient non estre filles dudit duc de [C]larence mais d'un chevalier nommé Audelay, lequelle [*sic*] depuis a esté cause par l'ordonnance dudit Roy Edouart le Tiers eut la teste coppee. Et ladicte dame s'en retourna en Irlande et maria ses dictes deux filles, l'une, c'estassavoir l'aisnee, au conte de Nothombellain, et la seconde a Messire Rogier de Mortemer conte de la Marche. Et dient lesdis Anglois pour monstrer que lesdittez filles n'estoient point filles dudit Messire Leonnel, que oncquez elles ne recoeillerent l'eritage ne la succession dudit Messire Leonnel, ne ne porterent son nom ne ses armes,[115] mais le nom et les armes de laditte contesse de Woulstre leur mere, qui est grande demonstrance qu'il y a quelque faulte de ce costé la.[116]

Le tiers fut Jehan surnommé de Gand pour ce qu'il avoit esté nez a Gand, et fut conte Derby et espousa Madame Blanche de Lancastre, fille et heritiere du grant duc de Lancastre nommé Henry, qui fist les drois d'armes, a cause de laquelle il eut la duchié Lancastre, et duquel mariage issi Henry conte Derby qui depuis fut[117] couronné roy d'Angleterre et fut Roy Henry IIIIe, et pareillement la contesse de Hontiton, mere du duc d'Excestre derreniere trespassee.[118]

|**17r**| En secondes nopces il espousa la fille du roy Pietre d'Espaigne, duquel mariage il eut[119] deux filles dont l'aisnee fut mariee au roy

---

Salisbury; her second son by the first marriage was John Holland, earl of Huntingdon, and later duke of Exeter (d. 1400).

[115] A replaces 'que oncquez elles ne recoeillerent l'eritage ne la succession dudit Messire Leonnel ne ne porterent son nom ne ses armes' with 'ne ne pourterent son nom ne ses armes, ne oncques ne recueillerent l'eritaige ne la succession dudit Messire Leonnel'.

[116] In 1342, Lionel married Elizabeth de Burgh and was subsequently recognized as earl of Ulster by right of his wife. Their only daughter, Philippa, married Edmund Mortimer, earl of March, with whom she had four children, including Roger Mortimer, earl of March, and Elizabeth, wife of Henry Percy, eldest son of the first earl of Northumberland (see p. 163, notes 83 and 84). For the claim that Philippa was illegitimate, see p. 24.

[117] A replaces 'fille et heritiere du grant duc de Lancastre [. . .] Henry conte Derby qui depuis fut' with 'du quel mariage issust Henry qui fist les droiz d'armes a cause de laquelle il eust la duchié de Lanstacle et puis conte Derby et aprés'.

[118] The first wife of John of Gaunt was Blanche of Lancaster, with whom he had three sons, two of whom died as infants, and two daughters. Henry IV (d. 1413) was the oldest child, and his sisters, Philippa and Elizabeth, married King João I of Portugal and John Holland, earl of Huntingdon and duke of Exeter. Elizabeth's son was John Holland, earl of Huntingdon and duke of Exeter (d. 1447).

[119] C omits a long section, from this point until the end of the paragraph reading 'de France, par les raisons dessus touchies puisse avoir aucun droit ne tiltre au royaume ne a la couronne de France' on p. 77 below, due to a missing folio.

Alphons d'Espaigne filz de Henry le Bastard, et l'autre fut mariee au roy de Portugal.[120]

Aprés il se en amoura d'une dame nommee Madame de Swinforde de laquelle il eut V enfans, c'estassavoir le conte de Sombreset qui fut l'aisné, le cardinal d'Angleterre qui fut le second, le conte Dorset qui fut le tiers, la royne de Norweghe et la contesse de Westmerland. Lesquelz cinq enfans furent mis soubz le poile et legitimez.[121]

Le quart filz du Roy Edouart fut messire Emond de Langlay conte de[122] Cambruge et depuis duc d'Iorc, lequel espousa la seconde fille dudit roy Pietre d'Espaigne, dont yssirent le duc d'Yorc le Gras qui morut a la bataille d'Agincourt et n'eut nulx enfans que le conte de Cambruge, qui eut la teste coppee a Hantonne quant le Roy Henry V[e] passa la mer pour venir a Harfleu.[123]

Le V[e] filz fut Messire Thomas de Wystok conte de Boguinquam et depuis duc de Clocestre, que l'en fist morir ou temps du Roy Richart a Calais entre deux covettez et n'eut aucuns enfans masles mais seulement deux filles, dont l'une fut |17v| mariee au conte de Harefort, et l'autre au conte de Staffort [pere du conte de Stafford][124] derrainement mort, lequel avoit esté fait duc de Boguinquam.[125]

---

[120] Gaunt's second wife was Constanza of Castile, daughter of King Pedro I of Castile. Their son, John, died in infancy and their daughter Katherine married King Enrique III of Castile.

[121] Following Constanza's death in 1394, Gaunt married Katherine Swynford, with whom he already had four children born between 1372 and 1377: John Beaufort, marquis of Somerset and marquis of Dorset; Henry Beaufort, bishop of Lincoln and then of Winchester; Thomas Beaufort, duke of Exeter; and Joan Beaufort, who married Sir Robert Ferrers and Ralph Neville, earl of Westmorland. These children were legitimated by papal bull and royal charter between 1396 and 1397, and in 1407 the patent of legitimation was reissued by Henry IV with a clause excluding them from the royal succession. The queen of Norway was in fact Philippa, daughter of Henry IV, who married Erik IX of Norway, Sweden, and Denmark in 1406.

[122] N adds 'Lambrughe ou de'.

[123] Edmund of Langley, earl of Cambridge and subsequently duke of York, married Isabella of Castile, sister of Gaunt's second wife, Constanza, in 1372. They had two sons: Richard, earl of Cambridge, who was executed for his role in the Southampton plot in 1415; and Edward, duke of York, who died at the battle of Agincourt shortly afterwards.

[124] B, along with AFO, omits 'pere du conte de Stafford'; LNQ omit 'et l'autre au conte de Staffort pere du conte de Stafford'.

[125] Thomas of Woodstock married Eleanor, daughter and co-heiress of the last earl of Hereford, Humphrey de Bohun (d. 1373). Thomas was made count of Buckingham in 1377 and then duke of Gloucester in 1385, but was murdered in 1397; two years later, John Hall confessed before parliament that he had suffocated the duke under a feather mattress. Thomas had one son, Humphrey, who died in 1399, and three daughters, Joan, Isabel, and Anne. Only Anne was married: firstly to Edward, earl of Stafford, father of Humphrey, duke of Buckingham (d. 1460); secondly to Edward's brother Edmund; and finally to Sir William Bourchier. The title of duke of Hereford was given to Henry Bolingbroke in 1397, but was never regranted after he became king in 1399.

Maintenant a venir au fait dudit Roy Edouart en tant qui touche son estoc de la lignie masculine. Il est filz de Richart duc d'Yorc, lequel fut filz de Emond de Cambruge qui morut a Hantonne ainsi que dessus est dit; lequel conte de Cambruge fut second filz de Emond duc d'Yorc, quatiesme filz de Edouart. Et par ainsi de ce branchage masculin, il n'est pas le plusprochain dudit Edouard le Quatresme[126] qui querela le royaume de France, mais est le plusprochain heritier dudit Roy Edouart le Tiers, le Roy Henry qui a present est. Car son pere Henry le Ve fut filz de Henry conte Derby et depuis roy, lequel estoit filz de Jehan de Gand duc de Lanclastre, tiers filz dudit Roy Edouart le Tiers.[127] Et ledit Roy Edouart qui est a present n'est descendu que du quart filz. Parquoy est tout cler posé que ledit Roy Edouart le Tiers eust eu aucun droit a la couronne de France ce que non par les causes moyens et raisons dessus dessus [*sic*] touchiez, si ne puet ledit Edouart qui a present est aucune chose y demander ne reclamer en especial a cause de ligne masculine. Et se aucun droit il y vouloit reclamer,[128] il convendroit que ce fust a cause de femme, non autrement.

|18r| Et pour venir a ceste matiere il est vray que ledit Roy Edouart pretend que son pere le duc Richart fut filz du conte de Cambruge dessusnommé et de Madame Anne de Mortemer, fille de Messire Rogier de Mortemer et de Madame[129] Phelippe, de qui maintient estre fille du duc de Clarence Messire Leonnel second filz du Roy Edouart, [et a ce tiltre pretend la couronne d'Angleterre luy appertenir comme yssu par fille de fille du second filz dudit Roy Edouart][130] le Tiers et par consequent plusprochain heritier dudit Roy Richart.[131]

Mais prenons orez qu'il fust ainsi, et qu'il fust plusprochain hoir dudit Roy Richart que ledit Roy Henry, et que a ceste cause la couronne d'Angleterre lui appartenist du debat et querellez desquellez parties on se deporte de present a parler pour ce que on n'a a besongnier que des querellez qui sont entre France et Angleterre,

---

[126] Only manuscripts B and J refer to Edward IV rather than Edward III; moreover, 'III[e]' has been inserted in a very small hand, different from that of the main scribe, immediately before 'Quatresme' in B.

[127] H omits 'qui querela le royaume de France [. . .] tiers filz dudit Roy Edouart le Tiers', perhaps because of a homoeoteleutic error, jumping from 'Edouard le Tiers' (the reading given in H, rather than Edouard le Quatresme in BJ) to 'Edouart le Tiers'.

[128] M omits 'Et se aucun droit il y vouloit reclamer'.

[129] A omits 'Anne de Mortemer, fille de Messire Rogier de Mortemer et de Madame', presumably due to an eyeskip from 'Madame' to 'Madame'.

[130] BF omit this material (here transcribed from K), perhaps because of a homoeoteleutic error, jumping from 'Edouart' to 'Edouart'.

[131] Richard, duke of York, was descended from Lionel of Clarence through his mother, Anne Mortimer, daughter of Roger Mortimer, son of Philippa, daughter of Lionel: see p. 74, n. 116 and p. 163.

si ne puet cela riens servir audit Roy Edouart touchant la querelle de France, car comme dit est dessus, ledit Roy Edouart qui a present est ne pretend droit aladicte couronne d'Angleterre qui par fille descendu de fille[132] qui ainçoires n'estoit point l'aisnee. Mais estoit la contesse de Nothombellain l'aisné, dont il y a enfans et sieute, et par consequent il est impossible que ledit Roy Edouart au moyen que dessus, c'est assavoir comme issu de la fille d'une fille[133] qui se disoit de Messire Leonnel et n'estoit point l'aisnee, et lesquellez filles heritent point a la couronne |**18v**| de France par les raisons dessus touchies,[134] puisse avoir aucun droit ne tiltre au royaume ne a la couronne de France.

Item et no[n] mi[e] seulement par la loy et coustume de France, ne par les drois positifz, ne par la Loy Salicque, ne par les prerogativez ottroyeez aux roys de France par les preeminences celestiellez et autrement, mais mesmement par la loy et coustume notoirement gardee en Angleterre quant telz cas avienent.

Et pour descendre au cas particulier, il est vray que en Angleterre en toutes successions qui chieent en taille les filles ne succedent point tant qu'il y'a aucun hoir masle descendant de la ligne. Et se practique chascun jour oudit royame, c'estassavoir que s'il y a ung homme qui ait deux filz et son heritaige soit en taille pour venir a hoirs masles et l'aisné a qui selon la coustume du pays la succession doit appartenir, va de vie a trespas delaissé une fille, laquelle fille ait ung filz et le pere desdittes deux filz voise de vie a trespas,[135] supposé que oudit royaume d'Angleterre il y ait representation par coustume ou par convenance especiale, si ne succedera point le filz de la fille ou prejudice du second filz, et aura le second filz toute la succession. Et est la raison pource que la fille ne puet |**19r**| succeder. Et par consequent ne puet transporter son droit a autrui ne par son moyen le filz ne puet venir a l'eritage.[136]

Puis doncquez que le Roy Edouart le Tiers confessoit la Loy Salicque vraye loy laquelle prive les filles de la couronne de France, et que jamais ne fut trouvé que fille ne hoir masle au moien de fille[137] recueillast la couronne ne le royame de France par droit de succession, et que la loy et coustume d'Angleterre, ouquel royaume lesdits Roy Edouart le Tiers et Edouart le Quart qui est a present ont esté nes, ilz vivent et pretendent prendent leur usage, si ordonne et establisse

---

[132] AO omit 'descendu de fille'.

[133] AHJNOPQ omit 'd'une fille'.

[134] N adds 'si est comme dessus impossible qu'il'.

[135] P omits 'delaissé une fille, laquelle fille ait ung filz et le pere desdittes deux filz voise de vie a trespas', perhaps because of a homoeoteleutic error, jumping from 'trespas' to 'trespas'.

[136] For the English legal device, the entail, see p. 25.

[137] P omits 'ne hoir masle au moien de fille', perhaps because of a homoeoteleutic error, jumping from 'fille' to 'fille'.

le semblable, eulx fondans expressement sur ceste regle de droit, *Nemo plus juris* &c,[138] il est bien cler que c'est a tort et contre raison que aux moyens pretendus par lesdits, Edouart le Quart qui est par trois moyens descendu de fille, ainsi comme dessus est declarié, puisse aucune chose demander ne reclamer a laditte couronne de France. Car puis que la loy et coustume de France[139] le prive de cela ouquel lieu l'eritage est situe et assiz, la loy aussi et coustume d'Angleterre dont il est natif, et le pape, l'eglise universel et tous les princes crestiens depuis VI^{XX} et XIIII[140] ans en ça regnans pendant icellui temps VI roys en France on[t] tenu, reputé, receu et approuvé tous ceulx qui sont descendus dudit Phelippe de Valois vrais |**19v**| roys et heritiers de la couronne de France, ce seroit chose bien estrange que ledit Roy Edouart peust apresent aucun droit pretendre ne reclamer en ladicte couronne, et convendroit en cellui cas soy fonder sur la foy payenne ou sur la coustume des estranges royaumes, qui n'ont riens commun ne habitude avec cellui de France, laquelle chose ne se pourroit soustenir en aucune maniere.

Et quant au Roy Henry et au droit qu'il pretend a la couronne ne au royaume de France, il est vray qu'il y pretend par deux moyens, l'un comme plusprochain hoir masle dudit Roy Edouart le Tiers,[141] l'autre a cause du mauvais traittié qui fut fais a Troiez en Champaigne l'an mil quatrecens et vingt. Par lequel traittié le Roy Charles le VIe, pere du Roy Charles le VIIe[142] et ayeul du roy qui est a present, par le conseil de ceulx qui lors estoyent avecques lui, adopta en filz le Roy Henry le Ve, pere du Roy Henry qui est au jour d'huy;[143] lui bailla sa fille en mariage, Madame Katherine mere dudit Roy Henry le VIe; declaira icellui Roy Henry le Ve estre et devoir estre, aprés son deces, vray heritier de la couronne de France; le fist regent du royame; et vouloit et ordonnoit que aprés son trespas la couronne et le royaume de France lui venissent et appartenissent et a ceulx qui ysteroyent de lui, en privant et deboutant de la dicte suc- |**20r**| cession du royame et de la couronne de France le Roy Charles le VIIe, lors daulphin, pere du roy qui est a present,[144] icellui exheredant et faisant contre

---

[138] AO omit '*plus*'; C offers '*juravit*' in place of '*juris*'. See p. 61, n. 49.

[139] Q omits 'Car puis que la loy et coustume de France', perhaps because of a homoeoteleutic error, jumping from 'France' to 'France'.

[140] K gives the figure as 'VI^{XX} et VIIII', while M offers 'VI^{XX} et IIII^{XX} ans'. See p. 2 above and p. 83 below.

[141] O omits 'hoir masle dudit Roy Edouart le Tiers'.

[142] JP omit 'pere du Roy Charles le VIIe'.

[143] CP omit 'Henry le Ve pere du roy'.

[144] O adds the following passage, which is underlined: 'par le conseil de ceulx qui estoient lors avecques lui adopta en filz le Roy Henry le Ve, pere du roy Henry qui est au jourduy lui bailla'.

lui pluiseurs grandes inhumaines et detestables declerations, contre Dieu, nature, raison et justice.[145]

Item et au moyen duquel traittié lequel les Anglois appellent le traittié de paix final entre France et Angleterre, le Roy Henry le Ve se nomma heritier de France et regent le royaume.

Et pour ce que le Roy Henry V[e] morut avant ledit Roy Charles le VIe, parquoy ne se peut pas faire couronner roy de France selon le pactions faittes oudit traittié, car il ne s'appelloit que heritier et regent, et ne se devoit faire couronner ne prendre tiltre de roy de France[146] jusquez aprés le trespas dudit Roy Charles le VIe. Voyant les Anglois icellui Roy Henry V[e] estre prevenu de mort devant ledit Roy Charles VIe, si tost qu'ilz l'ont peu faire passer deça la mer le Roy Henry VIe dessus nommé qui vit a present, ilz l'ont fait pour le faire couronner roy de France au moyen et traittié dessusdits.[147] Et a cause de ce que la ville et cité de Rains estoit en l'obeissance du Roy Charles le VIIe, lequel avoit esté la enoingt et sacré, et depuis couronné a |**20v**| Sainct Denis, ilz firent couronner ledit Roy Henry le VIe en la ville de Paris, non gardeez les solemnites tellez qu'il appartient et qu'il est requis a une telle dignité et mistere comme de enoingdre, sacrer et couronner les trescrestiens roys de France.[148]

Or maintenant fault il venir a respondre aux tiltres et drois dessus declaries que pretend ledit Roy Henry le VIe.[149]

Premierement au regard de ce qu'il pretend la couronne et le royaume de France lui appartenir comme plusprochain hoir masle du Roy Edouart le Tiers &c, la response est bien clere en ceste partie par deux moyens: l'un que ledit Roy Edouart le Tiers par les raisons dessus touchiez n'eut oncques droit a la couronne ne ou royaume de France. Doncques se ledit Roy Henry le VI[e] y vient a ce tiltre, il est cler que il n'y a riens.

L'autre moyen s'y est qu'il ne puet avoir plusgrant droit a la couronne au tiltre procedant dudit Edouart le Tiers que avoit ledit Henry le V[e] son pere, duquel le droit lui est venu en ceste partie, se aucun droit y avoit ce que non. Or est ainsi que ledit Roy Henry monstra bien |**21r**| clerement que en son vivant qu'il ne pretendoit aucun droit en la couronne au moyen dudit Roy Edouart le Tiers. Car

---

[145] For the treaty of Troyes, concluded on 21 May 1420, see *GTGCA*, pp. 100–115, and *EMDP*, II, pp. 629–636.

[146] P omits 'selon le pactions faittes oudit traittié, car il ne s'appelloit que heritier et regent, et ne se devoit faire couronner ne prendre tiltre de roy de France', perhaps because of a homoeoteleutic error, jumping from 'France' to 'France'.

[147] Q omits 'Voyant les Anglois icellui Roy Henry V[e]'.

[148] Henry V died on 31 August 1422, and Charles VI died on 21 October. Henry VI was consecrated as king of France at Paris on 16 December 1431. For Charles VII's coronation, see Malcolm G.A. Vale, *Charles VII* (London, 1974), pp. 194–217.

[149] C adds 'a la couronne et audit royaulme de France'.

lui informé quant il fut en France que la couronne ne le royaume de France ne tumbe point en la fille, n'y entre autre hoir masle descendant de fille, il se deporta incontinent de se nommer ne porter pour roy de France, mais seulement se dist heritier et regent de France, confessant par exprés que ledit Roy Charles le VIe estoit vray roy et heritier de la couronne de France.[150] Et par ce doncquez appert clerement que au moyen et tiltre dudit Roy Edouart le Tiers, il ne demandoit ne reclamoit aucun droit a la couronne ne au royame de France, si doncquez n'y avoit ne pretendoit avoir aucun droit ne tiltre au moien dudit Roy Edouart le Tiers. Par consequent il est bien cler que ledit Roy Henry le VIe, qui ne puet riens pretendre en ceste partie au moien dudit Roy Henry V^e son pere ainsi que dit est dessus, n'a ne puet avoir ne reclamer aucun droit ne tiltre en ladicte couronne de France[151] au moyen dudit Roy Edouart le Tiers.

[*Item* et qui plus est, ledit Henry le Ve confessoit ledit Roy Charles le VIe vray roy de France et le reputoit et avouoyt pour tel. Or est ainsi que depuis que le royaulme de France fut bourné et limité ainsi qu'il devoit demourer au temps que les partaiges furent faiz entre le Roy Charles le Chauve et ses freres jusques a present, il ne sera pas trouvé que au royaulme de France deux personnes en ung mesmez temps ayent jamez esté tenuz ne reputez par le pape et l'eglise universel, par les autres princes crestiens et par les subgietz du royaulme, pour roys de France. Ainçoys depuis icelluy temps a tousjours la dicte couronne de France demoure et reside en ung suppost et en une personne. Puis doncques que ledit Roy Henry le Ve confessoit ledit Roy Charles le VIe estre vray roy de France, il est tout cler qu'il ne avoit ne reclamoit aulcun droit ne tiltre en ladicte couronne.][152] Et pour plus conforter et justifier ceste matiere [et monstrer clerement que ledit Roy Henry confessoit que ledit Roy Charles le VIe estre vray roy de France et que durant sa vie il ne reclamoit aulcun droit ou tiltre a ladicte couronne],[153] soient veues en Angleterre les epytaphes dudit Henry le Ve tant en son palais de Westmonstre que par tout ailleurs ou royaume, il met expressement en ceste maniere aumoins en substance, *Henricus Quintus, dux Normanorum verusque* |**21v**| *conquestor eorum, heres Francorum decessit et rector eorum.*[154]

Soient aussi veues toutes les lettres patentez dudit Roy Henry donneez en France ou temps qu'il y estoit, et ne sera point trouvé

---

[150] O omits 'confessant par exprés que ledit Roy Charles le VIe estoit vray roy et heritier de la couronne de France', presumably because of an eyeskip from 'France' to 'France'.

[151] H omits 'si doncquez n'y avoit ne pretendoit [. . .] ne tiltre en ladicte couronne de France'.

[152] This material from A also appears in CMO.

[153] This material from A also appears in CMO.

[154] For the epitaph of Henry V at Westminster Abbey, see pp. 26–27.

qu'il s'appellast autrement que roy d'Angleterre, heritier et regent de France.[155]

Pareillement es lettres patentes dudit Roy Charles VIe depuis ledit traittié de Troyes, il a tousjours esté escript dessoubz en marge 'Par le roy a la relation du roy d'Angleterre heritier et regent de France'. Qui sont bien cleres demonstrances que ledit Roy Henry le Ve ne pretendoit aucun droit a la couronne de France par le moyen dudit Roy Edouart le Tiers ainçois se paravant y avoit pretendu, il est cler qu'il s'en desistoit et departoit, *quare* &c. *ut supra*.

Touchant l'autre moyen que ledit Roy Henry le VIe pretend en ladicte couronne de France a cause du traittié de Troies qu'ilz appellent le traittié de paix final comme dit est dessus, il est ainçoires plus cler que ledit moien est inutile et de nul effect et valeur que le moien precedent provenant a cause dudit Roy Edouart le Tiers.

|**22r**| Car premierement ledit Roy Charles le VIe estoit frappé de maladie telle comme chascun scet, parquoy il n'estoit point *compos mentis*, ne avoit faculté de disposer de son royaume en aucune maniere.[156]

Secondement il estoit en captivité et en la main et soubz la puissance dudit Roy Henry le Ve et de ses mortelz et anciens ennemis, despourveu du conseil et absent de la compaignie des principaulz princes et seigneurs de son sang, des gens des trois estas et autres notables gens de son royame, parquoy il est bien cler qu'il ne se povoit faire chose vaillable, ne qu'il peust avoir ne sortir aucun effect a l'avantaige ne prejudice de nul.[157]

Tiercement il avoit filz naturel et legittime, né et procree [*sic*] en leal mariage, qui jamais n'avoit fait chose digne de reprehention dont sondit pere deust estre malcontent, ne dequoy il eust deservi devoir estre desireté [desherité], or est il tout cler que la ou il y a filz de la condicion dessusdits, et fust orez en moindre seignourie cent fois

---

[155] C adds 'comme dessus est dit'. Following the treaty of Troyes, Henry V's royal style changed from '*rex Anglie et Francie et dominus Hibernie*' to '*rex Anglie et heres Francie et dominus Hibernie*': *EMDP*, II, p. 630.

[156] O adds 'que ce peut estre'; H omits this paragraph and begins the following paragraph 'Car premierement il estoit en captivité'. The argument that Charles VI did not have sufficient mental competence to agree to the treaty of Troyes was a common one amongst Valois lawyers and diplomats: see *EMDP*, II, pp. 642 and 650; Nicole Pons (ed.), *L'Honneur de la couronne de France*, pp. 119–120 and 128; Friedrich Schneider, *Der Europäische Friedenskongres von Arras (1435) und die Friedenspolitik Papst Eugens IV und des Basler Konzils* (Greiz, 1919), p. 186; Jean Juvénal, I, pp. 184–185 and 193 and II, pp. 55–60; Robert Blondel, *Oeuvres de Robert Blondel*, I, pp. 273 and 459.

[157] For earlier use of this argument, see *EMDP*, II, p. 640; Pons (ed.), *L'Honneur de la couronne de France*, pp. 119–120 and 123–124; Jean Juvénal, I, p. 185 and II, pp. 55, 57, and 133–134; Robert Blondel, *Oeuvres de Robert Blondel*, I, pp. 273–274 and 458–459; Christopher T. Allmand, 'Documents relating to the Anglo-French negotiations of 1439', *Camden Miscellany*, 24 (1972), p. 116.

que n'est la couronne de France, les filles ne le puent debouter de sa succession, ne le pere ne le puet deshireter sans cause,[158] et ainçores moins a la couronne de France que en nulle autre succession car ce n'est que une continuation de seignourie de pere en filz ou au pluspro- |**22v**| chain hoir masle, sans qu'il se puisse selon droit et raison changier ne transmuer deça ne dela et fault qu'elle voise tousjours la ou la ligne et consanguinité l'envoie, ne oncquez ne fut fait autrement.[159]

Et se le cas avenoit que Dieu ne vueille qu'il y eust aucun roy meu de faire aucune chose en telles matieres, si fauldroit il oyr partie et convocquier et appeller tous ceulx qu'il appartient; que le prince aussi fust en estat et acompaignié comme la matiere le requiert; et que toutes les solennitez qui doivent estre gardeez en tel cas si fussent gardeez,[160] lesquellez seroient bien fort a trouver.[161] Car il n'est pas leu depuis le temps du Roy Clotaire le Premier, contre qui ses deux filz se forfirent bien estangement, ainsi comme dist l'istoire, et dont l'abbaye de Jumegez fut fondee a ceste cause que jamais telles choses avenissent.[162] Et ne sera pas trouvé que en ceste matiere il y ait fondement pourquoy l'en peust dire que le [Roy Charles le VIIe dessus nommé filz dudit][163] Roy Charles le VIe deut estre exheredé ne privé de la couronne et succession du royaume de France, qui a bon droit et juste tiltre heredital paternel lui competoit et appartenoit ne qu'il y ait eu solennité gardee qui en riens lui peust prejudicier.

Item et meismez aprés ledit dampnable traittié fait a Troies, ledit Roy Henry le Ve tant |**23r**| en son nom comme dudit Roy Charles le VIe et de leurs adherens envoya solennelle ambassade a Romme devers le Pape Martin qui pour lors estoit, affin d'avoir la confirmation dudit traittié, et que le pape et l'eglise le voulsissent avoir aggreable et icellui emologuer et approuver.[164]

Et combien que le Roy Charles le VIIe, pour lors daulphin, fust bien foible de gens et eust beaucop de grans troublez, necessitez et adversaires, neantmoins lui oy ou son procurer pour lui en ses drois et justifications fut ledit traittié regetté et renvoyé sans aucune

---

[158] JKLOPQ omit 'ne le pere ne le puet deshireter sans cause'.

[159] C adds 'ne ne se peust faire'. This was a common argument amongst Valois writers, usually supported with Biblical and legal citations: Pons (ed.), *L'Honneur de la couronne de France*, pp. 120, 123–124, and 130–131, and also see Jean Juvénal, I, pp. 186–188 and II, pp. 55–56, and Robert Blondel, *Oeuvres de Robert Blondel*, I, pp. 273–274 and 458–460.

[160] ACP omit 'en tel cas si fussent gardeez'.

[161] For the earlier use of this argument, see Jean Juvénal, I, pp. 188–189 and II, p. 57.

[162] The abbey of Notre-Dame de Jumièges in Normandy was founded around 654 by St Filibert.

[163] This additional phrase relating to Charles VII from K also appears in AHJLMNOPQ but is omitted in BCF, though C makes more sense of the 'error' by correcting the reference from 'Charles le VIe' to 'Charles le VIIe'.

[164] This is presumably a reference to the embassy of June 1422, discussed in Beaucourt, I, p. 325n, and Margaret Harvey, 'Martin V and Henry V', *Archivum Historiae Pontificiae*, 24 (1986), p. 67n.

confirmation ne approbation; et tousjours depuis a esté baillié lieu audit monseigneur pour lors daulphin en court de Romme comme a filz et vray heritier de la couronne de France: et aprés la mort dudit Roy Charles VIe son pere, fut tenu,[165] reputé et receu en ladicte court de Romme, au Concille de Basle, et par tout ailleurs ou laditte eglise a esté assemblee et tous les princes crestiens, pour vray roy et heritier de la couronne de France; et lui a esté baillié, ou a ses ambassaders, le lieu tel et appellé et nommé par tous roy de France sans aucune difficulté au veu et sceu du roy d'Angleterre ou de ses ambassadeurs et procureurs, et de tous ceulx qui l'ont volu veoir et scavoir.[166]

Lesquellez choses dessus declaries monstrent |**23v**| bien clerement que ledit Roy Henry au tiltre et moyen dudit Roy Edouart le Tiers, ne au tiltre et moyen du traittié fait en Troyes en Champaigne, ne ne puet avoir ne reclamer aucun droit ne tiltre au royaume ne a la couronne de France. Ainçois aprés la mort dudit Roy Charles le Bel, roy paisible sans contredit aucun ou difficulté du royaume de France, Messire Phelippe conte de Valois a bon et juste tiltre recoeilla et prist la succession de la couronne et du royaume de France comme vray, legittime et plusprochain heritier habille a succeder a laditte couronne. Et a bon et juste tiltre le tint et posseda et l'ont tenu possedé ses successeurs l'espace de VI^{XX} et XVI ans, c'estassavoir depuis l'an mil III^C XXVIII jusques a l'heure presente que l'en comte mil IIII^C LXIIII.[167] Et recueilla le royame et la couronne aprés le deces dudit Phelippe de Valois, Jehan son filz ou premier degré, Charles le Quint ou second degré, Charles le VIe ou tiers degré, Charles le VIIe ou quart degré, et le Roy Loys qui a present est ou V^e degré. Et continueront au plaisir de Dieu, ceulx et la ligne de prochain en prochain, selon que le cas y escherra [comme vrais heritiers de la couronne et droituriers][168] roys de France, ainsi que selon Dieu, raison, et justice, et leur bon droit, le veullent jusques a la fin. Et n'y pevent lesdits Roy Edouart IIIIe de ce nom a present regnant en Angleterre, ne le Roy Henry VIe son compediteur aux tiltres et moiens pretendus, ne autre quelconques, y |**24r**| demander ne reclamer aucun droit ne tiltre en maniere quele qu'elle soit.[169]

---

[165] The transcription in M ends here, though there is a final paragraph: 'France/ Angleterre'.

[166] See Jean Juvénal, II, pp. 40 and 55–56, together with Jocelyn M. Dickinson, *The Congress of Arras: a study in medieval diplomacy* (Oxford, 1955), pp. 25ff; Christopher T. Allmand, 'Normandy and the Council of Basel', *Speculum*, 40 (1965), pp. 10–11; and Margaret Harvey, *England, Rome and the Papacy, 1417–1464: the study of a relationship* (Manchester, 1993). Also see p. 62, n. 82 above.

[167] H: 'mil IIII^C LXV'.

[168] This additional material from K does not appear in BF but is in ACHJLNOPQ.

[169] H adds a new paragraph: 'Fin de la premiere partie de ce present traittié'; Q adds a new paragraph: 'Cy fine la premiere partie du presen livre'.

CY COMMENCE LA SECONDE PARTIE DE CEPRESENT LIVRE.[170]

|**24v**| La seconde partie principale de la matiere dont de present est question[171] traittera du droit et des querellez que les Anglois pretendent en pluiseurs terres et seignouries particulieres du royaume de France a tiltre heredital et oultre, et par dessus[172] lesquelles ilz maintiennent estre leur propre heritage, oultre et par dessus les drois par eulx pretendus a la couronne et a la totalité dudit royame: et les responses que sur ce on y puet faire, ensemble les moyens comme elles ont esté reunyez et rejoinctez a bon et juste tiltre a la couronne de France, et comment elles competent et appartiennent au roy de France et non a autre.

Et pour entendre ceste matiere, est vray que les Anglois pretendent d'ancienneté les duchiez de Normandie et de Guyenne,[173] contez d'Anjou, du Mainne et Touraine, de Poitou leur competer et appartenir par droit de succession et heritage a eulx escheuz et avenus a cause de leurs predeccesseurs aux moyens cy aprés declariez.[174]

Et premierement dient lesdits Anglois que le Duc Guillaume de Normandie estoit duc paisible dudit duchié, et conquesta le royame d'Angleterre, et duquel tous les deux roys d'Angleterre qui a present sont, c'estassavoir Edouart |**25r**| et Henry, sont descendus en droitte ligne au moyen de femme, ainsi comme cy aprés sera declairié plusadplain.[175]

---

[170] This paragraph only appears in BLN. H prefers 'Fin de la premiere partie de ce present traittié' on fo. 21r and then, after a blank page, the following paragraph appears at the top of fo. 22r: 'Cy sensuit la seconde partie de ce present traictié qui traicte des singulieres terres et seignouries que les Anglois dient que a tiltre heredital leur compettent et apartient'. Manuscript Q offers 'Fin de la premiere partie de ce present traittié' in red ink on fo. 85r and then, at the top of fo. 86r, again in red ink, 'Cy commenche la seconde partie de ce livre qui parle des questions et quereles Anglois font au royaulme de France en aulcunes terres et seignouries'.

[171] O omits 'dont de present est question'.

[172] The phrase 'oultre et par dessus' only appears in BF.

[173] Cousinot followed contemporary French practice in using the term Guyenne to refer to the assemblage of territories held by the English king in the south-west of France, including Gascony. Under the Romans, this region was known as the province of Aquitania and included more than a dozen counties: Poitou and Berry in the north; La Marche, Limousin, Angoumois, Saintonge, Aunis, Bordelais, Périgord, and Uzerches in the centre; and Agenais, Quercy, Rouergue, and Auvergne in the south. Following the political confusion of the late ninth century, the counts of Poitiers won control of the duchy of Aquitaine, to which the previously independent duchy of Gascony was added in 1052.

[174] C adds 'et remonstrez de point en point'.

[175] William I the Conqueror (d. 1087) became duke of Normandy on the death of his father, Robert, in 1035 and conquered England in 1066.

Est vray aussi que ledit Duc Guillame, qui depuis par conqueste fut roy[176] d'Angleterre, eut quatre filz et une fille, desquelz quatre filz seront icy obmis les trois premiers pour cause de briefté, et que toute la succession tant d'Angleterre comme de Normandie[177] vint a Henry Beau Clerc qui fut le IIIIe filz.[178] Et la fille nommee Adelle fut mariee au conte de Chartres et de Blois, auquel conte de Chartres escheut depuis la conté de Champaigne, duquel mariage yssi le Conte Thibault de Champaigne, et Estienne conte de Blois qui depuis occuppa le royaume d'Angleterre.[179] Et dicellui Conte Thibault de Champaigne descendy une fille nommee Adelle qui fut marié[180] au Roy Loys le Piteux, pere de Phelippe le Conquerant autrement dit le Corageux. *Et nota propter subsequentia.*[181]

Dudit Henry Beaucler ne demoura que une fille qui eut nom Maheut l'emperris pour ce qu'elle fut femme a l'Empereur Henry le Quart, et depuis fut conjoincte par mariage en secondes nopces au conte d'Anjou, Geffroy Martel le Tiers, qui fut filz du Conte Fouquez le derrenier, lequel Fouquez en son tamps passa outre mer et fut |**25v**| le derrenier[182] roy de Jherusalem qui ait esté crestien.[183]

---

[176] In O, the phrase 'que ledit Duc Guillame, qui depuis par conqueste fut roy' is underlined and there is a marginal note in the same hand, 'Le Duc Guillaume de Normandie conquesta le royaulme d'Angleterre'.

[177] C omits 'tant d'Angleterre comme de Normandie'.

[178] In O, there is a marginal note in the same hand, 'La succession d'Angleterre et de Normandie vint a Henri Beauclerk filz dudit Guillaume'.

[179] C omits 'auquel conte de Chartres escheut depuis la conté de Champaigne'. Manuscript A replaces 'mariee au conte de Chartres et de Blois, auquel conte de Chartres escheut depuis la conté de Champaigne, duquel mariage yssi le conte Thibault de Champaigne, et Estienne conte de Blois' with 'mariee au conte de Flandre, escheut depuis la conté de Champaigne a Thibault conte de Bloys'.

[180] P omits 'au conte de Chartres et de Blois, auquel conte de Chartres [...] descendy une fille nommee Adelle qui fut marié'. This may be the result of a homoeoteleutic error, jumping from 'mariee' to 'marié'.

[181] William I had four sons: Robert Curthose, duke of Normandy (d. 1134); Richard (d. between 1069 and 1075); King William II Rufus (d. 1100); and King Henry I (d. 1135), who was also styled Henry Beauclerc from the fourteenth century. William I also had five daughters, including Adèle who married Etienne Henri, count of Blois; amongst their five children were Thibaud (d. 1152) and King Stephen of England (d. 1154). Philippe II Augustus (d. 1223) was the son of Louis VII (d. 1180) by his third wife, Adèle of Champagne. See pp. 97–98 below.

[182] O omits 'lequel Fouquez en son tamps passa outre mer et fut le derrenier', perhaps because of a homoeoteleutic error, jumping from 'derrenier' to 'derrenier'. There is also a marginal note in the same hand, 'Le Conte Geufroy Martel fust le dernier roy crestien de Jerusalem crestien'.

[183] Matilda (d. 1167) was the only legitimate daughter of King Henry I. She married the Emperor Heinrich V and then Geoffrey V Plantagenet (d. 1151), son of Foulques V, count of Anjou and Maine, and also king of Jerusalem following his marriage to Melisende, eldest daughter of King Baudouin II.

Dicellui mariage de l'Emperris Maheut et du conte d'Anjou Geoffroy Martel issy ung filz nommé Henry le Second, lequel a cause de sa mere heritiere du Roy Henry Beau Clerc fut roy d'Angleterre et duc de Normandie, de par son pere Geoffroy Martel fut conte d'Anjou, du Maine et de Touraine.[184]

Item icellui Henry le Second espousa la Royne Elyenor qui paravant avoit esté femme du Roy Loys le Piteux, filz du Roy Loys[185] le Gros et pere du Roy Phelippe le Conquerant dont dessus est faitte mention, laquel Elyenor pour certaines causes qui autrepart se declarront par l'auctorité du Pape Eugene le Second, ledit Roy Loys la repudia.[186] Et aprés ledit Henry le Second roy d'Angleterre l'espousa, et duquel issirent quatre filz et une fille.[187]

Le premier fut Henry qui fut couronné durant la vie de son pere et morut avant sondit pere;[188] et fut cellui qui fist martirisier Saint Thomas de Cantorbiery de l'adveu et consentement de sondit pere Henry le Second, et n'est point en nombre ledit jone Henry ou nombre des autres roys d'Angleterre.[189]

|**26r**| Le second fut Richart Cuer de Lyon qui succeda audit Henry le Second, mais il n'eut point de sieutte masle ne femelle.

Le tiers fut Geffroy qui espousa la contesse de Bretaigne dont issy ung filz nommé Artus et une fille appellee Elyenor.[190]

Le quart fut Jehan seigneur de Yeuniez et d'Arquez, lequel depuis recueilla la succession du pere de la mere, et forfist tout ce qu'il avoit en France, et commença la conqueste contre lui et lui fut tout osté.[191]

---

[184] The eldest son of Matilda and Geoffrey was King Henry II (d. 1189).

[185] H omits 'le piteux filz du Roy Loys', perhaps because of a homoeoteleutic error, jumping from 'Loys' to 'Loys'. Manuscript A offers a marginal note, 'Nota de Alienor'.

[186] In 1152, King Louis VII of France divorced Eleanor (d. 1204), daughter of Guillaume, tenth duke of Aquitaine and eighth count of Poitou (d. 1137): see pp. 100–101.

[187] The sons of Henry II and Eleanor were William (d. 1156); Henry the Young (d. 1183); Richard I the Lionheart (d. 1199); Geoffrey, duke of Brittany (d. 1186); and King John (d. 1216).

[188] N prefers 'Le premier filz doncques qui de ce mariage yssi ce fut Henry qui fut couronné du royaulme d'Angleterre durant encores la vie de son pere et si morut avant son pere'.

[189] Henry the Young was crowned as heir presumptive to the throne in 1170, during the lifetime of his father, Henry II. He was a ward of Archbishop Thomas Becket and there is no evidence that he played a role in his murder in 1170. Both Jean de Montreuil and Jean Juvénal blamed the murder solely on the king: Montreuil, II, pp. 182, 242, and 287, and Jean Juvénal, I, 206 and II, pp. 83 and 89.

[190] Geoffrey had a son, Arthur, duke of Brittany (d. 1203), and a daughter, Eleanor (d. 1241), by his wife Constance (d. 1201), heiress of Conan, fourth duke of Brittany (d. 1171). The names of the two children are not identified in manuscript C.

[191] It is not clear why John, count of Mortain and king of England, should be associated with these particular places. He was entrusted with the castle of Arques by his brother

La fille fut Dame Elyenor ou Margarite qui fut femme du roy d'Espaigne nommé Alphons, dont issy une fille nommee Blanche qui fut femme du roy Leon le Debonnaire,[192] filz du Roy Phelippe le Conquerant et pere de Sainct Loys. Et demoura laditte Blanche seule heritiere de son pere et de sa mere par ce que son frere aisné, Henry, morut ainsi qu'il appert par lettres auctentiquez estans ou Tresor des Chartres.[193]

A revenir doncquez a la matiere Richart Cuer de Lyon, deuzieme filz du Roy Henry le Second, pour ce que son frere aisné estoit mort sans hoir et avant son pere, aprés la mort dudit Henry le |**26v**| Second recueilla toute la succession, et fut a cause de son pere roy d'Angleterre, duc de Normandie, et conte d'Anjou, du Maine et de Touraine. Et a cause de sa mere Elyenor il fut duc de Guyenne et conte de Poitou, qui est a entendre touchant Guyenne[194] en tant que laditte duchié se extend es trois seneschaucees de Bordeaulx, les Lanes et Barades et non plus.[195]

Cestui Richard fut grant ami du Roy Phelippe le Conquerant ou temps que le Roy Henry le Second son pere vivoit, et se allierent ensemble ledit Roy Phelippe et ledit Richard pour lors conte de Poitiers, al'encontre dudit Roy Henry le Second pere dicellui Richard, et lui firent guerre et beaucop de oultrage, dont a ceste cause ledit Henry morut de courroux.[196]

Richard in 1194, and it was seized by Philippe Augustus in 1204. 'Yeuniez' may be Verneuil, also lost to Philippe in the same year.

[192] A has a marginal note, 'Louys'; O omits 'nomee Blanche'.

[193] Henry II and Eleanor had three daughters, including Eleanor, who married King Alfonso VIII of Castile. The children of Alfonso and Eleanor included King Enrique I of Castile, Berenguela, and Blanche, wife of Louis VIII of France (d. 1226), the son of Philippe Augustus. When Henry I died in 1217, Berenguela renounced any claim to the Castilian throne in favour of her son, Fernando III (see p. 174, n. 120).

[194] ACO omit 'et conte de Poitou, qui est a entendre touchant Guyenne', perhaps because of a homoeoteleutic error, jumping from 'Guyenne' to 'Guyenne'. Manuscripts AO add at the end of the sentence 'et aussi conte de Poitou', while C prefers 'et conte de Poictou et enjouyst paisiblement'. Richard paid homage to Louis VII for Poitou and Aquitaine in January 1169; his control of these lands remained contentious until his father, Henry II, died in 1189, whereupon his mother, Eleanor, resumed control of the duchy until her own death in 1204.

[195] Like other French diplomats, Cousinot was confusing areas of customary law with judicial and administrative boundaries. This description of Guyenne as encompassing the sénéchaussées of Bordeaux (presumably Guyenne), Landes, and Bazadais was long outdated, especially after 1399 when the English divided the duchy into the four sénéchaussées of Guyenne, Landes, Bigorre, and Agenais. See pp. 91–92 below and, for example, *L&P*, I, pp. 51–52 and 135, together with Malcolm G. A. Vale, *English Gascony, 1399–1453: a study of war, government and politics during the later stages of the Hundred Years' War* (Oxford, 1970), pp. 6 and 103n.

[196] Mounting tension between Henry II and his son during the 1180s gave Philippe II the opportunity to negotiate with Richard, culminating in his payment of homage to the French king for Normandy, Anjou, and Aquitaine in 1188, shortly before his father's death.

Mais tantost aprés que ledit Richard fut roy tant ou voiage de la terre saincte que firent ensemble ledit Roy Phelippe et lui, comme depuis icellui Richard s'accorda tresmal avecquez ledit Roy Phelippe et lui fist guerre, et commença deslors une partie de la confiscation, jasoit ce que n'est pas le droit fondement dont proceda depuis la declaration et la confiscation,[197] et pource l'istoire se taist a parler plusavant en ce pas de laditte matiere.[198]

|**27r**| Ledit roy Richard morut sans aucuns enfans et doit venir la succession a Artus et Elyenor, enfans de Geffroy qui fut filz dudit Roy Henry le Second, lequel espousa la contesse de Bretaig[n]e. Mais pour ce qu'ilz estoient jeunes et en bas eage, ledit Jehan, quart filz, prist le gouvernement desdits enfans et de leurs terres et seignouriez.[199]

Et pensant icellui Jehen que se sesdits nepveu et niepce estoient mors il seroit ung des plusgrans seigneurs de crestienté, il machina en la mort de son dit nepveu Artur, et le fist jetter par subtilz moyens du hault d'un chastiau du milieu de Chynon dedens la ville, et se rompy le col et tous les membres.

Et aprés icellui Jehan envoya ladicte Elyenor sa niepce, suer dudit Artur, a Wincestre en Angleterre, la ou il la fist tenir prisonniere jusquez a la mort, dont a ceste cause sa cronique d'Angleterre dit de lui en substance telles paroles: *Iste Johannes propter feloniam commissam in personis Arturii nepotis sui quem proditorie occidere fecit, et Elyenoris nepotis sue quam mancipatam ducit apud Winctonias, rex Francorum abstulit ei omnes terras omniaque dominia que et quas possidebat in regno Francie.*[200]

|**27v**| Toutesfois quoy que en deust avenir aprés les choses dessusdittes faittez, le devandit Jehan recueilla toute la succession de son pere et de sa mere et de ses freres, et se tint et porta pour roy d'Angleterre, duc de Normandie et de Guienne, conte de Poitou,

---

[197] O omits 'jasoit ce que n'est pas le droit fondement dont proceda depuis la declaration et la confiscation', perhaps because of a homoeoteleutic error, jumping from 'confiscation' to 'confiscation'.

[198] Jean Juvénal's account of the tensions between Richard I and Philippe II was based principally upon Rigord, in Jean Juvénal, II, pp. 90–92. This story was explored in great detail in *A declaracion of the trewe and dewe title of Henry VII*, pp. 176–184 below.

[199] Eleanor and her posthumous brother, Arthur, were the children of Geoffrey and Constance, duke and duchess of Brittany. Although many supported Arthur's claim to inherit the English throne from his childless uncle Richard I, the king had named his youngest brother, John, as his successor shortly before his death on 6 April 1199. See James C. Holt, 'The *casus regis*: the law and politics of succession in the Plantagenet dominions, 1185–1247', in Edmund B. King and Susan J. Reynolds (eds), *Law in Mediaeval Life and Thought* (Sewanee, 1990), pp. 21–42.

[200] It is not clear which 'cronique d'Angleterre' is the source for this improbable quotation. King John was charged with murdering Arthur in a number of French chronicles, including the *Grandes chroniques*, VI, pp. 306 and 358. Jean Juvénal claimed that the English king had strangled Arthur, citing this as one reason for the subsequent judgement against him by Philippe II, in Jean Juvénal, II, pp. 92, 95, and 138–139. Neither of these sources blamed John for the death of Eleanor, who was never imprisoned at Winchester.

d'Anjou, du Maine et de Touraine, et s'en mist en possession et saisine, et fist de grans rebellions, desobeissances, conspirations et traisons al'encontre dudit Roy Phelippe son souverain et naturel seigneur au regard des terres de France.

A l'occasion desquelz crismez et malefices, tant en cas de lese majesté de felonnie que autrement, il fut declairié par le roi et les barons de France, qui vault autant a dire comme les pers, avoir tout forfait et confisquié envers le roy. Et a ceste cause et par ce moyen fut privé, dejetté et debouté de toutes les terres et seignouriez dessus declareez[201] qu'il tenoit en France, et furent acquisez par tiltre de confiscaton au roy, et adjoinctez et reunies a la couronne comme le vray heritage et demaine du roy.[202]

Et ainçoires plus veu qu'il estoit ingrat al'encontre de son sang dont la succession lui devoit venir et par consequent indigne a venir a laditte succession comme sera touchié plus amplement cy aprés,[203] semble que le royame |**28r**| d'Angleterre devoit venir au plus prochain de laditte succession aprés ledit Roy Jehan.

Lequel plusprochain, se le royaume d'Angleterre puet tumber en fille ou en hoir masle descendant de fille, estoit le Roy Phelippe le Conquerant d'un costé et le Roy Sainct Loys de l'autre, car la mere dudit Phelippe le Conquerant estoit fille du Conte Thibault de Champaigne, nepveu du Roy Henry Beauclerc, et son plusprochain hoir hors mis l'Emperris Maheut. Et Sainct Loys estoit filz de Blanche d'Espaigne, niepce desdits Roys Richard et Jehan, et seule heritiere de ses pere et mere comme dit est dessus.[204] Et ne sera pas trouvé qu'il y ait nulz plusprochains hoirs de laditte succession aprés ledit Roy Jehan que ledit Phelippe le Conquerant et Sainct Loys. Toutesfoiz pour ce que ce n'est pas *presentis speculationis*, il fault revenir a la matiere subgette.

---

[201] N omits 'et seignouriez dessus declareez'.

[202] In April 1202, Philippe Augustus pronounced the confiscation of all the fiefs of John in France because of his refusal to attend court to answer charges levelled against him by his former ally, Hugues de Lusignan, who was angry at the way in which the English king had stolen his fiancée, Isabelle (d. 1246), daughter of Audemar, count of Angoulême, together with lands held by Lusignan and his brother, Raoul d'Exoudun. The French king then accepted Arthur of Brittany's homage for all John's lands except for Normandy. See p. 91.

[203] See pp. 90–91.

[204] Philippe II of France was the son of Louis VII (d. 1180) and his third wife, Adèle, daughter of Thibaud (d. 1152), son of Adèle and nephew of her brother Henry I of England. St Louis was the son of Louis VIII and Blanche of Castile, daughter of Alfonso VIII of Castile and Eleanor, daughter of Henry II and sister of Richard I and John. Jean Juvénal des Ursins had championed the right of Philippe II as closest heir to the murdered Arthur, nephew of John, in Jean Juvénal, II, pp. 139. Cousinot returned to the claims of Philippe II on pp. 97 and 99 below.

C'est assavoir que non obstant les choses dessusdittes, les roys d'Angleterre qui depuis ont esté tous iceulx descendus en droitte ligne masculine dudit Roy Jehan de Angleterre jusquez aux deux roys qui de present sont en Angleterre, Henry et Edouart, inclus dont ledit Henry en ligne masculine est plusprochain que Edouart car il est du tiers filz, et le Roy Edouart n'est que du |**28v**| quart,[205] ont tous volu quereler les terres et seignouries dessusdittes aux tiltres et par les moyens des successions dessus declarieez sauf les renuntiations qui furent faittes la premiere foiz par le Roy Henry le Tiers, filz dudit Jehan, et a la seconde foiz par le traittié de Bretegny.[206]

Et pour entendre plus avant ceste matiere, est vray que des le tamps du Roy Henry le Second, par le moyen de l'ayde que le Roy Loys, pere de Phelippe le Conquerant, lui fist au recouvrement du royaume d'Angleterre et de la duchié de Normandie que le roy Estienne de Blois[207] son cousin tenoit et occuppoit indeuement et contre raison, ainsi que disoit le Roy Henry, icellui Henry et sa mere l'emperris donnerent et transporterent audit Roy Loys tout le pays de Veqcin qui est entre les rivieres d'Ette et de Andelle, et pareillement la conté d'Evreux et toutes les terres de laditte conté et des environ, qui sont depuis la riviere d'Yton jusquez en Saine et en la conté de Dreux,[208] parquoy sans difficulté cela est le cler heritage du roy.[209]

Et quant au surplus combien qu'il n'est plus cler ne plus juste tiltre que confiscation quant il y'a matiere souffisant, et que les procés sont deuement fais, et ainsi l'ordon- |**29r**| nent les drois civilez et canons, la Loy Salicque et la coustume generale du royaume de France. Et mesmez en usent les Anglois en Angleterre par semblable et a ce moyen en tiennent tous les pays de Gallez et la pluspart du nord depuis la riviere du Humbre en tirant devers Escoce.[210] Et que la matiere de confiscation et forfaiture fut si clere al'encontre dudit Roy Jehan, tant en cas leze majesté comme de felonnie et autrement; et que ainsi eut

---

[205] See p. 76.

[206] By the treaty of Paris in October 1259, Henry III renounced all claims to Normandy, Touraine, Anjou, Maine, and Poitou. In May 1360, Edward III agreed the treaty of Brétigny by which he gave up all claims to Normandy, Touraine, Anjou, and Maine in return for the continued possession of Aquitaine, Poitou, Ponthieu, Guînes, and Calais and its march. See *EMDP*, II, pp. 618–621, and *GTGCA*, pp. 39–68, together with pp. 91–93 below.

[207] N replaces 'le roy Estienne de Blois' with 'le duc estoit conte de Blois'.

[208] O omits 'et toutes les terres de laditte conté et des environ'. ACO prefer 'd'Evreux' to 'Dreux'.

[209] The Norman Vexin was ceded to King Louis VII in 1144 by Geoffrey V Plantagenet, count of Anjou, father of Henry II, following the victory in the war with King Stephen for the control of Normandy: Daniel Power, *The Norman Frontier in the Twelfth and Thirteenth Centuries* (Cambridge, 2004), p. 392. Jean Juvénal had also connected this grant with the payment of homage by Henry II to Louis VII in August 1151, in Jean Juvénal, II, p. 88.

[210] See pp. 23–24 and 112–113.

esté solennelement declairié par ceulx a qui de droit il appartenoit de faire; et que pour ceste il y eut trois journeez solennelement[211] tenues en ce royaume, dont l'une fut a Estampez, l'autre a Chartres, esquellez deux journeez ledit Roy Jehan comparut en personne moyennant seureté qu'il eut dudit Roy Phelippe, et la tierce fut a Vendosme, la ou il ne se volu point comparoir, ainçois se fortiffia en toutez manieres a lui possiblez contre le Roy Phelippe. Auquel lieu de Vendosme la declaration fut solennelement faitte contre lui.[212]

Neantmoins Sainct Loys, filz du filz dudit Phelippe le Conquerant, desirant aler conquerir la terre saincte et cuidant mettre son royaume en paix par les moiens cy dessoubz declaries, et que aucun trouble pendant son absence ne lui fust donné, fist certain appointement avecquez |**29v**| ledit Roy Henry le Tiers, filz de Jehan, du consentement des deux filz dicellui Henry, c'estassavoir Emond et Edouart,[213] et de tous les princes, seigneurs et gens des trois estas d'Angleterre, par lequel par tiltre de pure, liberale et mere donnation, ledit Sainct Loys donna, quitta, ceda et transporta au dit Roy Henry le Tiers roy d'Angleterre, lequel en ceste forme, c'est a entendre par tiltre de don, le accepta pour lui et ses successeurs nez et procreez en leal mariage, la duchié de Guyenne ainsi que anciennement elle se comportoit, c'est a dire es trois seneschauceez de Bordeaux, les Lanes et Baradez.[214]

Et en augmentation et accroissement de seignourie, y adjousta ledit Sainct Loys le pays de Xantonge et de la Charente, et les pays, contés et seignouriez de Perregort, Agenez, Quercy, Rouergue et Lymosin, avecquez leurs appartenances et deppendances a icellui duchié et autres terres et seignouries[215] dessus declariez, avoir tenir et possider par ledit roy d'Angleterre et ses successeurs ainsi que dessus

---

[211] C omits 'declairié par ceulx a qui de droit il appartenoit de faire, et que pour ceste il y eut trois journeez solennelement', perhaps because of a homoeoteleutic error, jumping from 'solennelement' to 'solennelement'.

[212] In reality, Philippe Augustus ordered John to appear in 1202 in order to respond to charges brought against him and, when the English king failed to attend a conference arranged for 21 April, Philippe's court rendered a judgement against him as a contumacious vassal: François Delaborde (ed.), *Oeuvres de Rigord et de Guillaume Le Breton, historiens de Philippe-Augustus* (2 vols, Paris, 1882–1885), I, pp. 151–152 and *Grandes chroniques*, VI, pp. 260–261.

[213] Cousinot deliberately inverted the order of the two sons of Henry III, Edward I and Edmund of Lancaster. See p. 102, n. 255.

[214] O offers a marginal note in the same hand, 'La duché de Guienne donnee au roy d'Angleterre par le Roy Saint Louis'. The treaty of Paris (1259) did not define the duchy of Guyenne as encompassing the three sénéchaussées of Bordeaux, Landes, and Bazadais. See p. 87, n. 195 and p. 90, n. 206.

[215] JP omit 'de Perregort, Agenez, Quercy, Rouergue et Lymosin, avecquez leurs appartenances et deppendances a icellui duchié et autres terres et seignouries', perhaps because of a homoeoteleutic error, jumping from 'seignouriez' to 'seignouries'.

est dit, comme leur propre heritage, sauf la foy et l'ommage lige qu'ilz seroyent tenus d'en faire aux roys de France comme a leurs souverains en ceste qualité et le ressort et souveraineté ainsi que les autres duchiez et parriez de France.[216]

|30r| Et oultre donna, bailla et delivra ledit Sanct Loys audit Roy Henry d'Angleterre le paiement de V^C chevaliers avecquez leur sieute pour ung an entier, que cellui roy d'Angleterre devoit mener avecquez lui en la compaignie dudit Sainct Loys al'encontre des mescreans et ennemis de la foy, lequel paiement fut extimé a XII^C mille escus de la monnoye qui couroit pour lors, et tant lui en fut il payé, combien que de sa part il n'accomplist pas ce qu'il avoit promis ne n'y ala ne envoya en aucune maniere.[217]

Et au moyen desquellez choses ledit Roy Henry renonca pour lui et ses successeurs au prouffit dudit roy Sainct Loys et de ses successeurs a tout le droit que icellui Henry et ses predecesseurs avoient ou povoyent reclamer ou demander en la duchié de Normandye et es contés de Poitou, d'Anjou, du Maine et de Tourainne, et generalement a toutez les autres terres et seignouriez esquellez lui ou sesdits predecesseurs aux moyens dessus touchiez ne autrement ne povoient demander ne reclamer droit ou tiltre en quelque partie que ce fust du royaume de France, autres que en ce qu'il lui fut baillié par le traittié dessusdit, ainsi comme toutez ces chosez apperent clerement par lettres auctentiquez qui sont ou Tresor des Chartres.

|30v| Et fut faitte paix final entre lesdits deux roys de France et d'Angleterre, et devint ledit roy d'Angleterre a cause de laditte duchié de Guyenne acreue et augmentee ainsi que dit est homme et vassal du roy de France, et lui en fist la foy et le serement et l'ommage lige.[218]

Et pour oster l'erreur de ceulx qui cuident que lesdits terres, pays et seignouriez comprises oudit traittié oultre les trois seneschauceez ordinaires de Guyenne dessus declareez, c'estassavoir Bordeaux, les Lanes et Barades, soient d'ancienneté et de la duchié de Guienne,

---

[216] By the treaty of Paris, Henry III agreed to pay liege homage for the duchy of Aquitaine together with the additional lands that he was to receive, including the cities and diocese of Limoges, Cahors, and Périgueux, as well as the Agenais, Saintonge (south of the Charente river), and Cahorsin (southern Quercy), then held by Alphonse de Poitiers. See *EMDP*, II, pp. 618–621 and p. 93, n. 221 below.

[217] St Louis promised to fund 500 knights to serve Henry III for two years, either for the service of God or the profit of England: *EMDP*, II, pp. 619–620. Other polemical writers, including Montreuil and Jean Juvénal, had cited the treaty of Paris without providing the details of either the territorial arrangements or the allocation of knights. See Montreuil, II, pp. 75–77, 101–102, 185, 260, 286, and 311; Jean Juvénal, I, pp. 200–201 and II, pp. 97–100, 107, and 170.

[218] CJP omit 'devint ledit roy d'Angleterre', but only C inserts the phrase 'ledit roy d'Engleterre devint' before 'homme et vassal du roy de France'. H places this paragraph after the next two.

il est vray que ou temps que le Roys Loys[219] le Piteux espousa la Royne Elienor, le pere de laditte dame en cellui temps n'estoit si non conte de Poitou, et depuis la mort du duc de Guyenne, cousin germain dicellui conte, lequel morut sans hoir, ledit duchié de Guyenne escheut audit conte comme plusprochain heritier. Ainsi appert clerement que Poytou n'est pas d'ancienneté du duchié de Guyenne, mais est terre apart.[220] D'autrepart ou temps de Phelippe le Conquerant, filz dudit Loys le Piteux, le conte de la Marche estoit conte de Xangtonge, et le conte de Thoulouse estoit conte de Rouergue et de Agen, et le conte d'Auvergne estoit conte de Quercy, et en Pyerregort y avoit ung autre conte qui tenoit le pays, et en Lymosin viconte qui estoit seigneur dudit |31r| pays, parquoy appert clerement, posé que le roy d'Angleterre fust duc de Guynne d'ancienneté si n'avoit il aucun droit es terres dessusdittez si par le moyen dudit traittié.[221]

Duquel traittié dessus declarié, pluiseurs seigneurs et autre gens de divers estas de France furent tresmal contens, et ainçoires au jour d'huy a esté cause es marches de Pierregort, Quercy et autres d'environ, jasoit ce que Sainct Loys soit sainct canonisié par l'eglise, neantmoins ilz ne le reputent point pour sainct, et ne le festoient point comme on fait es autres lieux de France.[222]

Par le moien desquellez choses dessus declareez puet chascun clerement cognoistre que, en tant que touche la duchié de Normandie et les contés de Poitou, d'Anjou, du Maine et de Touraine, les Anglois a quelque tiltre que ce soit de succession ne autrement aux moyens par eulx pretendus d'ancienneté esdittez terres, consideré les

---

[219] In O, the phrase 'il est vray que ou temps que le Roys Loys' is underlined and there is a marginal note in the same hand, 'Dit comme la conté de Poitou n'est pas du duché de Guienne'.

[220] Eleanor married Louis VII in 1137, shortly after the death of her father, Guillaume, tenth duke of Aquitaine and eighth count of Poitou.

[221] Philippe Augustus reconquered Auvergne and Berry from Henry II in 1169 and these gains were confirmed by treaty in 1189. In October 1196, Richard I made peace with Count Raymond VI of Toulouse, renouncing all claims to the county of Toulouse and the subject county of Rouergue; Richard also returned Quercy and gave the Agenais as part of the dowry for his sister's marriage to Raymond. In 1199, Richard I was killed while fighting the rebel Viscount Aimar of Limoges, who was supported by Philippe Augustus. Following the judgement against King John in 1202, Philippe Augustus's forces invaded Poitou, La Marche, and Saintonge, though they were not able to establish a firm control over these lands. By 1249, all of these lands were in the hands of Alphonse de Poitiers (d. 1271): he had been assigned the counties of Poitou and Auvergne as an apanage by his father, Louis VIII, and he also inherited the lands of his father-in-law, Raymond VII, count of Toulouse and lord of Rouergue, Quercy, and the Agenais.

[222] O has a marginal note in the same hand, 'Es marches du pais de Perigourt, Quercy et es environs l'on ne repputa point St Louys Sainct'. Louis IX of France was canonized in 1297. For his cult, see Colette Beaune, *The Birth of an Ideology: myths and symbols of nationhood in later medieval France* (Berkeley, 1992), pp. 90–125.

renunciations, recompensez et appointemens dessusdits, n'y pevent aucune chose demander, reclamer ne quereler.

Item oultre plus, qui vouldroit reprendre pluiseurs anciens tiltres et moyens par |**31v**| lesquelz est fort apparant et cler que lesdittez[223] terres et seignouriez doivent par autre maniere competer et appartenir au roy de France, et qu'il y avoit matiere souffisant et bien fondee pour les rejoindre et reunir a la couronne long temps paravant le Roy Phelippe le Conquerant,[224] semble que en ce y ait belle matiere et que par pluiseurs manieres il se puet clerement monstrer et justifier.

Et premierement en tant que touche la duchié de Normandie est vray que c'est l'ancien heritage de la couronne de France des le temps que l'en appelloit ledit pays Neustrie, lequel les Normans aprés leur nom, quant laditte terre fut baillié a Rollo, nommerent Normannie, et aprés par corruptele de langue a esté appellee Normandie.[225]

Et pour savoir la maniere comment elle sailli hors de la couronne de France, et comme par raison long temps paravant qu'elle y ait esté reunie, elle y devoit revenir et estre rejoincte.

Est vray que ou temps de Charles le Simple ledit pays de Neustrie, *id est* Neufue Austrie a present appellee Normandie, fut baillié au Duc |**32r**| Rollo le Danois avecquez la fille dudit Roy Charles le Simple nommee Gille pour estre le propre heritage dicellui Rollo et des enfans qui ysteroyent dudit mariage.[226]

Or fut le cas tel que aprés ledit Rollo eut la possession de toute la terre et qu'il en fut paisible possesseur, il regetta de lui sa femme Gille et la fist morir piteusement et n'en yssirent aucuns enfans, et par consequent tant par droit de forfaiture comme selon la convenance du traittié, il est tout cler que aprés la mort dudit Rollo, laditte duchié de Normandie devoit retourner de plain droit au roy de France.[227]

---

[223] Q omits 'lesquelz est fort apparant et cler que lesdittez'.

[224] O omits 'long temps paravant le Roy Phelippe le Conquerant'.

[225] O offers a marginal note in the same hand, 'La reunion du duchié de Normandie a la couronne'. Neustria was the western portion of the Frankish lands of Clovis I that were divided amongst his sons and grandsons in the sixth century. It included the Seine and Loire regions together with lands to the north. This was a much larger area than the duchy of Normandy, whose origins are obscure. According to tradition, a Viking chieftain named Rollo (d. *c.*931) had settled with his followers around the city of Rouen. Rollo was supposedly baptized in 912 as a Christian, accepting the name Robert, and paying homage to Charles III the Simple, probably as count of Rouen or 'princeps Nortmannorum' rather than as duke of Normandy.

[226] This well-known story had been reported in much greater detail in Jean Juvénal, II, pp. 62–73, based largely on the account in Guillaume de Jumièges.

[227] JKLNPQ omit 'Gille', the name of Rollo's wife. The claim that Rollo had killed Gisla did not appear in the *Grandes chroniques* and this claim that the duke was a murderer is far more negative than that offered by Jean Juvénal or Noël de Fribois, who emphasized Rollo's positive actions as a patron of churches and as a law-giver: *Grandes chroniques*, IV,

Item et oultre plus, par autre moyen devoit elle retourner a la couronne de France, car ledit Rollo n'eut oncquez enfant masle ne femelle ne en mariage. Vray est que avant qu'il fust crestien il se enamoura d'une fille nommee Poupé, fille du conte de Bessin,[228] laquelle estoit crestienne et lui Sarrasin et eut sa compaignie dont, pendant le temps que l'un estoit Sarrasin et l'autre crestien, il issi ung enfant de eulx deux nommé Guillame Longue Espee, lequel estoit *ex dampnabili cohitu* par deux manieres. L'une pource que pour le temps de lors il n'avoit point espousé laditte Poupé, l'autre car l'eglise deffend tous |**32v**| mariages et copulations charnellez, soit en mariage[229] ou hors mariage, d'un crestien avecquez une femme non crestienne ou d'une crestienne avecquez un infidel. Ainsi que plusadplain est traittié XXVIII, *q. I, c. Sic enim neque, § hiis verbis versus cur fidelem,* et *c. Judei, eodum titulum et quasi per totum illum titulum.*[230] Et par consequent il estoit inhabile a succeder et a recueillier la succession dudit Rollo son pere, en especial en tant qu'il touche laditte duchié de Normandie.

Et pose que depuis ledit Rollo aprés la mort de laditte Gille reprist laditte Poupé et lespousast, non pour tant ne povoit ledit Guillame Longue Espee par ce moyen estre legittimé tant pour ce que ou temps de sa nativité son pere et sa mere estoient de divers sectez comme dit est, comme pour le mariage de Madame Gille qui avoit esté moien entre laditte nativité dudit Guillame Longue Espee et ledit mariage derrenier de Rollo et de laditte Poupé, ne si ne sera point trouvé en cronique ne histoire du monde que ledit Guillame Longue Espee fust jamais autrement legittimé.[231]

---

pp. 314–317, and Kathleen Daly, 'Villains into heroes? Some "French" and "Norman" attitudes to Norman history in the later middle ages', in Andrew Brown, Jean-Marie Cauchies, and Graeme Small (eds), *The Burgundian Hero. Proceedings of the Annual Conference of the Centre Européen d'Etudes Bourguignonnes (XIVe–XVIe siècles) at Edinburgh and Glasgow, 28–30 September 2000* (Neuchâtel, 2001), pp. 183–198.

[228] N prefers 'Veuquessin' to 'Bessin', and O offers 'Vessin'. Neither Jean Juvénal or Noël de Fribois had discussed Poppa. The story that she was the wife or mistress of Rollo and the mother of William Longsword originated in Dudo of Saint Quentin, pp. 38–39 and 57. It was taken up by Guillaume de Jumièges, whose work was known at the abbey of Saint-Denis: Elizabeth A.R. Brown, 'La notion de la légitimité et la prophétie à la cour de Philippe Auguste', in Robert-Henri Bautier (ed.), *La France de Philippe Auguste: le temps des mutations* (Paris, 1982), p. 82n.

[229] Q omits 'et copulations charnellez, soit en mariage', perhaps because of a homoeoteleutic error, jumping from 'mariages' to 'mariage'.

[230] *Decretum Gratiani*, C. 28 q. 1, c. 9, 6, and c. 10. The early church did not consider marriage between Christians and non-Christians to be invalid, especially when a person had been converted to the faith after such marriage. Objections mounted until the *Decretum* of Gratian established the requirement that all such marriages were invalid unless a dispensation had been obtained from the appropriate ecclesiastical authority.

[231] ACHO omit 'ne si ne sera point trouvé en cronique ne histoire du monde que ledit Guillame Longue Espee fust jamais autrement legittimé'.

Et oultre plus, selon la coustume d'Angleterre dont de present meismez on use oudit royame, laquelle anciennement fut apportee |**33r**| oudit royaume par ledit Guillame, dont a ceste cause plaident ilz ainçoires par dela par tout au jour d'huy en françois, et lequel Duc Guillame receut laditte coustume et ses predecessurs dudit Rollo, toutez et quantesfoiz que le cas avient que ung homme maintient une femme avant qu'il lespouse et qu'il en a des enfans et aprés il espouse laditte femme, les enfans nez ou mariage, posé qu'ilz soyent plus jonez, succedent entierement au pere et a la mere, et non point ceulx qui sont nez paravant le mariage. Et de cest article ne fault faire difficulté aucune car c'est le vray usage dont l'en use cotidiennement oudit royaume d'Angleterre.[232]

Au moien desquellez chosez congnoissant ledit Guillame Longue Espee qu'il n'estoit point legitismé et que de raison la duchié de Normandie ne lui devoit point competer ne appartenir, il desiroit tousjours et se disposa pour estre moisne et laissier le siecle. Et de fait l'eust esté, se ne fust le Conte Bernard de Senlis qui lui voloit ballier sa fille en mariage,[233] et aucuns de ses subgés de Normandie qui l'en destourberent, lesquellez chosez monstrent clerement que ledit Guillame Longue Espee n'estoit pas habille a recueillier laditte duchié de Normandie, ne laquelle ne lui devoit point competer ne appartenir: ainçois devoit |**33v**| selon raison deslors retourner a la couronne.

Et se l'en veult demander pourquoy ne se fist il oncquez response, en cellui temps les roys de France estoient si foblez et le royame si destruit et y avoit tant de broullis en icellui temps des grans seigneurs dudit royame les uns contre les autres, comme d'aucuns desdits seigneurs contre le roy, ainsi que l'en puet toutes ces chosez veoir et congnoistre clerement par les croniquez du temps de lors, qu'il eust esté trop fort et trop difficile de ce faire. Et a ceste occasion convint passer les choses par dissimulation jusquez au temps qu'il pleust a Dieu que laditte

---

[232] This English practice was contrary to medieval canon law, which did allow for the legitimization of children through the subsequent marriage of parents, as seen in commentaries on Gratian's *Decretum* as well as two papal decrees of Alexander III, dated 1172 and 1180, both incorporated into canon law as the *Liber extra*, X 4.17.6 and 4.17.1. See John Fortescue, *De laudibus legum Anglie*, pp. 92–100; Richard H. Helmholz, 'Bastardy litigation in medieval England', in *idem, Canon Law and the Law of England* (London, 1987), pp. 187–210; Litzen, 'A war of roses and lilies', pp. 44–48. The author of *Pour ce que plusieurs* carefully evaded this problem and instead cited canon law on the issue of marriage of Christians and pagans (see p. 95, n. 230 above).

[233] Duke William's decision to enter the monastery of Jumièges was recorded, for example, in *Grandes chroniques*, IV, pp. 329–331. Dudo of Saint Quentin claimed that William's son Richard was the nephew of Count Bernard while Guillaume de Jumièges, writing over a century later, argued that the mother of the duke's son was Sprota: Dudo of Saint Quentin, pp. 106–107 and *Gesta Normannorum Ducum*, I, pp. 78–79.

duchié de Normandie fust reunie a la couronne comme dessus est declarié.

Item y a pluiseurs autres moyens par lesquelz selon raison laditte duchié de Normandie, paravant la reunyon dicelle a la couronne, devoit semblablement revenir a laditte couronne; car le Duc Richard Sans Paour qui fut IIIIᵉ duc de Normandie aprés que le pays avoit esté baillié au Duc Rollo, forfist ladicte terre et seignourie en pluiseurs manieres al'encontre du roy de France qui pour lors estoit, ainsi que par la discution de la cronique de France et aussi de Normandie chascun puet veoir et congnoistre |**34r**| clerement.²³⁴

Pareillement le Duc Guillame estoit bastard filz de Robert duc de Normandie, ne jamais son pere ne fut marié, c'estassavoir ledit Robert ne ledit Guillame legittimé, et par consequent il estoit inhabile a succeder et deslors devoit venir au roy la duchié.²³⁵

D'autrepart ledit Guillame fist guerre ouverte au roy de France par pluiseurs foiz et forfist laditte duchié en maintes manieres, tant par descongnoissance de son seigneur comme par crisme de felonnie et de leze majesté *quare* &c.

En oultre ledit Guillame eut quatre filz et une fille dont l'aisné fut nommé Robert qui fut duc de Normandie, le second fut nommé Guillame le Rous qui fut roy d'Angleterre, le tiers fut Rogier nommé qui espousa le heritiere de Bertaigne, le quart fut nommé Henry qui fut envoié aux escolles a Paris et le voloit on faire homme d'eglise, et aprés fut surnommé Henry Beauclerc, et la fille Adelle, femme du Conte Thibault de Chartres, mere du Conte Thibault de Champaigne et grant mere de Adelle, femme du Roys Loys le Piteux et mere de Phelippe le Conquerant, ainsi comme dessus est ung en autre pas declairié.²³⁶

|**34v**| Ledit Guillame le Rous, roy d'Angleterre, second filz dudit duc Guilame, morut sans hoir, et aussi fist Rogier qui fut le tiers filz.

Aprés la mort desquelz Guillame le Rous et Rogier, pource qu'ilz n'eurent aucuns enfans et que le Duc Robert estoit oultre mer en la conqueste de la terre saincte, Henry Beau Clerc, son derrenier frere,

---

²³⁴ The rule of Duke Richard I (d. 996), supposedly the third duke of Normandy, was not described by Jean Juvénal, II, p. 73, but there was a favourable account of the duke in *Grandes chroniques*, IV, pp. 335–362 and V, pp. 10–15.

²³⁵ King William I the Conqueror was the son of Duke Robert (d. 1035) and Herleva, identified variously as the daughter of either an undertaker or a tanner from Falaise, and also as a woman of the ducal household. Writing in 1446, Jean Juvénal claimed that William was the illegitimate son of Duke Robert and a concubine, arguing that this meant that the duchy should rightfully have returned to the French crown but for the fact that King Henri of France supported his succession: Jean Juvénal, II, pp. 73–75. Noël de Fribois did not raise this issue.

²³⁶ In B, 'en' has been inserted in a different hand. Jean Juvénal erroneously argued that Robert was not the eldest son, in Jean Juvénal, II, pp. 80. See p. 85, n. 181 above.

prinst et occupa le royame d'Angleterre, lequel par raison devoit appartenir a l'aisné.[237]

Lesquellez chosez venues a la congnoissance dicellui Duc Robert, incontinent il retourna en toute haste en Normandie pour pourveir a ces choses. Et eurent lesdiz deux freres guerre ensemble pour laditte cause, et depuis firent paix moiennant certaines condicions qui icy sont obmises pour cause de briefté, lesquellez ledit Henry Beauclerc ne garda point, et par ce rencheirent en guerre. Et trouva maniere ledit Henry Beau Clerc par subtilz moyens, soubz couleur de paix et d'amistié, de prendre sondit frere aisné, le Duc Robert, et le constraingny a renoncier a tout ce qu'il povoit pretendre oudit royaume d'Angleterre, et extorqua en oultre de lui par forme de raenchon pluiseurs grans sommes de deniers.[238]

Et non content de ce, aprés ce que ledit Henry |**35r**| eut delivré sondit frere le Duc Robert, il passa en Normandie a puissance et lui fist guerre, et a la parfin jasoit ce qu'il fust son aisné et son seigneur de rechief, il le prinst et le fist morir et prist et occuppa par force et tyrannie la duchié de Normandie.[239]

Et oultre plus, pour ce que le filz dudit Robert se estoit retrait devers le conte de Flandres son oncle de par sa mere pour sa seureté, lequel conte de Flandres l'avoit envoié a Hesdin et lui avoit baillié ladicte place pour demourer et soy esbatre, ledit Henry Beau Clerc par conspiracions et machinations de longue main, voulans de tous poins estaindre, effacier et mettre au neant toute la sieutte dudit Duc Robert son frere aisné, ainsi que ledit filz et heritier dicelluy Robert se aloit[240] esbatre en une isle pres dudit Hesdin, il le fist de guet appensé par murtriers affaittiez, tuer et murtrir moult pitieusement.[241]

---

[237] When William I died in 1087, he had made no explicit arrangements for the succession beyond the designation of Robert as his heir in Normandy. At that time, there was no firm tradition of primogeniture for the English royal succession, and the inheritance of the throne by the eldest son had been uncommon ever since the time of King Alfred in the ninth century; moreover, Norman ducal practice held that all sons should have some share in the inheritance. Thus, at the instigation of William I and Archbishop Lanfranc, William Rufus became king of England though, four years later, the two brothers nominated each other as their successor in the absence of legitimate heirs.

[238] Robert Curthose was captured during the siege of Guillaume de Mortain's castle at Tinchebrai on 28 September 1106.

[239] Robert Curthose died in 1134, while under the custody of Henry I's illegitimate son, Robert of Gloucester. There is no evidence that he was murdered.

[240] O omits 'ainsi que ledit filz et heritier dicelluy Robert se aloit'.

[241] William Clito, son of Robert Curthose, was four years old when his father was captured. He took shelter at the court of Flanders and became count there in 1127, thanks to a claim inherited from his grandmother, Matilda of Flanders. William died the following year at Aalst while besieging the castle of Count Thierry of Alsace, his rival for the county of Flanders.

A l'occasion desquellez chosez est bien cler quant il n'y eust eu orez autre raison parquoy la duchié de Normandie deust est reunye a la couronne, que se il y avoit il assez cause par les moyens dessusdits.

Premierement par le crisme de felonnie |**35v**| commis en la personne de son frere aisné et son seigneur, lequel inhominieusement il avoit fait tuer et murtir et pris et occuppé sa terre mauvaisement et indeuement.

Secondement par crisme de lese majesté en tant que icellui Henry Beau Clerc estoit natif du royame de France et avoit attempté de son auctorité a ung des pers de France hereditaux et qui d'ancienneté se disoit premier per, en contempnant le roy son souverain seigneur et la majesté et auctorité royal.[242]

Tiercement comme indigne de venir a la succession de laditte duchié de Normandie attendu les cas par lui perpetrez contre son sang et lignage naturel, dont laditte succession lui devoit venir, et a cause de quoy il estoit inhabile de parvenir a icelle succession, et ne la povoit ne devoit selon raison escripte et coustumiere avoir ne recueillier en aucune maniere.

Or est ainsi que se selon raison ledit Roy Henry Beau Clerc estoit indigne par les moyens dessus touchiez de venir a la succession de laditte duchié de Normandie, comme il est tout cler que si estoit, il convenoit qu'elle venist au plusprochain hoir d'aprés qui estoit Adelle sereur desdits |**36r**| quatres freres, femme du conte de Chartres et mere du Conte Thibault de Champaigne, qui fut pere de Adelle, la seconde femme du Roy Loys le Piteux et mere de Phelippe le Conquerant.[243] Et par consequent est cler que laditte duchié de Normandie *nedum jure confiscationis sed etiam jure [recompensationis], renunciationis [et] successionis*, appartient et doit competer et appartenir au roy de France sans aucune difficulté.[244]

Or ça et que dirons nous des contés d'Anjou, du Maine, de Touraine, et de Poitou et de Pontieu.

Item il est cler du droit de confiscation par les moiens dessus touchiez et pareillement de renunciation, sauf en tant qu'il touche Pontieu dont

---

[242] The scope of treasonous actions was much wider in fifteenth-century France than in England: Simon Cuttler, *The Law of Treason and Treason Trials in Later Medieval France* (Cambridge, 1981), pp. 28–54.

[243] This acceptance of the possibility of the female inheritance of a French duchy, for rhetorical purpose alone, contrasts with the arguments that Cousinot later employed to resist Marie of Austria's claim to the duchy of Burgundy. See pp. 10–12 and p. 89, n. 204 above, regarding Philippe II's claim through the female line.

[244] The word '*recompensationis*' is only omitted from BF. C adds '*reprehensionis*' after '*jure*'; N omits '*sed etiam jure recompensationis, renunciationis*'; O omits '*et successionis*'. Such confusions would strongly suggest that this is not a common legal maxim but rather a creation of the author of the treatise.

cy aprés sera parlé. Mais ainçoires plus soient veuez les cronicques de France et celles d'Anjou il ne sere point trouvé que le premier consul d'Anjou nommé[245] Fouquez le Premier eust oncquez le conté d'Anjou en tiltre du roy de France, mais seulement en gouvernement et n'en fut jamais si non occuppateur et gouverneur.[246]

Et quant a la conté du Mainne semblablement elle n'avoit jamais esté baillié |**36v**| en tiltre, mais seulement a gouvernement a ceulx qui le tenoient ou temps que les Normans persecuterent si fort le royaume de France: mais pour ledit temps neantmoins soit en laditte conté du Mainne ou en celle de Tourainne, si ne sera il point trouvé hors mis les chasteaux de Loches et d'Amboise qui anciennement furent l'eritaige des contes d'Anjou par mariages, que iceulx contes d'Anjou[247] aient riens eu esdits contez du Mainne et de Tourainne si non par force et par occupation, et les ont osteez aux vrays heritiers; ne le roy de France n'y povoit donner prouvision pour la impuissance que pour lors il avoit.[248] Et par ainsi pource que indeuement leur estoient venues, Dieu par vray jugement les a remisez la ou elles devoient estre, et a bon et a juste tiltre comme dessus est declairié.

Touchant la conté de Poitou, comme dit est dessus, c'estoit l'eritaige de la Royne Elyenor laquelle estoit vassale et femme ou hommesse lige du roy, ainsi que on le vouldra appeller a cause des duchies Guyenne et conté de Poitou, et laquelle oultre plus fut femme et espouse du roy.[249] Et non obstant ce la, aprés pluiseurs forfaitures qu'elle fist contre son seigneur et espoux dont l'ystoire parle bien avant, non contente de ce perpetra ainçoires ung bien detestable cas, car ainsi que pluiseurs croniques dient, elle machina en la mort |**37r**| de son mari, et fist appointement avecquez le Soudan de Babilonne, estant sondit mari le Roy Loys le Piteux, et elle oultre de laissier et habandonner sondit mari

---

[245] Foulques is referred to as a 'conte' in manuscripts NO, and in O the words 'il ne sere point trouvé que le premier conte d'Anjou nommé' are underlined and a marginal note in the same hand reads 'Fouques Premier conte d'Anjou'.

[246] Foulques le Roux was a viscount administering the city of Angers on behalf of the French king until around 930, when he usurped the title of count. In Paul Marchegay and André Salmon (eds), *Chroniques d'Anjou* (Paris, 1866), there are two texts entitled *Chronica de gestis consulum Andegavorum* and *Historia abbreviata consulum Andegavorum, auctore Johanne, monacho majoris monasterii*, as well as the *Historia comitum Andegavensium, auctore Thoma Pactio, Lochensi priore*.

[247] O omits 'par mariages, que iceulx contes d'Anjou', perhaps because of a homoeoteleutic error, jumping from 'd'Anjou' to 'd'Anjou'.

[248] Touraine and Maine fell under the control of Foulques III Nerra, count of Anjou, and his son Geoffroy II Martel, by military and diplomatic means. The control of Maine by successive counts was challenged by the dukes of Normandy until the county was effectively united with Anjou by the first marriage of Foulques V and Eremburge, heiress to that county.

[249] In O, the words 'de Poitou, et laquelle oultre plus fut femme et espouse du roy' are underlined and there is a marginal note in the same hand, 'La confiscacion des duches de Poitou, et Guienne et reunion a la couronne'.

et s'en aler devers ledit Souldan pour estre sa femme, en soy fourfaisant non pas seulement contre son seigneur et mary et son souverain, mais contre Dieu, sa loy et la foy que nous tenons. Et fut prise en entrant dedens la gallee, voulant accomplir son dampnable propos, et voyage avecquez enseignemens d'eulz des choses dessusdittes,[250] et aussi furent ses complices et adherens en la ditte matiere. En quoy chascun puet bien veoir et congnoistre s'il y avoit confiscation de corps ne de biens, et se a ce moien la duchié de Guyenne et la conté de Poitou, quant orez il n'y eust eu autres moyens de de [*sic*] confiscation, par droit et raison devoit competer au roy et appartenir. Et pour ce que le Roy Loys le Piteux ne vouloit prendre vengance d'elle ainsi que la matiere le requeroit, et qu'il trouva autre maniere honneste du dyvorce d'entre eulx deux, on lui attribua le nom de Loys le Piteux.[251]

Doncquez par les chosez dessus declairees chascun puet veoir et appert clerement, non obstant tous les drois, actions et demandes que les Angloiz font es duchiez de Normandie et contez d'Anjou, du Maine, et de Tourainne et de Poitou, qu'ilz n'y ont aucun droit: ainçois a bon et juste tiltre, vray droit |**37v**| et canonicque, elles comppettent et appartiennent au roy de France et sont et doivent[252] estre reputeez le droit heritage de la couronne, a icelle venus et escheuz par divers tiltres et moiens justes et raisonnablez, sauf au regard de ceulx a qui le roy selon l'usage et coustume de France en a donné et departy a son plaisir selon que les cas si sont offers.

Et quant a la duchié de Guienne en tant qu'il touche les trois seneschauceez dessus declairieez par les moyens dessus touchiez, pluiseurs foiz elle est cheue en confiscation par avant le traittié Sainct Loys, et a ceste cause rejoindre et reunye a la couronne jusquez au traittié Sainct Loys[253] dont dessus est faitte mention. Et au regard des

---

[250] O omits 'et voyage avecquez enseignemens d'eulz des choses dessusdittes'.

[251] Louis VII divorced Eleanor of Aquitaine on the grounds of consanguinity in 1152. John of Salisbury suggested that the marriage was strained by Eleanor's affection for her uncle, Raymond of Antioch, during the Second Crusade, while William of Tyre implied that Eleanor had had an incestuous affair with him. By 1260, the *Récits d'un ménestrel de Reims* reported that Louis had prevented Eleanor fleeing to her lover Saladin, a salacious story that was repeated in numerous late medieval chronicles, including Pierre Cochon's *Chronique normande* and the *Geste des nobles françois*. None of these sources claimed that Eleanor had plotted to murder her husband, or used this accusation to argue that her inheritance in France was forfeit to the crown. See Peggy McCracken, 'Scandalizing desire: Eleanor of Aquitaine and the chroniclers', in John Carmi Parsons and Bonnie Wheeler (eds), *Eleanor of Aquitaine: lord and lady* (Basingstoke, 2002), pp. 247–263, and Daniel Power, 'The stripping of a queen: Eleanor of Aquitaine in thirteenth-century Norman historical tradition', in Marcus Bull and Catherine Léglu (eds), *The World of Eleanor of Aquitaine* (Woodbridge, 2005), pp. 127–128.

[252] O omits 'au roy de France et sont et doivent'.

[253] ACO omit 'et a ceste cause rejoindre et reunye a la couronne jusquez au traittié Sainct Loys', perhaps because of a homoeoteleutic error, jumping from 'Loys' to 'Loys'.

terres qui y ont esté adjoinctez par lesdittes traittiez, ilz ne furent
oncques aux Anglois ne ilz n'y pevent aucune chose demander par
tiltre de succession.

Touchant ledit traittié il est vray que aprés la mort de Henry le
Tiers roy d'Angleterre avecquez lequel Sainct Loys avoit fait ledit
traittié, Edouard le Premier de ce nom,[254] second filz dudit Henry
le Tiers,[255] fut roy d'Angleterre et duc de Guienne et fist hommage
lige dudit duchié au roy de France, Phelippe filz Sainct Loys, duquel
Phelippe il avoit espousee la fille nommee Madame Margarite et avoit
eu la conté de Poitou en mariage: |**38r**| mais ce non obstant, il ne
voulut ressortir[256] ou Parlement du roy de France et fist beaucop de
grandes desobeissances, dont a ceste cause grande partie de la duchié
de Guienne fut mise en la main du roy et aussi la ditte conté de
Pontieu.[257]

Depuis ces choses appointement se fist entre le roy de France et le
roy d'Angleterre du temps de Phelippe le Bel, filz de Phelippe[258] dessus
nommé, et firent paix ensemble, et pour icelle mieulx entretenir ledit
Roy Phelippe le Bel bailla en mariage a Edouart de Carnarinam, filz
dudit Edouart le Premier, sa fille nommee Madame Ysabel sa seconde
fille, et estoient cousins germains. Mais ce non obstant, quant ledit
Edouart le Premier son pere fut alé de vie a trespas, icellui Edouart
le Second dit de Carnarinam reffusa de faire aux roys de France
successeurs dudit Phelippe le Bel les devoirs qu'il leur devoit faire

---

[254] In O, 'second filz dudit Henry le Tiers, fut roy' is underlined and a marginal note in
the same hand reports 'Edouart Premier fust filz du Roy Henry le Tiers'.

[255] The claim that Edward I (d. 1307) was the second son of Henry III is undoubtedly
a reference to the Crouchback legend which held that Edmund of Lancaster (d. 1296)
was the elder brother of Edward I, but was excluded from the royal succession because
of his deformity. See Christopher Given-Wilson (ed.), *Chronicles of the Revolution, 1397–1400*
(Manchester, 1993), pp. 41, 43, 161, and 195–196, and see p. 91, n. 213, p. 159, n. 68, and
p. 160, n. 70.

[256] In O, 'voulut ressortir' is underlined, and a marginal note in the same hand reads 'La
confiscation du pais de Ponthieu'.

[257] Edward I paid homage to Philippe III on 6 August 1273. In 1279, Edward's first wife,
Eleanor of Castile (d. 1290), inherited the county of Ponthieu following the death of her
mother, Jeanne de Dammartin, and she paid homage for the county to the French king. In
1293, Edward was summoned to appear before the Parlement of Paris following a private
naval war between English and Norman sailors and it was in an effort to resolve that crisis
that the French king, Philippe IV, first suggested that Edward marry his sister Marguerite
(d. 1318); when Edward failed to answer the summons, the duchy of Aquitaine was declared
to be forfeit, triggering a war that was largely ended by his marriage to Marguerite in 1299.
An account of these events appeared in Jean Juvénal, II, pp. 107–109.

[258] P omits 'le Bel, filz de Phelippe', perhaps because of a homoeoteleutic error, jumping
from 'Phelippe' to 'Phelippe'.

a cause de laditte duchié de Guyenne et aussi de laditte conté de Pontieu.[259]

Et a ceste cause le conte de Valois, Charles frere dudit Roy Phelippe le Bel, et oncle desdits trois roys, fut envoyé en Guienne ou temps desdits trois roys. Et depuis sa mort y fut envoyé une autreffoiz Phelippe de Valoiz son filz qui depuis fut roy, lesquelz tant pour ce que ledit Roy Edouart de Carnarinam denyoit faire l'ommage |**38v**| de Guyenne et de Pontieu audit roy de France et ne le voloit faire, pour pluiseurs grandes rebellions, descongnoissances et desobeissances qui avoient esté faittez par ledit Roy Edouart de Carnarinam et ses officiers al'encontre du roy de France et des siens, prindrent et mirent en la main du roy la pluspart de la duchié de Guyenne et de la conté de Pontieu et en especial es terres qui avoient esté bailliez de crue audit roy d'Angleterre oultre les trois seneschauceez de Bordeaux, de Lanes et de Barades.[260]

Pour laquelle cause voyant les Anglois qu'ilz perdoyent toute Guyenne, fut advisé entreulx que le Roy Edouart de Carnarinam transporteroit laditte duchié de Guyenne a son aisné filz le Roy Edouart le Tiers autrement dit de Windezore, filz de Madame Ysabel de France et nepveu desdis trois roys freres, et qu'il en vendroit faire l'ommage au Roy Charles le Bel son oncle et essayer de recouvrer toutes lesdittes terres.[261]

En fournissant ausquellez choses ledit Edouart de Windezore, duc de Guiennc, passa la mer et vint devers le Roy Charles le Bel, son oncle, et par le moien de Madame Ysabel, mere dicellui Edouart, qui estoit lors avecquez ledit Charles le Bel, son frere, pour cause de cartaines divisions qui estoient adoncquez en Engleterre. Ledit Roy Charles |**39r**| le Bel dist audit Edouart son nepveu telles parolles en substance:[262]

---

[259] Isabella, daughter of Philippe IV, was first proposed as a wife for Edward I's eldest son in 1298. The wedding eventually took place in January 1308, on which occasion the newly crowned king of England, Edward II, paid homage to his father-in-law for the duchy of Aquitaine. Edward II also performed homage for Aquitaine and Ponthieu to King Philippe V in June 1320, but declined to swear fealty to his brother-in-law.

[260] The invasion of Aquitaine in August 1324 by Charles of Valois effected the confiscation of the duchy in June 1324 by King Charles IV, following the destruction of a French bastide at Saint-Sardos.

[261] By the treaty ending the war of Saint-Sardos on 31 May 1325, Charles IV agreed to return the Agenais, and Edward II promised to pay homage to the French king. But Edward claimed to be too ill to travel to France and transferred the duchy to his son, Edward of Windsor, so that he might perform the ceremony. An account of these events appeared in Jean Juvénal, II, pp. 110–111.

[262] O adds at the beginning of this speech, 'Pour bien entendre laquelle matiere est necessaire a congnoistre premierement'.

'Vostre pere a forfait et confisquié envers moy la duchié de Guienne et tout ce qu'il tient en France, et n'estoie point disposé de jamais lui en rendre riens, mais pour l'amour de ma sueur, vostre mere, et de vous qui estez mon nepveu, et que maditte suer m'a dit que vous ne voulez point user de mauvaises condicions que fait vostre pere et que vous me volez congnoistre vostre souverain touchant la duchié de Guyenne et les autres terres de France ainsi que les ducs de Guienne et autres mes subgés sont tenus et doivent recongnoistre les roys de France pour leurs souverains seigneurs, et que les pactions et convenances ont esté entre mes predecesseurs et les votres,[263] je vous rendz la duchié de Guienne et vueil que tout ce qui en a esté mis en ma main et aussi des autres terres vous soit rendu et restitué.'[264]

Desquellez choses ledit Edouart remercia tres humblement ledit roy son oncle et lui fist hommage dudit duchié de Guyenne et des autres terres de France, et demoura avecquez lui l'espace d'un an et plus.

Ne demoura gaires aprés ledit an que ledit Edouart |**39v**| le Tiers et la royne d'Angleterre sa mere repasserent en Angleterre et prindrent ledit Roy Edouart de Carnarinam et le firent morir piteusement et tous ceulx qui avoient auctorité entour lui, et prist icellui Edouart le [royaume] comme plusprochain hoir de son pere.[265]

Et ne tarda pas longuement aprés que ledit Roy Charles le Bel morut et vint Phelippe de Valois a la couronne de France; et le recongnut ledit Roy Edouart le Tiers pour tel et lui fist hommage a Amiens dudit duchié de Guyenne et des terres de Pontieu comme a vray roy de France, confermé ledit hommage depuis en Angleterre comme hommage lige ainsi comme dessus a esté touchié plusadplain en la premiere partie de ce livre.[266]

Mais ce non obstant, sans nulle cause aumoins raisonnable, ledit Edouart en venant contre son serement et sa feaulté meut guerre

---

[263] A adds 'vous les voulez tenir et observer'; O adds 'vueillez tenir et garder'.

[264] There is no record that Charles IV ever made this speech when his nephew paid homage to him on 24 September 1325. See Elizabeth A.R. Brown, 'The political repercussions of family ties in the early fourteenth century: the marriage of Edward II of England and Isabelle of France', *Speculum*, 63 (1988), pp. 573–595 and 64 (1989), pp. 373–379.

[265] Having brought Prince Edward to France, Isabella refused to allow him to return to England because of the influence that her enemies, the Despensers, had established over her husband. They finally returned together on 24 September 1326, alongside Isabella's lover, Roger Mortimer (d. 1330); following the forced abdication of Edward II, Edward III was crowned on 24 January 1327. His father died on 21 September 1327, and rumours quickly spread that the dethroned king had been murdered.

[266] JP omit 'depuis en Angleterre comme hommage', perhaps because of a homoeoteleutic error, jumping from 'hommage' to 'hommage'. N recasts the prose from 'conferme ledit hommage' to the end of the paragraph as 'conferme depuis fut ledit hommaige en Angleterre par le Parlement comme dessus a esté touchié en la premiere partie de ce livre'. For the previous discussion of the homage at Amiens, see p. 68.

contre ledit roy de France Phelippe, s'efforça de lui oster la couronne et
le royaume de France, et de esmouvoir tous les subgetz dudit royaume
al'encontre de leur souverain seigneur, le Roy Phelippe en confiscant
de rechief laditte duchié de Guienne et tout ce qu'il tenoit en France.
Ne en tout le monde n'y a plus cler moyen de confiscation que de
machiner en la |**40r**| mort de desheritement de son souverain et
naturel seigneur.[267] Pourquoy est cler, quelque transport de la duchié
de Guyenne qui eust esté fait par Sainct Loys au Roy Henry le Tiers
et a ses successeurs, ainsi que dessus est declairié, et de la conté de
Pontieu par le traittié du mariage dont dessus est faitte mention, il
y'a eu depuis tant de fourfaitures, ingratitudes, descongnoissances,
crismez et deliz commis et perpetrez par les roys d'Angleterre ducs de
Guienne et contes de Pontieu, successeurs dudit Henry le Tiers, qu'il
y a eu plus de dix moyens de confiscation et y eust il quatre foiz aussi
grant seignourie comme il yavoit et que a bon et juste tiltre le roy a
eu cause legitime de les prendre et reunir a la couronne de France
comme vray et droit heritage dicelle.

Et pour ce que les Anglois se vantent depuis toutes ces choses que au
traittié de Bretigny toutes ces questions et debas furent appointiez et
que par traittié de paix final, tant pour la delivrance du Roy Jehan de
France que pour assoper et pacifier toutes les querellez que ledit Roy
Edouart pretendoit tant a la couronne de France que es singulieres
partiez qu'il queroit dedens le royaume, laditte duchié de Guienne
ainsi qu'elle se estendoit par le traittié de Sainct Loys, ensemble les
contés de Poitou, Ponthieu, Engomez, Bygorre |**40v**| avec les ressors
d'Armignac, d'Abric et des autres seignouries de Gascoingne, les pays
aussi de Xantonge et [de]ça la Charente, Aunys, Mercq, Ouaye,[268]
Calais, Guynez et les autres terres et seignouries plusadplain contenues
oudit traittié, lui furent bailliez purement et absolument et sans
aucun ressort ou souveraineté et que a tort et sans cause on les en a
forclos et deboutés.[269]

Response. Le traittié de Bretigny a esté par tant de foiz debatu et
en tant de lieux et en la presence de tant de princes et de prelas et
meismez de nostre sainct pere et des legas et autrement que chascun
a peut assez et puet congnoistre que les Anglois n'ont aucune cause

---

[267] See pp. 70–73.

[268] N omits 'deça la Charente, Aunys, Mercq, Ouaye'.

[269] By the treaty of Brétigny, Edward III was assigned Guyenne and Gascony, together
with the counties of Poitou and Saintonge on both sides of the river Charente, and the
Agenais, Périgord and Périgueux, Limousin, Cahorsin, Tarbe, Bigorre, Gorre, Angoumois,
and Rouergue, as well as the homage of local lords such as the counts of Foix, Armagnac,
and L'Isle. In addition, Edward was to have the county of Ponthieu, the town of Calais, the
lordships of Marck, Sangatte, Coulogne, Ham, Le Wal, and Oye, as well as the county of
Guînes: *GTGCA*, pp. 39–68.

aumoins legittime de riens demander par vertu dicellui ne que ilz ne accomplirent ne entretindrent oncquez de leur part ledit traittié.[270]

Ainçois au premier point la ou ilz doivent renoncer a la couronne de France qui estoit le premier et principal point, ilz ne le volurent oncquez faire.[271]

Secondement ilz devoyent faire vidier les compaigniez hors du royaume de France,[272] dont semblablement ilz n'en firent riens. Et morut a ceste occasion plus de XX^{M} hommez |4ɪr| dudit royaume de France depuis ledit traittié et si eurent le roy et ceulx du royame dommage a cause des compaignez avant qu'il peust trouver moien de les jetter hors du royaume de France par autre facon que au pourchas et par le moyen desdits Anglois de plus de la valleur de six millions d'or, ainsi que par les discours et la matiere l'en puet veoir clerement qui vouldra lire les cronicquez et histoires dudit temps.[273]

Tiercement le prince de Gallez eses officiers depuis ledit traittié firent tant de maulz et d'excés aux subgetz de Guienne qu'ilz furent constrains d'appeller au Roy Charles le Quint comme a leur souverain seigneur, lequel ne le Roy Jehan son pere n'avoient jamais renoncé au ressort de Guyenne pour ce que ledit Roy Edouart par semblable n'avoit point renoncé a la couronne de France ainsi qu'il avoit promis et juré, lesquelles deux renuniciations se devoient faire l'une quant et l'autre. Et envoia ledit roy de France pour ceste cause aux jour et lieu qui sur ce[274] avoient esté enconvenenciez, gens notablez garnis de povoir souffisant de par lui de faire lesdits renunicions de sa part. Mais de la part du roy d'Angleterre nul ne si comparut jasoit

---

[270] The French case against the treaty of Brétigny was principally developed in a bill presented to the English early in 1369 that was included in the *Grandes chroniques de France* and circulated widely. This may have provided the framework for the speech that Charles V delivered when Emperor Charles IV visited Paris in 1378. See Roland Delachenal (ed.), *Chroniques de Jean II et de Charles V* (4 vols, Paris, 1910–1920), II, pp. 76–116 and 251–255, and III, pp. 123–145, and Montreuil, III, pp. 85–110, together with p. 109, n. 282 below.

[271] By articles 11 and 12 of the treaty of Brétigny, Jean II was to give up sovereignty and resort over the lands ceded to Edward III in return for the English king's renunciation of his claim to the French throne and to all remaining lands in France: *GTGCA*, pp. 36–37; Pierre Chaplais (ed.), 'Some documents regarding the fulfillment and interpretation of the treaty of Brétigny, 1361–1369', *Camden miscellany*, 19 (1952), pp. 1–84; and John Le Patourel, 'The treaty of Brétigny, 1360', in *idem, Feudal Empires: Norman and Plantagenet* (London, 1984), chapter 13. Also see p. 107, n. 275 below.

[272] O adds 'et chascun partie de royaume'.

[273] French diplomats and writers consistently argued that the English had not met their obligations under the treaty of Brétigny by failing to hand over certain fortified strongholds as well as by supporting the Companies that terrorized the kingdom: *Chroniques de Jean II et de Charles V*, II, p. 253; *Le Songe du vergier*, I, pp. 276 and 282; Montreuil, II, pp. 187, 198, 237, 283–285, 300–301, and 328 and III, 69–70, 80–81, 99–100, and 102–108; Jean Juvénal, I, p. 210 and II, p. 125.

[274] O omits 'aux jour et lieu qui sur ce'.

ce que deuement ledit roy d'Angleterre et les siens fussent appellez et at|41v|tendus comme par lettres auctentiques ces choses se puent clerement monstrer.[275]

Et par grande et meure deliberation de conseil ouquel les pers de France et tous les princes et prelas du royaume, et autres gens de grant estat furent convocquiez aprés la complainte faitte audit Roy Charles le Quint par les subgés de Guienne des tors, griefs et excés que les Anglois leur faisoient, fut dit et remonstré au roy par plusieurs grandes et evidentes raisons fondeez en chascun droit, que, sans charge de conscience, pertermission de son honneur et qu'il ne fust dit injuste et denegateur de justice a ses subgetz, il ne povoit reffuser lesdittes appellations.[276]

Aprés lesquelles choses le roy voulant obtemperer a raison croire le conseil de ses parens et subgés et administrer justice a ceulx qui l'en requeroient, receut lesdits appellations, bailla les provisions qu'il convenoit en laditte matiere. Et pour icelles mettre a execution garda toutes les solemnitez que ordre de droit usage stille et les communes observances du royame ordonnent et commandent.

En venant al'encontre desquelles choses ledit prince de Gallez, pour lors duc de Guyenne, |42r| fist prendre les officiers du roy, c'estassavoir un chevalier et ung clerc qui furent envoyes devers lui pour laditte matiere, et deschira les lettres royallez et fist mettre lesdits commissaires en prison et illecquez piteusement morir.[277]

Sur lequel attemptat ledit Roy Charles le Quint envoia de rechief autres comissaires devers ledit prince de Gallez, ausquelz fut fait comme aux premiers, et depuis n'y osa personne aler.

[275] French diplomats and writers blamed the English for failing to complete these renunciations. See, for example, *Chroniques de Jean II et de Charles V*, II, p. 253; Edouard Perroy (ed.), 'The Anglo-French negotiations at Bruges, 1374–1377', *Camden Miscellany*, 19 (1952), pp. 72–74 and 84; *Le Songe du vergier*, I, pp. 277–278 and 281; Montreuil, II, pp. 186–189, 199–200, 247–249, 284–285, 297–298, 301–302, and 327–329, and III, 61–64 and 66–69; Jean Juvénal, I, pp. 208–210 and II, pp. 122–124 and 133–134.

[276] On 30 June 1368, Jean I, count of Armagnac, and his nephew, Arnaud-Amanieu, lord of Albret, appealed to Charles V against a hearth tax that the Black Prince had imposed on Aquitaine. Having taken legal advice, the French king accepted the appeal and summoned Edward to appear before the Parlement of Paris. When the Prince failed to appear, he was declared to be a contumacious vassal on 2 May 1369 and the duchy of Guyenne was declared forfeit.

[277] For French accounts of the Black Prince's treatment of the officers, along with other crimes, see Perroy (ed.), 'The Anglo-French negotiations at Bruges, 1374–1377', pp. 81–82 and 84; *Chroniques de Jean II et de Charles V*, II, pp. 253–254; *Le Songe du vergier*, I, pp. 275, 279, and 282–283; Montreuil, II, pp. 189–190, 195, 212–214, 238, 285, and 294–295 and III, 67–69, 81–82, 93–94, and 99; Jean Juvénal, I, pp. 212–213 and II, pp. 127–131. Also see pp. 239–240 below, drawing upon the account in Froissart.

Et non content de ce, fist guerre ouverte contre ledit[278] Roy Charles le Quint en croissant tousjours et augmentant les excés, enterprisez et oppressions accoustumeez al'encontre du roy et des subgetz des terres et seignouries que iceulx Roy Edouart et prince de Gallez tenoient et avoyent en leur possession et obeissance[279] ou royaume de France: dont a ceste cause ledit Roy Charles le Quint fist faire les declarations contre lesdits roy et prince de Galles telles que ou cas appartenoit, et se leverent en pou de temps pres que tous les subgetz desdits Roy Edouart et prince de Galles tant en la duchié de Guienne que es contez de Poitou, Pontieu, Xantonge et ailleurs al'encontre d'eulx; et se mirent en la main et obeissance dudit Roy Charles le Quint leur |**42v**| souverain seigneur, ainsi que selon Dieu, raison et justice doivent faire.

Il y'a aussi pluiseurs autres choses dedens ledit traittié de Bretygny qui se devoit faire et accomplir de la part desdits Roy Edouart et prince de Galles lesquelles ne se accomplirent point, jasoit ce que de la part du Roy Jehan et du duc de Normandie qui puis s'appella le Roy Charles le Quint, toutes les chosez qu'ilz devoient faire par ledit traittié eussent esté accompliez, sauf en tant qu'il touchoit la renonciation du ressort de Guienne et autres terres dessusdittes, laquelle chose ne vint point a la deffaulte desdiz Roy Jehan et duc de Normandie, mais par le deffault des Anglois, ainsi que dessus a esté touchié. Ne en ce ne pevent lesdis Roy Jehan et duc de Normandie emporter raisonnablement aucun blasme, charge ou reproche.

Et pour ainçoires plus esclarcir ceste matiere, est vray que aprés les choses dessusdittes, l'Empereur Charles le Quart vint en France acompaignié de son filz, le roy des Rommains, autres grans princes et seigneurs, lequel recita au Roy Charles le Quint les complaintes et douleances que les Angloiz faisoient de luy a cause des appellations et reuniemens a la couronne des terres et seignouries dessusdittes ainsi que devant est declairié. |**43r**| Lequel Charles le Quint pria audit empereur qu'il lui pleust venir au palais en la chambre de Parlement pour illecques oyr plus amplement la response desdittes matieres et le demene dicelles.[280]

En obtemperant ausquelles choses se trouverent en laditte chambre de Parlement lesdits empereur et roy de France et des Rommains

---

[278] A replaces 'Et non content de ce, fist guerre ouverte contre ledit' with 'Et ce fist il au contempt dudit'.

[279] A replaces 'avoyent en leur possession et obeissance' with 'possidoient'.

[280] For the visit of Emperor Charles IV to Paris in 1378, see *Chroniques de Jean II et de Charles V*, II, pp. 193–278, and Françoise Autrand, 'Mémoire et cérémonial: la visite de l'empereur Charles IV à Paris en 1378 d'après les *Grandes chroniques de France* et Christine de Pizan', in Liliane Dulac and Bernard Ribémont (eds), *Une femme de lettres au moyen âge: études autour de Christine de Pizan* (Orléans, 1995), pp. 91–103.

acompaignies de grans nombres de princes, prelas, seigneurs et gens de divers estas tant de France que dAlemaigne, et en audience publicque et en la presence de tous ledit Roy Charles le Quint, en partie de sa bouche et en partie par la bouche de[281] Messire Jehan des Mares son advocat fiscal, dist et fist dire, reciter et remonstrer tout l'effect du traittié de Bretigny, en semble les querellez des Anglois et les justifications dicellui Roy Charles le Quint, avecques toutez les lettres, appointemens, evidences, sommations, requestez, procés et declarations qui avoient esté faittes touchant les choses dessusdittes.[282]

Et finablement tout oy, ledit empereur acompaignié et conseillié comme dessus dit, et declaira en publicque qu'il estoit bien joyeux d'avoir veu et oy ce que la avoit esté dit et remonstré[283] pour en parler plus au vray partout ou besoing seroit, et oster l'erreur de pluiseurs de diverses nations qui par sinistres rappors estoient autrement informés |43v| desdittes matieres, et que puis qu'il congnoissoit la verité dicelle estre telle, il conseilloit audit Roy Charles le Quint qu'il gardast son droit et sa prerogative comme roy ainsi qu'il appartenoit, et que veu son bon droit et sa bonne querele es choses dessusdittes, il lui aideroit a la conservation diceulx et lui donrroit en ceste partie tout le secours, confort et ayde qui lui seroyent possiblez. Et commanda des lors a son filz le roy des Rommains, que *ad quemcunque statum preveniret*, il fist le semblable, lequel promist de ainsi le faire.

Oultre plus ledit Roy Charles le Quint envoya deux fois en Avignon devers le Pape Clement le VIe pour ceste matiere, en la presence duquel et du concistoire des cardinaulx, les ambassadeurs d'Engleterre furent oys d'unepart et les François d'autre, et finablement ne fut trouvé ou fait dudit Roy Charles le Quint touchans lesdittes matieres aucune chose digne de reprehention mais demoura tousjours la matiere en cest estat, c'estassavoir la confiscation clere et toute pleniere al'encontre desdits Angloiz, et a la justification et bon tiltre de la part des Françoiz.[284]

---

[281] C omits 'en partie par la bouche de'.

[282] Charles V personally delivered a two-hour speech on the ongoing dispute with the English, drawing upon a lengthy dossier of documents prepared by Gérard II de Montaigu, the future *Garde du Trésor des chartes*. That dossier served as a template for the development of resources for diplomats and administrators, culminating in *Pour ce que plusieurs* itself. See André Artonne, 'Le recueil des traités de la France composé par ordre de Charles V', in *Recueil de travaux offerts à M. Clovis Brunel* (2 vols, Paris, 1955), I, pp. 53–63.

[283] ACO add 'touchant les choses dessusdictes'.

[284] In P, the original scribe had written 'Angloys' at the end of this paragraph, but this was later corrected to read 'Françoys'. Though Pope Clement VI did chair an important peace conference at Avignon, this took place in 1344, eight years before his death. Pope Clement VII (d. 1394) did not play any role in diplomatic negotiations between Richard II and Charles VI, in large part because he was one of two rival popes during the Schism and, being based at Avignon, was supported by the French crown.

Au moyen desquellez choses dessus declairiez est tout cler, notoire et manifeste que a bonne et juste querele non obstant le traittié |**44r**| de Bretigny, les predecesseurs du roy qui a present est depuis le temps du Roy Charles le Ve jusques a leur trespas et au droit et moyen d'eulx, le roy qui au jour d'huy regne a bon et juste tiltre en la duchié de Guyenne et en toutes les autres terres et seignouriez estans de present en son obeissance que les Anglois souloient tenir ou royaume de France,[285] ensemble es terres de Calais, Guynes et autres que iceulx Anglois tiennent ainçoires et occupent oudit royaume, et que a tort et sans cause lesdis Angloiz a cause dudit traittié de Bretigny ne autrement en font aucune question ou demande.

Et ainçoires en agravant le fait desdits Anglois ne doivent pas estre oublies les excés et inhumanités, forces et violences, oppressions et dampnables vices, crismes et malices que le Roy Henry le Ve et aprés lui Henry le VIe,[286] ou ceulx qui avoient le gouvernement d'Angleterre de par lui, ont depuis les choses dessusdittes, fait en ce royaume en prenant et occuppant la duchié de Normandie,[287] la ville de Paris et une grande partie de tout ledit royame, et eulx efforchans de priver et dejetter, debouter de tout le royaume les vrais et drois heritiers dicelluy.

En quoy y'a trois grandes et enormes faultez, l'une si est perseverance et continuation en la malice, desobeissance, et es crismez, faultez |**44v**| et delis des predecesseurs desdits Henrys V^e et VIe dont a ceste cause se aucun droit appartenoit a iceulx Roy Henry V^e et VIe es terres et seignouries dessus declariez, estans en France ce que non, ilz ont tout forfait et confisqué.

La seconde faulte si est que, pour leur ambition de seignourir a tort et contre raison, il est mort a ceste cause par leur moien et dampnable entreprinse plus de deux millions de personnez ou royaume de France, eglises destruitez, violees et demoliez, villes, chasteaulx et fortressez abatuez, destruitez et jetteez par terre, les villages et les champs demourez, inhabitez, incultivés et du tout en desert et en friche. Et tant d'oppressions, dommages et inconveniens avenus au royame de France que, se le royaume d'Angleterre et toutes les facultez, richesses et valeurs dicellui tant en meuble que en heritaige estoient toutez assembleez ensemble, elles ne seroient point souffisantez a reparer les choses dessusdittez.

La tierce cause si est que toute injuste bataille est deffendue et qui injustement fait guerre, justement on lui puet faire, non pas seulement en soy deffendant, mais en lui ostant tout le sien propre jusquez il ait

---

[285] O replaces 'ou royaume de France' with 'en leur obeissance'.
[286] A omits 'Henry le Ve et aprés lui'.
[287] C gives 'Guienne' in place of 'Normandie'.

deuement reparé l'offence qu'il a faitte. Et ainsi le mettent |45r| les
drois en la glose du decret *Domine noster*, et si est l'usage et la commune
observance de tous princes en tous les pays et contés du monde depuis
le temps des Rommains jusques a present.[288]

Or est il tout cler que a tort, contre Dieu, raison et justice, lesdits
roys Henry V[e] et VIe et leurs adherens, fauteurs et complices ont fait
guerre contre les roys de France Charles VIe et Charles VIIe de ce
nom, dont le roy qui au jour d'huy est a le droit la cause, parquoy
appert clerement que a juste et bon tiltre il leur loisoit en leur vie et
avoient cause raisonnablement quant le povoir y a esté joinct, et aussi
a le roy qui a present est par semblable, de prendre et applicquier
a eulx toutez les terres et seignouries que lesdiz roys d'Angleterre et
les leur avoient ou royaume de France.[289] Et non pas seulement ou
royaume de France mais[290] en Angleterre et partout ailleurs la ou les
siens les pourroyent recouvrer jusques a ce que traittié de paix soit
fait les tors injures[291] entre lesdits princes ou que ceulx d'Angleterre
ayent reparé les tors, injures et dommages qu'ilz ont fait ou royame
de France.

Et ainsi en concluant tout pertinamment selon la matiere subgette
et que l'en treuve les choses dessus declairiez veritables tant par |45v|
lettres auctenticques comme par cronicquez, histoires anciennes et
autres enseignemens, et en soy conformant aux drois canons, civilz
et a l'usage et coustume du royaume de France, il est cler, notoire
et manifeste, et n'en fault faire aucune difficulté que le roy a bon
et juste tiltre tient et posside les duchies de Normandie, Guienne,
contez de Poitou, d'Anjou, du Maine, Touraine et Pontieu, et toutes
les autres terres que les Anglois soloient occupper en ce royame. Et
oultre puet licitement recouverer tout le demourant quant son plaisir
sera de y entendre, et que bonnement le pourra faire sans aucune

---

[288] A marginal note in P offers 'I 23 q. 2', that is to say *Decretum Gratiani*, C. 23 q. 2 c. 2.
This famous authority explored the question of a just war fought to redress a legal wrong
or injury. Gratian's statements in this regard triggered debate because he did not make it
entirely clear whether a victim was only entitled to defend themselves against hostile attack
and to recover stolen property, or might go further and actively punish the evil-doers. Yet
Pour ce que plusieurs is here advocating an even more extreme interpretation, authorizing the
seizure of all the lands of an enemy, an action that exceeded the limits of proportionality
and self-defence. Such an argument was not made, for example, when this authority was
cited in *Le Songe du vergier*, I, pp. 289–290, 313, and 337, and it also contradicts the comments
on self-defence in John of Legnano, *Tractatus de bello, de represaliis et de duello*, ed. T.E. Holland
and trans. J.L. Birerly (Oxford, 1917), pp. 151–154. Also see Frederick H. Russell, *The Just
War in the Middle Ages* (Cambridge, 1975), pp. 63–68.
[289] C omits 'que lesdiz roys d'Angleterre et les leur avoient'.
[290] AN omit 'non pas seulement ou royaume de France mais'.
[291] The words 'les tors injures' only appear in B.

charge d'honneur ne de conscience, et avecquez ce leur faire guerre en Angleterre quant bon luy samblera.

Et au contraire que a tort et sans cause et a mauvaise et injuste querelle et sans aucun tiltre aumoins vaillable ne raisonnable les Angloiz pretendent aucun droit esdittes terres es seignouries.

Et ne pevent lesdiz Anglois raisonnablement alleguer ne maintenir aucune chose au contraire, car selon raison il fault qu'ilz sueffrent les loix, coustumez et usages des pays et contreez ou les choses sont scitueez et assisez, et pareillement de celles dont ilz usent tous les |**46r**| jours ensemble en leur royame.

Et pour ceste heure se deporte l'en icy a parler des loix, usages et coustumes de France en ceste partie, car ilz sont tous notoires a chascun. Mais en venant a celles d'Angleterre, oncques les Anglois n'eurent droit de succession ne transport ou pays de Galles, ne autre tiltre fors faulte d'hommage, desobeissance ou rebellion, et la guerre que les Gallois leur faisoient. Et a ce tiltre et non aultre tient le roy d'Angleterre tout ledit pays de Galles, tant de noort Gallez que soubz Galles et Poysland, que soloit tenir le Prince Cloellin, qui vault autant adire en françois comme Loys, lequel les Anglois firent morir piteusement et son frere David; et devoit venir la succession au conte de Montfort, filz de leur suer, dont sont descendus en partie les ducs de Bretaigne qui a present sont, et a ceste cause est leur propre heritage se ne fust la dicte confiscation.[292]

Pareillement les roys d'Escoce soloyent tenir la conté de Hontiton, Nothombelland, [Westmelland], Tindal et pluiseurs grans terres et seignouries en Angleterre,[293] lesquelles les Anglois par semblable leur ont osteez et les en ont privez et deboutés,[294] et puis doncques qu'ilz usent en pareil cas en ces choses, il est tout cler qu'ilz doivent

---

[292] AC omit 'se ne fust la dicte confiscation'. By the treaty of Montgomery on 29 September 1267, Henry III recognized Llywelyn ap Gruffudd (d. 1282) as 'prince of Wales and lord of Snowdon', following Llywelyn's establishment of control over Gwynedd Uwch Conwy and Perfeddwlad, and supremacy over the other Welsh rulers. Yet, within ten years, Llywelyn's principality had been dismembered by Edward I, and the Welshman was killed on 11 December 1282 in battle near Builth. His brother Dafydd ap Gruffudd assumed control and continued the struggle until his capture in the summer of 1283. Amaury de Montfort (d. *c.*1300) did not have any claim to inherit the principality by reason of his sister Eleanor's marriage to Llywelyn.

[293] There is no reference to Westmorland in B; ACO also add 'Combelland' to the list.

[294] King David I of Scotland (d. 1153) inherited the earldom of Northumberland and the honour of Huntingdon (comprising lands in the shires of Northampton, Huntingdon, Cambridge, and Bedford) through his wife, Maud de Senlis, daughter of Waltheof, earl of Northumbria. He also restored the southern border of his kingdom west of the Pennines to Westmorland, where it had run before 1092. But in July 1157, King Malcolm IV of Scotland paid homage to Henry II and gave up Cumberland, Westmorland, and Northumberland. Henry subsequently restored the honour of Huntingdon to Malcolm and gave the lordship of Tynedale to the latter's younger brother William.

souf- |**46v**| frir la semblable contre eulx, et qu'ilz ne sont a recevoir d'aucune chose alleguer ou demander au contraire, *quia patere legem,* &c.[295]

Pluiseurs cronicquez aussi et histoires dient qu'il y eut certain traittié japieca fait entre le roy d'Angleterre Henry le Tiers, filz de Jehan d'une part, et Messire Loys de France, pere de Sainct Loys, que depuis on appella Leon le Debonnaire d'autre, a cause et pour raison de la croisee qui avoit esté donnee par le pape contre lesdits roys Jehan et Henry son filz, et de la conqueste dudit royaume, ensemble du droit dicellui baillié, donné et ottroyé audit Messire Loys de France a l'occasion dessusditte. Lequel Messire Loys de France[296] a ceste cause passa en Angleterre et eut la possession de Londres, de Lincol,[297] et de pluiseurs autres cites, villes et chasteaulx dudit royame, et la foy et l'ommaige de presquez tous les prelas, seigneurs et barons dudit pays, qui lui firent le serement et feaulté comme a leur roy et souverain seigneur. Au moien desquellez choses,[298] ledit Messire Loys de France a ce tiltre se nommoit et portoit pour roy et droiturier seigneur du royame d'Angleterre.

Par lequel traittié et pour appaisier ledit discord les parties appointerent ensemble que les prisonniers d'unepart et d'autre seroient |**47r**| delivrez, paix final faitte entre eulx et grande somme de deniers baillié audit Messire Loys de France pour s'en retourner de ça la mer.[299]

---

[295] The full text of this citation from Cato, *Monosticha,* 49, is given in manuscript O: '*quia patere legem, quam ipse tulleris*'.

[296] CJP omit 'a l'occasion dessusditte. Lequel Messire Loys de France', perhaps because of a homoeoteleutic error, jumping from 'France' to 'France'.

[297] O omits 'de Lincol'.

[298] O adds the following passage that had already appeared on pp. 90–91 above: 'depuis la riviere du Humbre en tirant devers Escosse. Et que la matiere de confiscation et forfaiture fut si claire al'encontre dudit Roy Jehan tant a cause de leze majesté comme de felonnie et autrement, ce que ainsi eust esté solempnellement declairé par ceulx a qui de droit il appartenoit de faire, et que pour ceste il y eust trois journees solempnellement tenues en ce royaume, dont l'une fut a Estempes, l'autre a Chartres, esquellez deux journeez ledit Roy Jehan comparut en personne moiennant seurte qu'il eut du Roy Phelipes, et la tierce fut a Vendosme ou il ne se voulut point comparoir ainçois se fortifia en toutes manieres a lui possibles contre ledit Roy Phelipes. Auquel lieu de Vendosme la declaration fut solempnellement faitte contre lui. Neantmoins Saint Loys, filz du filz dudit Phelipes le Conquerant de France, desirant choses'. This same error was repeated in the printed editions, and translated by the Tudor respondent to *Pour ce que plusieurs.* See p. 29 above, together with p. 245, n. 361 below.

[299] English rebels invited the future Louis VIII to invade in 1216. Louis laid claim to the English throne through his wife, Blanche of Castile, but Pope Innocent III supported King John, who had surrendered the kingdom to papal overlordship two years earlier. Following John's death on 19 October, the English barons threw their support behind Henry III, and Prince Louis was defeated at the battle of Lincoln on 20 May 1217. Louis was then

Et oultre plus dit l'istoire que ledit roy d'Angleterre se soubzmist comme subget du roy de France a cause dudit royame d'Angleterre a venir au Parlement dudit roy de France[300] deux foiz l'an, et en cas qu'il auroit ensongne raisonnable de n'y point venir,[301] seroit tenu d'y envoyer gens notables garnis de povoirs souffisans de par lui en signe de recongnoissance qu'il se tenoit pour subget dudit roy de France. Et avecques ce, estoit tenu et se soubzmettoit de servir le roy de France en ses guerres avecques certain nombre de gens toutez et quantesfoiz que le roy de France le lui feroit savoir.

Et pour accorder les cronicquez de France et d'Angleterre en paix, il est vray que lesdiz cronicquez desdits royaumes s'accorderent bien en ce qui touche ladite croisee, le passage aussi dudit Messire Loys de France en Angleterre et toutes les autres choses, excepté sa submission dessusditte de venir au Parlement du roy de France et du service que le roy d'Angleterre estoit tenus de faire au roy de France toutes les fois qu'il lui seroit fait savoir, car la cronicque de France met expressement lesdittes submissions et la cronicque d'Angleterre n'en fait |**47v**| aucune mention.[302]

Et n'est pas merveille se laditte cronicque d'Angleterre taist les choses dessusdittes, car les Angloiz se dient souverains en leur royame, et ne congnoissent nul empereur ou aultre et s'ilz confessoient la submission dessusditte ce seroit trop a le prejudice.

Toutesfois consideré le droit que ledit Messire Loys de France avoit en Angleterre et la possession pluiseurs places et obeissance de grande partie des subgetz, il est plus a croire que en renonçant ausdittes choses, laditte submission fut faitte pour aucunement recompenser ledit Messire Loys de France, veu qu'il rendoit tout ce qu'il tenoit en Angleterre que autrement: laquelle submission s'il estoit trouvé avoir esté faitte par lesdits Anglois, comme il est vray semblable que si est, seroit bien clere demonstrance que toute la guerre que les Anglois ont depuis fait contre les roys de France est injuste et desraisonnable. Et que au moyen dicelle il est bien evident que les roys d'Angleterre

---

persuaded to abandon his claim to the throne in the treaty of Lambeth on 11 September 1217, in return for an indemnity of 10,000 marks and the release of prisoners without further ransom payments.

[300] O omits 'a cause dudit royame d'Angleterre a venir au Parlement dudit roy de France', perhaps because of a homoeoteleutic error, jumping from 'France' to 'France'.

[301] N adds 'et se [. . .] et que venir n'y peust'.

[302] Jean Juvénal had offered a more accurate account in 1446, admitting that Pope Innocent III excommunicated both Louis and his father, and also avoiding the fiction that Henry III was required to pay homage to the French crown by the treaty of Lambeth: Jean Juvénal, II, pp. 143–144. The notion that Henry III promised to pay homage does not appear in either *Grandes chroniques*, VI, pp. 366–368 or Hercule Géraud (ed.), *Chronique latine de Guillaume de Nangis de 1113 à 1300 avec les continuations de cette chronique de 1300 à 1368* (2 vols, Paris, 1843), I, pp. 153–155.

n'avoient pas seulement fourfait ne confisqui ce qu'ilz avoient en France ainçois tout le royame d'Angleterre et que a juste et bonne querelle le roy le pourroit demander leur faire guerre et mettre paine dicellui invader et conquerir.

|**48r**| Et quant orez laditte submission n'auroit point de lieu si est il cler et evident par les autres moiens dessus touchiez que a tort et contre raison les Anglois font demande des terres et seignouries particulieres qu'ilz querellent en ce royame dont dessus est faitte mention, et qu'ilz n'y ont droit ne tiltre qui soit vaillable. Et se par aucun temps ilz y en ont eu par tiltre[303] de succession ou autrement, ilz l'ont perdu, forfait et confisquié,[304] et a juste et bon tiltre le roy a pris, mis en sa main et reuny a la couronne toutez les terres et seignouries dessusdittes, et que justement, sainctement et licitement le pourroit faire et luy appartiennent de droit sans aucune reprehention. Et cecy est quant a la seconde partie de ce present traittié.[305]

---

[303] AC omit 'qui soit vaillable. Et se par aucun temps ilz y en ont eu par tiltre', perhaps because of a homoeoteleutic error, jumping from 'tiltre' to 'tiltre'.

[304] AC replace 'ilz l'ont perdu, forfait et confisquié' with 'qu'ilz ont forfait'.

[305] AC omit 'de ce present traittié'. LNP add 'en laquelle est faite mencion du droit que les Anglois pretendent en pluseurs terres et seignouries particulieres du royaume de France &c'. H replaces 'Et cecy est quant a la seconde partie de ce present traittié' with 'Fin de la seconde partie de ce present livre'. In J, fo. 68v finishes with the words 'Et cecy est quant a la', and fo. 69r begins 'Et pareillement' (from p. 116 below), thereby missing out five paragraphs.

CY COMMENCE LA TIERCE PARTIE DE CE PRESENT LIVRE[306]

|**48v**| Maintenant fault venir a la tierce partie principale de la matiere dont de present est question, c'estassavoir de la complainte que les Anglois font touchant la roupture des treves qui fut l'an mil CCCCXLIX, soubz confiance desquellez lesdiz Anglois dient qu'ilz ont perdu Normandie et Guyenne, et a ceste cause requierent prealablement et devant tout euvre en estre restituez.[307]

Pour bien entendre laquelle matiere, est necessaire congnoistre premierement le fondement dicelle et aprés les incidences, ou autrement on n'en pourroit avoir parfaitte ne clere congnoissance.

Et pour ce sera commencié a la naissance desdittes treves, lesquelles furent faittez et prises la premiere fois ou moys de jung mil IIII^C XLIIII et ce pour le temps et terme de XXII moys seulement.[308]

Et est vray que en icelles treves chascun des deux roys de France et d'Angleterre comprist de sa part ses alyes et subgetz. Et nommeement fut compris pour la part du roy de France entre les autres princes et seigneurs, ses subgetz le duc de Bretaigne qui lors estoit en son pays et duché de Bretaigne.

|**49r**| Et pareillement le roy d'Angleterre en ses treves recitant les alliez et subgetz du France, nommeement declaira[309] ledit duc de Bretaigne et son pays, comme subgetz dudit roy de France, estre compris esdittes trevez pour la part dudit roy de France, sans ce que ledit roy d'Angleterre reclamast, reservast ne feist quelque mention au contraire du fait dudit duc de Bretaigne ne de sesdittes pays et duchié.[310]

[306] ACFJOPQ omit 'Cy commence la tierce partie de ce present livre'. H prefers 'Sensuit la tierce et derreniere partie de ce present traittié faisant mention des trevez rompues a Fougieres par le feu Roy Charles que Dieux pardonist, comme les Anglois dient et en demandent avoir reparacion et restitution' and K offers 'Sensieut le derrenier traittié qui parle de la roupture des treves'. L prefers 'Cy finit la seconde partie du present livre et sensieuit la tierce et daraniere partie' and N states 'Sensieut le derrenier traictié qui parle de la roupture des treves'.

[307] In C, a marginal note in a different hand reads 'l'an mil IIII^C XLIX touchant la roupture des treves que furent faicte l'an mil IIII^C XLIIII'. For the events discussed in this final section of *Pour ce que plusieurs*, see Craig Taylor, 'Brittany and the French crown: the legacy of the English attack upon Fougères (1449)', in John Maddicott and David Palliser (eds), *The Medieval State: essays presented to James Campbell* (London, 2000), pp. 243–257.

[308] The truce of Tours was agreed on 28 May 1444 and ratified by Henry VI on 27 June. It was set to conclude on 1 April 1446.

[309] C omits 'Et nommeement fut compris pour la part du roy de France [...] les alliez et subgetz du France nommeement declaira'.

[310] See *GTGCA*, pp. 163 and 187.

Lesdittes treves de XXII moys furent depuis prorogueez de VII mois et aprés de V mois et depuis de VII mois, et ainçoires de rechief de XII mois.[311] Vray est que la derreniere prorogation de XII mois fut condicionelle, c'estassavoir en cas que le roy d'Angleterre delivreroit le Mans et les autres places qu'il tenoit en la conté du Mainne dedens le jour de la Toussains qui fut l'an mil IIII^C XLVII.[312]

Et pour ce que ledit roy d'Angleterre ne le fist pas ainsi, ou que ceulx qui tenoient lesdittes places n'y vouldrent pas obeir et a ceste cause y convint proceder par main armee ainsi que chascun a assez de congnoissance. Quant l'appointement du Mans fut fait pour oster la doubte qui eust peu cheoir esdits prorogations de treves, a cause de la condicion dessusditte non accomplie, |**49v**| et commissaires des deux princes roys de France et d'Angleterre se condescendirent de faire nouvelles treves durant deux ans, c'estassavoir jusquez au premier jour d'april, qui devoit escheoir environ la sepmaine saincte, l'an mil IIII^C XLIX selon l'usage de France, et selon celui d'Angleterre se contoit IIII^C L.[313]

Et esquellez treves le roy de France comprist de sa part le duc de Bretaigne et sondit pays et duché comme ses subgetz, ainsi qu'il avoit acoustumé de faire au paravant. Et quant les minutez furent accordeez entre les deux parties, ainsi fut il monstré, escript et accordé entre elles, sans que de la part des Anglois ledit duc y fut compris en aucune maniere, mais les Angloiz en usant de leurs cautelles, combien qu'il y eust de bien sages gens de la part dudit Roy Charles le VIIe, firent ung strategeme bien merveilleux, c'estassavoir pour ce qu'ilz disoient qu'ilz povoient mettre les gens de guerre de la part de France dedens la place du Mans s'y non de nuyt et ainsi le firent, et qu'ilz ne bailleroient point laditte place si non qu'ilz eussent les appointemens, et que la matiere requeroit celerité pour eviter pluiseurs inconveniens

---

[311] C omits 'et aprés de V mois et depuis de VII mois', and N omits 'et ainçoires de rechief de XII mois', perhaps because of a homoeoteleutic error or eyeskip. O replaces 'XII' with 'XXII', and repeats this substitution in the following sentence.

[312] The truce agreed by the truce of Tours was extended on 15 August 1445 for seven months (until 1 November 1446) and on 19 December 1445, it was renewed for another five months (until 1 April 1447). Three days later, Henry VI agreed to cede Maine by 30 April 1446, in response to pressure exerted by the French ambassadors, Guillaume Cousinot and Jean Havart. On 22 February 1447, the truce was further extended for nine months (until 1 January 1448) and on 1 December 1447 for twelve months (until 1 January 1449). The handover of Maine only took place in March 1448 under the threat of military action by the French.

[313] On 15 March 1448, the truce was extended for fifteenth months, until 1 April 1450. In England, the new year began on the 25 March, but in France it started on the date of Easter, which fell on 5 April that year. As a result, the truce ended in 1450 in England but 1449 in France.

qu'ilz estoyent fors a doubter de avenir, les commissaires desdiz deux princes appointerent que on bailleroit lesdittes |50r| appointemens d'unepart et d'autre, et feroit on la delivrance de laditte place quant et quant.

Et a ceste cause convint que feu Monseigneur le Partriarche de Poitiers et les autres commissaires de la part de France venissent environ minuit ou fons du fosse du Mans, ouquel lieu se trouverent semblablement les commissaires de la part des Anglois, et baillerent leur appointement d'unepart et d'autre sans chandeille ne regarder qu'il y avoit dedens,[314] et incontinent les gens d'armes entrerent dedens laditte place.[315]

Or est vray que lesdits commissaires de la part des Anglois en la treve qu'ilz baillerent, de leur part au dessceu et sans le consentement des commissaires de la part de France, comprindrent le duc de Bretaigne de leur part, comme le roy de France l'avoit compris de la sienne.[316] Et soit bien notté ceste cautelle, car c'est toute leur justification de la prise de Fougieres,[317] a laquelle cautelle sera respondu cy aprés ou lieu la ou le cas si adonne.

Ces chosez faittez ne demoura gaires aprés que le duc de Sombreset passa deça la mer qui eut tout le gouvernement de par le roy d'Angleterre es pays de son obeissance [en Normandie][318] et es autres |50v| terres adjacentes, estans de ça laditte mer.[319]

Durant le gouvernement duquel duc de Sombreset pluiseurs grans excés, enterprisez et attemptas se firent de ceulx de son parti, tant par son ordonnance que autrement contre la teneur desdittes treves. A l'occasion desquelles choses, le Roy Charles le VIIe que Dieux pardoinst envoia par diverses foiz devers ledit duc de Sombreset et

---

[314] ACO add 'cuidans les Françoys que la grosse desdits appoinctemens fut parelle a la minutes'. In manuscript P, there is a marginal note in a post-medieval hand, 'Ruse des Anglois au traicte'.

[315] Jacques Juvénal des Ursins was bishop of Poitiers and patriarch of Antioch, though at the time of the negotiations in 1448 he was archbishop of Reims. He was accompanied by Jean, count of Dunois, Pierre II de Brézé, Bertrand de Beauveu, and Jean du Mesnel-Simon.

[316] For the inclusion of Brittany as both a French and an English ally in the two versions of the truce, see *Foedera*, XI, pp. 200 and 206.

[317] ACO replace 'de la prise de Fougieres' with 'des Anglois touchant la prise de Fougieres dont cy aprez sera parle et'.

[318] BF omit 'en Normandie'.

[319] The return of Maine to the French directly affected Edmund Beaufort, duke of Somerset, because he had been made captain-general and governor of Maine in 1438 and had received the land rights to the county in 1442. Beaufort delayed taking up the post of lieutenant and governor-general of France and the duchies of Normandy and Guyenne until December 1447, when he had received a promise of 10,000 livres tournois a year from taxation in Normandy, which was fully paid until the outbreak of war in 1449.

furent pluiseurs journeez tenues par les commissaires d'unepart et d'autre touchant lesdittes matieres.[320]

Et oultre plus pour ce que on ne trouvoit pas grant raison ne justice avec ledit duc de Sombreset, le roy de rechief envoya en Angleterre devers le roy dudit royaume pour lui signiffier lesdits excés, entreprisez et attemptas, et que sur ce il lui pleust pourveoir ainsi que raison estoit, et que les treves le portoient.[321]

Lequel roy d'Angleterre rescripvy au roy son oncle qu'il avoit envoyé le duc de Sombreset de ça la mer expressement pour ceste cause, auquel il avoit baillié tout povoir pour y besongnier comme lui meismez eust peut faire, et ainçoires de rechief lui en escripvoit en signifiant au roy sondit |51r| oncle qu'il n'envoiast plus devers lui pour ceste cause, et que quant les cas y escherroient, l'en se tirast vers ledit duc de Sombreset, et que sans point de faulte il lui donneroit provision.

Mais non obstant toutes ces choses, aussi pou fut il donné de provision par ledit duc de Sombreset esdittes matieres comme auparavant, ainçoires en mettant a execution l'entreprise de Fougieres que ja avoit trayné ung an et demy, et estoit encommencee long temps paravant lesdittes treves faittes au Mans, ainsi qu'il appert par la deposicion de Messire François de Surienne dit l'Arragonnois, executeur de ladicte entreprise et de pluiseurs autres qui aidierent a icelle conduire, ou mois de Mars mil IIII[C] XLVIII selon l'usage de France,[322] et IIII[C] XLIX selon usage d'Angleterre. Icellui Messire François l'Arragonnois de sceu, adue et consentement du roy d'Angleterre, du duc de Suffolc, du duc de Sombreset, et de pluiseurs autres des principaulx d'Angleterre, partant[323] de Normandie et ayant illecquez charge de gens d'armes et de places de par ledit roy d'Angleterre, et portant son ordre de la jaretiere, prist d'emblee le chasteau et la ville de Fougieres, pylla, et ceulx qui avecquez lui estoyent ladicte ville tua gens en icelle, les autres prinst prisonniers, couru tout le pays d'environ, prist patis |51v| et bailla sauvegardes et

---

[320] In April 1448, Charles VII sent Guillaume Cousinot and Pierre de Fontenil to Rouen to complain about the actions of English captains who, retiring from Maine, had occupied and fortified the fortresses of Saint-James-de-Beuvron and Mortain on the Breton–Norman frontier, contrary to the terms of the truce. The following month, the French king sent Cousinot and Raoul de Gaucourt to Rouen.

[321] Charles VII sent Jean Havart, the Valois herald, to England in May and August 1448, which led to a series of meetings between representatives of the two kings, including Cousinot, at Louviers in August and November 1448 and January 1449.

[322] JP omit 'IIII[C] XLVIII selon l'usage de France, et'.

[323] C replaces 'Icellui Messire François l'Arragonnois de sceu, adue et consentement du roy d'Angleterre' with 'de l'ordonnance'; A omits 'du duc de Suffolc'; N omits 'autres des principaulx d'Angleterre, partant'.

saufconduis, et fist guerre ouverte en Bretaigne, ainsi que ennemis ont accoustumé de faire les uns contre les autres, au veu et sceu dudit roy d'Angleterre, et de ceulx de son conseil dudit duc aussi de Sombreset et tous ceulx qui avoient puissance et correction sus ledit Messire François, sans ce que par nul d'eulx aucune provision ou reparation y fust faitte ne donnee.[324]

Ains qui plus est le conforta ledit duc de Sombreset de gens d'artillerie et d'autres choses depuis laditte prinse et avoit ledit de Surienne les propres gens de la maison dudit duc de Sombreset avecquez lui a laditte prise et a faire le exploiz dessusdit.[325]

Voyant lesquelles choses ledit Roy Charles requis par le duc de Bretaigne, François, qui pour lors estoit, de lui donner provision, ayde et secours en ladicte matiere, envoya premierement Messire Guillame Cosinot chevalier et Pierre de Fonteny, ses conseilliers, devers ledit duc de Sombreset pour savoir son intencion et voloir touchant le fait de laditte prise, et s'il en voloit faire aucune reparation. Et avec ce envoya en Angleterre Jehan Havart devers le Roy Henry pour semblable cause. Mais d'unepart ne d'autre les ambassadeurs ne peurent obtenir provision.[326]

|52r| Et en tant que touche ledit Roy Henry, il remist la chose audit duc de Sombreset. Et a regart dudit duc de Sombreset,[327] il envoia devers ledit Roy Charles Messire Jehan Hennefort, chevalier Anglois, et Messire Jehan l'Enfant, pour lors son conseillier, pour excuser ladicte prise de Fougieres et la justifier a leur povoir.[328]

Lesquelz ambassadeurs dirent et exposerent audit Roy Charles pluiseurs choses touchans le fait des treves, complaignans de beaucop d'excés et attemptas qu'ilz disoient avoir esté fais par les gens de son

---

[324] On 24 March 1449, the Breton town of Fougères was captured by the Aragonese mercenary captain, François de Surienne. On 29 June 1449, French ambassadors described him as 'Messire François l'Arragonnois, chevalier de l'ordre de la Jarretiere [...] conseiller et pensionnaire dudit prince nepveu, et soubz le gouvernement et lieutenance du dit haut et puissant prince, duc de Somerset': *Narratives*, pp. 415–416, 436–437, and 441–442, together with *L&P*, I, p. 249. Also see André Bossuat, *Perrinet Gressart et François de Surienne, agents de l'Angleterre* (Paris, 1936), pp. 301–335. For the deposition of François de Surienne, see p. 7 above.

[325] See *Narratives*, pp. 441–443, 449–450, and 457–458, and *Chronique d'Escouchy*, III, pp. 225–242.

[326] Cousinot and Fontenil were already in Rouen to discuss recent violations of the truce, and left on 22 April without discussing the matter officially with Somerset. Jean Havart was sent to England in June 1449.

[327] N omits 'Et a regart dudit duc de Sombreset'.

[328] Jean L'Enfant and Sir John Handford met with Charles VII at Razilly on 23 April, but advised the king to raise the matter of Fougères directly with Henry VI because the matter was too important for Somerset to deal with on his own authority.

obeissance al'encontre et au dommage des subgés et obeissans du roy d'Angleterre et ou prejudice desdittez treves.

Et entre autre choses,[329] pour venir a la principale justification de laditte prise de Fougieres, dirent que le duc de Bretaigne estoit subget du roy d'Angleterre, compris de sa part esdittes treves,[330] lequel avoit pris et tenoit prisonnier Messire Gilles de Bretaigne son frere a tort et contre raison, et lequel Messire Gilles estoit homme lige et vassal dudit roy d'Angleterre, et ne voloit ledit duc de Bretaigne delivrer icellui Messire Gilles, ne le rendre audit roy d'Angleterre son souverain seigneur, jasoit ce que par pluiseurs fois il en eust est sommé et requis. Parquoy n'estoit pas merveilles se |**52v**| les amis dudit Messire Gilles avoient fait aucune entreprise sur ledit duc de Bretaigne.[331]

Et posé orez que aucun excés lui eust esté fait, se n'estoit ce point infraction de treve,[332] consideré ce que dit est disans en oultre qu'ilz voloient, pensoient que quant il vouldroit requerir reparation au roy d'Angleterre, ilz esperoient qu'il donneroit si bonne provision en ladite matiere que ledit duc de Bretaigne n'auroit cause de s'en doloir, voulans au moiens dessusdits attraire le duc et la duché de Bretaigne a leur obeissance comme leurs subgez, et l'oster hors de la main et de l'obeissance du Roy Charles, qui estoit ainçoires plusgrant entreprise et infration de treve XX foiz que n'estoit ladite prise de Fougieres.[333]

Sur quoy leur fut respondu que leur ouverture n'estoit pas raisonnable, ne ce qu'ilz maintenoient de leur part selon verité.[334]

Ausquelles choses et a chascune des complaintez par eulx faittez, ledit Roy Charles en la presence de pluiseurs princes, prelas et gens notables, leur fist respondre publicquement en telle facon et maniere, et ladite response si bien justifier par lettres et enseignemens auctentiquez, que chascun povoit bien congnoistre que a |**53r**| tort

---

[329] JKLNPQ insert 'dirent et exposerent audit Roy Charles pluiseurs choses touchans le fait des treves', which they remove from the preceding paragraph.

[330] In H, a marginal note in a post-medieval hand offers 'Messire Gille de Bretaigne prisonere'.

[331] Gilles de Bretagne, brother of Duke François I of Brittany, was arrested on 26 June 1446 for conspiring with the English and murdered while in custody at La Hardouinaie on the night of 24 April 1450.

[332] C omits 'se n'estoit ce point infraction de treve'.

[333] Duke François I had paid homage to the French king on 16 March 1446, ending a period of some uncertainty regarding the allegiance of Brittany; François's father, Jean V (d. 1442), had taken the English side in the treaty of Troyes, ratifying it on 8 October 1422 and on 3 July 1427. Regarding the strategy to win the duke to the English side, see Taylor, 'Brittany and the French crown', pp. 243–257.

[334] ACOP omit this paragraph.

et sans cause ilz faisoient lesdittes complaintes, et aussi que leur justification du fait de Fougieres ne se povoient soustenir.[335]

Et oultre plus leur fist remonstrer comme il avoit pluiseurs justes causes de se doloir du roy d'Angleterre et de ceulx de son obeissance, a l'occasion de pluiseurs grans excés et attemptas par eulx commis et perpetres ou prejudice desdittes treves, et aussi de pluiseurs autres choses accordees et promises par ledit roy d'Angleterre, dont riens n'avoit esté par lui fait gardé ne accomply.

Et combien que lesdiz excés et attemptas commis et perpetrez de la part des Anglois, autres que cellui de Fougieres, fussent si grans et si enormez que chascun povoit clerement congnoistre que lesdiz Anglois n'avoient aucune bonne voulenté a l'entretenement desdittez treves. Toutesfoiz pource que ce seroit bien longue chose a reciter tous les cas particuliers, icy seulement sera parlé du fait particulier dudit Fougieres, pour ce que les Angloiz, congnoissans que c'estoit clere infraction de treve, y insisterent plus que en tout le demourant.

Et pour venir a laditte matiere, leur fut remonstré que de toute ancienneté depuis le temps du Roy Clotaire le Premier, filz Clovis, jusquez |53v| a present, la duché de Bretaigne estoit du royame de France et subgette des roys de France.[336] Et mesmez Sainct Judicail, roy de Bretaigne, pource qu'il avoit desobey aux commissaires du Roy Dagobert, a cause de laquelle desobeissance ledit Dagobert[337] esmeut ses ostz pour aler contre lui, icellui Sainct Judicail vint devers le roy Dagobert, lui requerant mercy de la offence qu'il lui avoit faitte, le recongnoissant pour lui et pour ses successeurs son souverain[338] seigneur a cause dudit pays de Bretaigne, et tous les autres roys de France qui vendroient aprés luy.[339]

Et en particularisant plus avant lesdittes matieres selon les temps nouveaux, c'estassavoir depuis le tamps de Phelippe le Conquerant jusques au temps de lors, estoit cler et manifeste que tous les contes et ducs qui avoient esté en Bretaigne estoyent hommes du roy de France,

---

[335] No record survives of this meeting, but these statements echo the French position at subsequent meetings: *Chronique d'Escouchy*, III, pp. 225–239 and 245–251; *Narratives*, pp. 435–473, 482–493, and 502–512; *L&P*, I, pp. 243–264.

[336] In H, a marginal note in a post-medieval hand reads 'Pour l'hommaige de Bretaigne'.

[337] CO omit 'a cause de laquelle desobeissance ledit Dagobert', perhaps because of a homoeoteleutic error, jumping from 'Dagobert' to 'Dagobert'.

[338] P omits 'lui et pour ses successeurs son souverain'.

[339] This reference to Dagobert and Judicael echoes a statement in a memorandum produced by Cousinot and his colleagues in 1464 to justify the rights of Louis XI over the duchy of Brittany: Philippe Contamine, 'Méthodes et instruments de travail de la diplomatie française: Louis XI et la régale des évêchés bretons (1462–5)', in *idem*, *Des pouvoirs en France, 1300–1500* (Paris, 1992), p. 159. Note also that, on 29 June 1449, Cousinot and Charles, lord of Culant, set out the French case for the claim that the counts and dukes of Brittany had always been liegemen of the kings of France: *Narratives*, pp. 467–468.

et lui avoient fait hommage toutes et quantesfois que le cas estoit avenu de changement de seignourie fust de roy, conte ou duc, comme par lettres auctentiques ces choses apparissoient clerement a tous ceulx qui les vouloyent veoir et savoir. Et ressortissoit la duché de Bretaigne en la court de Parlement quant le cas y escheoit, tout ainsi comme les autres seignouriez du royaume de France, garde au duc |**54r**| son privilege selon que la matiere le requerroit, ainsi que on doit faire a chascune seignourie selon le privilege qu'elle a, et que de tout temps sans aucun contredit ou difficulté, le roy en estoit en juste possession et saisine.

Leur fut en oultre remonstré que le roy d'Angleterre ne povoit prendre cause d'ygnorance de ces choses, ne aucune chose alleguer au contraire aumoins qu'il fust vaillable, car il estoit tout notoire que ledit Duc François qui pour lors vivoit, en ensuivant ses predecesseurs, avoit fait hommage au roy au veu et sceu de tous ceulx qui l'avoient volu veoir et scavoir. Et y avoit au temps de lors, et y a ainçoires pluiseurs causes de la duché de Bretaigne introduites en la court de Parlement comme en derrenier ressort.[340]

Et oultre plus leur fut[341] dit comment ledit roy d'Angleterre par ses lettres patentes des premieres treves, lesquelles adonc furent leutez en publicque devant lesdits ambassadeurs de Sombreset,[342] comprenoit nommeement esdittes trevez ledit Duc François pour la part du roy de France comme son subget.[343] Parquoy estoit bien cler qu'il ne faisoit a recevoir de venir, quereler, maintenir ne demander icellui duc pour |**54v**| estre son subget, car il ne sera point trouvé que depuis la datte desdittes lettres il eust fait serement, promesse ne aucune suggession audit roy d'Angleterre, ne qu'il lait recongneu ne advoé son seigneur en aucune maniere. Aussi n'eust il peu au prejudice du roy quant orez meismez il l'eust volu faire sans le consentement dudit seigneur.

Et ainçoires qui plus est estoit vray que ledit Duc François recongnoissant ledit Roy Charles son souverain seigneur, doubtant pour aucunes chosez que on disoit avoir esté faittez avecquez les Anglois, tant par sondit feu pere comme par ledit Messire Gilles de

---

[340] This is a more blunt argument than that presented by previous polemical writers, including Jean Juvénal, who had admitted the complexity created by the past status of counts of Brittany as arrière-vassals of the French crown, paying homage to English dukes of Normandy. Moreover, Cousinot here ignores the fact that Duke Jean V had supported the treaty of Troyes and hence King Henry VI's claim to the French throne. See Paul Jeulin, 'L'hommage de la Bretagne', *Annales de Bretagne*, 41 (1934), pp. 411–418, and Jean Juvénal, II, pp. 69–71, together with p. 121, n. 333 above.

[341] N replaces 'Et oultre plus leur fut' with 'Et alors leur fut oultre ces choses'.

[342] AO add 'et tous les personnes [. . .]'; C adds 'et tous les aultrez present, et lesquelles [. . .]'.

[343] AO replace 'Duc François' with 'duc de Bretaigne'; C replaces 'Duc François pour la part du roy de France' with 'duc de Bretaigne'.

Bretaigne et autres subgetz dudit duc ou prejudice dudit Roy Charles
son souverain seigneur, que aucune chose lui en peust estre demandee
ou a ses subgetz en temps avenir prist icellui duc abolition dudit Roy
Charles comme de son souverain tant pour lui et ledit Messire Gilles,
que pour toute la duché, de toutes les choses qui par sondit feu pere
ledit Messire Gilles et ceulx de la duché[344] povoient avoir esté faittes
en ladicte matiere, qui estoit bien clere demonstrance que lui et sa
duché se reputoient subgetz du roy de France, et non point du roy
d'Angleterre en maniere quelconque.

|55r| Doncque puis qu'il estoit tout cler que ledit duc de Bretaigne
estoit homme et vassal du roy, et la duché de Bretaigne subgette a la
couronne de France, et que le duc jamais n'avoit baillié consentement
de sa part, ne le roy aussi de la sienne que icellui duc ne la duché
fussent subgetz du roy d'Angleterre, posé que cauteleusement et par
les moiens dessus touchies, les Angloiz eussent compris ledit duc de
Bretaigne de leur part es treves, aussi bien comme le roy l'avoit fait
de la sienne, si ne leur attribuoit cela aucun droit de seignourie ne
[subjection][345] sur ledit duc et duché de Bretaigne, lequel duc n'eut
oncquez la chose aggreable de sa part ne le roy de France de la sienne.

Et au regart dudit Messire Gilles de Bretaigne, il estoit aussi bien cler
qu'il n'estoit point subget audit roy d'Angleterre pour trois raisons.
L'une si estoit a cause de sa nativité car il fut nez en Bretaigne qui
estoit de l'obeissance du roy;[346] la seconde car ou temps qu'il fut pris,
il demouroit oudit duché et y estoit maryé et y faisoit sa residence;
la tierce car il tenoit et possidoit terres et seignouries oudit pays de
Bretaigne qui estoient de la foy et de l'ommage du duc en plain fief,
en arriere fief et derrenier ressort de la couronne de France. Et par
ainsi il estoit bien evident et povoit chascun clerement congnoistre
|55v| qu'il estoit homme, subget et de l'obeissance du roy. Et quant
il se fust voulu tenir homme et subget du roy d'Angleterre, il se fust
fourfait, et meismement pour le doubte qu'il avoit d'estre repris ou
temps advenir de la faveur qu'il avoit donné audit roy d'Angleterre[347]
volut il estre compris en l'abolicion dont dessus est faitte mention.

Et posé qu'il eust esté de si mauvaise et dampnable voulenté que
de vouloir descongnoistre son souverain seigneur le roy de France[348] et

---

[344] A omits 'que pour toute la duché, de toutes les choses qui par sondit feu pere ledit
Messire Gilles', perhaps because of a homoeoteleutic error, jumping from 'Gilles' to 'Gilles';
C replaces 'ledit Messire Gilles, que pour toute la duché, de toutes les choses qui par sondit
feu pere ledit Messire Gilles et ceulx de la duché' with 'sondit frere que pour ceulx de laditte
duchié de toutes les choses qui'.

[345] B offers 'succession'.

[346] A omits 'car il fut nez en Bretaigne qui estoit de l'obeissance du roy'.

[347] ACO add 'et ceulx de son party.'

[348] P omits 'seigneur le roy de France'.

son naturel seigneur le duc de Bretaigne, pour advoer ung autre prince estrangier a estre son seigneur, ennemy et adversaire de ses souverain et naturel seigneurs, si n'estoit pas en sa liberté ne en sa faculté de le faire ou prejudice de sesdits souverain et naturel seigneurs et sans leur consentement. [Ne pourtant des cas crismes ou malefices par lui commis devoient ou povoient perdre la congnoissance, ainçois leur demouroit sur luy tout droit de subjection et de seignourie comme les souverain et naturel seigneurs doivent avoir sur leurs vassaulx et subgetz, et de ses tors faiz la correction et pugnition et non a autres, chascun selon son regard].[349]

Au moien desquelles choses et par les raisons que dessus, et pluiseurs autres qui furent alleguees sont icy obmises pour cause de briefté, apparissoit clerement que ledit duc de Bretaigne et la duchié ensemble ledit Messire Gilles estoient subget du roy et non d'aultre. Et consideré ce que dit est que le roy d'Angleterre ne iceulx de son parti n'avoient aucune chose raisonnable soubz leurs couleurs dessus pre- |**56r**| tendues de prendre laditte place de Fougieres, et que c'estoit clere infraction de treve, attendu mesmement le lieu dont elle procedoit et par quel commandement, adveu et consentement elle avoit esté faitte. Et ainçoires plus grande infraction de treves en tant que ledit roy d'Angleterre et le duc de Sombreset vouloient efforcer contre la teneur desdittes treves de voloir attribier a eulx la subjection et obeissance desdits duc et duché de Bretaigne. Et par consequent estoient leurs ouvertures et remonstrances impertinentes et non recevablez, et leur justification moins raisonnable et moins vaillable, et ne se povoit soubstenir en aucune maniere.[350]

Et pour ce que ledit roy de France avoit tousjours desiré et desiroit que bonne paix et union peust estre trouvee, faitte et entrenue entre lui et ledit roy d'Angleterre son nepveu et les royames de France et d'Angleterre et autres leurs terres, pays et seignouriez, ne au deffault dudit roy de France n'avoit esté que ainsi ne fust fait, comme chascun povoit clerement veoir et congnoistre par les diligences qu'il y avoit faittez et le devoir en quoy il s'estoit mis de sa part, jasoit ce que de la part du roy d'Angleterre oultre les excés et attemptas commis et perpetrez par ceulx de son obeissance de son consentement et autrement |**56v**| ou prejudice desdittes treves, ainsi que plus adplain et plus particulierement il fut adoncquez declairié et remonstré, ledit roy d'Angleterre n'eut pas bien entrenu ses promesses et convenances faittez avec ledit roy de France, comme de passer deça la mer en personne pour le fait de la paix dont il avoit baillié ses lettres patentes

---

[349] BF omit the final sentence of this paragraph, here transcribed from K. ACO omit 'chascun selon son regard'.

[350] N omits 'en aucune maniere'.

en forme auctentique, que a icellui passage faire dedens certain jour
dequoy il ne fist riens; pareillement des fruis des eglises en chascun
parti et que durant lesdittes treves ceulx du contraire parti joyr comme
se ilz eussent esté d'une meismez obeissance, et ainsi le garda et le
fist entretenir ledit roy de France de sa part, ce que ne fut pas fait
en semblable de la part du roy d'Angleterre, combien qu'il y fust
obligé par ses lettres patentez.[351] Et avec ce que ledit roy d'Angleterre
n'eut pas gardé sa promesse[352] touchant la delivrance du Mans et des
autres places estans en son obeissance ou pays de Maynne, a quoy il
estoit obligié soubz son sing manuel et son seel de secret, confermé
depuis[353] par ses letters patentes en forme auctentique.[354] Et a ceste
cause y convint proceder en la forme et maniere qui adonc fut notoire
et manifeste a ung chascun, et que les chosez dessusdittes faittez et
commises de la part des Anglois n'estoit pas grande demonstrance
de voloir avoir paix ne bonne union avec ledit roy de France et ses
subgetz, ne a l'en- |**57r**| trenement desdittes treves.

Neantmoins icellui prince roy de France pour le bon et entier voloir
ouquel toudis il perseveroit ou fait de laditte matiere de paix, fist
dire et recongnoistre en oultre ausdits ambassadeurs que non obstant
les choses dessusdittes, en cas que lesdits roy d'Angleterre et duc de
Sombreset vouldroient faire reparer ledit cas de Fougieres et les autres
excés et attemptas commis par ceulx de leur parti ainsi que raison estoit
et que la teneur desdittes treves le portoit, il estoit content de sa part
d'entretenir lesdittes treves, exhortant lesdits roy d'Angleterre et duc
de Sombreset que ainsi le voulssissent faire, et au regart de lui il estoit
prest de sa part de faire tout ce qu'il appartendroit par raison. Et quant
aussi lesdits roy d'Angleterre et duc de Sombreset ne vouldroyent faire
faire [*sic*] ce que dit est, il estoit bien cler a congnoistre qu'ilz ne avoyent
aucune voulenté d'entendre a paix raisonnable ne d'entretenir de leur
part lesdittes treves. Et fauldroit en cellui cas qu'il eust adviz a ce qu'il
auroit a faire.

Ausquellez choses fut respondu par lesdits ambassadeurs qu'ilz
avoient dit audit roy de France ce que leur avoit esté chargié de
par leur maistre. Et qu'ilz apporteroient volen- |**57v**| tiers a leur

---

[351] For the negotiations for a personal meeting between Charles VII and Henry VI, see
Jean Juvénal, II, pp. 13–14. In 1449, the French complained that the English were not
upholding an agreement to allow clerics of each allegiance to receive revenues from their
lands controlled by the other king: Christopher T. Allmand, *Lancastrian Normandy 1415–
1450: the history of a medieval occupation* (Oxford, 1983), p. 280, together with Morice, II, col.
1430–1436, and *Chronique d'Escouchy*, III, pp. 212–216 and 218–225.

[352] The transcription in manuscript J ends here.

[353] O omits 'obligié soubz son sing manuel et son seel de secret, confermé depuis'.

[354] Henry VI agreed to cede Maine on 22 December 1445, and confirmed this promise in
a letter issued on 27 July 1447, *L&P*, II, ii, pp. [638]–[644].

dit maistre la response que ledit roy de France leur avoit faitte, ne que autre puissance n'avoient de besoingner esdittes matieres. Et a tant s'en departirent sans autre chose faire, sauf que d'un commun appointement desdits ambasseurs et des commis et deputez de par le roy, journee fut prinse pour convenir ensemble a certain jour au Port Sainct Ouyn lez Rouen, auquel lieu les ambassadeurs desdits deux parties garnis de povoir souffisant de par leurs maistres, se trouveroient pour besoingnier esdittes matieres.

En fournissant auquel appointement se comparurent de la part dudit roy de France au jour et lieu enconvenencez Messire Charles seigneur de Culant et ledit Messire Guillame Cousinot ses conseilliers, et pour la part du roy d'Angleterre se comparut messire ledit Messire Jehan l'Enfant, ung escuier Anglois nommé Sainte More, et un autre Anglois que on appelloit Maistre Jehan Cousin.[355]

Et pour ce que on doubtoit se la convention eust longuement tenu au Port Saintouyn qu'il en eu peut ensieuvir des inconveniens, attendu le feu qui estoit ja fort alumé entre lesdits parties, ledit lieu du Port Saintouyn du consentement des parties fut treschangié et transmué |58r| au lieu de l'abye de Bon Port lez le Pont de l'Arche.[356]

Auquel lieu de Bon Port les ambassadeurs et commissaires d'unepart et d'autre se comparurent pluiseurs jours et firent de grandes sommations, requestez, offres et protestations, chascun de sa part.

Et la parfin de la part du roy de France fut offert que se le plaisir du roy d'Angleterre et du duc de Sombreset estoit de rendre et restituer la ville et chasteau de Fougieres en la main et obeissance du duc de Bretaigne, subget et vassal du roy de France[357] et comme tel compris en ses treves, avecques les biens qui estoyent dedens ladicte ville et chastel ou temps de la prinse diceulx, ou la juste valleur et exstimation selon la commune renommee, qui estoit d'un million d'or ou plus, car c'estoit la plus riche ville de Bretaigne ou temps qu'elle fut prinse ainsi que chascun disoit, et se plus y avoit plus en seroit restitué, et se moins y avoit il en seroit d'autant deffalquié, le roy de France leur feroit restituer le Pont de l'Arche, Conchez et Gerberoy, ensemble le Seigneur de Fouquemberghe qui estoit prisonnier et tous les biens que selon la commune renommee l'en disoit qu'ilz avoyent

---

[355] The order of the discussion of the French and English ambassadors is reversed in manuscript N.

[356] The conference opened at Port-Saint-Ouen in late June 1449, and subsequently moved to Venable and the abbey of Bonport. Cousinot and the lord of Culant were the spokesmen on behalf of Charles VII, and the English embassy included Jean L'Enfant, Osbert Mundford, Jean Cousin, and Thomas de Sainte-Barbe, the bailly of Mantes: *Narratives*, pp. 399–514.

[357] C prefers 'du roy d'Angleterre'.

esté perdus dedens lesdittes places depuis laditte prinse de Fougieres et a l'occasion dicelle avoient esté prisez |**58v**| par aucuns eulx disans amis et serviteurs dudit duc de Bretaigne.

Et en ce cas que lesdits biens pris dedens Fougieres ne se pourroient promptement recouvrer ou la valeur et exstimation diceulx fut en oultre, offert que en baillant hostagez villes ou places ou autres choses raisonnablez a la valeur et exstimation desdits biens selon la commune renommee, jusquez a ce la certaineté en peust estre sceue, on estoit content d'entrenir les offrez dessus declaireez ensemble lesdittes treves, pour autant de temps qu'elles duroient selon leur forme et teneur.[358]

Lesquellez offres furent par lesdits ambasseurs et commissaires de la part d'Angleterre reffuseez, disans que sans le faire savoir au roy d'Angleterre ilz n'y oseroyent faire response.

Et pour ce que chascun congnoissoit l'entencion desdits Anglois lesquelz ne tendoient fors affin de dilation pour avoir armee et secours d'Angleterre et qu'ilz demouroyent tousjours saisis, faisans guerre ouverte continuellement oudit duché de Bretaigne, et que le Roy Charles estoit informé par pluiseurs tesmoings dignes de foy, prisonniers et autres,[359] qui avoyent deposé |**59r**| sollennellement en laditte matiere que les Anglois avoient disposé de prendre pluiseurs[360] bonnes villes en son obeissance, nommees et declareez es disposicions desdits tesmoingz, sur lesquellez ilz avoient entreprisez non obstant lesdittes treves, lesdis ambasseurs de la part de France dirent ausdits ambasseurs de la part d'Angleterre[361] comme comme [*sic*] representans ledit roy d'Angleterre et ledit duc de Sombreset, son lieutenant general, et desquelz ilz avoient povoir souffisant en lettres patentes pour besoingnier et appointier es offres et choses dessusdittes, ainsi que ceulx mesmes l'avoient monstré que veu les fuittez et delais que iceulx ambasseurs d'Angleterre prenoient sans voloir entendre a aucun appointement raisonnable. Lesquellez choses donnoient a entendre clerement a chascun que ceulx de la part d'Angleterre ne voloyent aucunement entretenir les treves ne trouver les moyens pource faire. Et que comme il estoit tout notoire ilz avoyent commencé la guerre de leur part et la continuoient chascun jour ouvertement ce qui ne se povoit plus dissimuler ne tollerer de la part dudit roy de France sans inconvenient irreparable pour lui et ses subgetz. Pour ces causes iceulx ambassadeurs de France pour la part du roy leur souverain seigneur

---

[358] Culant and Cousinot presented the final French offer on 4 July 1449: *Narratives*, pp. 508–512. Also see Morice, II, col. 1503.

[359] For the records of the French investigations into the events surrounding Fougères, see p. 130, n. 370.

[360] P omits 'les Anglois avoient dispose de prendre pluiseurs'.

[361] P omits 'de France dirent ausdits ambasseurs de la part', perhaps because of a homoeoteleutic error, jumping from 'de la part' to 'de la part'.

declaroyent ausdits ambassadeurs d'Angleterre³⁶² que |**59v**| que [*sic*] par le roy de France ne de sa part ne tenoit point que lesdittes treves n'estoient bien entretenues et qu'il se estoit mis en son devoir, et estoit prest de faire tout ce qu'il appartendroit par raison touchant laditte matiere.³⁶³

Mais puis que ainsi estoit que lesdits ambasseurs de la part d'Angleterre ne voloient acquiesser aux requestez ne accepter les offrez que les ambasseurs de France leur faisoient de la part de France, leur roy et souverain seigneur, iceulx ambasseurs de France protesterent du devoir en quoy le roy leur souverain seigneur se mettoient de son costé, et appelloient Dieu, le ciel et la terre a tesmoing, et aussi les notaires appostolicquez et imperialz et autres tesmoingz qui estoient la presens, que ce n'estoit point par le roy leurdit souverain seigneur que la guerre estoit commencee ne a sa deffaulte que les trevez n'estoyent entretenuez, et que tous justez et raisonnables appointemens n'estoient fais en ladicte matiere, et que de tous les inconveniens qui en pourroient ensuivir en quelconque forme ne maniere que ce fust, le roy leurdit souverain seigneur s'en tenoit honnourablement et raisonnablement deschargié.

|**60r**| Et requirent lesdits ambasseurs de France ausdits notaires appostolicques et imperialz lettres et instrumens de toutes les choses dessusdittes, lesquellez ilz leurs ottroierent. En iceulx instrumens, qui s'appellent le deslyen des treves, sont compris toutes les comparitions et assembleez desdits ambasseurs³⁶⁴ d'unepart et d'autre depuis qu'ilz vindrent au Port Sainctouyn jusquez a la fin des matieres. Et aussi toutes les sommations, requestez, responsez, offres et protestations d'unepart et d'autre³⁶⁵ en forme solennelle [lesquelz sont en nature pour en faire foy quant besoing sera].³⁶⁶

Et aprés ces choses ainsi faittez et lesdits ambasseurs de France retournez devers ledit Roy Charles et leur relation oyé, volut et ordonna ledit seigneur que la chose fust fort debatue en son conseil

---

³⁶² A omits 'pour la part du roy leur souverain seigneur'. O replaces 'sans inconvenient irreparable pour lui et ses subgetz [. . .] declaroyent ausdits ambassadeurs d'Angleterre' with 'desquelz les embaxadeurs declarerent a iceulx d'Angleterre'.

³⁶³ N adds 'cy dessus declairee'; P omits 'et qu'il se estoit mis en son devoir, et estoit prest de faire tout ce qu'il appartendroit par raison touchant ladicte matiere'.

³⁶⁴ H omits 'de toutes les choses dessusdittes, lesquellez ilz leurs ottroierent. En iceulx instrumens', perhaps because of a homoeoteleutic error, jumping from 'instrumens' to 'instrumens'; P omits 'toutes les comparitions et assembleez desdits ambasseurs'.

³⁶⁵ A omits 'depuis qu'ilz vindrent au Port Sainctouyn jusquez a la fin des matieres. Et aussi toutes les sommations, requestez, responsez, offres et protestations d'unepart et d'autre' perhaps because of a homoeoteleutic error, jumping from 'd'autre' to 'd'autre'.

³⁶⁶ BFH omit 'lesquelz sont en nature pour en faire foy quant besoing sera', here transcribed from manuscript K. For the dossier of the conferences of June and July 1449, see *Narratives*, pp. 377–514.

pour savoir s'il estoit souffisamment deslyé des lyen des treves, et se justement et licitement sans charge d'honneur et de conscience il povoit faire guerre contre les Anglois. Et en fut tenu ung conseil, premierent a Vendosme, secondement aux Roches Trenchelyon, et tiercement a Evreux ou a Louviers,[367] et volut le roy que chascun franchement en deist son oppinion, et en tous lesdits trois conseilz la ou il y avoit beaucop de gens notablez, tant de l'espirituel que du temporel, sambla a tous et furent d'oppinion que ledit seigneur estoit souffisamment deslyé |**6ov**| du lyen de treves et que justement et licitement, raisonnablement il povoit faire guerre aux Anglois non obstant que le temps contenu en icelles ne fust ainçoires expiré.[368]

Et oultre plus consideré le devoir en quoy il s'estoit de sa part, et le reffus et denee de droit qui avoyent esté fais de la part des Anglois, qui ne sembloit pas a ceulx qui estoient la presens, que ledit Roy Charles, lequel estoit tenus de faire raison et justice a ses subgetz et les garder d'oppressions indeuez quant aucuns les leur font, ainsi que tous roys raisonnablement doivent et sont tenus de faire, deust ne peust raisonnablement[369] et sans charge d'honneur et de conscience dissimuler lesdittes matieres, et qu'il ne s'exploitast comme prince vertueux doit faire a la deffense de ses subgetz l'expulsion de ses ennemis et a la conservation de la chose publicque de son royaume, ainsi que jure et promis l'avoit a son sacré. Desquellez choses ledit seigneur demanda lors lettres pour son honneur et sa descharge ou temps avenir, laquelle semblablement est en matiere comme dessus.

Pareillement aussi y'a pluiseurs procés, informations, depositions et tesmoingz et autres evidences notables en forme deue et |**6ir**| auctentique touchant la prise dudit Fougieres et dont elle proceda et le confort, conseil et le consentement que de la part du roy d'Angleterre du duc de Suffolc, du duc de Sombreset et des autres de leur parti furent donnez audit Messire François de Suryenne, la depposition aussi dudit Messire François et pluiseurs autres choses qui bien servent a la justification du fait du roy touchant icelle matiere.[370]

---

[367] ACO omit 'a Evreux ou'.

[368] The first assembly was held at the chateau of Roches-Tranchelion, near to Chinon, on 17 July 1449. The second took place at the same location on 31 July. See Beaucourt, IV, pp. 330–332.

[369] O omits 'doivent et sont tenus de faire, deust ne peust raisonnablement'.

[370] The record of the official inquiry into the attack on Fougères appears in Thomas Basin, *Histoire des règnes de Charles VII et de Louis XI*, ed. Jules Quicherat (4 vols, Paris, 1855–1859), IV, pp. 290–347. In addition, thirteen documents relating to François de Surienne, including his deposition, appear in BNF MS français 4054, fos 111r–131r, a collection that includes a number of materials directly associated with Guillaume Cousinot. This dossier also includes the verbal process of the meeting on 31 July and a statement of the English breaches of the truce, presented at the same time: *ibid.*, fos 153r–157r and 86r–91v.

Lesquellez monstrent bien clerement la conspiration de long temps faitte touchant ladicte prise de Fougieres et comme elle procedoit du sceu et consentement du roy d'Angleterre et de ceulx de son conseil, et que aprés icelle prinse, ilz conforterent et ayderent ceulx qui lavoyent faitte en ce qu'il leur fut possible.

Ainsi appert par les choses dessusdittes que les Anglois n'ont aucune juste ne raisonnable cause de faire complainte, querelle ne doleance de la roupture desdittes treves, pour donner ne imputer soubz ceste couleur aucune charge ou blasme audit Roy Charles le VIIe que Dieu pardoinst, ne que ladicte roupture soit commencié ne procedee de sa part en aucune maniere, ainçois vint, proceda et commença [de la] part les Anglois de la certaine science du roy d'Angleterre et de ceulx de son conseil, et de ceulx qui avoyent la charge et le gouvernement de par lui des pays de deça la mer |**61v**| estans en son obeissance, sans que jamais iceulx Anglois en voulsissent aucune reparation ne eulx mettre en leur devoir en ceste partie en maniere quelconquez.

Et est venu le tort de la part desdits Anglois et par eulx tousjours continué, et a la fin par le vray jugement de Dieu, comme raison estoit, leur est ledit tort demouré. Et ne fault faire doubte que en tous d'honneur soit en la presence du pape, du concille general et de tous les princes crestiens, la querelle du roy de France en ceste partie ne soit bien et deuement fondee. Et quant besoing sera, elle sera par tout si bien et si clerement deffendue et justifiee que chascun pourra evidamment congnoistre que les Anglois n'ont cause raisonnable d'eulx doloir de leur part de la roupture desdittes treves en imposant audit Roy Charles que la faute ait procede ou soit venue de sa part, et oultre que le roy de France qui a present est, a bon et juste tiltre, ne tiengne et posside ce que lesdiz Anglois ont perdu et qu'ilz tenoyent ou royaume de France ou temps desdittes treves.[371]

Mais pour ce que lesdits Anglois dient communement et publicquement que |**62r**| soubz confiance desdittes treves ilz ont perdu Normandie et Guienne, ce que autrement ilz n'eussent point fait car ilz y essent bien donné provision et remede &c, il fault ainçoires voir pour respondre a ceste raison.

Cellui qui parle demanderoit volentiers en quel temps commença la guerre ouverte de la part du roy de France contre les Anglois,[372] et il sera trouvé que ce fut le XIXe jour du mois d'aoust l'an mil CCCCXLIX, lequel jour la ville de Vernueil fut prinse.[373] Et atendy

---

[371] C omits 'et qu'ilz tenoyent ou royaume de France'.

[372] C replaces 'de la part du roy de France contre les Anglois' with 'desdits Anglois contre le roy de France'.

[373] On 19 July 1449, Robert de Floques and Pierre de Brézé led the forces that laid siege to Verneuil, defended by Jean de Surienne and Thommassin Duquesne, who had just fled from

ledit Roy Charles plus de V mois aprés la prise de Fougieres, qui fut ou mois de mars precedent,[374] pour savoir se les Anglois se vouldroient mettre en aucun devoir touchant la reparation dudit cas, avant qu'il leur voulssist faire guerre ouverte. Et depuis icellui temps posé que les trevez n'eussent point esté rompuez, si n'eussent elles duré que jusquez ou mois d'avril ensuivant.[375]

Demande maintenant ledit qui parle quant les Angloiz congneurent que le temps desdittes treves estoit expiré, et que a ceste cause ilz n'avoyent plus de seureté a cause desdittez treves, quel remede ne qu'elle provision donnerent ilz depuis ledit temps pour garder Normandie et Guienne, car ainçoires tenoyent |**62v**| ilz en Normandie les batailles de Caen et Contentin, aumoins les principales places, et si avoient desja eu advis de VII mois de l'ouverture de la guerre contre eulx, et si y avoit plus d'un an et demy que la conspiration de prendre laditte ville de Fougieres avoit esté par eulx faitte et toutesfois chascun a congneu le remede et la provision qu'ilz y ont mis.

Et est assavoir que depuis ledit premier jour d'april ilz prindrent la bataille de Formigny et tout ce qu'ilz tenoient en la basse Normandie, pareillement tout ce qu'ilz tenoient en Guienne et n'y seurent oncquez mettre ne donner remede. Parquoy appert clerement que ce ne sont que couleurs et allegations frivolez, *quare* &c.[376]

Et quant orez seroit ainsi qu'il y auroit aucune apparence de querelle ou complainte en ceste partie contre le Roy Charles, que Dieu pardonist, ou ceulx qui le representent, ce que non, si n'appartient point laditte querelle au Roy Edouart le IIIIe qui de present regne en Angleterre, car le treve ne fut oncquez prise entre le Roy Charles le VIIe et le duc d'Yorc, pere dicellui Edouart. Ainçois fut prise entre ledit Roy Charles et le Roy Henry son nepveu, pour icellui Roy Henry[377] et ses royaumes d'Angleterre, terres et seignouriez qu'il avoit et tenoit tant deça que dela la mer.

|**63r**| S'il est doncquez ainsi que maintient ledit Roy Edouart, c'estassavoir que le royame d'Angletere n'appartient point au Roy Henry ne les duches de Normandie et de Guyenne, mais lui appartiennent, et a ceste cause en fait demande et que ledit Roy Charles n'eut aucunes treves audit duc d'Yorc ne audit Roy Edouart qui est au jour d'huy, mais seulement au Roy Henry, il est tout cler

---

Fougères. The French forces entered the town on 19 August and the remaining defenders in the Grey Tower capitulated three days later. Cousinot may have been present at this action. See p. 13, n. 55 above.

[374] O omits 'aprés la prise de Fougieres, qui fut ou mois de mars precedent'.

[375] See p. 117, n. 313 above.

[376] The battle of Formigny, north-west of Bayeux, took place on 15 April 1450.

[377] C replaces 'ledit Roy Charles et le Roy Henry son nepveu, pour icellui Roy Henry' with 'le Roy Henri son nepveu'; P omits 'son nepveu, pour icellui Roy Henry'.

qu'il n'y a point de infraction de treve de la part dudit Roy Charles en prenant les duches de Normandie et de Guienne et tout ce que les Anglois tenoient deça la mer, car esdittes treves il n'y a compris que les terres seignouries et subgetz dudit Roy Henry. Puis doncques que Normandie et Guienne n'estoyent point au Roy Henry ainsi que pretend le Roy Edouart, il appert clerement qu'ilz n'estoient point comprisez es trevez et par consequent n'y a point de infraction de treve.[378]

Et fault dire de deux choses: l'une que se aucun droit devoit appartenir aux Anglois ce que non es duches de Normandie et Guienne et que ledit droit competaist et appartenist audit Roy Edouart comme il pretend, et non point au Roy Henry, ledit Roy Edouart ne puet ne lui loist raisonnablement ne n'a aucune action pour riens y demander par infraction de trevez. Car oncquez ledit Roy Charles n'eut treves ne |**63v**| a lui ne a son pere. Et se au contraire ledit droit devoit appartenir audit Roy Henry, ledit Roy Edouart n'est pas cappable pour en faire poursieute [ainçois en appartendroit la poursieute][379] audit Roy Henry ou a son filz le prince, lesquelz quant ils la vouldront faire, les responses sont si cleres et si evidentez en laditte matiere, et fondeez en si bonne raison, que chascun pourra clerement congnoistre qu'ilz n'ont cause ne occasion raisonnable d'aucune chose en demander.

Cy doncquez faisant conclusion sur les trois poins principaulx de la matiere subgette dont a present est question et sur laquelle ce present traittié est fait et composé, c'est assavoir du droit de la couronne et totalité du royaume de France, et des responsez qui y sont; le second de terres et seignouryes particulieres que les Anglois pretendent ou royaume de France, et des responsez qui y sont;[380] et le tiers de la complainte que les Anglois font de la roupture des trevez ainsi que dessus est declairié, et des responses que licitement et raisonnablement on y puet faire. Appert clerement par les moyens dessus touchiez es trois parties de ceditte traittié que les Anglois, en chascun des poins dont dessus est faitte mention, sont incappablez d'aucune chose y demander, requerir ne reclamer et |**64r**| que atort sans cause et contre tout droit et raison, ilz font lesdittes querellez, demandez et reclaims, et n'y sont a recepvoir en aucune maniere.

[378] H omits 'au Roy Henry ainsi que pretend le Roy Edouart, il appert clerement qu'ilz n'estoient point', perhaps because of a homoeoteleutic error, jumping from 'point' to 'point'.

[379] BNOP omit 'ainçois en appartendroit la poursieute', here transcribed from K.

[380] CO omit 'le second de terres et seignouryes particulieres que les Anglois pretendent ou royaume de France, et des responsez qui y sont', perhaps because of a homoeoteleutic error, jumping from 'y sont' to 'y sont'; A replaces 'que les Anglois pretendent ou royaume de France, et des responsez qui y sont' with 'particulieres comme Guyenne, Normandie et autres ou ilz pretendent droit de honeure'.

Et au contraire, parce que dit est dessus, appert clerement que le roy de France, qui a present est, a juste et bon droit et tiltre raisonnable et bien fondé a la couronne de France et a la totalité du royaume, pareillement aux singulieres terres et seignouries dudit royaume[381] que les Anglois par aucun temps y ont tenues, possideez et occuppeez, et que pour cause de l'infraction des treves qui furent entre le Roy Charles son pere et le Roy Henry d'Engleterre, laquelle infraction vint et proceda de la part des Anglois, et non pas de celle dudit Roy Charles, ainsi que plusadplain a esté dessus declarié, n'en sont le roy de France qui a present est, ne ses successeurs, tenus en aucune maniere, ne par raison n'en pevent estre blasmez, chargiez ne reprochiez, et que la querelle dudit roy de France al'encontre desdits Anglois es matieres dessusdittes est bonne, juste, sainte, canonicque et raisonnable et n'est nul qui selon raison y doyve faire aucune difficulté, et comme ses predecesseurs l'ont bien et justement conduite jusquez icy, lui et ses successeurs le feront pareillement jusquez a la fin.

Amen.[382]

---

[381] C omits 'pareillement aux singulieres terres et seignouries dudit royaume', perhaps because of a homoeoteleutic error, jumping from 'royaume' to 'royaume'.

[382] CHNOPQ omit 'Amen'. C gives 'Explicit. Fut l'an de grasse mil IIII^C LXXIe au mois de juillet XVII'; H prefers 'Fin de la tierce et derniere partie de ce present traitié'; L gives 'Explicit le traicté du droit que les Englois pretendent ou royaume de France en aucunes terres et seignouries & amen'; N offers 'Explicit le debat de France et d'Angleterre'; O offers 'Explicit le traictié d'entre les roys de France et d'Angleterre comme les filles ne pevent succeder a la couronne de France' together with a note in a similar hand, 'Ce livre est a Jehan Budé conseillier du roy. Fait XXIe Decembre, MCCCIIII^{XX} VI. Budé'.

A DECLARACION OF THE TREWE
AND DEWE TITLE OF HENRY VIII

|**6r**| A declaracion of the trewe and dewe title of the right high excellent and most vertuous, my moost dredde soverayn lord Henry, by the grace of God king of Englond and of Ffraunce and lord of Irelond,[1] to the corones of Ffraunce and of Navarre, and to the duchies of Normandie and of Guyan and Gascoyn, and to the counties and cuntries of Angeo, Mayne and of Torayn, Poytow, Ponthieu, Champayn and of the Provynce, with the superiorite and dominion of Bretayn by dewe succession of heritage. And answeryng to the false objections, surmises and imaginacions made and put in prynte by the Ffrenshmen against the said title grounded upon a surmitted lawe called Lawe Salique.

|**6v**| Ffor asmoche as many persones speke upon and of the title of enheritaunce of the corone and reame of Ffraunce and of the duchies of Normandie and Guyan and of other particuler hereditamentes of the king of Englond in those parties which have not redde or knowen the trewe groundes of the same. And the Ffrenshmen of late and daily have, doo practique and put in printe dampnable matier and especially of late have compiled a boke put in printe conteynyng many objections and surmyses imagined and dampnably fayned in favour of the partie of the Valoys usurpers of the corone of Ffraunce, divided by matier into III principall partes. Wherof the first part treatith matier to extinctissh and adnichillat the title of the king of Englond to the corone and reame of Ffraunce. And the secund treatith in likewise by false imaginacions to extinct and adnichillat the title also of the kinges of Englond to the duchies of Normandie and Guyan and to other dominions of ther hereditamentes in the parties of beyond the see. And the third part treatith in falsely excusing of the Frenshmen of the breche & rumpure of the trews taken betwen King Henry the VIth and Charles the VIIth in the yere MIIII[C] XLIIII and at severall tymes contynewed and proroged unto the yere MIIII[C] XLIX |**7r**| and objecting the same breche to be on the part of the Englisshmen. I have put me to serche and see the croniques and histories of diverse famous

---

[1] For Henry VIII's royal title, see Clifford S.L. Davies, '"Roy de France et roy d'Angleterre": the English claims to France, 1453–1558', *Publications du Centre Européen d'Etudes Bourguignonnes (XIVe–XVIe siècle)*, 35 (1995), p. 125.

historiens aswel of Ffrenshmen as of other which make mencion of the accidentes and dedes of suche cases and grounding my matier of the same have framed this werke to answer and impugne the said contentes of the said printed boke and the objections and surmyses in the same, and have divided my said werke into certayn chapitres heraftir by nombres noted.

|7v| First of the issue and descent of Phelip le Beale somtyme king of Ffraunce and of Navarre, and of his III sones Loys [Hutin],[2] Phelip le Long and Charles le Beale also successively kinges of Ffraunce and of Navarre. And hough Phelip de Valoys happened to the corone of Ffraunce. And of the supposed Lawe Salique. And hough the reame of Navarre and the countie of Champaine happened to the said Phelip le Beale. *Capitulum primum.*

Item of the discent of kinges of the Ffrenshmen from Pharamont ther first king. And hough that Pepyn ffather of the Imperor Charles le Graunt and also Hugh Capet severally succeded to be kinges of Ffraunce by female blode. *Capitulum secundem.*

Item of the inconvenientes which might ensewe if the corone of Ffraunce shuld descende to female blode. *Capitulum III.*

Item of the supposed homage to be doon by King Edward the III^{de} to Phelip de Valois. *Capitulum IIII.*

Item hough King Edward the III^{de} first claymed the corone and reame of Ffraunce. And of his alliance with Almaynes and Fflemynges. And of the acquitaunce made by King Edward the III^{de} to the Fflemynges as king of Ffraunce. And of the condicions of Englisshmen and of the Frensshmen. *Capitulum V.*

|8r| *Item* of the issue of King Edward the III^{de} and of the mariage of his V sones. And of thissue of King Henry the Thridde. *Capitulum VI.*

Item of the objection against the title of King Edward the Fourth for the corone of Ffraunce. And of the mariage of Duc Leonel to the countes of Ulster with other matiers. And hough King Phelip de Valoys was but of the half blode to King Charles le Beale wherfor he might not be his successor. *Capitulum VII.*

Item of the title of King Henry the VI for the corone of Ffraunce. And of the treatie made betwix King Henry the Fift and Charles the VI. *Capitulum VIII.*

Item of the corone and reame of Navarre and of the countie of Champaine and of the cuntre of Province which the kinges of Ffraunce opteyned by succession of female blode and by like blode descended to King Edward the III^{de}. *Capitulum IX.*

---

[2] The scribe consistently gives the name as 'Louis Lutin' but, to avoid confusion, this will be corrected to 'Hutin'.

Item of the issue of William Conquerror and of the succession of the duche of Normandie. And of Ffulco king of Jerusalem and of Geffrey his brother erle of Angeo which espoused the doughtir of King Henry Beauclerk. And of King Henry the Secund and of thenheritaunce of Guyan by his wief. *Capitulum X.*

|**8v**| *Item* of King Richard Coer de Leon, and of King John his brother and of the voiage of King Richard to the Holy Lond. And of the homage of Bretayn, and of the deth of Arthur of Bretayne. And of the losse of Normandie by falshode of Frenshmen. *Capitulum XI.*

Item of the cuntre of Vulguissyn which is supposed King Henry the Secund shuld transporte to the king of Ffraunce. *Capitulum XII.*

Item of appointementes supposed to be had betwix Saint Loys and King Henry the III^{de} by which is alledged King Henry the III^{de} shuld accept of the gift of Saint Loys the duche of Guyan and other londes, for which he shuld transport the duche of Normandie and other to Saint Loys. And of the oppression of the than kinges of Ffraunce. *Capitulum XIII.*

Item of the cuntre of Xantonge, of Charente, Agen, Perregourt, Quercy, Rouergue and Lymoges. And of the descent of the dukes of Guyan. *Capitulum XIIII.*

Item of Rollo first duke of Normandie and of his II wiefes and of William Longespee his sone. *Capitulum XV.*

Item of Richard Saunz Paoure III^{de} duc of Normandie and of thoppression doon to him by the king of Ffraunce in his tender age. *Capitulum XVI.*

Item of William Conquerror and of testament of his father. And of debate betwix the king of Ffraunce & hym. *Capitulum XVII.*

|**9r**| *Item* of the cause why Henry Beauclerk was preferred to the corone of Englond befor his elder brother Duc Robert of Normandie. And of the succession of the same Henry Beauclerk to the said duche of Normandie. *Capitulum XVIII.*

Item of the title and discent of Angeo, Mayne and Torayn and hough they joyned by succession of heritage. *Capitulum XIX.*

Item of devorce betwix Loys somtyme king of Ffraunce and of Alianore his wief heriteresse of Guyan and Gascoyn and of Poytow. And of the espousels betwix King Henry the Secund and the said Alianore. *Capitulum XX.*

Item of the appertenauntes to the duche of Guyan and of the first mariage of King Edward the First to the doughtir of Castille heritiresse of Ponthieu and other londes. And of his secund mariage to Margaret doughtir of Ffraunce. And of the mariage of King Edward the Secund of Carnarvan to Quene Isabel aftir heritiresse of Ffraunce and of thoppressions of the kinges of Ffraunce and of diverse other thynges. *Capitulum XXI.*

Item of the treatie of Bretigny and of the breche and rumpure therof by the Ffrensshmen. *Capitulum XXII.*

Item of the werres of King Henry the V and King Henry the VI in Ffraunce. *Capitulum XXIII.*

Item of a supposed treatie betwix King Henry the III^de and King Loys father of Saint Loys. |9v| And of the werres of the same Loys in Englond with the rebellion of the barones of Englond to have made the same Loys king of Englond. And of his disconfiture and of his treatie to depart owt of Englond. And of his promyses upon the same treatie. And of the occasion of the entirdight of Englond with dyverse other matiers. *Capitulum XXIIII.*

Item of the breche and rumpure of the trews made betwix King Henry the VI and Charles the VIIth the yere MIIII^C XLIIII and proroged by tymes unto the yere MIIII^C XLIX. And thoccasions of the same. *Capitulum XXV.*

|11r| *Capitulum primum*[3]

Ffirst where in the former part of the said imaginacions of the Ffrenchmen making mencion of the corone and the right which that the king of Englond pretendith to the totalite of the reame of Ffraunce is surmitted that King Phelip le Beale somtyme king of Ffraunce & of Navarre shuld have had III sones, that is to saye Loys Hutyne, Phelip le Long & Charles le Beale, and also III doughtres of whom thelder named Margaret shuld have bene maried to Ffernand elder sone of Sance king of Castille, the secund Isabel wief of King Edward the Secund of which mariage issued King Edward the Thridde that aftir quarelled the reame of Ffraunce, and the thridde doughtir shuld be named Kateryne which died unmaried. And that the said Loys Hutyne shuld be aftir his father king, and had a sone named John which decessed in goyng towardes Reims there to have ben sacred king, and shuld have had a doughtir which shuld have ben maried to the counte d'Evreulx. And for that the same King Loys Hutyne and John his sone hadde none issue male, Phelip le Long brother to the same Loys shuld have succeded to the reames of Ffraunce and Navarre, which semblably shuld have had oon doughtir which shuld have ben maried to the erle of Arthois. And by like meane aftir the deth of the same Phelip, Charles le Beale his brother shuld have opteyned the succession of the reames of Ffraunce and Navarre. And that Charles de Valoys brother to

---

[3] Folio 10 is blank. The chapter headings appear in the left-hand margin. This chapter summarizes and responds to *Pour ce que plusieurs*, pp. 55–62 above, and redrafts material found in T, fos 5r–6v.

the aforenamed Phelip le Beale had issue II sones, that is to saye Phelip which aftir was king |11v| and Charles counte de Alencon which died at Crecy. And that so shuld have happened that the said Charles le Beale died without havyng eny children, but that he shuld have left his wief great of a doughtir which shuld have to name Blanche which shuld aftir have ben maried to Phelip duc of Orleaunce brother to King John. And that by occasion of defalt of havyng issue male shuld have meved great trouble and questions to the reame of Ffraunce aswel duryng the grossure of Quene Jahane of Burgoyne wedow of the said Charles le Beale for to have knowen who shuld have had the governaunce of the ventre as the next heir, as aftir whan the doughtir shuld have ben borne to have knowen to whom the reame ought to have apperteyned. And that the thre Estates General of the reame shuld have assembled to gether with the notable clerkes, doctoures and other persones of estate expert in knowlege of such matieres. To which Estates shuld have presented hymself Phelip de Valois sone and heritier of Charles counte de Valois brother of the said King Phelip le Beale. The which Phelip as counte de Valois and as cosine germain in ligne masculine of the said III kinges brothern, Loys Hutin, Phelip le Long and Charles le Beale, for that they had noon issue male nor other heritieres which shuld have descended in ligne masculine so nere as he, sayeng and meyntenyng the reame and corone to apperteyne to hym. And that on the other part shuld have appered to the said III Estates Edward the Thrid king of Englond, sone of Edward the Secund otherwise called Carnarvan and of Quene Isabel suster of the said III kinges brothern. Which Edward pretended to the |12r| contrarie, for that he shuld saye that he was male of the III kinges abovesaid, for he was ther nevew, sone of ther suster germain Dame Isabel as is aforesaid, and by consequent most next of those III kinges, and for that cause meyntened that the said reame and corone shuld apperteyn to hym.

And that for the justificacion of the right in that partie many great reasons shuld have ben there allegged of thoon partie and thother, aswel of the lawe and custume of Ffraunce in soche cases, as of the usages which shuld have bene kept whan soche case shuld have fortuned. Likewise also of the ordenance of the Lawe Salique which shuld have commencement in the XIIth yere of the regne of King Pharamont first king of Ffraunce soche tyme as the Frensshmen inhabited them upon the river of Rine.

And that, for that the said Lawe Salique shuld be the veray lawe of the Ffrensshmen,[4] every of the said parties and also their

---

[4] The English author omits the brief discussion of the relevance of the *Libri feudorum* and Roman law to the debate over the French royal succession (which did appear in

assistens shuld have grounded them upon the same Lawe Salique principaly, and also the said parties shuld have moche rested upon the usage kept whan soche case shuld have happened. And upon those II poyntes the said Phelip de Valoys shuld saye in somoche as towchith the Lawe Salique, titulo *De aloede*, LXII *capitulo* which shuld speke these woordes, *Nulla porcio hereditatis de terra saliqua mulieri veniat, set ad virilem sexum tota hereditas perveniat*, that by those woordes he shuld pretend the corone & reame of Ffraunce to aperteyne to hym.[5]

And for that which shuld towche the usage kept in soche case the said Phelip de Valoys shuld saye that it shuld |**12v**| be clere for his partie, for by that that King Loys Hutin and John his sone had noon issue male, the succession cam to Phelip le Long brother of the same Loys Hutin, and in likewise from Phelip le Long to Charles le Beale. And that if it shuld have ben so that doughtres shuld have succeeded to the reame and corone, the doughtir of Loys Hutin shuld have ben preferred afore Phelip le Long, Charles le Beale and the said King Edward. Concludyng that by the said II meanes without dificultie the reame and corone shuld apperteyne to the said Phelip de Valoys.

And that also is there alledged that the said King Edward on his partie shuld confesse to be trew that doughtres shuld not succede to the corone of Ffraunce, and if it shuld be saide that he descended of a doughtir, that shuld not serve to the case. Ffor the Lawe Salique wherby it shuld owe to descende to the heires males spekith none otherwise but onely the next heir male shuld come to the succession, and that he was next heir male *quare* &c. And that towching the usage, the said King Edward shuld saye that which is aledged of the said III kinges shuld mak nothyng to the matier, for that it shuld be trew that the doughtres shuld not succede to the corone of Ffraunce, and for that cause the succession was come to the said brothern to the oon aftir the other, for that at the deth of every of them ther doughtres shuld have no children male. But hymself shuld be male, and although his mother might not succede to the corone, yet hymself as male next to the said King Charles le Beale at the tyme of his deth shuld saie that the reame and |**13r**| corone shuld apperteyne to him.

T, fo. 5v) and also abbreviates the history of the Salic Law, omitting any mention of the first 'dictateurs' and its subsequent development under Charlemagne, as recounted in *Pour ce que plusieurs*, pp. 58–59 above.

[5] The English author retains Cousinot's insertion of the words '*terra saliqua*' into the citation of the Salic Law, but ignores the extensive Latin glosses and commentaries that argued that the Salic lands were synonymous with the kingdom of France: pp. 59–60 above, together with p. 145 below.

And that the said Phelip de Valoys for his part replieng amonges other argumentes shuld conclude that if the case were suche that if the sone of a doughtir might succede to the corone of Ffraunce, than shuld it have ben soo that the doughtir of the said Loys Hutin at the deth of the said Charles le Beale shuld have had a sone which aftir was king of Navarre, which shuld have ben preferred afore the said King Edward.[6] And in likewise, Margaret which is supposed to be the elder doughtir of the said Phelip le Beale, wief of Fferdinand the elder sone of the king of Spaine, shuld have ben preferred afore the said Isabel, which shuld have ben but the secund doughtir of the said Phelip le Beale.

Trew it is that the said Phelip le Beale had issue the said III sones, Loys Hutin, Phelip le Long and Charles le Beale, all III kinges of Ffraunce and of Navarre by trew succession of enheritaunce, thoon as next heir to thother therof.[7] But for trouth, the same Phelip le Beale besides oon doughtir which died infant, had but oon doughtir, the said Isabel, maried to the said Edward the Secund otherwise called of Carnarvan, king of Englond, of which mariage descended |**13v**| the said King Edward the III^de, and had no suche doughtir named Margaret or other maryed to the said Fferdynand sone of Spayne as is surmytted and that is sufficiently declared in diverse histories.[8]

And the said Loys Hutin had no soche doughtir in lauful mariage maried to the countie d'Evreulx nor eny other, nor eny other infant or issue but oonly the afore rehersed John which was borne soone aftir the dethe of his father and died the XV day of his age.[9]

Ffor of trouth the said Loys Hutin beyng king of Navarre by the transport and in the lief of his father King Phelip le Beale had to his wief Margaret thelder doughtir of [. . .] duke of Burgoyn, which

[6] This brief sentence summarizes the material from pp. 61–62 above, omitting 'other argumentes' against cognate succession, including legal authorities and maxims such as *Digest*, 50.17.54 and 8.3.7.1.

[7] Marginal note: 'Les cronikes de l'Evesque de Burges translates de Latin in Frauncois par Frere Jehan Golein des Carmes, maister in theologie, rubriche de Philip le Quinte roy de Ffraunce [. . .] ffo CCCLXIIII'.

[8] Marginal note: 'Et ce Ffernand de Castille espousa Constance fille de Denis roy de Portyugale, *eadem historia*, rubrico de Ffernand roy de Castille et rubrico de Denis roy de Portugale'. The three daughters of Philippe IV were Marguerite (d. 1300), Blanche (d. 1294), and Isabella (d. 1358). The proposed marriage between Marguerite and Fernando IV of Castile was prevented by her death.

[9] Marginal note: '*eadem historia* rubric de maister cesty Loys'. In reality, Louis X did have a daughter named Jeanne who married Philippe, count of Evreux, though the Tudor writer's insistence on this point may be due to the fact that she was not mentioned in *Les Chroniques d'Espagne ou de Burgos*, II, c. 787 (BL MS Royal 1 E vi, fo. 457r). See p. 56, n. 25 above.

Margaret was detect of encest and adulterie.[10] Ffor which and for lyke encest and adulterie by the wief of the aforenamed Charles countie de Valoys and mother to the said Phelip de Valoys usurpor of the corone of Ffraunce in the yere of our lord MCCCXIIII, by jugement of the said King Phelip le Beale and decree of his counseill, Sir Phelip de Alney and Sir Walter de Alney, knightes brothern germaines, were excoriated quik, and so excoriated, decapited or beheded, dismembred and aftir brent to asshes, and the said ladyes comytted to perpetuel prison, where they contenewed in myserie to the dethe.[11] And the same Loys Hutin aftir the deth of the said Phelip le Beale his father was coroned king of Ffraunce in the yere MCCCXV, and aftir that beyng devorsed by the lawes of the chirche from the said Margaret his wief, he espoused Clemence doughtir of the king of Hungarie, and dyed the Vth day of Junn in the yere MCCCXVI, leving the same Clemens his wief grosse with childe of a |14r| sone the said John, which as is declared afore dyed the XV day of his age. Which proveth wele that the said Loys Hutin had no soche doughtir in lauful mariage maried to the counte d'Evreulx as is surmytted or eny other.

And the said Phelip le Long brother to the same Loys Hutin and secund sone of the said Phelip le Beale succeded to the same Loys Hutin and John his sone to the corounes of Ffraunce and of Navarre, and also to the countie of Champayne, by due course of enheritaunce. Which he shuld not have done, and in especial to the reame of Navarre and the counte of Champayne, if the same Loys Hutin had had eny doughtir.[12] And in likewise the said Charles le Beale, brother of the said Phelip le Long and yongest sone of the said King Phelip le Beale, succeded the said Phelip le Long to the said corounes and reames of Ffraunce and of Navarre and to the countie of Champaine by due course of enheritunce. Which he shuld nor ought to have done and in especial to the said corone and reame of Navarre and countie of Champayne if the said Loys Hutin or Phelip le Long had had eny doughtir as is surmytted. Ffor it may not truly be denyed

---

[10] Marginal note: '*inter historias voc^a fflores historiarum apud Saint Edmundes Bury de anno domini MCCCXIIII*'. In 1284, Philippe IV married Jeanne, heiress to the kingdom of Navarre and the county of Champagne, and their eldest son, Louis, inherited these lands when she died in 1305. Later that year, Louis married Marguerite, daughter of Robert II, duke of Burgundy. In April 1314, Margurite and her cousin Blanche of Artois, wife of Louis's brother Charles, were accused of being the lovers of Philippe and Gautier d'Aunay.

[11] Marginal note: '*cronica episcopi inter historias voc^a fflores historiarum*'. None of the three wives of Charles of Valois was implicated in the adultery scandal. Moreover, Philippe VI was the son of Charles's first wife, Marguerite of Sicily, who had died in 1297, seventeen years before the events in question. Nevertheless, this claim did appear in the *Flores historiarum*, III, p. 167.

[12] In fact, the kingdom of Navarre did pass to Jeanne and her husband Philippe, count of Evreux, in 1328, though Philippe VI retained the counties of Champagne and Brie which were incorporated into the royal domain in 1361.

that the corone and reame of Navarre with the counte of Champaine descended from Henry somtyme king of Navarre to his oonly doughtir and heir Jahane, wief of the said King Phelip le Beal and mother of the said Loys Hutin, Phelip le Long, Charles le Beale and of Isabel mother of the said King Edward the III^{de}, and in the right of the same Jahane the said King Phelip |14v| le Beale possessed the coroune and reame of Navarre and the counte of Champaine. And the said Loys Hutin, Phelip le Long and Charles le Beale successyvely possessed and enherited aswel the corone & reame of Navarre and the countie of Champaine by due succession of enheritaunce descended from ther said mother as the corone and reame of Ffraunce by lyk succession descended from their said father.

The said Phelip le Long espoused Jahane an other doughtir of the said [. . .] duke of Burgoyn and died without issue.[13] And the said Charles le Beale had III wyefes wherof the former was named Blanche doughtir of the erle of Arthois and for that she kept full ill hir mariage, she was also imprisoned to the deth. And aftir devorce sued the same Charles le Beale secundly espoused [. . .] doughtir of the Imperor Sir Henry de Lucemburgh by whom he had a yong sone, which sone with the same his mother died suspeciously in Berry at Issodon. And thridly the said Charles le Beale espoused Jahane doughtir of the countie d'Evreulx and aftir died the yere MCCCXXVII, leving the same his latter wief grosse with childe of a doughtir, which died sone and shortly aftir hir birthe.[14] And the said Charles le Beale afore his deth, beyng therof langiussunt by thexortacion of Sir Robert of Arthois, havyng than undir and for the same King Charles the regimen and principal governaunce of the reame of Ffraunce, which Sir Robert than had espoused the suster of the said Phelip de Valoys, the same Charles le Beale by his testament assigned |15r| the said Phelip de Valoys to have the governaunce of the said reames of Ffraunce and Navarre and of the ventre of his wief and of the infant whan it shuld be borne, until the same enfant shuld be of age to governe the same.[15] And by that meane the said Phelip de Valoys opteyned the possession of the said reames of Ffraunce and of Navarre and of the counte of Champayne, and thois

---

[13] Philippe V had a son named Louis, who died in 1317, together with four daughters by his wife Jeanne, daughter of Otto IV, count of Burgundy. See p. 56, n. 26.

[14] Blanche was born on 1 April 1328, two months after the death of her father, Charles VI, and lived until 1358. This account of the wives of Charles IV strongly echoes the comments of Jean Froissart, though the chronicler did not claim that Blanche died soon after her father. See Lettenhove, *Froissart*, I, pp. 211–212, and Berners, *Froissart*, I, p. 71. The draft in T, fos 4v–5r, did not identify Charles IV's first wife as Blanche, but did report that she was imprisoned in Château-Gaillard.

[15] Froissart had described Philippe of Valois's appointment as regent and later reported that Robert of Artois, husband of Charles's sister Jeanne, had played a key role in these events: Lettenhove, *Froissart*, II, pp. 212–215 and 297–298, and Berners, *Froissart*, I, pp. 71–72 and 81, together with p. 156 below.

helde as governor and regent therof until the deth of the said doughtir of the said Charles le Beale, which was in the rogacion dayes next aftir the deth of the said Charles le Beal. Aftir the deth of which doughtir, the right and title of the said reames and corones of Ffraunce and of Navarre and of the countie of Champaine descended to the said King Edward the III^{de} as cosin and next heir therunto. And the same King Edward the III^{de} than beyng but of thage of XV yeres and occupied with werres to subdue the Scottes which than rebelled against hym, and beyng ignorant than of his title to the said reames and corones of Ffraunce & Navare, and the said Phelip de Valoys, as is aforesaid havyng the regimen and subjection of the same reames, was coroned for king of Ffraunce in the day of the fest of the Holy Trinite next aftir the deth of the said Charles le Beale,[16] and that with the more spede by the counseill and procurement of the said Sir Robert of Arthois, dowting the clayme of the said Kyng |**15v**| Edward the III^{de}. At which tyme the same Phelip de Valoys, by the counseil aforesaid, had not determyned what to doo with the reame of Navarre and perceyved that the said King Edward the III^{de} not as than nor by a certain tyme aftir made no clayme to neyther of the said reames, sone aftir that gave to the counte d'Evreulx, his half brothers sone, the corone and reame of Navarre, and held to hymself the countie of Champaine.

By the which it is manifest and clerely apparent that the said surmyses and all other surmyses in that behalf conteyned in the said pamplet or printed book, with the supposed allegacions, reasons, argumentes, relies and supposed confessions made afore the said III Estates of Ffraunce in eny point by or for the said King Edward the III^{de} be falsely and dampnably fayned, imagined and untruly contrived contrarie to the trouth, as is theffect of all the said prynted book.[17] And so that the right and title of the said reames and corones of Ffraunce and of Navarre, and of the countie of Champayne, truly descended by dew course of enheritaunce to the said King Edward the III^{de} and is now descended to the excellent and most vertuous, my most dred sovereyn lord, Henry the VIIIth, by the grace of God king of Englond and of Ffraunce and lord of Irelond.

And as for the Lawe Salique, supposed as is aforesaid to be made by King Pharamont in the XIIth yere of his regne, all the bookes of histories and cronikes seen shal apere for trouth |**16r**| that the same

---

[16] The coronation took place on 29 May 1328: Lettenhove, *Froissart*, II, p. 216 and Berners, *Froissart*, I, p. 72.

[17] The draft account in T, fos 5v and 6r, denied that either Edward III or any one of his agents had appeared before the Three Estates in this matter. This argument appears on p. 151 below.

king Pharamont dyed in the XIth yere of his regne,[18] and that he had his habitacion and regne in Germanie at Ffrankford and thereabowtes upon the water of Rine, and in no part of that which is now nor was the tyme of the deth of the said Charles le Beale, or afore or aftir in Gaule nor undir the dominion of the corone of Ffraunce. By which apperith that the said Pharamont ordeyned no such Lawe Salique in the XII yere of his regne, which regned not full XI yeres. And if he had ordeyned eny soche lawe eny tyme of his regne, he cowde not bynde eny londes owt of his dominion, which was not in eny part of the reames of Ffraunce nor yet in Gaule. And though it shuld so doo, the wordes of that Lawe as *Nulla porcio hereditates de terra saliqua mulieri veniat set ad virilem sexum tota hereditas perveniat* makith every wey good title for the said King Edward the III^de.[19] It may not be denyed but that the same King Edward was *virilis sexus* as every man is. And those woordes or menyng therof were of nor to other entent if eny soche were, but that the corone and regalie shuld be governed by the man or heir male next of blode, and that ought to be the said King Edward the III^de to the said Charles le Beale. For he was his susters sone, and the said Phelip de Valoys was but his uncles sone, and that but of the half blode which may not succede by enheritunce as shalbe declared hereaftir. And the suster is nerer than the uncle though he were of the hole blode.[20]

|16v| *Capitulum II*[21]

And where in the same first or former part is there alledged that if all the cronikes of Ffraunce were seen from the tyme of the said Pharamont first king of Ffraunce, that unto the tyme of Phelip le Beale[22] shuld not be founde eny defalt of ligne masculyne aftir Clodio the Hery, which Clodio shuld have dyed without heire male. And for that cause the succession shuld have comen to Meroveus, father of Chilperik and grauntfather of King Clovys, first christien king, as next heir male of the said Clodio, jugyng also the Lawe Salique. And that there shuld not be founde of all the descendantes

[18] Marginal note: '*cronica episcopi de Burges, rubrio* del commencement des roys de Ffraunce'. In T, fo. 6r, the author defended the same argument by citing the authority of the 'said cronikes aswel of Ffraunce as of thempire'. *Les Chroniques d'Espagne ou de Burgos* actually stated that Pharamond was king of France for six years: BL MS Royal 19 E vi, fo. 234v.

[19] See p. 140, n. 5.

[20] The Tudor author returns to the question of 'half blode' on p. 165. He also ignores the arguments against cognate succession in *Pour ce que plusiers*, pp. 61–62.

[21] This chapter summarizes and responds to material from *Pour ce que plusieurs*, pp. 62–63 and 71. It greatly extends the discussion in T, fos 8r–8v.

[22] *Pour ce que plusieurs* actually referred to 'Charles le Bel' (see p. 62).

of Charlemayn and of Hugh Capet that ever doughtir shuld have succeded to the corone of Ffraunce nor other male by meane of a doughtir.[23]

It is sufficiently declared afore that what so ever the Lawe Salique be if suche were, it can not be trew that it was ordeyned in the XII yere of the regne of Pharamont as is surmytted for he reyned not so long, but died in the XI yere of his regne. Nor the said Clovys was not the first christien king, for at that tyme christendome was great in the est parties at Jerusalem and in those parties, and the kinges therof christened. Also christendome was that tyme in Englond, than called Bretayne, and was long afore that. And so was in Armorik, Bretaine, Burgonie and many other places.[24] And all histories and cronikes wele seen shal not be founde hough King |17r| Meroveus was next heire male to Clodio the Hery nor therof make a trew pedigre by ligne masculine nor by ligne femynyne. And it is to be supposed that the said Meroveus toke upon him to opteyne the dominion and people of Clodio by conquest rather than by succession of enheritaunce, for he called his subgettes *Merovingi* as Meroveismen, and so contenewed the name by succession unto the tyme of the regne of King Pepin, father to Charles le Graunt, and afore that tyme were not called Frensshmen.[25]

And from the tyme of the said Meroveus unto the tyme that Chilperik, last king of Meroveismen afore Pepin, was professed monk, the lyneal descent by ligne masculine suche as it was failed not, though they were not laufully begoten. Ffor Childerik sone of the said Meroveus, being chaced out of his reame, made his abode and dwelling with his freend King Bissine of Thoringe. The same Childerik toke soche familier acqueyntaunce of Basine, wief of Bissine aforenamed, that whan the same Childerik was restored to his dominion, the same Basine forsoke hir husbond Bissine and cam to the said Childerik.[26] Which Childerik begate on hir Clovys, whom they suppose to be the first christien king, the said Bissine beyng in pleyne lief.[27]

---

[23] The English translator omits the restatement in *Pour ce que plusieurs* of the arguments justifying the exclusion of the daughters of the last three Capetian kings (see pp. 63–64).

[24] The French treatise in fact argued that Clovis was the first Christian king of France. This statement did not appear in T.

[25] This argument did not appear in T. See p. 63, n. 58.

[26] Marginal note: 'Rubrico de Merovee & de Childerisi roys de Ffrauncois [...] fo. CCCIII'.

[27] Gregory of Tours was the first chronicler to report that Childeric had stolen his wife, Basina, from Basinus, king of Thuringia. The implication of the story was that Clovis was illegitimate, though official French accounts reported that Childeric had married Basina before the birth of their son: *Grandes chroniques*, I, pp. 27–35, and also see Pascale Bourgain, 'Clovis et Clotilde chez les historiens médiévaux des temps Mérovingiens au premier siècle Capétien', *Bibliothèque de l'Ecole des Chartes*, 154 (1996), pp. 53–85. A rare example of a French chronicle that did claim that Clovis was illegitimate is a short history of the French kings

And for trouth, whan that the afore rehersed King Chilperik was professed as is aforesaid monke, the said King Pepin was taken as next heir to the same Chilperik and to the corone, and that by meane of a doughtir, that is to saie Lotharie the Secund, |**17v**| sone of Chilperik, sone of Lotharie, sone of the said Clovys had issue a sone named Dagobert and a doughtir named Batilde.[28] That Dagobert had issue Clovys which had issue III sones, Lothaire, Therry and Childerik.[29] That Lothaire and Childerik died without issue. The said Therry had issue III sones, Clovys, Childebert and Lothaire.[30] Those Clovys and Lothaire died without issue and Childebert had issue Dagobert and Chilperik, which Chilperik had none issue and Dagobert had issue Therry and the afore rehersed Chilperik last king afore Pepin.[31] Which Therry and Chilperik died without issue and than the said reame and corone desconded to the said Pepine as next heire therunto as descended of the said Batild. Thus the same Batild was espoused to Ausebert erle of Andwerp and by hym had issue Arnold also erle, which had issue Saint Arnold which had issue Ausegelides, which Ausegelides by Saint Begge his wief had issue Pepyn the Lesse, which had issue Charles Martell, which had issue the said King Pepin.[32]

And in lykewise happened whan that King Loys last issue by ligne generall faulted of male and died without issue, and that Charles duke of Lorayne his uncle for soche heynous great & abhominable treasons as he had doon and committed against the person of the same King Loys his nevew and soverayn lord was disabled to succede as heir to

---

written by a pro-English cleric in Normandy between 1422 and 1436: BNF MS français 10468, fo. 105v, cited in Sanford Zale, 'Unofficial histories of France in the late middle ages', (PhD thesis, Columbus, OH, 1994), pp. 196–206. This argument did not appear in T.

[28] From the ninth century onwards, the usurpation of the French throne by Pepin the Short in 751 was sometimes justified by the claim that he had been a descendant of Blitilde, a fictional sister of Dagobert I and daughter of Clotaire II, son of Chilperic I, grandson of Clotaire I and great-grandson of Clovis. See Elizabeth A.R. Brown, 'La généalogie capétienne dans l'historiographie du Moyen Age: Philippe le Bel, le reniement du *reditus* et la création d'une ascendance carolingienne pour Hugues Capet', in Dominique Iogna-Prat and Jean-Charles Picard (eds), *Religion et culture autour de l'an mil: royaume capétien et Lotharingie* (Paris, 1990), p. 200 and *idem*, 'Vincent de Beauvais and the *reditus regni francorum ad stirpem Caroli imperatoris*', in Monique Paulmier-Foucart, Serge Lusignan, and Alain Nadeau (eds), *Vincent de Beauvais: intentions et réceptions d'une oeuvre encyclopédique au Moyen Age* (Montreal, 1990), pp. 170, 176, and 185.

[29] Dagobert I had two sons, Sigebert III and Clovis II, and the latter had three sons: Clotaire III, Theuderic III, and Childeric II.

[30] The three sons of Theuderic III were Clovis III, Childebert III, and Clotaire IV.

[31] Childebert III had one son, Dagobert III, whose son Theuderic IV was succeeded temporarily by the mayor of the palace, Charles Martel (d. 741), until rebellions forced the restoration of a Merovingian to the throne between 743 and 751, that is to say, Childeric III, grandson of Childeric II.

[32] Charles Martel, father of Pepin the Short, was the illegitimate son of Pepin II of Heristal, last of the Pippinid or Arnulfing mayors of the palace. Pepin II was the son of Begga, husband of Ansegisel, daughter of Arnulf, bishop of Metz.

the same Loys, Hugh Capet was admitted as next heir to the corone and reame of Ffraunce and to the same King Loys, and so reputed and taken. And that also by meane of a doughtir, that is to saie as sone and heir of Haovide, wief of Hugh le Graunte, |**18r**| doughtir of the Imperor Loys, sone of the Imperor Arnold, sone of Charlemayn king of Germanie, sone of the Imperor Loys, son of Charles le Graunt.[33]

By which proveth wele that the usage or custome of Ffraunce was never other but that the next heir male, though it were by maternall blode, shuld enherite to the corone and reame of Ffraunce. And never was otherwise used until the usurpacion of the said Phelip de Valoys. And so is apparent that the right & title of the corone and reame of Ffraunce aftir the deth of the said Charles le Beale descended by due succession to the said King Edward the III[de] by enheritaunce as to the nex heir. And in affirmance therof, the acquitaunce made by the same King Edward the III[de] as king of Ffraunce to the Fflemynges, was to them good and vaillable against the said Phelip de Valoys and every other claymyng to be king of Ffraunce, in discharge of soche bondes, promyses and peynes as they stode bounde to the kinges of Ffraunce in the somme of XIIM sentes upon certain condicions, as the acquitaunce of the trewe king of Ffraunce. And the Fflemynges therby were and yet be discharged aswel of the censures of the chirche as of every other penalite conteyned in ther said bondes.[34]

Capitulum III [35]

And where it is also alledged in the said first partie in color for the part of the said Phelip de Valoys that if the corone of Ffraunce

---

[33] Hugues Capet usurped the French throne in 987 following the deaths of the last Carolingian kings, Lothaire and Louis V. In the thirteenth century, the Capetians were presented as a continuation of the Carolingian dynasty in a number of ways, including the notion that Capet's mother, Hawide, had been a descendant of Charlemagne: Elizabeth A.R. Brown, 'La notion de la légitimité et la prophétie à la cour de Philippe Auguste', in Robert-Henri Bautier (ed.), *La France de Philippe Auguste: le temps des mutations* (Paris, 1982), pp. 95–96 and 101, and *idem*, 'La généalogie capétienne dans l'historiographie du Moyen Age', pp. 203–204. At the start of the fifteenth century, Jean de Montreuil argued that Hugues Capet was descended from Charlemagne through his father, and from the emperor via his mother: Montreuil, II, pp. 68, 80, and 93, and IV, appendix III, pp. 323–332.

[34] The account of Edward III's negotiations with the Flemings appeared in *Pour ce que plusieurs*, p. 71, and the Tudor author returns to this topic in chapter five, pp. 155–156.

[35] This chapter responds to *Pour ce que plusieurs*, pp. 64–65, though the Tudor author ignores a significant number of Cousinot's points, including the arguments that cognates could not inherit the throne because a corrupt tree cannot produce good fruit (p. 63), and that a woman could not rule in France because of God's judgement against Eve (p. 63), because she might marry a commoner (p. 64), and because of the unique status of the French crown as a sovereign power without a superior (pp. 65–66). He also ignored the

might descende to a woman, she might take to hir husbond at hir pleasur and that so might fortune she wold take to husbond the hede enemy of the reame. And that it might be possible that a king of Ffraunce might |**18v**| have XII doughtres and than the reame shuld be devided in XII partes and to have so many kinges than might it be demaunded who shuld bere the oriflambe at the bataill, who shuld saye the gospell of Cristemesse where the pope shuld be, as the kinges of Ffraunce owe and be bounde to doo, and which of them shuld be most christen prince. And noon of them shuld be called king of Ffraunce, but king in Ffraunce.

As to that for the first point if thenheriteresse of Ffraunce shuld take to husbond the hede enemy of the reame, she shuld of an enemy make a freend. And histories wele seen shalbe founde that it have ben used politikely for comon welth to have the enfantes and heritiers of devided dominions to entirmarie to cause therby peas and unite betwix them. And for the devision of the reame, the reame & dominion of Ffraunce in the tyme aftir Meroveus and Clovys, whom they saye to be the first king cristicn king, diverse kinges of the Ffrensshmen divided ther region in to IIII partes at diverse times as the croniques make manifest mencion.[36] And if the case happened as undoubted the cause is otherwise used ffor the superiorite of regalie is not used to be devided for the elder doughtir or suster where dominion having regalie descendeth by enheritaunce to be preferred to the hole enheritaunce therof.[37] And that is now used in every region and regalies. And so happened of the cuntries of Hollond, Henaud, Selond and Ffriselond soche as the IIIIth William erle of the same cuntries was ded without issue, his elder suster Margaret the imperesse, wief the Imperor Loys de Bavier, was preferred and posseded the hole enheritunce of those cuntries. And Phelip quene |**19r**| of Englond, wief of the said King Edward the III[de], hir yonger suster, opteyned nor chalenged no part

<hr>

detailed justification of why the fleurs-de-lis, the holy ampulla, and the oriflamme could not be held by a woman (p. 66), as well as the dramatic description of how both the Three Estates and the church ruled for Philippe of Valois in 1328 (p. 67). This chapter develops upon the material in T, fos 8r–9r.

[36] Marginal note: '*Cronica episcopi de Burges in diversis locis*'. Following the death of Clovis in 511, his lands were divided equally amongst his four sons and only reunified by the last surviving brother, Clotaire I. At his death in 561, the kingdom was again split into the four distinct regions of Neustria, Austrasia, Burgundy, and Aquitaine, held by his four sons, Charibert I, Sigibert, Guntram, and Chilperic I. The realm was reunited by Chilperic's son Clotaire II in 613. This argument did not appear in T.

[37] In the first draft of this treatise, the Tudor author had also cited the example of the earldom of Chester: following the death of Earl Ranulf in 1232 without issue, his four sisters became co-heirs to his extensive lands, but his nephew, John the Scot, inherited the title of earl of Chester. See T, fo. 9r.

therof by cause of the regalie.[38] And the said Imperor Loys posseded the said cuntries in the right of his said wief as his owne. And so a woman heriteresse of a region or regalie taking a husbond, the same hir husbond shal use and opteyne the same as king and sovereyn therof as his owne in his wiefes right as doyng justice, bering the armes and doyng every other thing as king, and helyng the escroilles, which grace is geven and lent by God to every cristien king enoynted of other regions aswel as of Ffraunce.[39]

Capitulum IIII[40]

And also where in the said first partie is alledged that the said King Edward the III[de] shuld have departed from his pursuite which he shuld have made to the corone and reame of Ffraunce, and that he shuld have knowleged the said Phelip de Valois to be his naturell and sovereyn lord by cause of the duche of Guyan, in that the same King Edward shuld have doon homage to the said Phelip de Valois at Amiens, and shuld have there geven lettres in that behalf.[41] And for that there was som difficultie upon the forme of the doyng of that homage for that, that the king wold have had homage liege. And the said King Edward duc of Guyan shuld have saide that he ought not to doo homage without the |19v| assent of the Parliament of Englond, he refused the doyng therof in soche maner. Therfor it shuld have ben in couvenant betwix the said King Phelip and hym that upon that poynt, the same King Phelip shuld sende his ambassade into Englond, to shewe lovingly there the appurtenantes of the right. And that the Englisshmen shuld doo in lykewise of ther partie, to thende to conduct this

[38] Philippa of Hainault, wife of Edward III, was the daughter of Count Guillaume III of Hainault, Holland, and Zeeland. Her brother, Count Guillaume IV, died without issue in 1345 and, despite the opposition of Philippa and Edward III, the lands passed to her sister Marguerite, wife of Emperor Ludwig IV of Bavaria. In 1349, Marguerite appointed her son, Guillaume, as count of Holland-Zeeland and he also inherited Hainault when his mother died in 1356. Edward III continued to pursue Philippa's claims in Hainault, Holland, and Zeeland, especially after Guillaume V went mad in 1358.

[39] The Tudor author offers an extremely limited attack upon the claims of the French 'roi très chrétien', though there is no mention here of the temporary promise of Pope Julius II in 1512 to transfer this title to Henry VIII. See David S. Chambers, *Cardinal Bainbridge in the Court of Rome, 1509 to 1514* (Oxford, 1965), pp. 38–41, and Davies, 'Roy de France et roy d'Angleterre', p. 127, together with the reference in the conclusion to T, p. 269 below.

[40] This chapter responds to *Pour ce que plusieurs*, pp. 68–69, and closely resembles the draft in T, fos 9v–10r.

[41] This translation omits the statement that the letters were preserved in the French *Trésor des chartes*, p. 69.

matier in good love and union and to eschew all causes of werre and discord. And that in furnisshing of those thinges in the yere MIII^C XXXI, the said King Phelip shuld have sent his ambassade in to Englond where the matiers shuld have ben wele debated at lengthe, which ambassadours shuld have brought the lettres of the said King Edward passed in his Parliament and of auctorite, which they shuld have delyvered to the said King Phelip, touchyng the duche of Guyan. By the which he shuld have knowleged the said Phelip king of Ffraunce to be his sovereyn lord by cause of the duche of Guyan, and by that cause he shuld have ben his man and vassal liege.[42]

It is declared afore the aforenamed Charles le Beale died aftir Estir in the yere MCCCXXVII and left his wief grosse with childe of a doughtir and by his will at the especiall labour and counseill of Sir Robert of Arthois assigned the said Phelip de Valois to have the rule and to be regent of the ventre and of reame of Ffraunce during the grossure. And that the same doughtir sone aftir the birth in the rogacion daies next aftir died, and aftir hir deth the said Phelip de Valois was coroned king contrarie to |20r| right in the day of the fest of the Holy Trinite.[43] And of that tyme the said King Edward the III^{de}, not beyng enformed of the deth of the said doughtir and beyng but than of thage of XV yeres and occupied in werres to subdue the Scottes for their rebellion, and not than advertised of his title, never made of a long tyme eny apparence or pursuite afore the III Estates of Ffraunce as is in the first article supposed.[44] So that he never departed from soche pursuite aftir he began it, and in soche his yong age, the same King Edward the III^{de}, having communicacion with the said Phelip de Valois at Amiens in the yere MCCCXXVIII, by protestacion savyng his right and to be restored to soche londes as were of his enheritaunce, he knowleged homage to be dewe for the duche of Guyan and the counties of Poytew and of Ponthiue, which doyng of homage for that tyme was respected.[45] And aftir the said King Phelip sent his ambassade to the said King Edward in to Englond by the bisshop of Chartres and other to treate with the counseill of the

---

[42] Again, no mention is made here of the documents in the *Trésor des chartes*, nor the subsequent legal arguments regarding the consequences of a vassal's disobedience towards his lord, p. 69.

[43] See pp. 143–144.

[44] In May 1328, the bishops of Worcester, Coventry, and Lichfield were sent to Paris to put forward Edward III's claim to the French throne, though the English king never attended the assembly that ruled in favour of Philippe of Valois.

[45] Edward III paid simple homage to Philippe VI at Amiens on 6 June 1329: Lettenhove, *Froissart*, II, pp. 231–233, and Berners, *Froissart*, I, p. 78.

said King Edward upon the same homage, and for the same taried in Englond all a wynter tyme and aftir unto the monyth of Maii, and had for ther answere that ther was dewe to the corone of Ffraunce homage for the said duche and counties, and otherwise ded not doo homage.[46] By which is manifest that the said King Edward the III[de] never ded expressely homage to the said Phelip de Valois, nor knowleged the same Phelip to be king of Ffraunce or his sovereyn lord, nor was his man or vassal liege, and in knowleging of homage it was but by protestacion saving his right. By which protestacion he |20v| saved his enteresse and right and title aswel to the corone and reame of Ffraunce as to every other parcell of his enheritaunce. And the said King Edward the III[de] never ded eny thing to estoppe or barre hym of his title therof or of eny part therof unto the tyme of the treatie of Breticgny concluded at Calais betwix him and King John, sone of the said Phelip. Which treatie the Ffrenshmen falsely and dampnable brak and violated to ther most reproof and shame as heraftir shalbe declared sufficiently at length in place according.[47]

Capitulum V[48]

And where it is in the said first part also surmytted that aftir that Sir Robert of Arthois, which had ben at the assemble aforesaid of the III Estates of Ffraunce and oon of the V principall which gave his oppinion to the proufit and entent of the said Phelip of Valois,[49] was banisshed out and from the reame of Ffraunce, desiring to bere domage and prejudice to the said king his sovereyn and naturell lord, had geven to entende and graunte more great right in the said matier. That the thing wherupon the Englisshmen shuld grounde them most shuld be whan Sir Robert of Arthois had ben in Englond and offred to them the aliaunce of the erle of Henaude and of Sir John of Henaude and also of the dukes of Braban & Guerles, the erles of Clyves & Julers, tharchebisshopes of Cologne, Treves and Destrabaurg, with the Gantois and almost of

[46] In the draft version of this treatise in T, fo. 9v, the French embassy was listed as including not just the bishop of Chartres but also the bishop of Beauvais, Louis, duke of Bourbon, the earl [count] of Harcourt, and the earl [lord] of Tancarville. This accorded with the description of the embassy in Froissart, as well as the letters patent that Edward III had issued on 30 March 1331, recognizing his homage to Philippe VI as liege: Lettenhove, *Froissart*, II, pp. 234–236, and Berners, *Froissart*, I, pp. 79–81.

[47] See pp. 225–241.

[48] This chapter translates and then responds to *Pour ce que plusieurs*, pp. 69–73, and expands upon T, fos 10r–11r (which is incomplete because of a missing folio between fos 10v and 11r).

[49] *Pour ce que plusieurs* simply stated that Robert of Artois was one of the principal men who had supported the succession of Philippe VI (see p. 70).

all |21r| Almayne. And that the said King Edward the III^de shuld not have named hymself king of Ffraunce, nor in his werres shuld not have borne the armes of Ffraunce escarteled or quartered with the armes of Englond, but onely shuld have borne the III leopardes, until that the Fflemynges shuld saie to him that without he shuld entitle hym and bere the armes of Ffraunce, they shuld not dare aide or folowe hym. For that by the werres which before had ben betwix the kinges of Ffraunce and the Flemynges, aftir the bataill which was betwix them at Mons in in [*sic*] the tyme of King Phelip le Beale,⁵⁰ the Fflemynges submitted and bond them undir the censures of the chirche of Rome and upon of excomenqement and of XII^C sentes of the mony that shuld be currant for the tyme, they shuld never aftir make werre to the kinges of Ffraunce nor rebelle ageinst them. And in case they shuld, *ipso facto* they shuld renue in sentence of excomenqement and ther cuntre in entirdict without ever to be assoiled without the consent of the king of Ffraunce. Ffor the which cause, Jacques d'Artevell, Ganthois, the yere MCCCIIII^XX II,⁵¹ shuld saie openly afore all the princes, prelates and lordes abovenamed, that it shuld behove the said King Edward to intitule him king of Ffraunce, or otherwise the Ganthois nor ther adherentes shuld not folowe him nor allie them to him. By occasion of which thynges and also by thenortement of the said lordes which wold of all thinges have the Fflemynges with them and of ther alliaunce, the said King Edward toke the name and armes of Ffraunce which he shuld contenew without eny other grounde.

And that it shuld be wele to note in that matier that soche shuld be the condicion of Englisshmen, and what suretie there shuld be with them, and in thing which they |21v| shuld promyse. Ffor that the said King Edward shuld have avowed and knowleged the said King Phelip to be trew king of Ffraunce, and shuld receyve of hym as suche king the duche of Guyan, and shuld have made to hym othe of fealtie and delivered lettres patentes aftir confermed in his Parliament touching that matier. And that the said King Phelip of his grace shuld have yelded to hym many londes and seignories in the duche of Guyan, which had ben taken by his predecessoures kinges of Ffraunce by auctorite of justice for lak of doyng of homage.

⁵⁰ *Pour ce que plusieurs* did not identify the name of the battle of Mons-en-Pévèle (18 August 1304), and the reference to the 'time of King Philippe the Fair' only appeared in certain manuscripts (see p. 71).

⁵¹ In fact, Cousinot had reported that Jacques van Artevelde was the father of Philippe, who was killed at the battle of Roosebeke in 1382 (see p. 71).

And that notwithstonding all these thynges, as sone as the said King Edward shuld see that he had fote on that side the see and aliaunce to invade the reame, not havyng regard to right reason and justice, and directly against his faith, othes and promyses, he shuld have inforced him to invade the said reame and his veray and naturell sovereyn lord by cause of the said duche of Guyan. The said King Edward shuld have entred within the said reame of Ffraunce and shuld there have doon so many ill dedes wherof the voix and renome yet shuld endure. And that not onely of people nor of arme which shuld have come out of Englond nor of Almaines, but also of londes and subgettes of the said duche of Guyan, and namely of suche as the said King Phelip shuld have yelded to him whan he shuld have doon homage to him. And that it shuld not be to merveille of, ffor the said King Phelip shuld saye in signifieng or describing the propirte & condicion of Englisshmen:[52] *Angelus est cui nunquam credere fas est, dum tibi dicit ave tanquam ab hoste cave.* And that of thother partie Englisshmen shuld saie that they shuld have prerogative and that right usage, that alweyes |**22r**| and as often that they shuld see ther evident proufit, they shuld not be subgettes to othes nor to promyses which they shuld make.

Trew it is that the said Sir Robert of Arthois was at the ellection of the said Phelip of Valois to be king and of the most fervent oppinion aswel in counseill as in labour, and the former of the V principall which with him gave oppinion for the said Phelip to be preferred to the corone of Ffraunce. And that was for the favour he had to him and had espoused his suster, and not of right, and by the matier supposed the same Phelip de Valoys was not so preferred by true title, but by favour and extreme labour of suche V principall of his affinite, the said King Edward next and trew heritier therunto beyng of thage but of XV yeeres than and not advertised of his right therunto. But for the parciall meende of the said Sir Robert of Arthois and labour which he extremely made to disherite the trew enheritor the said King Edward the III^de in favour to preferre oon of wrong to usurpe the corone of Ffraunce, God suffred hym to be rewarded with the reward accident to suche case, that is unkyndenesse and will of destruction, and therof thexperience faileth not, ffor it was not long aftir that the said Phelip de Valois toke suche hate and extreme malice to the said Sir Robert of Arthois, that he laboured greatly his destruction and to have caused him to have ben murdred as the croniques declareth at large. So that

---

[52] Cousinot had attributed this quotation, which also appeared in Walter Bower's *Scotichronicon* and John Ireland's *Vraie chronique d'Escoce*, to Bede rather than to King Philippe VI: see pp. 72–73.

the same Sir Robert of Arthois might not abide in no place beyond the see for the pursuite |**22v**| of the seid Phelip de Valois, that he was of force dreven to come into Englond for his refuge to King Edward aforesaid. And havyng remorse in his conscience of his said labour against the same King Edward and of his disheritaunce, he confessed and knowleged the same and as a penitent yelded himself to the same King Edward and in satisfaction became his man and offred to aventure to lyve and dye with him in the conquest and recovere of his right of the corone and reame of Ffraunce.[53]

And the alliance betwix the said King Edward and the aforesaid erle of Henaud was not by the said Sir Robert of Arthois. For long afore that the same King Edward had espoused Phelip oon of the[54] doughtres of the said erle of Henaud, which erle had to wief the suster of the said Phelip de Valois.[55] But for all that, the same erle wele undirstonding that the true title of the corone and reame of Ffraunce apperteyned to the said King Edward and not to the said Phelip de Valois, the said erle lyke a trew knight favoured the rightfull clayme of the same King Edward against the injurious pretense of the said Phelip de Valois.

And the Fflemynges also wele undirstonding that the said King Edward had the right of the said corone and reame of Ffraunce, offred to him to serve hym as to the veray king of Ffraunce. And the same King Edward, as king of Ffraunce of his grace especial, without other condicion, by his lettres patentes remytted and quiteclaymed to the Fflemynges all the peynes and other demaundes wherin they stood bounde to the corone of Ffraunce or kinges of Ffraunce by reason of eny of ther bondes, promyses or othes wherin they |**23r**| stode charged for eny of the premisses. Which lettres of remyse and quitances from that tyme hetherto have ben good and vaillable to

---

[53] The draft version in T, fo. 10v, provided more detail: 'the said King Phelip de Valoys toke suche hate to the same Sir Robert so that if he might have taken him, he wold have caused the same Sir Robert to dye. The love of his wief, suster of the said King Phelip, had no place. Ffor whan the same Sir Robert was voided the reame of Ffraunce first to the countie of Namur and aftir to the duke of Braban, the said King Phelip de Valoys imprisoned straitly his said suster with her II sones, and so procured against the said erle of Namur and duc of Braban for the favoryng of the said Sir Robert, that the same Sir Robert, beyng penytent of his former dede, cam to the said King Edward the Thrid and confessed to him that by his labor the same King Edward was desherited from the coroune of Ffraunce, and offred to hym for that to become his man, to lyve & dye with him to conquest of his said right of the corone and reame of Fraunce.' This echoes Lettenhove, *Froissart*, II, pp. 297–300, and Berners, *Froissart*, I, pp. 81–82 and 91. Also see p. 143, n. 15 above.

[54] The words 'susters of the said erle of Henaud' are crossed out in the manscript.

[55] Philippa of Hainault, wife of Edward III, was the daughter of Count Guillaume III of Hainault, Holland, and Zeeland and his wife Jeanne, sister of Philippe VI. Her father died in 1337. See p. 150, n. 38.

the Fflemynges against the said Phelip de Valois and every other king for the premisses, aswel in the court of Rome as in every other place, as the lettres made by the trew and veray king of Ffraunce. And the Fflemynges therby were and yet ar clerely discharged of the premisses aswel of the censures of the churche, as of every other penaltte conteyned in the said bondes and promyses.[56]

And as is answered afore the said King Edward never made homage to the said Phelip de Valois directly, but tended homage by protestacion, savyng his right. By which protestacion, if he had made homage yet, he savyd his right and cleyme therunto and might at all tymes clayme, demaunde and entirprise the recovere therof, the same homage notwithstonding. And the same King Edward never made promyse, covenante or otherwise ded to barre hym of his said title, wherby Frensshmen shuld have cause or may trewly saye that the said King Edward had avowed or knowleged the said Phelip de Valois to be trew king of Ffraunce, or that he shuld receyve of him the duche of Guyan but that he contenewed his possession therof, nor never made to hym othe of fealtie or delivered to him lettres patentes therof or that confermed by auctorite of Parliament, nor the same King Edward against his othes nor othirwise ded eny thing wherby eny persone of trouth may object eny thing to his rebuke or reproche, the report or discryving of the said Phelip de Valois or eny other persone his adverse partie notwithstonding.

|23v| But for trouth, the histories of croniques of antiquite and of new wele seen, it shal not be found eny breche, rumpure or coloured thing doon by the kinges of Englond to the breche or violating of eny treatie, promyse or couvenaunte by them with the kinges of Ffraunce or Ffrensh kinges, or eny other prince. The contrarie shal appiere of the partie of the Ffrensshmen, and of the Scottes ther adherentes and rebellions of Englond, for they have observed but very fewe or none treatie, couvenant or promyse. But by cautelles, for as nigh as they can, in every soche treatie they wol have a sterting hole to take and leve at their libertie and by comon experience, whan they shewe themself to be moost faithful, they shalbe founde at lengthe most false, if they see likelyhode for their avauntage.

And it is manifestly confessed in the said allegacion & sufficiently declared that the said Phelip de Valois was preferred to the corone and reame of Ffraunce by the synyster labour of V principall persones specially, wherof the said Sir Robert of Arthois was the chief, which may not be denyed. But it was of wrong and not of right and so the said Phelip opteyned the same by usurpacion, and his successoures from thens hetherto usurpe the same from the trewe heritiers therof, the

---

[56] See p. 148.

noble kinges of Englond. Which is the suffraunce of God for a tyme, which with his pleasure and grace shalbe redressed, I trust, and the right high and excellent and most vertuos prince, my dred sovereyn lord Henry the VIIIth, by the grace of God king of Englond & of Ffraunce and lord of Irelond, therunto restored with the other of his hereditamentes.

|24r| *Capitulum VI*[57]

And where it is further supposed in the said first partie that the said King Edward the III[de] had V sones which all V came to the age of perfection and every of them was maried. The elder was prince of Wales which shuld espoused the countes of Saresbury, of whom shuld have descended King Richard which had none children. And the secund sone was Sir Leonell that shuld have ben duc of Clarence, which espoused madame the countesse of Ulster in the cuntre of Irelond, of the which countes shuld have issued II doughtres which that many Englisshmen shuld saye not to be the doughtres of the said Duke Leonell but of oon knight named Audeley, which aftir for that cause by the ordenaunce of King Edward of Englond shuld have ben behelded. And the same dame shuld have retorned into Irelond and shuld have maried the said II doughtres, that is to saye thelder to the erle of Northumbirlond and the secund to Sir Roger Mortymer erle of Marche. And that Englisshmen shuld saie to shew that the said II doughtres shuld not be of the said Sir Leonell and shuld not bere his name nor his armes, but the name and the armes of the said countesse of Ulster ther mother, which shuld be demonstraunce that there shuld be som defalt in that side. The thrid sone was John surname of Gand, erle of Derby, and espoused Blanche of Lancaster, doughtir & heir of the gret duke of Lancastre Henry, by whom he had the duche of Lancaster, which shuld have made the rightes of armes, by cause wherof he shuld have had the duche of Lancaster and coroned king of Englond and shuld have ben called King Henry the III[de].[58]

---

[57] This chapter translates and then responds to *Pour ce que plusieurs*, pp. 73–75. There is no parallel in T, though this may be because of the missing material between fos 10v and 11r.

[58] This is an extremely confused translation of the French account of John of Gaunt and his heirs, from p. 74. Cousinot had reported that Gaunt married Blanche of Lancaster, daughter of Duke Henry of Lancaster, and that from their marriage came Henry, count of Derby, the future King Henry IV. The translator omits the reference to their son Henry, count of Derby, and reconceives the passage as an argument for Duke Henry of Lancaster becoming king of England as Henry III. The English author also omits the discussion of Gaunt's second and third marriages in *Pour ce que plusieurs*, pp. 74–75.

And that the IIIIth sone was Sir Edmond of |24v| Langley, erle of Cambregge and aftir duke of York, which espoused the secund doughtir of king Petir of Spayne, of whom issued the duke of York which died at Ageincourt, which had no children, and also the countie of Cambregge.[59] The Vth sone shuld be Sir Thomas of Wodestok, erle of Bukingham and aftir duc of Gloucester,[60] which shuld have had II doughtres, wherof the one shuld have ben maried to the erle of Hereford and the other to the erle Stafford.

Here is taken a great businesse to imagine this matier by way of a pedegre cautelously, falsely and untruly intending therby to conveye false titles to the corone of Englond, to have and stere division amonges the Englisshmen, to thentent that by suche division, rebellions and werres might growe, therby to geve place & tyme to the usurpours of Ffraunce to contenew possession of the same, and Englisshmen shuld not have tyme or be able to aide the king of Englond to pursiew for his right of the corone and reame of Ffraunce and thother his enheritaunce in those parties.

But trew it is that the said King Edward the III[de] had issue the said V sones besides other III sones which died enfantes. And that the said Prince Edward was the elder, which espoused Johane doughtir and heritier of Edmond of Wodestok, somtyme erle of Kent, yonger sone of King Edward the First, and had issue the said Richard the Secund, aftir the said King Edward the III[de], king of Englond and heir of the premisses, which Richard died without issue.[61]

And |25r| the said Duke Leonell the secund of the said V sones was duc of Clarence, and espoused Elizabeth, doughtir and heir of John of Burgh, erle of Ulster, and of Elizabeth, oon of the sustres and heires of Gilbert erle of Gloucestre, and had issue by his said wief onely one, Phelip his doughtir and heir. Which Phelip was maried to Edmond Mortymer, erle of Marche, which Edmond and Phelip had together issue a sone named Roger aftir erle of Marche, and one doughtir named Alice, maried to Henry Percy erle of Northumberland.[62] And

---

[59] The English author tactfully omits the statement that Richard, count [earl] of Cambridge, was executed at Southampton by Henry V (see p. 75).

[60] Again, the Englishman does not mention the murder of Thomas of Woodstock in 1397, as reported on p. 75.

[61] In fact, Edward of Woodstock, the Black Prince, had two sons, Edward and Richard, by his wife Joan of Kent. See p. 73, n. 114.

[62] Lionel married Elizabeth de Burgh, daughter of William de Burgh, third earl of Ulster, and his wife, Matilda, daughter of Henry, third earl of Lancaster. Their daughter, Philippa, married Edmund Mortimer, earl of March, and was the mother of two sons, Roger and Edmund Mortimer, and two daughters, Philippa and Elizabeth, wife of Henry Hotspur Percy, son of Sir Henry, first Earl of Northumberland. See p. 74, n. 116 and p. 163.

the said Elizabeth wief of Duc Leonell died in the yere MCCCLXIII and lieth buried at Brusyard in Suffolk.[63] And aftir hir decesse the same Duc Leoncll secundly espoused the suster of Galeace than duc of Melain and there sone aftir died.[64] And aftir that in the tyme of the regne of the said King Richard the Secund, for that the same King Richard the Secund had none issue, the said Roger erle of Marche as next heir apparant to the same King Richard and to the premisses was taken & reputed. By which aperith wele that the said matier supposed of the ymaginat adulterie of the said Elizabeth duchesse of Clarens was of a dispightfull and dampnable meende, falsely imagined and conspired. And it shal not be founde in any trew historie, cronique or recorde in all the time of King Edward the III[de] that for suche cause or any other, eny of the name of Audeley was executed or put to eny peynefull deth by jugement, decree or otherwise but by thaventure of werres.[65]

And as for the name or bering of the armes of the said duc Leonell, the same Leonell was by his father the said King Edward the III[de] created |25v| him duc to have that name to him and to his heires males of his body laufully begoten, so that whan he deyde he had none issue male, nor but one doughtir, and she cowde not have that name, but alwey she bare his armes.[66] By which &c.

And the said John the III[de] of the said V sones espoused Blanche doughtir and heir of Henry duc of Lancaster, but that Henry was never coroned king of Englond, nor was not he which was called King Henry the III[de].[67] Ffor King Henry the III[de] was that King Henry sone of King John. And that King Henry had issue II sones, that is to saie Edward which was king aftir him and was called King Edward the First, and thother sone was named Edmond whom the said King Henry the III[de] his ffather created erle of Lancaster, and that had the counte of Lancaster.[68] And aftir the forfaite of Simon Mountfort erle

---

[63] Elizabeth de Burgh died in Dublin in 1363 and her body was buried in her family mausoleum at Clare Priory in Suffolk. Bruisyard was the site of a Franciscan nunnery founded by her husband; it was also the home of a secular college originally founded at Campsey Ash in Suffolk by her mother, Matilda, to staff a chantry offering prayers for the souls of her two husbands. Matilda was living at Bruisyard by 1366 and was buried there after her death in 1377. See pp. 46–47.

[64] Lionel married Violante Visconti, sister of Giangaleazzo, first duke of Milan, in 1368.

[65] See p. 24.

[66] In 1362, Lionel was created duke of Clarence, meaning the town, castle, and honour of Clare.

[67] See p. 157, n. 58.

[68] Edmund, known as Edmund Crouchback, was the second son of King Henry III. He was styled earl of Leicester from 1267, and earl of Lancaster from 1276.

of Leicestre, the said King Henry the III^{de} gave to the said Edmond his secund sone, the erledom of Leycestre. And for the forfaite of Sir Robert de Fferrarys somtyme erle of Derby, his said father King Henry the III^{de} gave to him the same Edmond the erledom of Derby.[69] And so the same Edmond was erle of Lancastre, Leycestre and Derby and was a noble man, and was with his said elder brother Edward the First in the lief of ther father in the Holy Lond and there ded valiant dedes, and retorned into Englond afore his brother sone aftir his fathers deth in the yere MCCLXXII.[70] And many in the north parties rebelling, the same Edmond with Roger Mortemer subdued them, his said brother Edward beyng in Guyan and not retorned in to Englond.[71] And in the yere MCCLXXIIII, the same King Edward the First retorned in to Englond fro his journy out of the Holy Lond |26r| and the same yere the XIIII kalend of Septembre, he was coroned king of Englond in Westminster and Quene Alianore his wief was the same tyme coroned quene.[72] And the said Edmond erle of Lancaster was for the same King Edward his brother deputie of Guyan, and the same Edmond had to wief Avelyne doughtir and heir of William de Ffortibus erle of Albermarle and of Holdernesse and of Devonshire and lord of the Isle of Wight, and by hir had II children which died enfantes and the same Avelyne died.[73] The said Edmond espoused secundly Blanche quene of Navarre somtyme wief of Henry king of Navarre and suster of the erle of Arthois and mother to Jahanne quene of Ffraunce and of Navarre, wief of King Phelip le Beale, by the which quene Blanche the said Edmond had issue III sones, Thomas, Henry and John.[74] The same Thomas was aftir his father erle of Lancastre, Leycester and Derby and espoused Alice doughtir and heir of Henry Lacy erle of Lincoln and of Saresbury, and had by the same Alice

[69] Edmund was granted the lands previously held by Simon de Montfort, earl of Leicester, in 1265 and in 1266 he received the lands and honour of Derby, forfeited by the rebellious Robert de Ferrers.

[70] Henry III had taken a crusading vow in 1250 but it was his son Edward, the future Edward I, who carried his father's cross to the East in 1270. Edmund followed in the spring of 1271, and was in the Holy Land from August of that year until March 1272, where he earned the nickname Crouchback.

[71] *Flores historiarum*, III, p. 32.

[72] *Flores historiarum*, III, p. 44. Edward I was crowned on 19 August 1274.

[73] The first wife of Edmund was Avelina de Forz [Fortibus], daughter of William de Forz, count of Aumale, who had held honours in Holderness and had been married to the heiress of the earl of Devon.

[74] Edmund's second wife was Blanche of Artois, daughter of Robert (I), count of Artois, and widow of Henry, king of Navarre, with whom she had a daughter named Jeanne, who married Philippe IV in 1284. Edmund and Blanche had three sons – Thomas of Lancaster, Henry of Lancaster, and John – and a daughter named Mary.

his wief the erledomes of Lincoln & of Saresbury.[75] And so the same erle Thomas was erle of Lancaster, Leycester, Derby, Lincoln and Saresbury, but he had none issue. And the said Henry the Secund sone was lord of Monenine by the gift of his said father and espoused the doughtir of Sir Patrice Chaworth and had issue the said Henry first duke of Lancaster, father to Blanche, wief of the said John of Gand, thrid sone of the said King Edward the III[de].[76] And John yonger sone of the said Edmond erle of Lancaster abode and dwelled with the said Quene Jahane of Ffraunce and of Navarre |**26v**| his suster on the mothers side.

And the said Edmond of Langley IIIIth of the said V sones of King Edward the III[de] espoused Isabel secund doughtir of King Petir of Spayne and had issue as is alledged.[77]

And the aforenamed Thomas of Wodestok yongest sone of King Edward the III[de] espoused [. . .] oon of the doughtres and heires of Sir Humfrey Bohun erle of Hereford and had by hir issue oon sone named Humfrey which[78] died without issue, and II doughtres of whom thoon died unmaried and thother named Anne which was first maried to [. . .] erle of Stafford and aftir his deth was secundly maried to William Bourghchier, lord Bourghchier.[79]

Capitulum VII [80]

And where also in the said first partie is objected against the clayme of King Edward the IIIIth that if so were that King Edward the III[de] shuld have had right to the corone and reame of Ffraunce, yet King Edward the IIIIth shuld not demaunde or clayme therunto

---

[75] Thomas of Lancaster married Alice, daughter and heir of Henry de Lacy, earl of Lincoln.

[76] Henry of Lancaster was lord of Monmouth and first married Maud, daughter and heiress of Patrick of Chaworth, and then Alix, daughter of Jean de Joinville. In total, he had seven children, including his son and heir, Henry of Grosmont, first duke of Lancaster.

[77] Edmund of Langley and his wife, Isabella of Castile, had two sons: Edward, duke of York, and Richard, earl of Cambridge, both of whom died in 1415. See p. 75, n. 123.

[78] The words 'was killed and' are deleted.

[79] Thomas Woodstock married Eleanor, daughter and co-heiress of Humphrey de Bohun, earl of Hereford. Their son Humphrey died in 1399 and they had three daughters, including Anne, who married Edward, earl of Stafford, then his brother Edmund, and, thirdly, Sir William Bourchier. See p. 75, n. 125.

[80] This chapter translates and then responds to *Pour ce que plusieurs*, pp. 76–77 above. The English author omits a brief statement of the rival claims of Edward IV and Henry VI, the 'plusprochain heritier dudit Roy Edouart le Tiers'. There is no parallel in T, presumably because of the missing material between fos 10v and 11r.

in especial by ligne masculine. And if he shuld clayme eny right, it shuld be by the woman and not otherwise. And that the same King Edward the IIIIth shuld pretende that his father the duke of York shuld be sone of the erle of Cambregge and of Dame Anne Mortemer doughtir of Sir Roger Mortemer and of Dame Phelip which is meintened to be doughtir of the duke of Clarence, Sir Leonell, secund sone |27r| of the said King Edward the III[de], and by that title shuld have taken the corone of Englond, and by consequent he shuld be next heir to King Richard the Secund. And that though it were soo that he were nerest to the same King Richard and by that cause the corone of Englond shuld apperteyne to hym, yet it shuld not serve to the said King Edward the IIIIth touching the quarell of Ffraunce, and that for that as it is saide before that the said King Edward the IIIIth shuld not pretende to the corone of Englond but by a doughtir, which shuld not be the elder, but the countesse of Northumberlond shuld be the elder, of whom there shuld be children and issue. And so by the consequent, it shuld be impossible that the said King Edward by the said meane, that is to saie by the doughtir which he shuld saye to be of the said Sir Leonell and shuld not be the elder, and the whiche doughtres shuld not enherite to the corone of Ffraunce for the reasons above towched, shuld, may have or clayme eny right or title to the corone of Ffraunce. And that not onely by the lawe and custome of Ffraunce, nor by the lawe kept in Englond whan suche case shuld happen.[81]

And for to descend in particuler case, that it shuld be trew that in Englond in all successions that happen in taill, the doughtres shal not succede if there were eny heir male descended in ligne, and that shuld be practiqued every day in the said reame of Englond. That is to saie that if there shuld be eny man which shuld have II sones and his heritage be entailled to come to the heir masle, and thelder, which aftir the |27v| custome of the cuntre shuld have the succession, dye, and have a doughtir, which doughtir shuld have a sone, and the father of the II sones decesse, that in the said reame of Englond there shuld be no representation by custome or by covenaunte especial, the sone of the doughtir shuld not succede in prejudice of the secund sone. But the secund sone shuld have all

---

[81] The English author ignores a brief reference to the Salic Law, p. 77.

the succession, the reason to be for that the doughtur shuld not succede.[82]

Trew it is that the said King Edward the IIIIth claymed the corone of Ffraunce as next heriter therunto by discent and fro the said Duc Leonell, in somoche as the aforesaid Prince Edward elder sone of the said King Edward the III[de] and Richard his sone were dede without issue. Ffor the same Duke Leonell had issue but onely one doughtir, the said Phelip, maried to Edmond erle of Marche, and had no doughtir maried to the erle of Northumbirlond as is surmytted. And the same Phelip, by the same Edmond, had issue a sone named Roger aftir hym erle of Marche and a doughtir named Alice maried to Sir Henry Percy erle of Northumbirlond of whom is descended the now erle of Northumbirlond.[83] And the said Roger erle of Marche had issue II sones and II doughtres. The elder sone was named Edmond and was erle of Marche aftir his father and died without issue. The secund sone was named Roger and died without issue in the lief of his brother. The elder of those |28r| II doughtres was named Anne and was maried to the aforenamed Richard erle of Cambregge. And the secund of those II doughtres was maried to the erle of Devonshire but she died without issue.[84] The said Richard erle of Cambregge had issue by the said Anne, Richard duke of York, ffather to the said King Edward the IIIIth. By which is apparent that the same King Edward the IIIIth was next heir[85] to the said King Richard the Secund and by the consequent to the corone and reame of Ffraunce.

And it is sufficiently declared afore that there was not ordeyned for the reame of Ffraunce eny Lawe Salique to bynde eny of the heritaunces in Ffraunce. For King Pharamond was never king of nor in Ffraunce nor of eny part of the londes undir the corone of

[82] This omits the claims that the exclusion of women meant that no cognate could inherit the French throne, based on the authority of the Salic, Roman, and English law, as well as the prescriptive right created by the fact that Edward III, the papacy, the church, and all Christian princes had acknowledged Philippe VI and his five successors as the rightful rulers of France: pp. 77–78.

[83] Philippa and her husband, Edmund Mortimer, earl of March, had four children: Roger Mortimer, earl of March; Sir Edmund Mortimer; Elizabeth, who first married Henry Percy, son of the first earl of Northumberland, and then Sir Thomas Camoys; and Philippa, who was married three times. See pp. 158–159, as well as p. 74, n. 116. Henry Algernon Percy was fifth earl of Northumberland from 1489 to 1527 and his son, known by the same name, was the sixth earl until his death in 1537.

[84] The four children of Roger Mortimer, earl of March, and his wife, Eleanor Holland, were: Edmund, earl of March and Ulster; Roger Mortimer; Anne, wife of Richard, earl of Cambridge; and Eleanor, who married Sir Edward Courtenay, son of the earl of Devon.

[85] The word 'male' is crossed out.

Ffraunce, wherby his ordenaunces, if eny he made, cowde not be of effect.[86] And the usage in Ffraunce for soche case make substancialy for the said King Edward the III[de] and King Edward the IIIIth and ther heires for ther title to the corone and reame of Ffraunce, in that the same descended to king Pepin by a woman, Batildes, suster of King Dagobert, and in lyke wise by a woman the same corone and reame of Ffraunce discended to Hugh Capet as is declared afore truly & sufficiently.[87] And by the same title the said King Edward the IIIIth hath good right to clayme and take the corone and reame of Ffraunce as the trew heritier of the same, which title and right is now discended to the right excellent and most vertuous, my moost dred sovereyn lord Henry the VIIIth, by the grace of God king of Englond and of Ffraunce and lord of Ireland, |28v| eny allegacion or other thing to the contrarie notwithstonding.

And as for the use of tailles in Englond, is but the lawe of Englond but late made for particuler londes and can not bynde londes of other cuntrees but in Englond. And the supposel objected afore for usage of tailled londes in Englond makith not against the title of the kinges of Englond. And there is diverse maner of tailles in Englond aftir the myendes of the makers or ordeynors of suche tailles. Ffor some mynde to preserve the possession of soche londes in the surname of the donee therof for ever, and that is entended whan the donor gevith to the donee and to the heires males of his body laufully begoten eny londes. Here the doughtres sone shal not enherite for the doughtir hath chaunged hir surname by hir husbond, whois surname the sone shal use and not the donores, his grauntfathers surname. And that is taken in the lawe of Englond for that by his gift is expressed of whois body the heir male must discend. And in eny other taill the generall heire shal be heritier.[88] And if the surmytted Lawe Salique were, it was never entended to hold eny surname and that was extinct long afore now. For the surname of King Pharamond were ferre to seke and so were the surname of Clodio the Hery or Criniens, for that he had heris on his bak like a swyne. And the surname of Meroveus were also ferre to seke, and the surname of King Pepin were ferre to seke. And if it shuld take effect at Hugh Capet, the surnames of the Ffrenssh king now usurpers of the corone of Ffraunce shuld be Capettes |29r| and not Valois. For the surname of Valois toke original at the father of the said Phelip de Valois, Charles counte de Valois, but it is apparent that

---

[86] See pp. 144–145.

[87] See pp. 147–148.

[88] This argument relating to the English practice of entail was presented early in the first draft of the treatise, immediately following the discussion of Pharamond and the Salic Law. See T, fos 6v–7r.

the surname of great princes be by reason of his maneres or valiaunce, or of the place of ther nativite, or of ther offices or condicions.[89]

And it is to be noted that the said Phelip de Valois was not nor by eny meane might be heire to the said Charles le Beale nor to eny of the said Loys Hutin or Phelip le Long his brothern, by cause the same Phelip de Valois was not of their hole blode, but of the half blode.[90] Thus King Phelip sone of Saint Loys espoused first Isabel, doughtir of the king of Aragon, and had issue by hir Loys and King Phelip le Beale.[91] Which Phelip le Beale had issue the said Loys Hutin, Phelip le Long, Charles le Beale and Isabel mother to the said King Edward the III[de]. And the said Phelip sone of Saint Loys, aftir the deth of the said Isabel of Arragon his wief, secundly espoused Marie, suster of the duke of Braban, and by hir had issue the said Charles counte de Valois, father to the said Phelip de Valois, and II doughtres, the elder doughtir Margaret which was secund wief of King Edward the First, and thother doughtir was maried to the duke of Austriche.[92] And aftir the deth of the said King Phelip sone of Saint Loys, the said Marie his secund wief was maried to the counte d'Evreulx and by hym she conceyved a sone also counte d'Evreulx which had issue a sone which by the color of the said |**29v**| Phelip de Valois usurped the corone and reame of Navarre.[93] And for that the same Phelip de Valois was but of demy sang of the said Loys Hutin, Phelip le Long and Charles le Beale and not of ther hole blode, the corone and reame of Ffraunce ought in nowise to aperteyne to hym the same Phelip de Valois.

Capitulum VIII [94]

And where also in the said first partie is objected against the right which King Henry the VIth pretended to the corone and reame of Ffraunce that it shuld have ben by II meanes, the one as next

[89] This curious argument had appeared in T, fos 7r–7v. Also see p. 146 above.

[90] This false claim that Philippe VI was 'half-blood' also appeared in T, fo. 7v. Also see p. 145 above.

[91] In reality, Charles of Valois was the third son of Philippe III and Isabella of Aragon, and brother of Louis (d. 1270) and King Philippe IV the Fair.

[92] Philippe III and Marie of Brabant had one son and two daughters. The son was Louis, count of Evreux, who married Marguerite of Artois and fathered Philippe of Evreux, husband of Jeanne, daughter of King Louis X and queen of Navarre. The two daughters of Philippe III and Marie were Marguerite, wife of King Edward I, and Blanche, who married Rudolph of Austria, king of Bohemia.

[93] The English author continues to ignore the fact that Philippe, count of Evreux, was married to Jeanne, daughter of Louis X. See pp. 141–142.

[94] This chapter translates and then responds to *Pour ce que plusieurs*, pp. 78–80. There is no parallel in T, presumably because of the missing material between fos 10v and 11r.

heir therunto, the other by vertue of the treatie which was made at Troyes in Champaine the yere MIIII^C XX. By the whiche treatie King Charles the VI by his counsaill shuld adopte King Henry the Vth father to the said King Henry the VIth to be his sone and gave to him in mariage his doughtir, Madame Katherine, mother to the same King Henry the VIth, and graunted that to the said King Henry the Vth aftir the deth of the same Charles the VIth shuld apperteyne the corone and reame of Ffraunce and for his lief duryng made the same King Henry the Vth regent of Ffraunce. And also that the said Charles the VIth shuld have willed and ordeyned that aftir his decesse the corone of Ffraunce shuld come and apperteyne to the said King Henry the Vth in disheriting Charles his sone than dolphine and shuld have doon against hym many detestable and inhumaines declaracions against God, nature, reason and justice. By meane of which treatie, the said King Henry the Vth shuld have named hymself heritier of Ffraunce and regent of the reame. And that for that the said King Henry the Vth shuld have decessed afore the said Charles the VIth, by the which he might not be coroned king of Ffraunce according to |30r| pactions made in the said treatie, for that he shuld have called hymself but heritier and regent and shuld not be coroned nor take title of king of Ffraunce until aftir the deth of the said Charles the VIth. And that the Englisshmen, perceyving that prevent of deth of the said King Henry the Vth afore the deth of the said Charles the VIth as sone as they cowde, they shuld have caused the said King Henry the VIth to passe over the see to corone him king of Ffraunce by reason of the said treatie. And for that the cite of Reims shuld be that time in the obeissaunce of King Charles the VIIth which shuld afore then there be enoynte and sacred and aftir coroned at Saint Dionise, they shuld have doon the said King Henry the VIth to be coroned in the towne of Parys, not keping the solemnitees suche as apperteyned and shuld be requisite to enoynte a man to be sacred and coroned the most christien kinges of Ffraunce.[95]

And also that the said King Henry the Vth shuld be enformed whan he was in Ffraunce that the corone and reame of Ffraunce shuld not happe to a doughtir nor to other heire descendyng of a doughtir, he shuld have departed incontinent from the name of king of Ffraunce and named hymself but onely heritier and regent

---

[95] The English author omits the repeated statement that Edward III had no claim to the French throne to pass on to Henry V and Henry VI, p. 79.

of Ffraunce, confessing expressely that the said Charles the VIth shuld be trew king and heritier of the corone of Ffraunce, and for soche shuld have reputed and avowed hym. And in proof that the said King Henry the Vth shuld have confessed the said Charles the VIth to be trew king of Ffraunce, he shuld not have cleymed the corone of Ffraunce by the meane of the said King Edward the III[de] but by the said treatie of Troyes in Champaine.[96]

|30v| Trew it is that the said King Henry the VIth pretended title and right to the corone and reame of Ffraunce and had therof possession and was enoynted, sacred and coroned king of Ffraunce in the cite of Parys, the principall of all reame of Ffraunce, with asmoche solemntees and ministration of divine observances as eny king of Ffraunce had ever afore hym or aftir. Though it were not doon at Reins, the place is not materiall, nor all the kinges of Ffraunce afore that tyme were not enoynted and sacred at Reins nor coroned at Saint Dionises and yet they have ben taken, reputed and obeyed as kinges of Ffraunce nor eny part of his right therof for soche cause mynisshed. As Loys Balde and Charlemaine were enoynted, sacred and coroned at Parys in the monastre of Saint Petir and not at Reins. And Loys sone of the first Phelip was enoynted, sacred and coroned at Orleance and not at Reins.[97]

And trew it is that the said Charles the VIth by thadvise, assent and consent of all his lordes and estates of the reame of Ffraunce and of his Parliament of & at Parys, for the horrible, detestable and abhominable crimes, enormitees, trespasses, murdres and treasons doon in the reame of Ffraunce by the said Charles the VIIth than called the dolphin of Vienne, aswel against the persone of his father, naturel and sovereyn lord, the said Charles the VIth than opteynyng the corone of Ffraunce, as of his naturell mother and his sovereyn lady the quene, and also for the detestable, inhumaine and shamefull murdre committed by the said Charles dolphin of Vienne in the persone of John duke of Burgoigne cosin germaine of the said Charles the VIth and than regent of Ffraunce for and

---

[96] The English author ignores the remainder of the first section of the French treatise, including the description of the epitaph on Henry V's tomb at Westminster and the extensive arguments against the treaty of Troyes, pp. 80–83.

[97] In fact, Charlemagne was crowned at Noyon in 768, and in 800 at Saint Peter's in Rome; the coronation of Charles the Bald as king of Lotharingia took place at Metz in 869; and Louis VI the Fat was crowned at Orléans in 1108. From the eleventh century onwards, most French royal coronations took place at Reims and Henry VI was the only medieval monarch to be crowned in Paris as king of France.

undir the same King Charles the VIth.[98] Which duke than at the request of the said dolphine, by his lettres comprehending false, dissimiled amite, presented hymself to the same dolphine in the castel |31r| of Monstrian and kneling afore the same dolphine upon his kne in reverence of the same dolphine at his first comyng, was piteuously by the same dolphine murdred to the dampnable and shamefull reproche of the same dolphine.[99] And for many other disobeissances, insurrections, murdres and destructions committed by the said dolphine associat with the Armynakes, graunted, decreed and ordeyned that the same Charles dolphine of Vienne shuld be for ever disabled to cleyme eny thing of the corone or reame of Ffraunce.[100] And further aggreed, treated, promysed, decreed and graunted, by the assent and auctorite abovesaid, that the said King Henry the Vth shuld espouse and take to wief in mariage Madame Katherine doughtir of the said Charles the VIth.[101] And that for the pacifyeng of the debat and werres which that the same King Henry the Vth had and made, aswel for the recover of the possession of the corone & reame of Ffraunce as of thother his particuler hereditamentes in the parties of beyond the see, considering the great recoverees and conquestes of the same King Henry the Vth in that behalf likely by force to have opteyned all the same his right, as he had than by conquest and victories opteyned Normandie his anncient heritage, the said King Charles the VIth, by the assent, consent and auctorite aforesaid, treated with the said King Henry the Vth at Troyes in Champaine, moving the same King Henry the Vth to be contented

[98] On 17 January 1420, Charles VI addressed a letter to the people of France, citing the transgressions and crimes that had made his son, the Dauphin Charles, unworthy to inherit the throne; these charges were repeated in the treaty of Troyes on 21 May 1420. The latter was transcribed in *Chronique de Monstrelet*, III, pp. 390–402, and *Chronicles of Monstrelet*, I, pp. 439–442; also see *EMDP*, II, pp. 629–636.

[99] Monstrelet described the efforts of the Dauphin Charles to persuade the duke of Burgundy to come to Montereau-faut-Yonne, together with the subsequent murder committed by Sir Tanneguy du Châtel and other conspirators at the bridge by the castle on 10 September 1419: *Chronique de Monstrelet*, III, pp. 338–346, and *Chronicles of Monstrelet*, I, pp. 422–424.

[100] The treaty of Troyes did not explicitly bar the Dauphin Charles from the royal succession but, on 23 December 1420, he was summoned to appear before a lit de justice, in the presence of Charles VI and Henry V, to answer for the murder at Montereau. When he failed to appear by 3 January 1421, he was declared guilty of lèse-majesté, which was presented as rendering him incapable of succeeding to the French throne: *Chronique de Monstrelet*, IV, 17–20 and 36–37, and *Chronicles of Monstrelet*, I, pp. 450–451 and 458.

[101] The marriage was celebrated on 2 June 1420, after being agreed in the first article of the treaty of Troyes: *Chronique de Monstrelet*, III, p. 390, and *Chronicles of Monstrelet*, I, pp. 439–440. Also see *EMDP*, II, p. 630.

that the said King Charles the VIth might occupie and peasibly enjoye the name and corone as king of Ffraunce for terme of his lief, for that he had regned amonges them by a long tyme and had ben to them good and gracious. And that the said King Henry the Vth |31v| shuld have the regimen and governaunce of the reame of Ffraunce and to be contented onely with the name of king of Englond and of heritier and regent of Ffraunce, and that the corone and reame of Ffraunce and the name of king of Ffraunce shuld come and apperteyne to the same King Henry the Vth and his heires ymmediatly aftir the deth of the said King Charles the VIth for ever, according to the clayme and former right of the said King Henry.[102] Wherupon the same King Henry, considering that by the contynewaunce of his werres, the reame of Ffraunce and his other particuler hereditamentes in those parties might fall into ruyne and desolation, and moche homicide shuld be therby committed, and therof having in his mynde compassion and will to spare that if he might conveniently opteyne to his right which had ben and than was deforced from his progenitoures and him, and the rather with the love of his dew subgettes of Ffraunce than by rigour if he in eny wise might, aggreed and was contented upon that offre to suffer the said King Charles the VIth to contynew and enjoye the name of king of Ffraunce for terme of his lief, upon auctentique writinges and assurances to be made upon that ther couvenantes, promyses, agrementes and grauntes. So that aftir the deth of the same Charles the VIth, the possession of the corone and reame of Ffraunce without difficultie, lette or disturbance shuld come to the said King Henry the Vth and to his heires for ever. Which covenantes, promises, agrementes and grauntes were concluded and confermed with auctentique writinges, soleme othes and assured promyses, made, sealed and solennely declared, publisshed and denounsed, and by auctorite of the Parliament of Parys confermed for the sure |32r| entirteynyng of the same. And that the said King Henry the Vth to be contented for the terme of lief of the said King Charles the VIth for all the premisses other than he was in possession of tyme of the same treatie, onely to use within the reame of Ffraunce the regimen of the same reame of and in the name of the said Charles the VIth, and the same King Henry to use within the same reame the name of Henry king of Englond, heritier and regent of Ffraunce. As by the tenur of

---

[102] Articles 7 and 8 of the treaty of Troyes declared that the French crown would pass to Henry V and his heirs upon the death of Charles VI, and entrusted the regency of France to Henry until that time. Neither made any reference to Henry's previous claims to the throne. See *Chronique de Monstrelet*, III, p. 392, and *Chronicles of Monstrelet*, I, p. 440, together with *EMDP*, II, p. 631.

the same treatie in the first volume of the croniques of Enguerain Monstrellet appierith more at large.[103]

By which it appierith clerely that the said King Henry the VIth was not estopped to clayme, use, enjoye and possede laufully the corone and reame of Ffraunce by the one or thother of the said II meanes. For the oon destroyed not thother, but the same King Henry the VIth had good and just right to holde, possede and enjoye the corone and reame of Ffraunce in his owne and proper right by owther of the said II meanes, the prevent of deth or the deth of the said King Henry the Vth or the said Charles the VIth, eny informacion to the same King Henry made as is supposed, using of name, departing from name, reputing or avowing of name, auctorite, possession, power, confession, omission of clayme or eny other thyng objected, alledged or surmitted to the contrarie notwithstonding.

|32v| *Capitulum IX*[104]

And if the case were soche that the corone of Ffraunce were of soche nature as it is not that it ought not to descende by female ligne as is objected, yet there be diverse dominions and cuntrees which were in possession of the aforenamed Charles le Beale and were no parcel of the corone of Ffraunce, and descended to the same Charles le Beale from his auncestres by female blode, which the said Phelip de Valoys usurped with the corone of Ffraunce, that ought to have descended to the said King Edward the III[de] as next heir therunto. That is to saye the corone and reame of Navarre and the countie of Champaine, as is declared in the first chapitre afore.[105]

Also the cuntre and dominion of the Province which descended to Phelip sone of Saint Loys by thenheritaunce of his mother [...] wief of the same Saint Loys, elder doughtir of Raymond erle of Province. As thus Alphons somtyme king of Arragon opteyned and was lord of the countie of Province as parcell of Arragon, and gave the same countie of Province to Alphons his yonger sone, which Alphons the sone had issue Raymond erle of Province aftir hym.[106] Which Raymond

---

[103] Article 22 of the treaty of Troyes stipulated that Henry V would be known as 'nostre très chier fils, Henry, Roy d'Angleterre, héritier de France' and '*Noster precarissimus filius, Henricus, Rex Anglie, heres Francie*': *Chronique de Monstrelet*, III, p. 397, and *Chronicles of Monstrelet*, I, p. 441, and also see *EMDP*, II, p. 633.

[104] This is the only chapter that does not begin with a preçis of material from *Pour ce que plusieurs* and that does not respond directly to any statement in the French treatise. This material does not appear in T.

[105] See pp. 142–143.

[106] The house of Barcelona ruled Provence until 1245 when count Ramon Berenguer, son of Alfonso II, died. In the absence of male heirs, the county passed to his fourth daughter,

had issue III doughtres of which thelder doughtir named [...] was maried to Saint Loys king of Ffraunce, which by hir had issue Phelip, which had issue Phelip le Beale, which had issue the aforerehersed III brothern kinges, Loys Hutin, Phelip le Long and Charles le Beale, and Isabel quene of Englond, mother to the said King Edward the III^{de}. And for that the same III brothern, Loys Hutin, Phelip le Long and Charles le Beale were dede without issue, the said countre of Province ought to have descended |33r| to the said King Edward the III^{de} and not the said Phelip de Valois which cam but of the yonger brother of the said Phelip le Beale, as is confessed in ther allegacions and as is manifest declared in the croniques.

Capitulum X[107]

[A]nd[108] where in and for the secund part of the said matier of imaginacions conteyned in the said printed boke by which is made mencion against the right and title of the king of Englond to the particuler seignories and londes and cuntries in the reame of Ffraunce, over and besides the corones and reames of Ffraunce and of Navarre and the countie of Champaine.[109] Is alledged and objected that the Englisshmen shuld saye that Duke William of Normandie was in peasible possession of the duche of Normandie and conquered the reame of Englond. And that the II kinges late of Englond, Edward the IIIIth and Henry the VIth shuld be discended of right ligne by meane of a womman, as it shuld be theraftir declared. And declared that the said Duke William which by conquest was aftir king of Englond, shuld have IIII sones and oon doughtir, of which IIII sones he omittith in his allegacion the first III for brieftie. And that |33v| all the succession aswel of Englond as of the duche of Normandie shuld come to Henry Beauclerk which was the IIIIth sone. And the doughtir shuld be named Adelle, which shuld be maried to the erle of Chartres and of Bloys, to which erle of Chartres shuld have descended the countie of Champaine. Of which mariage shuld have issued the erle Theobald of Champaine & was erle of Bloys, which aftir shuld

---

Beatrice, and her husband, Charles I of Anjou. Louis IX was married to Beatrice's sister, Marguerite of Provence.

[107] This chapter translates and then responds to *Pour ce que plusieurs*, pp. 84–87.

[108] The scribe has left a two-line gap for the initial, just as at the beginning of the response to the third section of *Pour ce que plusieurs*, p. 256 below.

[109] The French treatise listed these lands as Normandy, Guyenne, Anjou, Maine, Touraine, and Poitou: see p. 84.

have occupied the reame of Englond.[110] And that of that Erle
Theobald shuld have issued a doughtir named Adelle which shuld
have be maried to King Loys the Peteous, father to King Phelip the
Conquerraunt. And that there shuld have ben but one doughtir
of the said Henry Beauclerk named Matildis the Imperesse, for
that she was the wief of the Imperour Henry the IIIIth, and aftir
maried to the erle of Angeo, Geffrey Martell the III[de], which shuld
be sone of the last Ffulco, which shuld be the last christien king of
Jerusalem. And that of that mariage of the Imperesse Matildes and
of Gefferey erle of Angeo shuld have issued a sone named Henry
the Secund, which by cause of his mother, heir of King Henry
Beauclerk, was king of Englond and duke of Normandie, and by
his father Gefferey was erle of Angeo and of Maine and of Torayne.
The same King Henry the Secund shuld have espoused the Quene
Alianore which afore had ben wief of the said King Loys the Peteux,
sone of King Loys the Grosse. Which Alianore, for certain causes
by auctorite of Pope Eugenie the Secund, the same King Loys
shuld have forsaken hir. And aftir the said King Henry the Secund
king of Englond shuld have espoused hir, of which mariage |34r|
shuld have issued IIII sones and oon doughtir. The first sone shuld
be Henry which in the lief of his father was coroned king and died
afore his father.[111] The secund sone shuld be Richard Cuer de Leon
which succeded the said King Henry the Secund, but he had none
issue. The III[de] sone shuld be Gefferey which shuld have espoused
the countesse of Bretayn of whom shuld have issued Arthur and
Alianore. The IVth sone shuld be John, which shuld have recuilled
the succession of his ffather and of his mother.[112] The doughtir shuld
be named Alianore or Margaret which shuld be wief of the king
of Spaine named Alphons, of whom shuld have issued a doughtir
named Blanche, which shuld be wief of King Loys sone of the said
Phelip the Conquerrant, father of Saint Loys. And that the said
Blanche shuld be onely heir of hir father and mother for that hir
elder brother decessed.

Trew it is that the said William duke of Normandie aftir by his conquest
and by right of transport of Saint Edward the Confessour, somtyme
king of Englond, was king of Englond and in peasible possession of

---

[110] The English throne was inherited by Stephen (d. 1154), brother of Thibaud, count
of Champagne, as identified in most manuscripts of *Pour ce que plusieurs* (see p. 85).
[111] The English author omits the false French statement that it was this Prince Henry
the Young who killed Thomas Becket in 1170 on the orders of his father (see p. 86).
[112] This ignores the French claim that John had forfeited all of the French lands which
were subsequently confiscated from him by Philippe Augustus (see p. 86).

the duche of Normandie,[113] and that the said II kinges, Edward the IIIIth and Henry the VIth were bothe descended of him lyneally by a woman. And it is trew that the same William the Conquerror had issue IIII sones, but he had also V doughtres, of which the eldest named Cecilie was abbesse |34v| of Cane. The secund, Constaunce, was maried to Alain Ffergant erle of Bretayn. The III[de] doughtir, Adelle, was maried to Stephen erle of Bloys. The IIIIth doughtir, Matildis, was promysed in mariage to Harold sone of Godwin, which usurped the corone of Englond. And the Vth doughtir named [. . .] was promysed in mariage to Alphons king of Galice.[114] The said Stephen erle of Bloys had issue Theobald erle of Bloys and King Stephen which occupied the corone of Englond.[115]

And there was but one doughtir of the said King Henry Beauclerk, the said Matildes Imperesse which was maried to the Imperor Henry the IIIIth and secundly maried to the said Gefferey Plantagenet erle of Angeo, elder brother afore the said Ffulco king of Jerusalem.[116] And of that mariage descended the said King Henry the Secund and also one Gefferey Plantagenet, which Henry the Secund by cause of his said mother, heir of the said Henry Beauclerk, was king of Englond and duc of Normandie, and by his said father was erle of Angeo, Maine and Torayne. And the same King Henry the Secund espoused Alianore, doughtir and heir of William duc of Guyan and Gascoign and erle of Poytew, and by hir had the same hir heritages of Guyan, Gascoign & Poytew. Which Alianore was afore maried to the said King Loys the Petoux, and for cosinage and consanguinite devorsed.[117] And the said King Henry the Secund had by hir issue the said IIII sones and III doughtres,[118] of which III doughtres, the elder named Matildes was maried to Henry duc of Saxonie, of whom descended Henry duc of Saxonie and Othes the Imperor, of whom be descended the dukes of Saxonie with moche suer progenie.[119] The secund doughtir

[113] See pp. 209–210.

[114] The known daughters of William I were Adelida, Cecilia, Matilda, Constance, and Adèle, countess of Blois, though the order of their birth is not certain.

[115] William I's daughter Adèle was married to Etienne Henri of Blois, and their five children included Thibaud II of Champagne and King Stephen of England.

[116] The only legitimate daughter of King Henry I was Matilda, who married the Emperor Heinrich V and then Geoffrey V Plantagenet.

[117] The two sons of Geoffrey V Plantagenet and Matilda were King Henry II and Geoffrey, count of Nantes. Henry II married Eleanor of Aquitaine in 1152. See pp. 217–218.

[118] The sons of Henry II and Eleanor of Aquitaine were William, Henry the Young, Richard I, Geoffrey, and John, and their daughters were Matilda, Eleanor, and Joanna. See p. 86, n. 187 and p. 87, n. 193.

[119] Matilda married Heinrich the Lion, duke of Bavaria and Saxony. Their eldest son, Heinrich, assumed the title of duke of Saxony on his father's death, became count palatine of the Rhine in 1196, and died in 1227. His brother Otto was elected emperor in 1198 and crowned at Rome in 1209, but died without children in 1218.

named Alianore was |35r| maried to Alphons king of Castille, which had issue II sones, Ffernand and Henry, and V doughtres, wherof the elder named Berenger was maried to the king of Leon in Spaine, the secund Vracam maried to the king of Portuigale, the III^{de}, the said Blanche, maried to the said King Loys of Ffraunce, the IIIIth maried to the said king of Arragon, and the Vth Constance nonne in the abbey of Olgys.[120] And the III^{de} of the doughtres of the said Henry the Secund named Johane was first maried to William king of Cecile and secundly to Raymund erle of Tholouse.[121] By which aperith the false imaginacion of the Frensshemen in the premisses.

Capitulum XI [122]

And where in the same secund partie is also alledged against the right which the king of Englond pretendith of his said particuler heritages which that the said Richard Cuer de Leon opteyned by succession of enheritaunce aftir the deth of the said King Henry the Secund his father and of the said Alianore his mother.[123] Ffor that that aftir the possession of the same Richard therof, the same Richard aswel in the tyme of his voiage with the said King Phelip called the Conquerant king of Ffraunce to werre in the Holy Lond against the infideles, as aftir his comyng home, shuld make werre against the same King Phelip. And than shuld have begon a confiscacion of the said heritages.[124]

And for that the said King Richard decessed without issue |35v| and the succession therof shuld have comen to Arthur and Alianore, children and issue of Gefferey III^{de} sone of the said King Henry the Secund. And John the IIIIth sone of the same King

---

[120] Eleanor married King Alfonso VIII of Castile, and they had twelve children including: Fernando; King Enrique I of Castile; Berenguela, wife of King Alfonso IX of Leon, who renounced her claim to the Castilian throne in favour of her son Fernando after the death of her brother Enrique; Urraca, wife of King Alfonso II of Portugal; Blanche, wife of King Louis VIII of France; Eleanor, wife of King James I of Aragon; and Constanza, abbess of Las Huelgas.

[121] The word 'Raymond' was inserted into the text by the same scribe. Joanna married William II, king of Sicily, and then Raymond VI, count of Toulouse.

[122] This chapter translates and then responds to *Pour ce que plusieurs*, pp. 87–89. It is largely based upon the material in T fos 11r–15r, though that section of the manuscript is badly damaged and the author heavily edited his own text, crossing out eighteen lines on fo. 12v and replacing them with two small folios sewn into the manuscript at a ninety-degree angle.

[123] In *Pour ce que plusieurs*, Richard's inheritance from his father, Henry II, was identified as England, Normandy, Anjou, Maine, and Touraine, together with Guyenne and Poitou from his mother Eleanor (see p. 87).

[124] The English translator ignores the statement that Richard had allied with King Philip against his father, Henry II (see p. 87).

Henry, for that the said Arthur and Alianore shuld be yong of age, shuld have taken upon him the governaunce of the same Arthur and Alianore and of ther londes & lordshippes. And thinking the same John that if his said nevew & nece were dede, he shuld be oon of the most great lordes of christientie, he therfor shuld have imagined the deth of his said nevew Arthur, and shuld have doon him to be cast by subtile meanes from the height of the castel in the mydd of Chinon within the toun to breke his nekke and all his membres.[125]

And aftir the said John shuld have sent the said Alianore suster of Arthur to Winchester in Englond where he shuld have caused hir to be kept prisoner unto his deth. And aftir the thinges abovesaid doon, the said John shuld have opteyned the succession of his ffather and of his said mother and of his brothern, and so shuld holde him for king of Englond, duke of Normandie and of Guyan, erle of Poytow, Angeo, Maine & of Torayne, and put him in possession and season therof. And shuld have made great rebellions and disobeissances, conspiracions, treasons against the said King Phelip his sovereyn lord to the regard of his londes in Ffraunce. By and for occasion of which crimes and ill dedes, aswel in casc of leze of the roiall majesté of felonie as otherwise, he shuld be declared by the barons of the reame of Ffraunce, which shuld be asmoche to saie as the peres, to have confisqued and forfaited against the king. And for that cause and by that meane shuld be deprived and put owt of all the londes and seignories above declared which he helde in the reame of Ffraunce and shuld be acquisite by title of |36r| confisquacion to the king and adjoint and reuined to the corone as to the great heritage and domane of the king.

And over that, seen that he shuld be unkinde to his blode from whom the succession shuld have comen and by consequent unworthy to have come to the said succession, it shuld seme that the reame of Englond ought to have comen to the moost next of the said succession aftir the same King John. Which most next, if the reame of Englond may come by a doughtir, shuld be the said Phelip called the Conquerrant of oon side, and the said King Saint Loys on thother side. For the mother of the said King Phelip shuld be doughtir of Erle Theobald of Champaine, neve of the said King Henry Beauclerk and his next heir except the Imperesse Matildes. And that Saint Loys shuld be the sone of Blanche of Espanie, nece of the said kinges Richard and John, and onely heir of hir father

---

[125] This translation also omits the quotation from the unidentified 'chronique dAngeleterre' quoted by Guillaume Cousinot when discussing the fates of Arthur and his sister Eleanor (see p. 88).

and mother, as shuld be aforeseid. And that it shal not be founde that there shuld be noo nerer heir of the said succession aftir the said King John.

Trew it is that the said King Richard Cuer de Leon succeded by trew heritage and was possessed of the corone & reame of Englond and of the duchies of Normandie and Guyan and of the counties of Poytew, Angeo, Maine, and Torayn, and also of the superiorite of dominion of Armorik Bretain by good and trewe title and by discent of enheritaunce. As thus of the corone and reme of Englond and of the duche of Normandie and superiorite of Armorik Bretain as next heir |36v| to his said father King Henry the Secund, the same King Henry beyng sone of Matildes Imperesse, doughtir of the said King Henry Beauclerk, sone of William duke of Normandie, conquerror of Englond, of which duchie of Normandie the cuntre of Bretain was than, and yet is holden in fee without resort to the corone of Ffraunce as hereaftir shalbe declared.[126] And of the counties of Angeo, Maine and Torayn also as next heir therof by his father King Henry the Secund, the same King Henry beyng sone of Gefferey Plantagenest, erle of those counties of Angeo, Maine and Torayne by olde enheritaunce, and of the duchie of Guyan and Gascoign, and of Alverne, and of the countie of Poytew, as next heir to his mother the said Quene Alianore, doughtir and heir of William duke and erle therof by anncient enheritaunce.[127]

Which King Richard never ded rebellion or eny thing against the said King Phelip or other king of Ffraunce wherby to confisque or confisqued eny thing. Albe it the same King Phelip ded to him many and dampnable injuries as may appere in the histories. Ffor the same King Richard and King Phelip in the yere MCIIII^{XX} X at [. . .] Saint Remy allied and couvenanted to gether in the quarell of our faith to passe into the Holy Lond to recovere the same out of the hondes of the infideles.[128] And by those couvenantes and alliance was promysed and sworne, auctorised by ther writing, that eyther of the same kinges the honour of thother shuld serve and kepe and to hym faith bere of lief and membre and erthely honor, and that neyther of them shuld fayle other in his journeyes or causes. But the king of Ffraunce shuld so help the king of Englond to defend his londes as he wold his cite of Parys defend if it were assieged. |37r| And the king of Englond shuld help the king of Ffraunce to defend his londes as he wold his cite of

---

[126] See pp. 203 and 259.

[127] See pp. 201–202.

[128] This paragraph is taken from the *Chronica Hovedene*, III, pp. 30–31, which reported that the treaty was agreed by Richard and Philip at '*Vadum Sancti Remigii*' on 13 January 1190.

Roan defend if it were assieged. And furthermore that if owther of
the same kinges shuld dye in their pilgrinage, the other which shuld
lyve shuld have the mony & men of him that shuld be dede to doo the
service of God. And the same alliaunce and couvenantes were by the
othes affermed and by writinges undir ther sealles in the fest of Saint
Hillarie. And the archebisshops and bisshops promysed *verbo veritatis*,
and the erles and barones of eyther reame, by their solenne othes that
they shuld kepe inviolated the said alliaunce, peas and couvenantes,
and that they shuld not depart from the faith of ther said kinges
nor shuld move werre duryng the tyme of their said pilgrimages.
And the archibisshops and bisshops promysed to geve sentences of
excommenqement against the violatoures of the same alliaunce, peas
and couvenantes.

And therupon in the same yere, mette at Virilak where the reliquies
of the body of Saynt Marie Magdalene rest, and departed from thens
in the Octabris of the Nativite of Saint John Baptist and went to
Lenur sur la Rone, where for the multitude of ther people by oon
assent departed ther companies.[129] And the king of Ffraunce with his
retenue went the nere wey to Geane. And the king of Englond with
his retenew went by Marsille, where he rested VIII daies, attending
for his navie. And for that his navie were not come, he conducted
and hired X carriques and XX galees and departed from Marsile the
VII day of August, and cam to Geane the XIII day of August |**37v**|
and there spak with the king of Ffraunce, and departed and sped his
jorney.[130] So that the XXIII day of Septembre, King Richard came to
Messane in Sisilie, where he fond the king of Ffraunce which had taken
the nerer wey.[131] And there King Richard treated with King Tancrede
of Sicile to have delyveraunce out of his custodie his suster, which was
wedow of William afore that king of Sicile, and had hir delyvered.[132]
And there were further couvenantes of leage and amyte made betwen
the same King Richard and King Tancrede and concluded.

And the said king of Ffraunce, envious of the same King Richard,
of prive and close malice, excited thinhabitauntes and citesines of
Messane to make debate with King Richardes people. By whois
mocion they killed many of King Richardes men, the same king

---

[129] *Chronica Hovedene*, III, p. 37. The two kings met at Vézelay, where some of the remains
of Mary Magdalene were housed, on 2 July 1190. After travelling to Lyon ('*Leonum supra
Rodanum*' in Howden's account), Richard and his forces went to join his fleet at Marseille,
while the French travelled to Genoa.

[130] *Chronica Hovedene*, III, p. 39.

[131] *Chronica Hovedene*, III, p. 55.

[132] *Chronica Hovedene*, III, p. 55. King William II of Sicily had died in November 1189
and was succeeded by his illegitimate cousin, Tancred of Lecce. William's widow, Joanna,
sister of Richard I, was held in custody by Tancred, who refused to release her dower.

of Ffraunce and his people loking on without eny rescue or confort
or helping the Englisshmen, wherin he violated his said couvenantes
and was therfor perjured.[133] Neverthelesse the grudges therof were
pacified the VIII day of Octobir and ther former couvenantes
newe confermed by bothe kinges and their lordes by their solenne
othes upon holy reliquies of saintes, that thoon of them shuld aide
thother in that pilgrinage goyng and comyng according to the same
ther former couvenantes, with many other statutes there made for
the sale and gayne of vitailles and to kepe ther people in good
governance.[134]

And all this notwithstonding the same king of Ffraunce, Phelip,
not having regard to his othes or promyses, nor yet to the service
of God in that pilgrinage, entending the destruction of the said king
of Englond, sent and directed his lettres to the said King Tancrede of
Sesile by the hondes of [. . .] duke of Burgoign.[135] By which he wrote to
him that King Richard shuld be a traitour |38r| and shuld not have
kept his peas with him, and offred by the same that if King Tancrede
wold doo bataill with King Richard or by night wold invade King
Richardes host, that himself, the king of Ffraunce, shuld aide him to
destroye King Richard and his host. Which lettres of the same kinges
of Ffraunce King Tancrede shewed and delivered to King Richard,
and offred that if the said duke of Burgoign wold denye that he
delyvered not to him the same lettres on the behalf of the said king of
Ffraunce, he wold prove it by the hondes of oon of his dukes. Wherof
King Richard greatly merveilled of that the king of Ffraunce was
of suche false imaginacion, not observyng his oothes nor promyses,
and by that somwhat moved forbare somwhat of his countenance
towardes him. And he the same king of Ffraunce, inquiring the cause,
King Richard, by the erle of Fflaundres, sent him direct notice of
the matier. And the king of Ffraunce, somwhat astonyed, denyed his
lettres. But nevertheless he expressely uttred somwhat of his malice
and said that if King Richard wold not espouse his suster Alice, as was
promysed in his fathers tyme, he wold be his enemye all his lief. And
whan that was shewed to King Richard, he answered therunto that
he might not espouse the said Alice for that his father King Henry the

[133] *Chronica Hovedene*, III, pp. 56–57. Roger of Howden did not blame the French king
for these tensions, but did criticize him for failing to assist Richard.

[134] *Chronica Hovedene*, III, pp. 58–60.

[135] Marginal note: '*hec omnia continentur in cronica magistri Roger de Hovedon ad totum & plura
alia in itinere ipsorum regis Ricardi Anglie & Philippi Ffrancie accedent versus Jerusalem ibidem &
revertendo*'. This story was reported in *Chronica Hovedene*, III, p. 98, which did not identify the
duke of Burgundy as Hugues.

Secund had begoten a sone upon hir, and offred to prove it.[136] Wherof the erle of Fflaundres made relacion to the said king of Ffraunce, which pacified his meend in that partie by the counseil of the same erle.

And aftir that there at Messane, new accord was made betwix the same kinges of Ffraunce and of Englond and upon that agrement amonges other. |38v| And to please King Richard, the same king of Ffraunce, Phelip, by his lettres undir his seall graunted and confermed for hym, his heires and successoures for ever, to the said King Richard, that the duche of Bretayn shuld for ever to apperteyne and belong to the dominion of the duche of Normandie. And that the duc of Bretayn and his heires and successoures shuld be liegemen to the dukes of Normandie. And that the dukes of Normandie shuld answer to the kinges of Ffraunce aswel of the duche of Bretain as of the duche of Normandie. And therupon the peas was confermed.[137]

And aftir that in the tyme of beyng of the said kinges as the siege of the cite of Acon, the said erle of Fflaundres decessed at that siege. Aftir whois deth the said king of Ffraunce made meanes by all colores he coude imagine to depart from that siege of Acon homewardes into Ffraunce, in trust at his retorne home not oonly to have opteyned the countie of Fflaundres, but also to oppresse from the said king of Englond the duche of Normandie.[138] And notwithstonding the great and solemie oothes, couvenantes and promyses of the said king of Ffraunce afore rehersed, the same king of Ffraunce without assent, will or agrement of the said King Richard, departed from the cite of Acon homewardes, leving the said King Richard in the werres against the infideles. Albe it afore his departing from Acon, afore all the princes there, the same king of Ffraunce made open and solenne oothes upon the holy evangelies that he shuld not invade, nor cause to be invade, eny of the londes or dominions of the said King Richard, nor doo, nor procure to be doon to the same King Richard eny hurt or dommage.[139]

---

[136] *Chronica Hovedene*, III, pp. 98–99. Richard I had been betrothed to Philippe's sister Alix in 1169 but, by 1191, he was planning to marry Berengaria, daughter of King Sancho VI of Navarre. The only evidence that Alix had been seduced by Richard's father, Henry II, is the testimony of Roger of Howden, though 'it is hard to see why [Richard] would invent an unnecessary lie': John Gillingham, *Richard I* (New Haven, CT, 1999), p. 142n.

[137] Marginal note: '*ibidem*'. See *Chronica Hovedene*, III, pp. 99–100, together with p. 259 below.

[138] *Chronica Hovedene*, III, p. 111. Count Philippe of Flanders died at Acre on 1 June 1191 and Philippe Augustus was the heir to his county of Artois.

[139] *Chronica Hovedene*, III, pp. 123 and 125–126. Philippe declared his wish to return to France on 22 July 1191 and departed on 31 July, accompanied by Roger of Howden.

And by confort and example of the same king of Ffraunce, many other princes and noble men beyng |39r| in the said pilgrinage also departed out and from the same and from the service of God. And notwithstonding the said othes and promyses of the said king of Ffraunce, at his retorne in to Ffraunce, he the same king of Ffraunce by his especiall ambassade procured and treated with the Imperour Henry[140] that if the said King Richard shuld retorne homewardes within his power, that he shuld be taken prisoner, and besides defamed the same King Richard of diverse infamies dampnably and untruly, wherof the same King Richard aftir declared hymself.[141]

And further the said king of Ffraunce with armed power invaded and made werre in and upon the londes of the same King Richard in Normandie and assieged and toke by force the castel d'Evreulx and assieged Roane, and toke also by force the castelles of Vaureall and Vernoly and destroyed abbeyes and churches there.[142] For the which his werres and destructions made in King Richardes londes, which was than pilgrine and in the service of God, the same king of Ffraunce was by Pope Celestine excommunicat.[143]

And aftir that the said King Richard being taken prisoner and by the duke of Austriche delyvered to the prison of the said Imperor Henry,[144] the said king of Ffraunce abetted and procured the said John, brother of the said King Richard, to usurpe the corone and reame of Englond, and offred to the same John in mariage his said suster Alice, and therfor promysed to delyver to hym Normandie and thother his brothers hereditamentes.[145] And the same king of Ffraunce of his further malice persiewed to have in mariage the doughtir of the king of Denmark and to have with hir soche title as the Danes had to Englond, and to have aide with shippes and men for the recovere therof for a yere, though ther title were right nought. |39v| It was denyed to hym. Neverthelesse he espoused the said doughtir of Denmark named Botild

---

[140] The name 'Henry' may have been inserted into the text later, by the same scribe. Marginal note: '*cronica Magistri Rogeri de Hoveden*'. See *Chronica Hovedene*, III, p. 167.

[141] Marginal note: 'Inter fflores historiarum'. Richard's response to the charges laid against him by Emperor Heinrich VI was recorded in the *Flores historiarum*, II, p. 107.

[142] The frontier castle of Gisors fell on 12 April 1193 and, the following year, Philippe temporarily captured Evreux, which was sacked, and Vaudreuil, and again laid siege to both Rouen and Verneuil: *Chronica Hovedene*, III, pp. 206–207, 251–252, 255, and 257.

[143] *Chronica Hovedene*, III, p. 187.

[144] *Chronica Hovedene*, III, pp. 185–186 and 195–196. Richard I was captured near Vienna in late December 1192 by Leopold of Austria.

[145] *Chronica Hovedene*, III, pp. 198 and 204. In January 1193, John paid homage to Philippe for Normandy and all of Richard's other lands, and also promised to marry Alix and to hand over Gisors and the Norman Vexin to the French king.

and had with hir XM marc. But aftir one night lyeing with hir, he forsoke hir, wherfor he was excomunicate and his londes enterdict.[146]

And over and besides, the said king of Ffraunce, aftir that the said King Richard was agreed with the said imperor for his raunsom to be delyvered out of his prison, the said king of Ffraunce sent his ambassade to the imperor, offring to geve to the same imperour fyfty thousand markes so that he shuld kepe King Richard in prison unto Michelmesse next aftir that, or elles to geve for every monyth he shuld kepe the same King Richard in prison M li[vres], or elles if the imperor wold delyvere the same King Richard to the prison of the king of Ffraunce, he wold geve for hym CCM markes, which taried his delyveraunce.[147]

And aftir whan the said King Richard was by his redempcion out of the imperores prison and was retorned into Englond, and had taken from his brother John all his londes for his rebellion and unkynde will of usurpacion, and had redressed many injuries doon in Englond in his absence, he passed the see into Normandie, and at the castel of Brins, the said John his brother havyng than nothing to lyve by and refused of the king of Ffraunce, yelded himself mekely and lamentably to the said King Richard which pardoned him there of fraternal pitie.[148] And aftir that King Richard recovered all his londes and castelles which the said king of Ffraunce had oppressed from him in the tyme of his said pilgrinage. And in that his recovere the said king of Ffraunce wold in nowise abide King Richard but fleddc from him, and sent his IIII ambassadoures to King Richard to treate with him to put ther variaunces upon |**4or**| the jugement of V persones of eyther partie. Wherunto the same King Richard was aggreable with that that the same king of Ffraunce shuld be the Vth persone for his partie, and King Richard to be the Vth persone for his partie, which the king of Ffraunce refused.[149]

[146] Marginal note: '*Si anno MCIIII^{XX} XIII*'. See *Chronica Hovedene*, III, pp. 224–225 and 307, and IV, pp. 112–113. In 1193, Philippe Augustus married Botilda, more commonly known as Ingeborg, daughter of King Waldemar I of Denmark. The following day, the French king sent his new bride away, and quickly replaced her with Agnes de Méran.

[147] Marginal note: '*Cronica magistri Rogeri de Hoveden*'. See *Chronica Hovedene*, III, p. 229, which reports that the offer was made by both Philippe and John.

[148] Richard landed at Sandwich on 13 March 1194 and forced the last of John's garrisons to surrender by the end of March, before crossing to Normandy in the middle of May. Roger of Howden did not identify the location of this meeting with John, but the *Flores historiarum*, II, p. 110, stated that it took place at Bruis (Brix) and described the fraternal mercy that Richard showed to his weeping brother.

[149] The story of the proposed combat was not reported by Roger of Howden, but did appear in the *Flores historiarum*, II, p. 110.

Notwithstonding aftir that in the fest of Saint Hillary in the yere MCIIII^XX XVI, the said II kinges of Englond and Ffraunce, Richard & Phelip, treated at Loviers where it was aggreed betwix them in this wise. The said King Phelip quitecleymed to the said King Richard Yssoden, with thappertonances and all the right which he had in Berry and in Alverne and in Gascoign, and yelded also frely to the same King Richard & quitely the castel of Arches and the counte of Albermarle and many other castelles which the said king of Ffraunce had occupied aftir his retorne from the cite of Acon. And the said King Richard quiteclaymed to the said King Phelip the castel of Gizorre. And for thassurraunce of the premisses eyther of them fond pledges to other, which were bounde that he which shuld violate that pacte and peas to forfaite to thother XVM markes.[150] And whan King Richard was in possession of the premisses according to that pact, the said King Phelip sone aftir repented him of that his pacte and remyses, assembled his armee, and besieged and toke again the castel of Albermarle and also hired and conducted XV persones and sent them to Chinon in Angeo to have by som subtile meane murdred the said King Richard which than kept his court there. Which XV persones cam boldly and pread to have goon into the kinges chamber, but they were espied of ther entent and taken. Which confessed that the said King Phelip had |40v| hired them and sent them to Chinon to have murdred the said King Richard. Ffor which causes the same King Richard seased the possessions of the abbottes of Clugny, of Charite and of Saint Denys, which were plegges for the part of the said King Phelip for the performans of the said pacte at Loviers, and of them levied the forfait of XVM marc.[151]

And the said king of Ffraunce, contenewing his oppression by werres upon the londes of King Richard, the same King Richard in resisting the same tirannie of King Phelip assembled his armee and subgettes, and he with his power had like to have mette with the said King Phelip betwix Garmes and Vernoll. But King Phelip wold not attend, but fledde in to Vernon and toke that for his refuge. And aftir likewise

---

[150] *Chronica Hovedene*, IV, p. 3 and *Flores historiarum*, II, p. 114. By the treaty of Louviers in January 1196, Philippe resigned all his conquests except the Norman Vexin and six further castles on the Norman-Capetian border. He gave up his claim to Issoudun, which he had attacked two months earlier, and other strongholds in Berry, together with territories in Auvergne and Gascony, the castle of Arques, and the county of Albemarle. In T, fo. 12r, there is a marginal note next to this statement referring to the '*chronica de Bury*', though the date of the treaty is given as 1197 in the text.

[151] *Chronica Hovedene*, III, p. 283, though Roger of Howden did not explicitly connect the attempted assassination of Richard in 1195 with the siege of Aumale the following year: ibid., IV, pp. 4–5. In T, fo. 12r, there is a marginal note next to this statement, '*chronica Bury*'.

shuld have mette betwix Curtolles and Gizorre, but King Phelip fledde into Gizorre.[152]

Aftir that the said King Phelip supplied to the Pope Innocent the III[de], enstauncyng the pope to procure the peas betwix the said King Richard and the same King Phelip, supposing his pursuite to King Richard to have ben in veyne for that he had never kept appoinctement with him. And at the instaunce of the said King Phelip, the said Pope Innocent the III[de] directed his elegant epistole to King Richard, by the legacie of Petir Capeten, deken cardinal, prayeng him instantly at his desire to be favourable and agreable in treating for peas to be had betwix him, the same King Richard and the said King Phelip. And the same King Richard, not willing to make werre but in defence of his londes and right, was conformable therunto. Wherupon bothe the same kinges with the said cardenal mette and peas taken in the yere MCIIII^XX XVIII |41r| for the entircourse of merchaundise to be without interupcion. And aftir in the fest of Saint Hillarie in the yere MCIIII^XX XIX, the same kinges Phelip and Richard couvented betwix Andely and Vernon, and spak there personelly to gether, and by the meane of the said cardenal and of bothe their counseilles, peas was taken and concluded betwix the same II kinges, their subgettes and cuntrees, for the terme of V yeres to come from that fest of Saint Hillarie.[153] That notwithstonding, contrarie to the tenur of that peas, sone aftir the said king of Ffraunce edified of new a castell betwix Butenant and Gualln and the fforest of the kinges of Englond, which he promysed to cause to be broken down again.[154]

And within a litle aftir that, the said king of Ffraunce *seminator discordiarum*, sent to King Richard and certified him that John erle of Moretaine, his brother, had geven hymself to the said King Phelip and in proof therof sent the forged lettres supposing to have ben the lettres of the same John. Which King Richard beleved *prima facie* and therfor seased again into his handes all the londes that were the same John. And the same John, demaunding to knowe the cause therof, was objected against him the premisses. Wherupon the said John sent II

---

[152] *Chronica Hovedene*, IV, pp. 55–56. In early September 1198, Richard inflicted a small defeat on a French raiding party into the Norman Vexin, between Jumièges and Vernon; later that month, he captured Courcelles and then drove the French back towards Gisors early in October.

[153] *Chronica Hovedene*, IV, pp. 73 and 79–80. Roger of Howden did not suggest that King Philippe had called for the papal intervention represented by the letter of Innocent III, issued on 13 August 1198, calling for a crusade and announcing the mission of Peter of Capua. The Tudor writer closely follows Howden's report of the subsequent truce agreed on 13 January 1199.

[154] *Chronica Hovedene*, IV, p. 80. According to Howden, Philippe erected a new castle between the English and French strongholds of Buttevant and Gaillon, and destroyed a forest that belonged to Richard.

of his knightes in his name and for him in to the court of the king of Ffraunce, which II knightes in the same court of the king of Ffraunce shewed that the said John was not gilty in that behalf and offred to verifie and deresue it as the king of Ffraunces court shuld awarde. And he was not found in all that court, king nor other, which wold receyve therof proof or defence. And in consideracion therof, the same King Richard ever aftir loved his said brother |**41v**| John the bettir, and never aftir gave credence to the king of Ffraunce.[155]

And not long aftir that, the said King Richard, beyng hurt and not trusting of lief, made his last will and gave and bequithed to the same John his brother, the succession of his londes, aswel of the reame of Englond as of his londes in the parties of beyond the see. And afore his deth, caused as many of his lordes and subgettes as were there present to doo and swere fealtie to the same John. And commaunded that all his castelles with the III^{de} part of his treasour shuld be delivered to the same John, and an other part to be disposed to his familier servantes and to pore people, and the thrid part to be taken to the Imperor Othes, his nevew, for the meyntanance of his werres for the title of the impire.[156] And the same King Richard decessed the VIII Idus of Ffebruarie MCIIII^{XX} XIX.[157]

Aftir whois deth, the said John than erle of Mortain, his brother, than beyng in Normandie the sonday octavis Pasche, the VII kalends of Maij and Saint Markes day the same yere, MCIIII^{XX} XIX at Roane, was girde with the swerde of the duche of Normandie in the cathedrall chirche by the archebisshop of Roane, and the same archebisshop put upon his hede as duke a circulet of gold with golden roses.[158] And meyntenant the same duke John put hymself in possession of all the other, his brothers londes in the partes of beyond the see. And the VI kalends of Junij in the day of the feest of the Holy Ascencion aftir, the same yere, was coroned king of Englond at Westmynster by the handes of Hubert archebisshop of Cauntirbury, and sone aftir retorned into Normandie.[159] And ymmediatly were stablisshed trewse |**42r**| betwix the said King Phelip of Ffraunce and the said King John of Englond until the morow aftir the fest of the Assumpcion of Our Lady.[160] And on the same morow of the fest of the Assumpcion of Our Lady, the same King Phelip and King John couvented betwix Butenant and Guletut

[155] *Chronica Hovedene*, IV, p. 81. Howden's account was written after John had succeeded to the English throne.

[156] *Chronica Hovedene*, IV, p. 83. Howden reported that Richard committed three quarters of his treasures to John and the remaining quarter to his nephew Otto IV.

[157] *Chronica Hovedene*, IV, p. 84. Richard I died on 6 April 1199.

[158] *Chronica Hovedene*, IV, p. 87. John was acclaimed duke of Normandy at Rouen on 25 April 1199.

[159] *Chronica Hovedene*, IV, p. 90. John was crowned as king of England on 27 May 1199.

[160] *Chronica Hovedene*, IV, p. 93.

and spak to gether by ther proper mouthes. But than King John cowde not opteyne at that tyme of further trewse, for King Phelip made gret quarell to him for that he had ben gird with the swerd of Normandie without his licence and none other at that tyme. And the same King Phelip alledged against him that he shuld have comen to hym and have made request to hym to be accepted as duke of Normandie, and to have done to him homage therfor. And for that crueltie of King Phelip and for his wrongful quarell to King John, diverse of his erles and barones, supposing he wold doo likewise to them, forsoke him and bycame men of the said King John.[161] And notwithstonding the same King John tended homage to the same King Phelip, the same King Phelip with a gret armee entred and toke by force many castelles of the same King John and destroyed them.[162]

And in Octobre aftir that, by the labour of the said cardenall Petir Capeten, trewse and peas was concluded betwix the said King Phelip and King John until the fest of Saint Hillarij.[163] At which fest of Saint Hillarie the yere MCC, the same II kinges, Phelip and John, couvented betwix Andely and Gualluin, and there was comoned and aggreed that Loys elder sone of the same King Phelip, shuld have in mariage the aforenamed Blanche doughtir of Alphons king of Castill, nece of the said King John, |42v| his susters doughtir, and the same King John to geve with hir XXXM marces. And was desired further than of King John that he shuld not geve eny aide to the Imperor Otho, his elder susters sone, of men nor money to purchas the impire, which King John refused.[164] And for that, the said treatie toke delaye until the octavis of the Nativite of Saint John Baptist and so departed. And in meane tyme Quene Alianore went in to Castill and at hir retorne brought with hir the said Blanche and delyvered hir to King John.[165]

And afore the said octavis of Saint John, the said kinges of Englond and Ffraunce, John and Phelip, couvented and treated betwix the said Butenant and Guletut. In which treatie, the same King Phelip yelded to the said King John the cite of Devereulx and all the countie and all the castelles, citees & londes which the same Phelip had occupied by werres of the londes of the kinges of Englond. And there King

[161] *Chronica Hovedene*, IV, pp. 94–95. Howden reported that the Frenchmen who pledged their support to John after the meeting on 16 and 17 August 1199 had previously been the liegemen of Richard.

[162] *Chronica Hovedene*, IV, pp. 96–97. In T, fo. 14r, the author stated that Arthur of Brittany joined the French king in these attacks.

[163] *Chronica Hovedene*, IV, p. 97.

[164] *Chronica Hovedene*, IV, pp. 106–107. In T, fo. 13v, the author left a gap in the text for the insertion of the name of the daughter of Alfonso of Castile, and he also followed Roger of Howden very closely in omitting any claim that John refused to promise not to support his nephew Otto IV.

[165] *Chronica Hovedene*, IV, pp. 107 and 114.

John became man and ded homage for that and all other his londes in those parties to the said King Phelip and delivered to the said Loys sone of King Phelip, the said Blanche. Which Loys espoused the same Blanche the X kalendes of June in the yere MCC at Purmore in Normandie, which were solempnised by the archebisshop of Burdeulx at that tyme, by cause the reame of Ffraunce was than in interdict for the refusell of the doughtir of Denmark whom the said King Phelip had espoused.[166] And than the same II kinges Phelip and John lovingly to apparence owtwardes went to gether to Verun. And there at Verun the said Arthur erle of Bretain, sone of Gefferey brother of King John, |43r| became liegeman of the same King John his uncle for the cuntre of Bretain by the consent, advise & agrement, and in the sight of the said king of Ffraunce Phelip, and of his said sone Loys, and sware fealtie and ded also homage therfor to the same King John. And at the instant desire of the same King Phelip, the same King John aggreed to suffre and licence the said Arthur to resort to the king of Fraunces court and to tarie there for a tyme, and King John promysed than that he shuld not mynyssh eny of the londes of the said Arthur not fees of Bretain but by jugement of his court at Roane.[167]

And in all the treaties and couvenantes than and afore betwix the said II kinges, the said King Phelip affermed, knowleged and avowed the said King John to be veray heire to his said brother King Richard, and that by his lettres patentes and writinges under his seale by these wordes: *Johannes rex Anglie rectus heres Ri[c]a[rdi] imper[io] fratris sui.*[168] And in that latter treatie was couvenanted further that if the same King John shuld decesse without issue of his wief in lauful mariage, he shuld geve to the said Loys sone of the said King Phelip, moche of his londes as is made mencion expressely in the same treatie.[169] And in this treatie, nor in eny other afore, the said King Phelip never quarelled nor made title for the said Arthur nor for eny other cause but onely for that he was gird with the swerd of the duche of Normandie without

---

[166] *Chronica Hovedene*, IV, pp. 114–115. By the treaty of Le Goulet, agreed on 22 May 1200, John was accepted as Richard's rightful heir and paid homage to Philippe II, also granting the French king a relief of 20,000 marks. In return, Philippe restored the county of Evreux, the whole Norman Vexin except Les Andelys, and the lordships of Issoudun, Graçay, and Bourges in Berry. Roger of Howden reported that these lands were assigned by John as the dowry for Blanche on her marriage to the future Louis VIII on 23 May 1200. See pp. 180–181 above.

[167] *Chronica Hovedene*, IV, p. 115.

[168] In the treaty of Le Goulet in May 1200, John was referred to as '*Johannes dei gratia rex Anglie, dominus Hibernie, dux Normannie, Aquitannie, comes Andegavie*': *EMDP*, II, p. 615.

[169] *Chronica Hovedene*, IV, p. 150. The treaty explained that Louis should receive these lands in the event of the death of John because they had been assigned as a dowry to Blanche.

his admission, and that was no quarel of right. Nor therfor eny thing belonged to the king of Ffraunce but onely homage and fealtie, and those were not dewe afore he was laufull duke.

And at |43v| the tyme of the making of the said treatie King John thought hymself wele in the favor of the said King Phelip and put his trust to him, thinking that the said mariage of the said Blanche his nece to Loys the sone of the said King Phelip, shuld be occasion of such trust. And by the counseill of the same King Phelip, King John pursewed divorce betwix him and his wief Dame Hawes, elder doughtir of the erle of Gloucestre for consanguinite and was aftir maried to Isabel doughtir of the erle of Angelesme in the same yere MCC.[170] And in colouring to be in like trust in the next yere MCCI, the said kinges of Englond and Ffraunce mette betwix Andely and and had there by semblaunce loving meting & convocacion and aftir III daies beyng there to gether, the king of Ffraunce made especial and instant requestes for King John to ride with him for recreacion of confort to Parys. And so he ded and was there tryumphantly receyved, fested and lodged in the proper palaice of the said King Phelip with as good semblant as if the same King John had ben naturel father to the said King Phelip. And the same King Phelip was for the tyme elleswhere lodged in reverence of the said King John.[171]

But King John was not advysed nor toke regarde to these II verses. *Ffistula dulce canit volucres dum decipit auceps. Impia sub dulci melle venena latent.*[172] Ffor in Lent next aftir that the said II kinges Phelip and John mette, trusting to King John for amyte. But the same King Phelip, armed with mortall hate and envie as a mortall ennemye to King John, not regarding to his othes nor promyses, quarelled with the same King John and wold have enforsed him with violent and opprobrious woordes |44r| to yelde to the said Arthur, sone of Gefferey, Normandie, Torain, Angeo, Maine and Poytew, with moche other thinges unreasonable.[173] And furthwith abetted and gave aide to the same Arthur to make open werre against the said King John his soverayn lord, as he ded and toke by force the castel of Mirabel, except the great towre therof, which the said Quene Alianore defended to

---

[170] *Chronica Hovedene*, IV, pp. 119–120. Having divorced Isabella of Gloucester, John's marriage to Isabella of Angoulême took place on on 24 August 1200.

[171] *Chronica Hovedene*, IV, p. 164 and *Flores historiarum*, II, p. 123. John visited Paris at the end of July 1201.

[172] These two verses derive from *Disticha Catonis*, 1.27.2 and Ovid, *Amores*, 1.8.104, and were cited in the *Chronica Hovedene*, I, p. 227, under the year 1165, in the context of the dispute between Thomas Becket and Henry II: '*Crede mihi; si credis ei, tu decipieris: / Fistula dulce canit volucres dum decipit auceps; / Impia sub dulci melle venena latent.*' See David Corner, 'The earliest surviving manuscripts of Roger of Howden's *Chronica*', *EHR*, 98 (1983), pp. 307–308.

[173] *Flores historiarum*, II, p. 124, though this did not mention Maine.

the comyng of King John hir sone. Which at his comyng reskewed hir and toke the said Arthur armed with baner displayed against him as a traitor and rebell contrarie to his dutie of allegeaunce by reason of the countie of Bretain, as is aforerehersed.[174] And also the said King John toke all the knightes and men whiche were with the same Arthur, not oon escaping, and sent them to be kept in diverse prisones in Englond.[175] And led with him the said Arthur his nevew to Roane, and also the same tyme made further werre against the said King John and assieged and toke the castel of Butenant and diverse other castelles and townes, and assieged Radepont and Arches. But at bothe those castelles, he was confused by the comyng of the said King John.[176]

And notwithstonding the same rebellions and treasons doon by the said Arthur against his said sovereyn lord King John, the same King John at his comyng to Roane called afore hym the said Arthur and demaunded of him if he wold theraftir take the same King John as his uncle and sovereyn lord, and no more to folowe the deceitful counseil of the king of Ffraunce. And the same Arthur proudly and dispightfully answere him with opprobrious wordes, claymyng aswel the reame of Englond as the other |44v| londes in the parties of Ffraunce. And therfor the said King John committed the same Arthur to prison in the castel of Roan, which prison the same Arthur toke impaciently of a proude mynde, and not long aftir, in forbering his mete for anguissh and proude hert, there died.[177] And the seid Alianore his suster abode as a vowes not professed in the nonnery of Ambresbury, and there lyved until the yere MCCXLIII, and than died there and lyeth buried in the quere amonges the nonnes there. And she gave afore hir deth to those nonnes the maner of Melkesham and also long afore hir deth, she relessed, remytted and transported unto King Henry the III[de], sone of the said King John, frely all the right if eny she had aswel of the reame of Englond as thother londes in the parties of beyond the see, aswel the duche of Bretayn as all other, to hold and succede to him, his heires and successoures for ever.[178]

[174] See p. 176.

[175] *Flores historiarum*, II, p. 125. Arthur was captured on 1 August 1202, while besieging Mirebeau in Poitou, where his grandmother Eleanor of Aquitaine was taking refuge.

[176] *Flores historiarum*, II, pp. 124–125. The *Flores* reported that Philippe's sieges of Buttevant and Radepond took place before the capture of Arthur, who was initially taken to Falaise.

[177] *Flores historiarum*, II, p. 125. The *Flores* also acknowledged that the common view both in France and amongst his own men was that John had murdered Arthur.

[178] Following her capture at Mirabeau in August 1202, Eleanor was held in a series of locations in England until her death at Bristol in 1241. She was buried in Saint James's Priory, Bristol, but her body was later moved to Amesbury in Wiltshire. There is no evidence that she renounced any claims in favour of King John or his son Henry.

By which it apperith wele and is sufficiently declared that the said King John was dew, trew and laufull king of Englond, duke of Normandie and of Guyan, and erle of the counties of Angeo, Maine, Torayn and of Poytowe, and by confisquacion of the said Arthur of the demeane of the countie of Bretain. And of thother besides the demeane of Breteyn, he was so takyn, reputed and avowed by the said King Phelip of Ffraunce and in his court at Parys approved by his auctentique writinges undir his seale, and also by the said Arthur and every other persone. And therof was in quiet possession, peasibly, without interupcion or clayme of the said Arthur or eny other persone, from the deth of the said King Richard his brother which was the VIII Idus of Ffebruarie in the yere MXIIII^{XX} XIX, until the |**45r**| Lente tyme in the yere MCCII, which tyme as is aforesaid the said king of Ffraunce and Arthur pretended title therunto for the same Arthur, contrarie to right and against ther solenne othes; at which tyme the said Arthur rebelled as is declared afore, and wold as a traitor have subdued his sovereyn lord, the said King John, his uncle. And for the takyng or prisonyng, nor yet for the deth of the same Arthur, if he had ben executed as a traitor to the deth as he was worthy and yet was not but died of froward and anguisshant meende, no quarell or other chalenge may of right belong nor owith to apperteyne to the said king of Ffraunce nor other erthely prince. For somoche as the same Arthur was subget and liegeman to the said King John aswel by reason of the countie of Bretayne as of his naturell birth, and was in nowise subget to the said king of Ffraunce, nor otherwise liege or servant, but as the same King John left him in custodie of the said king of Ffraunce at the desire of the same king of Ffraunce. Ffor the same king of Ffraunce Phelip, if eny right he had, it was but the rerofee of Breteyn, and that he had quitecleymed and remytted to King Richard aforsaid and graunted to the same King Richard that the same countie of Bretain shuld for ever apperteyne to the dominion of the duche of Normandie, and that the erles of Bretain and his heires and successoures shuld be liegemen to the dukes of Normandie for ever, and that the dukes of Normandie shuld answer to the kinges of Ffraunce for Bretain aswel as for Normandie. By which the said |**45v**| King Phelip of Ffraunce and all his successoures ar stopped to clayme eny thing of or in Bretayne as kinges of Ffraunce. And if the said Arthur had ben of soche dampnable mynde to disavow his naturell lord, it was not in his power so to doo. And for that the said King Phelip toke the same Arthur and aided him and conforted him against the said King John, he therby falsly violated his treaties and oothes to the contrarie made. And it is sufficiently declared afore that King John never toke upon him the governaunce of the said Arthur, nor for him of any his londes, nor imagined not the deth of the same Arthur, nor murdred him as is alledged and objected, but departed with the custodie of him and left him in custodie with the said king of Ffraunce as his subget.

And so appierith that the said King John came duely and laufully to the succession of all the premisses by the gift and transport of the said King Richard his brother, and in his lief was put in possession therof by the commaundement of the same King Richard. And it shal not be duly proved that the said King John ever made eny rebellion, treason or insurreccion, or unlauful disobedience against the said King Phelip in eny poynt, though he had many occasions. But of force and of necessite he was drevyn to kepe and defend his londes against the tirannie of the said King Phelip as laufull was for hym to doo, *Quia injuriam armis irrogatam, armorum propulsare remedia leges et jura permittunt.*[179]

And also it apperith that the said King John was never unkinde to the said Arthur nor to eny other of his blode, but onely to |46r| the King Richard his brother, and that was by the procurement of the said King Phelip of his cautelous imaginacion to have begiled them bothe. And against the unkyndenesse, rebellion and treason of the said Arthur his nevew, he wold lovingly have reconsiled him as his dere nevew, but of obstinat and proude mynd refused it as is saide afore. So that the same King John ought not to be accounted indigne to opteyne his said succession nor eny thing therof to confisque to the king of Ffraunce.

And it is manifest that the said king of Ffraunce Phelip, aswel in the tyme of the regne of the said King Richard as of the tyme of the regne of the said King John, was ever cautelously imaginyng to oppresse from bothe the same kinges Richard and John of ther enheritaunces on the parties to his regne adjoynant.

And it is here to be noted especially the cautelous mynde of the same King Phelip against the said King John at and aftir the making of the said treatie betwix the same kinges Phelip and John betwix Butenant and Guletut the yere MCC, hough dissimylatly and gilefully the same King Phelip used him to begile King John. He considered that King John was strongly than in the favor of his subgettes and that the counte de Engolesme had but oon onely doughtir to be his heir, which than was promysed in mariage to a great baron of Poytow named Hugh Brim within hir yeres of laufull assent. And to thentent to have occasion to cause the said Hugh Brim with his freendes in Poytow which were the substance of Poytevins, |46v| to withdrawe ther loving hertes from the said King John, the said King Phelip undir swete utteraunce of speche moved and exorted King John to sewe devorce

179 This maxim also appears on pp. 222, 225, and 251–252.

betwix him and the said Hawes doughtir of Gloucester, his wief, and to espouse the said Isabel, doughtir and heir of Engolosme. By whois mocion he soo ded, by occasion wherof the said Hugh Brim with his affinite of the Poytevins rebelled against the said King John.[180] And that by the said King Phelip prevented, he caused the said Arthur sone of Gefferey to make the said rebellions against the said King John as is afore declared, which was not for eny love or favor that he bare to the same Arthur, nor for eny zeale of justice, but onely to make weye and place to him to oppresse from them bothe the said londes of the heritage of Englond, *Dolosi semper querunt occasionem nocendi.*[181] Ffrensshmen and Scottes never were nor yet be otherwise to trust but whan they be moost plesaunt in their speche and promyses than they were and ar most falsest lest to truste.[182] And the said King Phelip of further cautell, exorted and procured the barones of Englond to move quarelles[183] and therupon to rebelle against King John to thentent the same King John shuld be so noyed with suche rebellion in Englond that he shuld not have tyme nor confort or sufficient aide to resiste the tirannie and oppression of the said king of Ffraunce in taking the londes in those parties of Ffraunce.[184] So that without resistence, the same King Phelip oppressed |**46*r**| from the said King John, Normandie, Angeo, Maine and Torayne, and a great part of Guyan and of Poytow. Wherfor might be saide to the than Englisshmen rebelles: *Quid ociosa gens pondere immanum scelerum oppressa, quid semper civilia prelia sitiens. Et te domesticis in tantum debilitasti motibus qui cum prius longe posita regna potestati tue subdidisses. Nec velut bona unica degenerata in amaritudinem versa patriam coniuges liberos nequeas ab inimicis tueri? Age ergo age civile discidunt parum intelligens evangelicum illud: 'omne regnum in se ipsum divisum desolabitur, et domus supra domum cadet'.*[185] *Quia ergo regnum tuum in se ipsum divisum fuit quia furor civilis discordie et livoris firmius mentem tuam hebetant, quia superbia tua uni regi tuo obedienciam ferre non permisit. Cernis ergo hereditatem tuam Normannie, Britannie, Andegavie, Cenomannie, Turonie, Pictanee, Acquitannie, Vasconie & Pontiue ab injurious tuis depredatam.*[186]

---

[180] See p. 89, n. 202 and p. 170, n. 170. Howden did not explain why Philippe II had advised John to marry Isabella of Angoulême.

[181] *Non inveni.* See p. 240.

[182] Marginal note: '*Gallorum ficta gens subdola gens maledicta*'. This maxim was repeated in the main text on p. 252.

[183] Marginal note: '*Nunquam Gallorum cessabit fraus patruorum*'. This maxim was repeated in the main text on p. 251.

[184] Marginal note: '*Notet*'.

[185] Luke 11: 17: '*omne regnum in se ipsum divisum desolatur et domus supra domum cadet*'. This verse was also cited at the very end of the draft treatise in T, p. 270.

[186] This quotation appeared at the end of the following section in T, fos 18r–18v: 'But here may be said of the Englisshmen and Normans Englissh as was wretin of the Bretons

And if the case were soche as is objected that the said King John shuld have ben for the causes alledged unworthy to have comen to the succession of his said brother King Richard Cuer de Leon, and that the reame of Englond ought to have comen owther to the said Phelip the Conquerant or to Saint Loys, it may not be denyed but that the said King Edward the III^de was next to bothe of them as is declared afore, so that none of the Valoys can eny thing clayme, nor have colour to clayme eny thing on that behalf. And if the said King John had ben unworthy, yet the said Alianore suster of Arthur and doughtir of Geffrey was not unworthy, so that the kinges of Englond have had good right to hold the premisses as next heires to hir aftir hir decesse, which was long aftir the deth of King John, and also by the the [sic] gift of the same Alianore to King Henry the III^de.

|46*v| *Capitulum XII*[187]

And where also in the said secund partie is surmytted that for the aide which that Loys somtyme king of Ffraunce, father to the said King Phelip called the Conquerrant, shuld have made to the afore named King Henry the Secund Fitz Imperesse, father to the said King John, against King Stephen which injustly occupied the reame and corone of Englond from the said King Henry the Secund and the Imperesse his mother, the same King Henry shuld have geven and transported to the said King Loys all the cuntre of Vulguissin which shuld be betwix the reviers of Dele and Delle, and also the countie d'Evreulx, which cuntries for that cause shuld be the veray heritage of the king of Ffraunce.

It is manyfestly noted and declared and may not be trewly denyed but that Eustace sone and heritier apparent of the said King Stephen, the same Stephen beyng by usurpacion king of Englond, espoused and had in mariage Constaunce doughtir of the said King Loys by his secund wief, doughtir of Alphons king and imperor of Spaine.[188]

of this lond what tyme they lost the deadem therof, *Quid ociosa gens pondere immanum scelerum oppressa, quid semper civilia prelia sitiens. Et te domesticis in tantum debilitasti motibus qui cum prius longe posita regna potestati tue subdidisses. Nec velut bona unica degenerata in amaritudinem versa patriam coniuges liberos nequeas ab inimicis tueri? Age ergo age civile discidunt parum intelligens evangelicum illud: 'omne regnum in se ipsum divisum desolabitur, et domus supra domum cadet'. Quia ergo regnum tuum in se divisium fuit quia furor civilis discordie & livoris firmius mentem tuam hebetant, quia superbia tua uni regi obedienciam ferre non permisit. Cernis ergo hereditatem tuam vicinis desolatam.'* See p. 200, n. 218.

[187] This chapter translates and then responds to *Pour ce que plusieurs*, p. 90, paragraph 2, omitting the preceding discussion, which emphasized the superiority of the Lancastrian claim to the English throne. This account builds upon the discussion in T, fos 15r–15v.

[188] Marginal note: '*Cronica magistri Rogeri de Hoveden de anno gratiae MCXLVIII*'. Eustace was betrothed to Constance, sister of King Louis VII, in 1140, and the wedding was cited by

Which Constaunce aftir the deth of the same Eustace was secundly maried to Raymond Erle of Tholous. And by reason and occasion of hir former mariage to the said Eustace the said King Loys hir ffather was extreme enemye to the said Imperesse and hir sone King Henry the Secund, for upon that mariage the duchie of Normandie was put to the possession of the said Eustace.[189] And for that the said Imperesse and Geffrey Plantagenest gave & transported the right of the same duche[190] to the |47r| said King Henry the Secund by force whereof the same Henry entred in to the same duche.[191] The said King Loys in aide of the said Eustace with the same Eustace and a gret armee made werre against the said King Henry and so contenued by a long tyme. And aftir in the yere MCLII the said Eustace died aftir whois deth in the yere MCLIII was made concorde betwix the said King Stephen and the said King Henry the Secund at Walyngford in this forme, that the said King Stephen shuld contenew king of Englond for terme of his lief and shuld adopte the said King Henry to be his heir to succede aftir his deth to the same.[192] And in the yere MCLIIII the said King Stephen decessed and in the same yere MCLIIII a litil afore the deth of the same King Stephen, peas was treated and had betwix the said King Loys and the said Henry than beyng duke of Normandie. By which treatie the said King Loys yelded to the same duke Henry Vernol and Noefinerke and the duke gave to the same King Loys MM markes of silver.[193] By which it is apparent and manifest that the said King Loys gave no soche aide to nor for the said Henry nor his mother to deserve to have the said cuntrees afore rehersed geven or transported to him, nor for suche cause or eny other it shal not be proved that the same Henry or his mother gave nor transported the said cuntrees to the said King Loys[194] as is surmytted.[195]

Howden under the year 1148, indicating that it had taken place earlier: see *Chronica Hovedene*, I, pp. 210–211 and also see p. 196.

[189] Eustace paid homage to the French king for Normandy in 1137, three years before the engagement.

[190] The words 'by force wherof the' are crossed out.

[191] *Chronica Hovedene*, I, p. 211. Henry, son of the Empress Matilda and Geoffrey Plantagenet, was invested as duke of Normandy in 1149.

[192] Marginal note: '*secundum Rogeri de Hoveden obiit anno MCLIIII*'. See *Chronica Hovedene*, I, p. 212. Roger did not mention the death of Eustace in August 1153, nor the location of the meeting between Stephen and Henry II at Wallingford [*recte* Winchester]; the latter was given in *Flores historiarum*, II, p. 71.

[193] *Flores historiarum*, II, pp. 71–72, which reported that Louis VII gave Verneuil and the '*Novum Mercatum*', or Neufmarché, to Henry, in return for 2,000 marks.

[194] The words 'for soche cause' are crossed out.

[195] The words 'or eny other' are crossed out.

|47v| *Capitulum XIII*[196]

And where also in the same secund partie is surmytted that Saint Loys king of Ffraunce sone of King Loys sone, of King Phelip the Conquerrant desiring to goo in help to conquere the Holy Lond and to put his reame of Ffraunce in peas in his absence and that no trouble shuld be in his absens, certain appointement shuld have ben made by hym with King Henry the III[de] sone of the aforerehersed King John by the consent of the II sones of the same King Henry, that is to saie Edmond and Edward, and of all the princes and men of the III estates of Englond. Wherby of pure and free will and deliberacion, the said Saint Loys shuld have geven, quited and transported to the said King Henry the III[de] king of Englond, which by title of gifte shuld have accepted for him and his successoures procreat in laufull mariage the duche of Guyan as it shuld have ben in olde tyme, that is to saie in III seneschalcies or stewarshippes of Burdeaulx, Les Lannes and Baxades, and in augmentacion and encresse of seignourees the same saint Loys shuld have unied and geven the cuntre of Xantonge and of Charente and the cuntre, countie and seignories of Perregort, Agenes, Quercy, Rouergue and Lymosin with ther appertenances and appendacies to the same duche and othe londes and seignories above named, to have, holde and possede by the said King Henry and his successoures as ther proper heritage sauf the loy and homage liege which they shuld be bounde to doo to the kinges of Ffraunce as to ther sovereynes.[197] And over that, that the said Saint Loys shuld have delyvered to the said King Henry the payment of XIM escutz for wages of V[C] knightes with ther suite for oon hole yere which the same King Henry shuld bring with him against the myscreantes and enemyes of the faith, which the same |48r| King Henry shuld not have accomplisshed.[198] And that for the premisses the same King Henry shuld have revoked for him and his successoures to the proufit of Saint Loys and of his successoures all the right that the same King Henry and his predecessoures had or might clayme & demaunde in the duche of Normandie and in the counties of Angeo, Maine, Torayne and Poytew, and generally to all other londes and seignories in the reame of Ffraunce other than were assigned by the said treatie.

---

[196] This chapter translates and then responds to *Pour ce que plusieurs*, pp. 91–92, omitting the discussion of the judgement against King John which appears below, pp. 244–245. The Tudor author develops the material in T, fos 15v–19r.

[197] The Tudor author omits the statement in the French treatise that this amounted to sovereignty and resort (see p. 92).

[198] The figure of 11,000 also appears in T, fo. 16r, even though Guillaume Cousinot had reported that the payment amounted to 12,000 écus.

It is notoriely knowen and mencioned in histories agreable that the said King John father to the said King Henry the III^de was in businesse with the werres by devision and rebellion of his subgettes the barons of Englond. And the same division and werres duryng, the aforenamed King Phelip called the Conquerrant, undir false pretended coloures, invaded and made werre upon the londes of the said King John in the parties of beyond the see, and as a tirant and not as a conquerror opteyned and oppessed from the same King John, whom he had taken for his homager, the duche of Normandie and the counties of Poytew, Angeo, Maine and Torayn, and a gret part of Guyan which the said King John cowde not resiste nor defende by occasion of the division in Englond.

And over and besides that the same King Phelip sent his sone Loys with a great armee to have usurped the reame of Englond.[199] Which Loys by the space of III yeres with his fautoures and adherentes, diverse of the barones of Englond, traitores to ther sovereyn lord, made werre and destructions |48v| in Englond, for which the same Loys with his adherentes were excomunicat and accursed by the Pope Innocenonis Tertius, and that notwithstonding contenewed ther werre until aftir the deth of the same King John.[200] And that King Henry the III^de his sone, than of thage of IX yeres, was coroned king of Englond in the yere MCCXVI, and aftir in bataille veynquisshed the said Loys and his adherentes and chaced the same Loys confused out of Englond.[201] But yet sone theraftir the same Loys with a great armee came out of Ffraunce and with the aide of som of the barons of Englond the next yere aftir and made newly werre against the said King Henry the III^de. And on the vigile of the Holy Trinite, he was estsones veniquisshed and moche of his people slayn and hymself the same Loys was in soche distresse that he sewed to Gualo the popes legate than beyng in Englond to be meane to treate for peas and to have licence to departe out of Englond and to be absolved of the sentence of the chirche wherin he was daungered.[202] Wherupon in the vigil of the exaltacion of the holy crosse in the same yere MCCXVII, the said

---

[199] See pp. 244–252.

[200] *Flores historiarum*, II, p. 154. The Tudor author neglects to mention that Innocent III and the Fourth Lateran Council excommunicated Louis and the English rebels because they were acting against the king of England, '*Romanae ecclesiae vassallum*'. Prince Louis's expedition to England in May 1216, despite the prohibition issued by the papal legate, Guala, was reported in *ibid.*, II, pp. 158–160. This account of the actions of Prince Louis is almost exactly reproduced below, pp. 249–251.

[201] *Flores historiarum*, II, pp. 162–164. Henry III was crowned on 28 October 1216 and Prince Louis abandoned the siege of Dover Castle and returned to France in February 1217 to seek reinforcements.

[202] *Flores historiarum*, II, pp. 164–165. Louis was defeated at Lincoln on 20 May 1217.

Loys was absolved of the said sentence by the said legat Gualo upon peas treated betwix King Henry the III^de and the same Loys, which was moche plesaunt to the same Loys, *timens detiora*.[203] And upon that treatie in sight and heering of the said legat and of all the noble men of eyther partie, the said Loys first sware upon the holy evangelies that he shuld stond to the jugement of the chirche and that he with his armee shuld depart out of Englond never to retorne into it again to doo in it eny domage. And |49r| that the same Loys shuld to the best of his power induce his father the said King Phelip to restore to the said King Henry all his rightes of enheritaunces which were oppressed and taken from the said King John or the same King Henry. And that whan the same Loys shuld come to be king of Ffraunce, the same Loys without dissimilacion or difficultie shuld resigne and restore to the said King Henry the said duche of Normandie with thothe his said hereditamentes of Poytew, Angeo, Maine, Torayn and Guyan in his former right of enheritaunce.[204]

And the said King Phelip his father died the yere MCCXXIII and the said Loys his sone was coroned king of Ffraunce, and therupon the said King Henry the III^de sent the archebisshop[205] with III other bisshopes to the same King Loys instantly requiring him to yelde to him the said duche of Normandie with thother of his enheritaunces the premisses in likewise as the same Loys had graunted, promysed and sworne to doo for and upon the said treatie made at his departing owt of Englond as is aforesaid. Which the same Loys refused and obstinatly denyed to doo and in that refusell he dampnably and falsely violated his othes and was forsworne and perjured.[206]

And the same King Loys dowting that the same King Henry the III^de wold invade and enter in to the premisses, the duchee of Normandie and thother, of a new cawtell and of covine banisshed Sir Simon Mountford a baron of Fraunce which came in to Englond to the said King Henry the III^de and he used hymself so plesauntly to the same king |49v| Henry to get into his favor that the same King Henry gave to hym his suster in mariage with the erledome of Leycestre. Which Sir Simon after was occasion of many and dyverse rebellions in Englond against the said King Henry, and by process toke and kept the same King Henry in prison.[207] And beside that with mony geven

---

[203] Marginal note: '*in cronices fflores historiarum*'. See *Flores historiarum*, II, p. 165.

[204] *Flores historiarum*, II, pp. 165–166. The *Flores* did not identify the lands that Louis would return to Henry.

[205] There is an insertion above the line, possibly in a different hand: 'of Cant[erbury]'.

[206] *Flores historiarum*, II, pp. 177–178.

[207] Marginal note: '*in cronices appelle fflores historiarum*'. See *Flores historiarum*, II, pp. 224, 447, 449, and 496, and III, p. 251. Simon de Montfort travelled to England in

by the said King Loys to the erle of Chester and other of the barones of Englond, the same erle of Chester with other of his affinite made also rebellion against the said King Henry ther sovreyn lord, and so used him with werres of rebellion and insurrections that he cowde not attend or have tyme or aide to pursiew the recovere of his said heritage beyond the sea.[208]

And that also gave place and time to the said King Loys to invade and oppresse further from the said King Henry of his hereditamentes in those parties. And the same King Loys assieging Rupelle, lettres came to him from the said erle of Chester and thother rebellions of Englond, conforting him in his said oppression and stirying him to persever therwith in those parties and they shuld so occupiethe said King Henry in Englond that he shuld have no tyme to passe the see with eny power to resiste the said King Loys. And they of Rupell that undirstonding, not trusting therfor of eny socour out of Englond by occasion of the said division, yelded themself to the said King Loys and in example thereof ymmediately all Poytow yelded them to the same King Loys, which put out therof all the officiers of the said King Henry and deputed in all Poytew new officiers for hymself.[209]

And after that in the |50r| yere MCCXXVI the pope by Maister Romanus his legat in Fraunce preched a croise to be had against the erle of Tholosan and his adherentes called Albigenses for ther heresies. And therupon the said King Loys graunted to take the croyse so that he might be assured that the said King Henry shuld not in his absence invade his londes in Fraunce. Wherupon the pope directed his epistles of prohibicion to the said King Henry prohibiting him not to invade with eny power armed the londes or possessions of the said King Loys in his absence. And therafter the same King Loys tok his jornay against the said Albigenses in which jorney he died of poyson.[210]

1230 to pursue his claim to the earldom of Leicester and in 1238 married Eleanor, sister of King Henry III, and widow of William II Marshal. Montfort played a leading role in the subsequent baronial opposition to his brother-in-law, culminating in the defeat and capture of the king at the battle of Lewes in 1264. This discussion of Simon de Montfort does not appear in T, fo. 17r.

[208] *Flores historiarum*, II, pp. 179–180. Ranulf de Blundeville, earl of Chester, was an opponent of the unpopular justiciar of Henry III, Hubert de Burgh, especially when he demanded a general resumption of royal rights and property at Christmas 1223. The *Flores* did not claim that Ranulf was financed by the French crown.

[209] *Flores historiarum*, II, pp. 179–182, reported that Louis VIII's successful siege of La Rochelle in Poitou in July 1224 was encouraged by Falkes de Bréauté, a former supporter of King John, who launched a revolt in England.

[210] *Flores historiarum*, II, pp. 185–186. In T, fo. 17v, the author followed the *Flores historiarum* in reporting that during the campaign, 'the same King Loys, by the procurement of the

And that notwithstonding the rebellion contenued in Englond and in effect during all the lief of the said King Henry the III^de, somtyme against the same King Henry ther sovreyn lord and sumtyme thoon against thother, and moche by occasion of envy for the having of the gret offices and rowmes about the king, the said King Henry, and for the kinges favor which was to som more than to other. Which rebellion and division ded not onely take from the said King Henry the III^d and also from the said King John his father tyme, helpe, corage and substaunce necessarie for the recover and keping of the hereditamentes in the parties of beyond the see, but also gave tyme, help, corage, substaunce & place to the kinges of Fraunce, the said kinges Phelip, Loys and Saint Loys, to invade the premisses and those to |50v| oppresse from the kinges of Englond, and also toke from the trew mynded subgettes and officers of the kinges of Englond in the parties of beyond the see, their corages, conforte and aide or trust out of Englond of havying aide or confort or help for the keping of the same.

For in the yere MCCXXIX, the said King Henry the III^de keping his Cristemesse at Excester, came thether to him the archibisshop of Burdeulx sent from the noble men of Guyan and Gascoign and Poytow and solenne massengers out of Normendie, and all ther requestes were that the said King Henry the III^d shuld goo into those parties and acertained him perfitely that all the noblemen of the said cuntries unmutably wold aide, serve and abide with him for the recover of all his right of the premisses which his father and he had lost and were holden from him by the King of Fraunce or eny other. And for the business that the said King Henry was in by occasion of the said division and rebellion, he coude not attonde to the said requestes. And the said massangers tarieng long for anwer and had none, departed and retorned into ther places thinking themselves ill used.[211]

And after that in the yere MCCXLVIII, the said Saint Loys taking his voyage towards the Holy Land he passed by the pope [. . .] which than laye at Lenur sur la Rosne and of him purchased the same popes prohibion directed to the said King Henry the III^de therby prohibiting him that he |51r| shuld not mak were upon the possession of the said Saint Loys in his absence beyng in the service of God to were upon the enemyes of our faith.[212] In which jorney the same Saint

erle of Champaine which adultered with Quene Blanche his wief, was poisoned, wherof he died'.

[211] *Flores historiarum*, II, p. 194, though this account began with the statement that Henry's court was meeting at Oxford rather than Exeter. The same error appears in T, fo. 18r.

[212] Marginal note: '*fflores historiarum*'. See *Flores historiarum*, II, pp. 353–354. Saint Louis met with Pope Innocent IV at Lyons.

Loys in pleyn bataill without stroke or wound of his partie or of eny his subgettes in his retenew yelded themself to the Surresines and many of them apostated the faith in rebuk therof as moche as in them was and of the chirche in everlasting their opprobrie.[213] But in the same bataill William Longespee than erle of Saresbury of Englond with Sir Robert Vere and many other worshipful men of Englond with their retenue by example of the said William Longespee faught against the Surresines in that conflight to the deth, which bataill was doon in the yere [M]CCL.[214] By which premisses it is apparent that there was no soche treatie betix the said Saint Loys and the said King Henry the III^{de} the tyme of taking the said jorney or voiage nor afore, for if there had ben Saint Loys wold not nor shuld have neded pursewe to the pope for the said prohibicion. And by that is evident that all the matier in the said article of surmyse is but fayned and falsely imagined.

Neverthelesse it is declared in histories that in the yere MCCLX, upon certain apoyntementes, the said Saint Loys shuld have restored to the said King Henry all the duche of Guyan and the counties of Angeo, Maine, Toraine and Poytow which had ben taken from the same King Henry and King John his father, and shuld delyver to the same King Henry also other londes to the yerely |51v| value of XXM by yere in recompence for the duche of Normandie. And for the same the said King Henry the III^{de} shuld have quiteclaymed to the said Saint Loys the duche of Normandie. And for that that the same Saint Loys yelded not to the same King Henry the said counties of Angeo, Maine, Torayn and Poytow nor other londes to the yerely value of XXM li[vres] by yere in recompence for the duche of Normandie, the same duche of right shuld have reverted to the said King Henry the III^{de} and his heires.[215]

By which matiers afore in this answere declared apperith manifestly that the said kinges of Fraunce have opteyned the said duche of Normandie and the counties of Angeo, Maine and Torayn and Poytow not by any just, trew, lawfull or reasonable title by adquisicion, right or otherwise but only by oppression and tirannie soche tyme as the kinges

---

[213] Marginal note: '*fflores historiarum*'. See *Flores historiarum*, II, p. 365.

[214] *Flores historiarum*, II, pp. 365–366. T, fo. 18v, also reported, thanks to the *Flores*, that their 'names undoubted rest notid in the book of lief as apperid by vision to the mother of the said William Long Spee somtyme countes of Saresbury than abbesse of Laycote [Laycock] in the night of the said bataill'. See Simon Lloyd, 'William Longespée II: the making of an English crusading hero', *Nottingham Medieval Studies*, 35 (1991), pp. 41–69 and 36 (1992), pp. 79–125.

[215] *Flores historiarum*, II, p. 440, which reported that Henry III renounced any claim to Normandy in return for unspecified lands and financial considerations, as well as the promise of Poitou, upon the death of St Louis.

of Englond were in gret businesses by reason of the said rebellions and divisions of the lordes of Englond which were seized, conspired and procured by the said kinges of Fraunce of cautell so that the said King Henry the III^de shuld have but litil tyme, confort, aide or help of his subgettes to defend or recover his said hereditamentes. And for the same the said King Phelip owith not nor is digne to be called a conquerant, but to be called King Phelip the Tirant for oppressing his homagers from ther right²¹⁶ without eny cause whom he shuld defended, socoured and aidid. *Rex dum bene regit, tiranno dum Phillippi sibi subditu* &c²¹⁷ and *Nichil quod vi & violencia adquiritur juste ab ullo possidetur.*²¹⁸

|52r| *Capitulum XIIII* ²¹⁹

And where it is also surmitted in the said secund partie that it shuld be entended that the cuntre of Xaintong and of Charente and the cuntre of Perrigourt, Agenes, Quercy, Rouergue and Lymosin shuld not of olde tyme have ben parcel of the duche of Guyan.²²⁰ And that the ffather of the said Quene Alianore wife of King Henry the Secund shuld not be but erle of Poytow and that by the deth of the than duke of Guyan his cosin germain, which shuld have died without heir of his body, the said duche of Guyan shuld have descended to the said erle as next heir. And the said cuntres, counties & seignories of Xaintonge, Ageneis, Quercy, Rouergue and Lymosin shuld not be parcel of the same duche.²²¹

---

²¹⁶ The words 'whom he ought to' are crossed out.

²¹⁷ This citation appears to be based upon Henry de Bracton, *On the Laws and Customs of England*, ed. G.E. Woodbine and trans. S.E. Thorne (4 vols, Cambridge, MA, 1968–1977), II, p. 305: '*Dicitur enim rex a bene regendo et non a regnando, quia rex est dum bene regit, tyrannus dum populum sibi creditum violenta opprimit dominatione*'.

²¹⁸ These conclusions appear early in the section in T, fos 18r–v, and the statement that Philippe II of France should rightly be called a tyrant was supported by a marginal note, '*quid nichil quod vi & violencia adqueritur juste ab ullo possidetur qui violenciam intulit [et] irresponsabilem causa pretendit*' (which was also cited in an abbreviated form in the main body of the text of T, fo. 19v). The main text continued with the extended quotation cited on p. 191, n. 186.

²¹⁹ This chapter translates and then responds to *Pour ce que plusieurs*, pp. 92–93, and builds upon the material in T, fos 19r–v.

²²⁰ In fact, this section of *Pour ce que plusieurs* began with the statement that Guyenne comprised the *sénéchaussées* of Bordeaux, Landes, and Bazadais (see p. 92).

²²¹ The Tudor author omits Cousinot's argument that Saintonge, Rouergue, Quercy, Périgord, and the Agenais were in the hands of French noblemen during the reign of Philippe II and therefore were not part of the duchy of Guyenne, together with the statement that the inhabitants of Périgord and Quercy did not recognize Louis IX as a saint because of his alienation of those lands in the treaty of Paris (see p. 93).

The duchie of Guyan or Acquitaine is lymyted and was a region somtyme by itself and oon of the IIII principall partes of Gaule and kinges were therof without eny sovereyn under God, and was inhabited by Gothes and not by Trojanes nor Frensshmen, as the histories mak pleyn mencion.[222] And the same duchie for the most part environned with the rivier Leyr, in which duchie be conteyned many particuler provinces and seignouries and amonges the said cuntrees and seignories of Xaintonge, Charente, Perregourt, Agenois, Quercy, Rouergue and Lymosin be parcell of the same duche |52v| of Guyan.[223] And the same duche extendith from the river of Leyre to the water of Geronnde, and stretchith out of the est from the river of Rosne unto the west ocean. And from the water of Geronne to the [sea] of myddel erthe and to the mounteynes Pirenes which be the great hilles of Spain, and that part is Gallia Narbonensis, wherof part have ben called Gothea and part Vasconia.[224] And as for Gascoign, Burdeulx and Bayone were of olde tyme no part of Gallia Acquitanica, for the duc of Guyan which founded Clugny purchaced the same Gascoign, Burdeulx and Bayon of Sance somtyme king of Castill,[225] and were holden in fee of eny king of Fraunce until that the afore named Sir Simon Mountfort erle of Leycest which of cautell as is touched afore was banisshed and came into Englond, gave counseil and enticed the said King Henry the third to doo homage thefor to Saint Loys and by that to exclude the king of Castel from the fee therof which claymed to be holden of him, and that was doon tyme of the said treatie in the yere MCCLX.[226] And William duke of Guyan which founded and began to edifie Clugny was duke of Guyan and of Alverne by anncient heritage, and died without issue of his body.[227] Aftir whois dethe the same descended to Hellewyn erle of Poytow in the tyme of the regne

[222] The four Roman provinces of Gaul were Gallia Aquitania, Gallia Narbonensis, Gallia Lugdunensis, and Gallia Belgica.

[223] This sentence does not appear in T, fo. 19v.

[224] In 297, Emperor Diocletian split Gallia Aquitania into three provinces, with the territory south of the Garonne river becoming a province called Novempopulana. After 600, Basque clans took control of Novempopulana, which became known as Vasconia.

[225] The independent duchies of Gascony and Guyenne (Aquitaine) were united under the control of Guillaume VIII in 1058, but Cluny had been founded in 909 by Guillaume I the Pious, duke of Guyenne and count of Auvergne, as recorded in *Flores historiarum*, I, p. 479, under the year 901. The reference to Cluny does not appear in the account in T, fo. 19v.

[226] The Tudor author had discussed Simon de Montfort on pp. 196–197, without exploring his role in the treaty of Paris. Montfort was not mentioned at all in the account in T, fo. 19v, which instead argued that the treaty 'was by force and not willingly nor of right and *Nichil quod vi vel violencia adquirit juste ab ullo possidetur ut autra*'.

[227] This second reference to Cluny does not appear in the account in T, fo. 19v.

of Odon which regned in Ffraunce as tutor to Charles Simplex, in the yere DCCCCX,²²⁸ which Hellewyn espoused [...] doughtir of Rollo first duc of Normandie,²²⁹ and by her had issue William Chief Rumpe, which had issue Geffrey, which had |53r| issue William, which had issue William which espoused the onely doughtir of the erle of Tholous, and by hir had issue William ffather of the said Quene Alianore wief of King Henry the Second.²³⁰

By which is manifest that the said duchie of Guyan and the countie of Poytow were reunied together by olde enheritaunce long tyme afore the tyme of the ffather of the said Alianore.²³¹ And that the said cuntreis of Xaintonge, Charente, Perrigourt, Agen, Quercy, Rouergue and Lymosin with their appendacies and diverse other provinces, cuntrees and seignories were of antiquite and owe to be parcell of the said duche of Guyan in fee or in demeane. And is also manifest the injuries, oppressions and tirannies of the said kinges of Fraunce, Phelip, Loys and Loys doon to the said kinges of Englond, John & Henry the III^de in taking and oppressing from them their dew and veray hereditamentes of Normandie and other the premisses without title, good consciens or lawfull or reasonable cause, and that by false cautelles, coloures and fained imaginacions.

*Capitulum XV*²³²

And where in the said secund partie is furthermore objected that in the tyme of the regne of Charles Simplex somtyme king of Fraunce, the cuntrie of Neustrie now called Normandie shuld be

²²⁸ Charles III the Simple became king of France in 898, after the death of Eudes, count of Paris, who had ruled after the death of Charles II the Bald in 887. The date is given as 1010 in T, fo. 19v.

²²⁹ Guillaume III, count of Poitou and duke of Aquitaine (d. 963) married Gerloc, later renamed Adèle, daughter of Rollo, duke of Normandy. There is no mention of this marriage in T, fo. 19v.

²³⁰ This is an extremely confused and unreliable genealogy, largely repeating the *Genelogia ducum Acquictainne* transcribed in the same hand at the beginning of this manuscript, W, fo. 1r – though that version recorded that Guillaume I the Pious died in 1016, rather than 918. The husband of Rollo's daughter Adèle was in fact Guillaume III, count of Poitou and duke of Aquitaine, son of Ebles-Mancer who died in 934. Guillaume IX, count of Poitou, married Philippa of Toulouse and died in 1126; their granddaughter was Eleanor of Aquitaine.

²³¹ This sentence appears at the end of the section in T, fo. 19v.

²³² This chapter translates and responds to *Pour ce que plusieurs*, pp. 94–95, omitting the preliminary statement that Normandy was part of the ancient heritage of the French crown, originally called Neustria and renamed Normandy after it was given to Rollo. The author also builds upon the discussion in T, fos 20r–21r.

delyvered to Rollo the Dane with the doughtir of the same King Charles named Sigille, to be the proper heritage of the same Rollo and of thissue which shuld descend of that mariage. And that for that the same Rollo aftir he shuld |53v| have possession of all that lond shuld have put the said Sigille his wief in prison and shuld have caused hir there to dye, and shuld have had none issue by hir, for which cause aswel by right of forfaiture as aftir the couvenant of treatie, it shuld be clere that aftir the dethe of the said Rollo, the duche of Normandie ought to have retorned to the king of Ffraunce. And also shuld retorne in lykewise for that the said Rollo shuld have had none issue male or female borne in mariage. And so alledgith bastardie in William Longespee his sone.[233]

The trouth is that the said Rollo with a great power of Norwagiens beyng gentiles and infideles conquered the said cuntre of Neustrie and subdued Bretayn in the yere DCCCIIII^{XX} V, and named that cuntre of Neustrie Normandie and made Berengier and Alain lordes of Bretain his subgettes.[234] And was seased and possessed of Normandie with the dominion of Bretain and had also conquerred diverse other londes in Ffraunce. And the said Charles Simplex to have peas, gave his doughtir Gille to Rollo in mariage and for the same mariage releassed, remitted and quiteclaymed to the said Rollo and his heires all Neustrie than called Normandie of new, with Bretain and all the righte, title and clayme which he, his heires or successoures might have in the same.[235] And therupon the said Rollo was christened and named Robert. And the said Gille died by the visitacion of God by naturell cause of deth, and aftir her decesse the same Rollo espoused |54r| Poupe doughtir of Guido counte de Sarnz,[236] by whom he had issue the said William Longespe aftir him duke of Normandie and

---

[233] The Tudor author omits the lengthy justification of the charge of bastardy levelled against William Longsword (see pp. 95–97).

[234] It is not clear what source was being used for this account of Rollo and his paternity of William Longsword, which does not appear to derive from the accounts in the *Flores historiarum*, I, pp. 475–476 and 483–484, or the very brief references in the *Chronica Hovedene*, I, p. 42 and II, p. 239. Berengarius and Alan were common figures in the story of Rollo as seen, for example, in the *Gesta Normannorum Ducum*, I, pp. 64–66, and Wace, *The Roman de Rou*, ed. Anthony J. Holden and trans. Glyn S. Burgess (Saint Helier, 2002), pp. 36 and 40. The account in T, fo. 20r, did not name Berengarius and Alan but simply referred to the 'erle of Armorik and Bretain'.

[235] The emphasis placed upon Brittany here is largely explained by its relevance to the debate over the breach of the truce in 1449, discussed in chapter twenty-five, p. 259.

[236] Poppa was identified as the daughter of Berengar in the *Flores historiarum*, I, p. 483, following a tradition reflected in Dudo of Saint Quentin, pp. 38–39, *Gesta Normannorum Ducum*, I, p. 58, and Wace, *Roman de Rou*, pp. 24 and 40. T, fo. 20r, reported that Poppa was 'suster of Lambert and Berenger, somtyme kings of Hungarie'.

also a doughtir which was maried to the aforenamed Helwyne counte of Poytow and aftir duke of Guyan as is made mencion afore.[237] And although that the same William Longespe as is supposed had ben born afore mariage solempnised betwix Rollo and Poupe, yet insomoche as they entirmaried aftir and the said William Longespe succeded unto the same duche of Normandie with Bretain as heir to his said father Rollo and therof was possessed all his lief and the same descended to Richard his son as his heir therunto and so reputed and taken as duke by succession thoon aftir thother, it may not be contraried but that the said William Longespee was therof heir to his father. And that is consonant to the lawe of Englond which is supposed to be brought by the aforenamed William duke of Normandie Conquerror of Englond, which he shuld have receyved of the usage of his predecessoures and from the said Rollo. For the lawe of Englond in soche case is, if a man have II sones, and thelder be a bastard and the yonger sone be mulier, and the father decesse, and his bastard sone entir into the heritage as heir to his father and so possedith during his lief and have issue and dye and that issue enter therin by succession, in this case the secund sone, which was mulier, is without remedie and estopped to clayme or saie but that his said elder brother though he were bastard |**54v**| in dede was right heir to his father.[238] By whiche proveth wele that the heritage of the duchie of Normandie and Bretain succeded duly to the said William Longespee from the said Rollo, and from that William to Richard Sanz Paour his sone and that they were laufull dukes of the same.[239]

---

[237] See pp. 201–202.

[238] This is a very careful statement of the legal problem, which rests upon the possession of the heritage by the illegitimate son, rather than his inheritance of the same, which was not valid under English common law: Richard H. Helmholz, 'Bastardy litigation in medieval England', in *idem, Canon Law and the Law of England* (London, 1987), pp. 187–210. Also see p. 96, n. 232 above.

[239] T, fos 20v–21r, concludes this section with a response to the rhetorical question of why the French kings failed to do anything about the inheritance by William Longsword (see p. 96): 'And thanswer in that partie made to a question or demaunde of that why the king of Ffraunce claymed not the duchie of Normandie in the tyme of lief of the said William Longespee is rehersed that the kings of Ffraunce were so feble and the reame so destroyed and were than so many broilles and troubles in the same aswel amongs the great lords of that reame thoon against thother, as somme of those lords against the king, that it was to difficlle to doo for which it behoved to passe the tyme under dissimyllacon unto other tyme. It apperith wele that the kings of Ffraunce than made no soche pretense or clayme to the said duchie of Normandye wherby in that partie they now ar estopped to cleyme eny thing therof in that partie for the reasons aforehersed.'

Capitulum XVI [240]

And where it is alledged further in the said secund partie that the said Richard Saunz Paour duke of Normandie aftir the countre shuld have ben delyvered to hym shuld have forfaited the same duche in diverse against the king of Fraunce.

The same Richard Saunz Paour never forfaited against the king of Ffraunce in eny poynt nor made to hym eny werre or made occasion as is alledged. At the deth of the said William Longespe which was shamefully & cautelously murdred by Arnold than erle of Fflaundres undir false dissymylacion,[241] the said Richard was very yong of age an infant and aftir by assent of all his barons of Normandie and Bretayn he and his duche were in tutele of Bernard le Danois and oon Osmont a knight, which II had faithfully served his father the said Duc William.[242] Loys than king of Ffraunce, sone of Charles Simplex, hering of the said murdre of William Long Espee, cam to Roane where he was honorably recyved by the Duc Richard at the provision and ordenance of the said II knightes Bernard and Osmond, and lodged in a |55r| faire inne making great semblant of great amyte, honor and feest to the said duc, alledging that he ought so to doo for the love of the said Duc William which was the chief aide and confort to the same Loys in his recover and comyng to the corone of Ffraunce and possession of the reame aftir the deth of his father Charles Simplex at the desire of Athelstan than king of Englond, his uncle.

And there at Roane than the same King Loys receyved of the said Duke Richard homage for the duche of Normandie and of Bretain, and there than the same King Loys put the same Duc Richard in possession of all his londes, forteresses and seignories of Normandie and of Bretain, and of great height the same King Loys afore all the barons there sware that he shuld venge the deth of Duc William Longespe and shuld punyssh the erle of Flaundres, and shuld aide Duc Richard to defend his right and his honour against all men, and saide that he wold assiege Arras where the murdrers were and required aide of the Normans. And required of them that for somoche as ther duc the said Richard was but yong and had as than but litel

---

[240] This chapter translates and responds to *Pour ce que plusieurs*, p. 97, and builds upon a much shorter narrative in T, fos 21r–21v. This colourful account of the reign of Duke Richard I was not taken from either the *Flores historiarum* or the *Chronica Hovedene*, and it is not clear what the author means by the 'croniques of Normandie' referred to below, p. 207.

[241] William Longsword was murdered on the instructions of Count Arnulf of Flanders in 942, leaving a young son, Richard, who was taken into custody by King Louis IV of France. See, for example, Dudo of Saint Quentin, pp. 99–100.

[242] The discussion of the tutelage of Richard is omitted in T, fo. 21r.

seen, if it shuld seme to them good that Duc Richard shuld be in the companie of Lothaire his sone at Laon to lerne aftir his estate. And the said King Loys spak so plesauntly to the Normans that they aggreed therunto.[243]

And so Duc Richard was conveyed honourably to Laon and had with him to attend daily upon him the said Osmont to see his governance. All that notwithstonding oothes nor promyses nor amyte nor trust, not long aftir the said King Loys imagined the destruction and disherision of the same Richard and of his duchie of Normandie and Bretain, commaund to Duc Richard and Osmond that for thing which shuld fortune the same |55v| Duke Richard shuld not issue the towne of Laon, and to Osmond that he shuld suffer the same Richard of the issue of the toun upon peyne of his lief. And that notwithstonding Duc Richard loved wele hunting and hawking and happened him oon day to see his hawk flye, tok his hors and rode owt of toun to see his hawk flye and resorted to serve the king at soper. And the king having knowlege that Duc Richard had ben out of the toun contrarie to his commaundment called the same duc and the said Osmond afore hym and saide to them, 'I have defended you the issue out of the toun and upon my defence you have issued and you Osmond have consented ye shal be punysshed therfor derely, for I see wele that you Richard whan yo shalbe great, ye shal doo no thing for me and your people held me in subjection at Roane and it was faire for me whan I was from them.'

Than Duc Richard kneled and saide to him, 'Sir, ye be my lord and I am your man and am hether come at your commaundement if I went to sporte me ye shuld not beleve that I so ded to disobeye you. Ye shal ordeyne of me and of Osmont at your pleasur and we shal obeye you. So we beseche you that ye wol tak displeasur against us'.

'By my faith' saide the king, 'your same langage shal not help you. I shal holde you fast ynow.' Whereupon the said Duc Richard & Osmont were moche abasshed and hevy for the king had ordeyned that Duc Richard shuld be kept in a chamber by VI men therto assigned, but Osmont lodged in the toun. Which Osmont aftir that conveyed the same Duc Richard secretly thens and brought him into his duche of Normendie.[244]

---

[243] The account in T, fo. 21r, merely states that 'in that his yong age, Loys than king of Ffraunce, hering of the said murdre, cam to Roane and there revested the same enfant Richard of the duché of Normandie and aftir led him to Laon to be norisshed.' Louis receives a much less cordial reception in Dudo of Saint Quentin, pp. 100–102, and Wace, *Roman de Rou*, pp. 56–60.

[244] This is a reworking of the story originally recounted in Dudo of Saint Quentin, pp. 104–106. A different version appears in the *Gesta Normannorum Ducum*, I, pp. 102–104,

Wherfor the said King Loys than was moche sorowfull that he had lost the said Duc Richard and tok the VI men that |56r| were assigned to kepe him and caused them to be hanged. And sent for Hugh le Graunt counte of Parys and graunted to him if he wold help him to conquerre Normandie, he wold geve of same duche all the cuntre betwix Saine and Bretayn, and the king to have thother part.[245] Wherupon the said King Loys assieged and tok Roan, and Hugh le Graunt assieged Bayeux. And sone aftir by processe conquerred all Normandie. But that was of a great cautel as the croniques of Normandie make especial mencion.[246]

And sone aftir King Herald of Denmark cam with a great power of Danes in relief of the said Duc Richard and with the same King Herald all Normans comones and other arose and went with him in aide of their duke and went nere to Roane were in bataill he veynquissed and toke the said King Loys and destroyed his power there and killed his knightes and held him prisoner in Roane until he was delyvered by treatie and for his redemption. By which treatie the said King Loys yelded to Duc Richard, Normandie and Bretayne quitely wuthout to reteyne upon or for those cuntrees homages, seignories or eny soveraynte, and besides sware that he shuld never demande thing of the said Duc Richard nor to bere him domage, but shuld ever aide him with all his power, and so was delyvered.[247]

This nothwithstonding, sone aftir the same King Loys called to his aide his wiefes brother, the Imperator Otho and the said Arnold erle of Fflaundres, and entred and distroyed Duc Richardes londes

---

and Wace, *Roman de Rou*, pp. 62–64. The account in T, fo. 21r, does not include the lengthy story of Richard's rescue from Laon, simply reporting that 'oon kings of Normandie named Edmond, douting and suspecting the same king of Ffraunce of straite keping of the said Richard, conveied the same Richard secritly into his owne duchie of Normandie amongs his own men.'

[245] Louis IV negotiated with Hugues the Great, count of Paris, who took control of Bayeux. This account is loosely based upon Dudo of Saint Quentin, pp. 110–111, and Wace, *Roman de Rou*, pp. 66–68. The account in T, fo. 21r, is different: 'And for displeasure therof the said King Loys gaf from the said Richard of that his enheritaunce the londs of Evreulx and Baieux to Hugh le Graunt than erle or duke of Parys, father to kings Capet, to thentent he shuld help and aide the same King Loys to take from the said Duke Richard the duchie and londs of Normandie'.

[246] This reference to the conquest of Normandy and to the 'croniques of Normandie' does not appear in T, fo. 21r.

[247] Richard was assisted by the Viking leader, Harald of the Bassin. These events were described in Dudo of Saint Quentin, pp. 114–117; *Gesta Normannorum Ducum*, I, pp. 110–116; and Wace, *Roman de Rou*, pp. 74–76. In the account in T, fos 21r–21v, the leader of the 'men of werre of Denmerk and Norwey' was identified as 'Aglode'.

and assieged Roane where Duc Richard put them to flight. And for anguissh the said king Loys sone aftir died.[248]

And aftir that Lothaire his sone king of Ffraunce, with Theobald countie of Chartres, by cautellous meanes imagined the destruction of the said Duc Richard and invaded his londes with armees |56v| and made many destructions in Normandie. But Duc Richard so defended them and vencquisshed them that the same King Lothaire sent the bisshop of Chartres to treate with Duc Richard for peas, to whom Duc Richard saide that he was content to be in peas, but he wold never trust King Lothaire in eny point, nor to mete him but in armes without suretie. But neverthelesse at the instant labour of the said bisshop, Duc Richard was content King Lothaire shuld come to Saint Clere upon Ette at a certain day, and so there they mette and peas was treated and concluded.[249]

By which it is manifest the injuries and oppressions doon by the said kinges of Ffraunce falsely doon to the said Duc Richard, and that the same Richard never made werre against them but to defend his right as lawfull was for him to doo.

Capitulum XVII[250]

And where also is surmytted in the said secund partie that William duc of Normandie, conquerror of Englond, shuld be bastard sone of Robert somtyme duc of Normandie. And that the same Duc Robert his father shuld never be maried nor the same William legittimat, wherfor he shuld be inhabill to succede, and for that cause the said duche shuld have come to the said reame. And that also the same Duc William shuld have made open werre to the king of Ffraunce many tymes and by that cause shuld have forfaited the said duchie.

|57r| As is saide afore, the kings of Ffraunce nor eny of them of eny tyme of all the succession of the said duche of Normandie until the tyme of King John never made eny clayme to the said duche for eny cause afore alledged nor other, nor in the tyme of the said King John but in colour for the deth of Arthur his neveu. And therfor they and

---

[248] Louis IV died in 954. This is a loose summary of the events described in the *Gesta Normannorum Ducum*, I, p. 118, and Wace, *Roman de Rou*, pp. 80–88. The account in T, fo. 21v, ends here and does not mention Arnold of Flanders.

[249] Duke Richard swore allegiance to Lothair I at Gisors in 965. The events leading up to the peace agreed at the river Epte are described in Dudo of Saint Quentin, pp. 162–163.

[250] This chapter translates and responds to *Pour ce que plusieurs*, p. 97, and builds upon the material in T, fos 21v–22v.

all ther successours ar estopped to take eny avauntage by reason of that bastardie.[251]

Also aftir the birth of the same William, matrimonie was solempnised betwix his father and mother, and also the said Duc Robert adopted him to be his heir of all the said duchie. And also afore his voiage towardes Jerusalem in his pilgrinage, he called all his barons of Normandie and of Bretayne at Ffuscamp. And in that counseill gave to the said William the same duchie and all his hereditamentes and made him there his heir and put him than in season and possession therof, and there assigned Alain of Bretain, seneschal of the duchie and londes until that the same William shuld be of resonable age, and ordeyned Erle Gillebert to be tutor of the same William, and the same tutor with his sone to be under tewicion of Henry than king of Ffraunce.[252] And as the said Duc Robert in his voiage went by the same king of Ffraunce and led with him the said William, and in the presence of the same Duke Robert the said king of Ffraunce Henry receyved homage of the same William for the duche of Normandie and Bretayne, and afore that in the sight of the same Duc Robert, the prelates and barons of Normandie and of Bretain made their homages to the same William and receyved the same William to be ther lord.

And the said Duc Robert died in that |**57v**| his said pilgrinage.[253] And aftir his deth the lordes of Normandie, by the comocion of oon Guy, a Burgonion of nacion, cosin to the said Duc William, toke upon them and every of them by him self to have severall divisions in the said duche without to have suffred the said Duke William or eny other for him to have dominion over of them. And therupon they killed the said tutour the Erle Gillebert and empoisoned Alain of Bretain seneschal of Normandie and soche werre contenewed until that the said Henry king of Ffraunce, *tutor tutoris* for the trust he was put in by the said Duc Robert, subdewed at Walesdomes XXXM Normannes, and aftir revested the said William duke of Normandie and affermed the same William to be veray duc of Normandie as heir to his said father.[254] And so aftir that regned peasibly duc of Normandie without

---

[251] This argument does not appear in the version in T, fo. 21v.

[252] William was formally designated as Robert's heir in January 1035, when the Norman nobles swore fealty to him. This account of William the Conqueror's succession to the duchy of Normandy is similar in some respects to that in the *Flores historiarum*, I, pp. 553–554, but this was probably not the direct source because there is no mention of Alan of Brittany or the marriage of William's parents, and the chronicle paid little attention to subsequent events in Normandy except insofar as they related to the invasion of England. There is no mention of Alan of Brittany in the account in T, fos 21v–22r.

[253] Robert died at Nicaea in July 1035, while returning from his pilgrimage to the Holy Land.

[254] A chronology of the early years of William's tenure as duke is difficult to establish. At least two of his guardians were killed around 1040 and, around 1046, William's position was challenged by Count Gui of Brionne, grandson of Duke Richard II. The challenge was

contradiction of eny man unto his death,[255] and aftir his deth, Robert his elder sone succeeded and was duke of Normandie by course of enheritaunce.[256]

And the said Duke William never made werre or rebelled against eny king of Ffraunce to forfaite eny thing therfor, hough be it in the tyme and aftir that the said Duke William was to conquerre the reame of Englond, which he than claymed to have by thassignement, transport and gift of Saint Edward the Confessour, his cosin afore king of Englond.[257] And the tyme he was subduying the same, King Phelip of Ffraunce, sone of the said King Henry, mayntened and procured certain lordes in Normandie to intende and rebell against the said Duc William, and also procured Robert Curthose his elder sone to make werre against the same William his father, the same his father beyng than in the north parties of Englond to resiste and |58r| and subdew Malcolme than king of Scottes.[258] And other werre the same William never made to the same King Phelip nor other king of Ffraunce nor other thing ded contrarious to his dutie, wherby to forfaite eny thing to the king or corone of Ffraunce, though he had many occasiones.

Capitulum XVIII [259]

And where in the said secund partie is furthermore alledged that the said William Conquerror shuld have had IIII sones and but oon doughtir, of which IIII sones thelder was named Robert aftir him duke of Normandie, the secund named William le Roux which was aftir king of Englond, the thrid shuld be named Roger which shuld have espoused the heritiresse of Bretayne, and the IIIIth was named the aforetime named Henry Beauclerk which was also king of Englond. And the said doughtir shuld be named Adelle maried to the the [sic] counte Theobold of Chartres and mother to

ended by the victory of William and the French King Henri I at the battle of Val-ès-Dunes in 1047.

[255] According to T, fo. 22r, William reigned as duke of Normandy for fifty years.

[256] See p. 212.

[257] This famous argument appeared, for example, in the *Flores historiarum*, I, p. 579, and the *Chronica Hovedene*, I, pp. 237 and 241.

[258] The first revolt of Robert Curthose in 1078 was followed in August and September 1079 by the devastation of northern England by King Malcolm of Scotland. See, for example, the *Flores historiarum*, II, pp. 6 and 8, and the *Chronica Hovedene*, I, pp. 126 and 133.

[259] This chapter translates and responds to *Pour ce que plusieurs*, pp. 97–98, and reorganizes and extends the discussion in T, fos 22v–23v, that had offered a heavily abbreviated translation of the French treatise.

Theobald erle of Champaigne and graunt mother to Adelle wief of King Loys the Peteux and mother to King Phelip the Conquerrant.

And that the said William Roux secund sone of the said IIII sones shuld have died without issue, and that also shuld so have died without issue the said Roger the thrid sone. And that aftir the deth of the same William le Roux and Roger, for that they had none issue and that the Duc Robert was in the parties of beyond the see in the conquest of the Holy Lond, the said Henry Beauclerk ther yonger brother shuld have occupied the reame of Englond, which by right and reason shuld owe to have aperteyned to ther elder brother |58v| the said Duke Robert. Which things comen to the knowlege of the same Duke Robert, the same Duke Robert incontinent shuld have retorned into Normandie to purvoie for all his thinges. And for the same cause the same II brothern shuld have had great werre to gether. And that therupon shuld theraftir peas have ben had upon certain condicions omitted for brieftie, which the said Henry Beauclerk shuld not have performed. And for that cause the werre shuld be revived. And that the same Henry Beauclerk shuld have founden the meanes undir colour of peas as amyte to have taken the said Duc Robert his elder brother and have constreyned him to have renounsed all that which he might pretende to the reame of Englond, and shuld have extorted of him many great somes of money. And not contented therwith, aftir that the said King Henry shuld have delivered the said Duke Robert out of his keping, he shuld have passed into Normandie with great puissance and have made to him werre, and at the last though he were his elder and his lord estsones he shuld have taken him and have made him to dye, and shuld have taken and occupied by force the duche of Normandie.

And furthermore for that the sone of the said Duke Robert was goon to the erle of Fflaundres his uncle of his mothers side for his suretie, which erle of Fflaundres shuld have sent him to Hedyn which place he had delyvered to him for his abiding there for his [deduit?], the same Henry Beauclerk by conspiracions, willing in all poyntes to destroye the ligne of the said Duke Robert his brother, and as the said sone and heritier of the said Duc Robert shuld have ben for his recreacion in an isle nere to Hedyn, he shuld have caused murdrers |59r| to have lyen in awayte for him which shuld have killed and murdred him petouxly.[260]

---

[260] The English translator omits the lengthy closing statement in *Pour ce que plusieurs*, which argued that the duchy of Normandy should have been reunited with the French crown after King Henry I had murdered his elder brother, Robert Curthose, thereby

Trew it is that the said William Conquerror had IIII sones, of whom thelder was the said Robert Courthose duke of Normandie, and the secund was named Richard which [died] without issue in the same forest that William Rufus was killed in, the thrid sone was the same William Rufus, and the IIIIth sone was the said Henry Beauclerk and had no sone named Roger. The said William Conquerror had also V doughtres of which V doughtres theldest was named Cicilie and was abbesse of the nonnery of Cane of his mothers foundacion, the secund was named Constance and was maried to Alain Ffergant erle of Bretayn, the third doughtir was named Adelle maried to Stephen erle of Bleyse and not to Theobald erle of Chartres as is surmytted. Of thother II doughtres, thoon afore the conquest Harold which aftir the deth of Saint Edward usurped the corone of Englond promysed to espouse to his wief, and thother was promysed to Alphons king of Galice in mariage, which II doughtres died unmaried.²⁶¹

And trew it is that the said William Rufus or le Roux died without issue the tyme that the said Duc Robert Courthose his elder brother was in the Holy Lond, and that the said Henry Beauclerk aftir the deth of the said William Rufus opteyned the corone and reame of Englond. And the cause why he so ded was upon this ground and reason, for that the same Henry Beauclerk was begoten and borne in Englond aftir the conquest by his father therof and so was not |**59v**| the said Duke Robert but borne in Normandie long afore the said conquest, for which cause and by that reason the barones and counseill elected the said Henry Beauclerk to be king of Englond.²⁶²

And the said Robert Courthose duke of Normandie beyng that tyme at Jerusalem at a Estir tyme, he with other princes havying in ther hands cierges²⁶³ unlight abiding aftir olde usage the misteries of God for light to be sent from heven, the cierge which the same Duke Robert held than in his hond was illumyned by misterie, by which he was than elected to be king of Jerusalem. And the same elect Duke Robert havyng newly tidinges of the deth of the said William Rufus his brother king of Englond gave his mynde rather to be king of Englond for the felicite of the world than to be king of Jerusalem with glorie in the service of God, and so refused the gift of grace to be king of

committing lèse-majesté by attacking a peer of the realm and acting against the king and the royal majesty and authority. The French treatise argued that, given Henry's unworthiness to inherit the duchy, it should have passed to Philippe Augustus as the rightful heir of the sister of Henry I. See p. 99.

²⁶¹ See pp. 172–173.

²⁶² Henry I was indeed born in England, possibly at Selby, in either 1068 or 1069, though this was not cited as a justification for his 'election' and coronation as king on 5 August 1100.

²⁶³ A 'cierge' was a large wax candle used in religious ceremonies.

Jerusalem. And from thens ymmediatly retorned into Normandie and prepared his power and so with his armee cam into Englond to have destroyer his brother King Henry Beauclerk.[264] But by mediation of the counseill of bothe parties, peas was treated betwix them and the same King Henry yerely to paie his brother the said Duke Robert IIIM marcs, aftir which treatie the same Duke Robert retorned in to Normandie. And aftir that passed against into Englond for recreacion & visitation of his brother the said King Henry, and assigned the same his yerely pencion of IIIM marc to be paied to Quene Matild wief of the Henry Beauclerk, and so for that remitted to the same King Henry the same pencion for ever.[265]

|60r| And not long aftir the same Duke Robert was retorned into Normandie by the counseill of counte d'Albmarle, the counte du Perche, le countie de Mortain and of Henry Harecort, he entred and seased in to his hondes the cuntries of Damfront and Constantine which the said King Henry held in gage of the londes of Normande for certain mony that he had lent to the said Duc Robert towardes his voiage of Jerusalem which he had not repayed. For the recover wherof, the said King Henry assembled his hostes and passed into Normandie. And in bataill the same King Henry toke the said Duke Robert his brother and kept him prisoner, and seased in to his hondes the said cuntrees of Damfront and Constantin and besides that caused governores to be appointed in the duche of Normandie to the use of William sone of the said Duke Robert which than was in Fflaundres with his cosin Robert erle of Fflaundres.[266] Which aftir the deth of the same Robert erle of Fflaundres was as next heir taken and created erle of Fflaundres and durst not abide in Normandie for drede of his uncle the said King Henry, but taried in Fflaundres until that Derik sone of Derik duke of Elsatever, very right heir therof afore the said William, in bataill for the recovere of his right in pleyne bataill wounded the said William, wherof he died.[267] Aftir whois deth all the inhabitantes

[264] Robert's refusal to accept the kingdom of Jerusalem was mentioned in the *Flores historiarum*, II, pp. 32 and 35, drawing on a wider tradition, which recounted this event and the pope's judgement that Robert's subsequent imprisonment was God's punishment for the duke's refusal of God. See, for example, William of Malmesbury, *Gesta regum Anglorum: the history of the English kings*, eds R.A.B. Mynors, R.M. Thomson, and M. Winterbottom (2 vols, Oxford, 1998–1999), I, p. 702, and Henry, Archdeacon of Huntingdon, *Historia Anglorum*, ed. Diana E. Greenway (Oxford, 1996), pp. 442–443 and 454–455, together with Charles W. David, *Robert Curthose* (Cambridge, MA, 1920), pp. 198–200.

[265] The treaty of Winchester and the pension of 3,000 marks were cited in the *Flores historiarum*, II, p. 35, though this did not report an assignation of the pension to Queen Matilda.

[266] Robert was captured in 1106, during Henry I's seige of Tinchebrai.

[267] William Clito was chosen as count of Flanders in 1127, but died the following year while besieging the castle of Aalst, held by his rival, Count Thierry of Alsace. T, fo. 23r,

of the duche of Normandie, not trusting of the deliveraunce of the said duke out of prison nor greatly tarying therfor for the manifold imposicions he put his subgettes unto, yelded them as subgettes to the said |6ov| King Henry as to the next heir of the same.

And the Pope Calixtus came personelly into Normandie with an angry and fell meende to couvente the same King Henry for the imprisonyng of the said Duke Robert whom he named to be pilgrine of the Holy Sepulcure. But the answer and probable argument of the same King Henry and the trouth declared afore the same pope was by the same pope king Henries cause demed good and the imprisonyng of the same Robert to be of his just desertes.[268]

By which premises is manifestly declared that nothing owe to be objected against the said King Henry for taking and imprisonyng of the said Duke Robert. And he murdred him not, for the same Duke Robert beyng in prison, the said King Henry sent unto him a bonet for his hede soche as was bought for himself, but whan he assaied it, it was somwhat to straite. And whan the said Duke Robert knew that it was the refuse of his brother, toke it to great disdeyne and never aftir wold for impaciens ete no meate, but died of anguissh.[269] And by the premisses is declared that the said William sone of the same Duke Robert was never killed or murdred by the procurement or commandement, will or assent of the said King Henry, wherfor eny thing owith to be objected against him to disabill him of eny of his hereditamentes.

|61r| *Capitulum XIX*[270]

And where it is also surmitted in the said secund partie that Ffulco which shuld be the first erle of Angeo shuld not have had the same countie of Angeo by title of the king of Ffraunce, but onely in

reports: 'The trouth is that the same William sone of Robert Cuthose, aftir the deth of Charles erle of Fflaunders, usurped the same countie of Fflaunders and held it XV monyths until that Dirik sone of Dirik duke of Elsaten right heir therof in bataill [...] hurt the said William wherof he died.' These accounts of his death are very different from the shorter versions in the *Flores historiarum*, II, p. 53, and *Chronica Hovedene*, I, pp. 182 and 184.

[268] The judgment of Pope Calixtus II is presented at the start of this section of T, fos 22v–23r, which does not recount the capture of Robert, but instead concludes with the statement that 'But he was by the same King Henry vemquisshed and committed to perpetuel prison, and that as I have rehersed the rightful suffrant of God for that he wold rather performe his sensual meende for erthely covitise, than to performe the will of God whan he was elect by miracle and divine misterie to be king of Jerusalem.'

[269] This famous story was repeated in the *Flores historiarum*, II, p. 56.

[270] This chapter translates and responds to *Pour ce que plusieurs*, p. 100, and extensively revises the material in T, fos 23v–24v.

governaunce, and that he shuld be but occupiour and governour.
And in likewise the countie of Maine shuld not be geven in title
but onely in governaunce to them which shuld have holden them
the tyme whan the Normans persecuted strongly the reame of
Ffraunce.[271] And that neverthelesse be it in the countie of Maine
or in that of Torayne, it shuld not be founde except the castel of
Loches and of Amboise which shuld of olde tyme the heritages of
the erles of Angeo, having no thing in the said counties of Maine
and Torayn but by force and by occupacion, and shuld have put
owt therfro the trew heritiers. And that the king of Ffraunce might
not at that tyme geve therof permision for the impuissance that
was than.[272]

There were severall erles of Angeo, of Maine and of Turayn of
antiquite. And the said Ffulco which is supposed shuld be the first erle
of Angeo was therof erle by lyneall discent and of his heritage in his
owne right, and nothing shal be proved or shewed of auctorite to the
contrarie, and held the same by service of the erle of Poytow as may
appere by histories where mencion is made against Geffrey Martel
sone of the same Ffulco erle of Angeo for taking and imprisonyng
|6rv| of the erle of Poytow his soverayn lord.[273] And Angeo is within
the partie of Gallia Acquitanica. And the countie of Maine is in fee
parcel of the duche of Normandie and in subjection of the duc of
Normandie as is specified in the histories.

And Gefferey Plantagenet father to King Henry the Secund was
by heritage erle of Angeo, Torayn and of Maine by descent from his
progenitores as thus. The said Ffulco the Elder erle of Angeo had issue
the said Geffrey Martell and a doughtir maried to the erle of Torayn
[...] Plantagenest. The same Gefferey Martell was a moche cruell
man and died without issue, aftir whose deth the same countie of
Angeo descended to his suster, wief of the erle of Torayn, and he was
erle of Torayn and in the right of his wief erle of Angeo.[274] Which erle
of Torayn by his wief heiresse of Angeo had issue Gefferey and Ffulco
Rechin. That Gefferey thelder sone was erle of Angeo & Torayn aftir
the deth of his father and mother and died without issue.[275] And Ffulco

[271] The summary of the argument in *Pour ce que plusieurs* ends here in T, fo. 23v.

[272] The Tudor author omits the French argument that the loss of Anjou, Maine, and
Touraine at the end of the Hundred Years War was God's judgement on the English kings'
lack of a good and just title (see p. 100).

[273] Geoffrey II Martel was the son of Foulques III Nerra. He captured Guillaume VI,
count of Poitiers, and held him prisoner until 1036.

[274] The sister of Geoffrey II Martel was Ermengarde, who married Geoffrey, count of
Gâtinais.

[275] The sons of Ermengarde were Geoffrey III le Barbu and Foulques IV le Réchin.

Rechin his brother succeeded and was also erle of Angeo and Torayn and had also issue Gefferey and Ffulco.[276] But aftir the birthes of those II sones, the king of Ffraunce Phelip sone of King Henry of Ffraunce toke Bertrand wief of the same Ffulco Rechin and begate on hir II sones and a doughtir, for which he was excommunicat and his londes in entredict by Pope Urban the Secund.[277] The said Geffery sone of Ffulco Rechin was also erle of Angeo and Torayn aftir his father and died without issue and to him succeded Ffulco his brother to bothe those counties of Angeo and Torayn, and had issue Gefferey |62r| Plantagenest father to the said King Henry the Secund and also Ffulco which was king of Jerusalem,[278] and also II doughtres. Thoon of those II doughtres was maried to William sone and heir apparant of the said King Henry Beauclerk, which William was drowned in the see in the lief of his said ffather, and thother doughtir was maried to William sone of the said Robert Curthose sone of William Conquerror.[279]

And the said countie of Maine was parcel of the duche of Normandie and holden in fee of the duke of Normandie. Ffor Richard Saunz Paour duke of Normandie gave the same Maine to oon Hugh whom he made erle therof to hold of him and his heires dukes of Normandie. Which Hugh erle of Maine had issue a sone named Herbert which succeded the said Hugh and was also erle of Maine.[280] That Herbert died without issue, aftir whois deth the same countie of Maine descended to the said Gefferey sone of Ffulco Rechin as cosin and heir therunto, that is to saie sone to the said Bertrand wief of that Ffulco Rechin, suster of the said Hugh, father of the said Herbert erle of Maine. Neverthelesse the Duke William of Normandie Conquerror

[276] The sons of Foulques IV le Réchin were Geoffrey Martel le Jeune and his brother Foulques V, who was count of Anjou from 1109 to 1129 and became king of Jerusalem in 1131.

[277] In 1092, King Philippe I repudiated his wife, Bertha, and married Bertrade de Montfort, fourth wife of Foulques IV le Réchin. Between 1094 and 1104, Philippe was excommunicated and then absolved. The bigamous marriage produced two sons, Philippe and Florus, and a daughter named Cecile. The account in T, fo. 24r, does not name the wife of Foulques nor the pope.

[278] Geoffrey V Plantagenet, father of King Henry II, was in fact the son of Foulques V.

[279] Henry I's son, William the Aethling, married Matilda of Anjou, daughter of Foulques V, and she became a nun after her husband's premature death in 1120. Her sister, Sibyl, married William Clito three years later. In T, fo. 24r, the author reminds us that Geoffrey married Henry's daughter, Matilda, who was the mother of Henry II and two other sons.

[280] This sentence is omitted from T, fo. 24r. The counts of Maine were Hugues I, his son Hugues II, his son Hugues III and grandson Herbert I Wakedog, Hugues III's brother Herbert Baco, Herbert Wakedog's son Hugues IV and grandson Herbert II, another grandson of Herbert Wakedog named Hugues V, and then a third grandson named Helias, whose daughter Eremburge married Foulques V and was the mother of Geoffrey V, count of Anjou and Maine. See the complex genealogical table in Richard E. Barton, *Lordship in the County of Maine c.890–1160* (Woodbridge, 2004), pp. xii–xiii.

of Englond entred into the countie of Maine claymyng the same by revercion for that there was none issue than of that descended of the body of the said Hugh father of Herbert, which had the gifte therof of the said Richard Saunz Paour to him and his heires and not in taill, and held the possession by a long tyme. But aftir, Ffulco father to the said Geffrey Plantagenest and yonger sone of Ffulco Rechin opteyned the possession therof agayn, and so it descended with thother to his sone |**62v**| the said Gefferey Plantagenest. Albe it the same Ffulco gave the same countie of Maine to William the said sone of Henry Beauclerk in mariage with his said doughtir.[281]

By which it is manifest that the said counties of Angeo, Torayn and Maine descended to the said Gefferey Plantagenest by due succession of heritage, and the right therof is now descended with thother to thexcellent and most vertuous my most dred sovereyn lord King Henry the VIIIth king of Englond and of Ffraunce and lord of Irelond, and that the allegacions and objections made to the contrarie be false and untrue, dampnably imagined.

Capitulum XX [282]

And where also in the said secund partie is surmytted that Quene Alianore wief of King Henry the Secund shuld have confisqued the countie of Poytow hir heritage for certain causes there[283] supposed by hir to be doon against King Loys somtyme hir husbond, they both beyng in the Holy Lond.

The same is falsly and dampnably imagined to the reproche of the same lady and dishonor of the said King Loys.[284] Ffor the same King Loys and Quene Alianore than his wief retorned from the Holy Lond unto the reame of Ffraunce the yere MCXLIX and contenued ther espousels |**63r**| unto the yere MCLIIII that is to say by V yeres aftir those causes shuld have ben done. If they had ben trew the same King

[281] The account in T, fo. 24r, merely stated that William the Conqueror was unable to obtain the county of Maine by right because Herbert had left it to his heir, Geoffrey Martel (without specifying the familial relationship), and because the lords of Maine had approved this.

[282] This chapter summarizes and responds to *Pour ce que plusieurs*, pp. 100–101. There is no equivalent in T.

[283] The words 'falsly and dampnably imagined' are crossed out.

[284] The adultery story did not appear in either the *Chronica Hovedene* or the *Flores historiarum*, though Matthew Paris did repeat it in his *Chronica majora*, ed. H.R. Luard (7 vols, London, 1872–1883), II, p. 186, and *Historia Anglorum*, ed. F. Madden (3 vols, London, 1866–1869), I, p. 288. See also p. 101, n. 251 above.

Loys wold not have contenewed with hir so long.[285] But the trouth was the same King Loys by the advise of his counseill for that he had contenewed with hir in espousels of a long tyme havying by hir no sone but II doughtres sewed divorse betwix them for consanguinete and none other cause nor colour of cause.[286] And also she and the said King Henry the Secund hir laufull husbond contenewed by all ther liefes with the possession of the said counte of Poytow and of the duche of Guyan also of hir heritage, without eny chalenge of the said King Loys or eny thing objected for eny soche or other cause of confisquacion.

Capitulum XXI [287]

And where in the said secund partie is furthermore supposed that the duche of Guyan in so moche as touchith the III seneschalcies afore rehersed shuld by the meanes afore touched and declared many tymes fall into cause of confisquacion afore the treatie of Saint Loys wherof is made mencion afore, and to the regard of the londes which shuld be adjoinct by the same treatie shuld never have ben to the Englisshmen. And that they shuld not may pretende eny thing therof by title of succession. And that it shuld be trew that aftir the deth of the said King |**63v**| Henry the III[de] king of Englond with whom the said Saint Loys shuld have made the said treatie, Edward the first duke which shuld be named secund sone of the seid King Henry the III[de] was king of Englond and duke of Guyan and shuld have doon homage liege to the king of Ffraunce Phelip [son] of Saint Loys.[288] Of which Phelip he shuld have espoused the doughtir named Margaret and shuld have had the countie of Ponthieu in that mariage. And that notwithstonding that he shuld not have willed to resort to the Parliament of the king of Ffraunce and shuld have doon many great disobediences and for that cause great partie of the said duche of Guyan shuld have ben put into the kinges handes and also the said countie of Ponthieu.

And that aftir those thinges, appoinctement shuld have ben had betwen the kinges of Ffraunce and of Englond in the tyme of Phelip

[285] In fact, the divorce took place in 1152.

[286] After their return from Jerusalem, Louis and Eleanor had two daughters, Marie and Alix, who married Henri, count of Champagne, and his brother Thibaud, count of Blois.

[287] This chapter translates and responds to *Pour ce que plusieurs*, pp. 101–104, and redrafts the confused account in T, fos 24v–27r.

[288] T, fo. 24v, begins the recapitulation of *Pour ce que plusieurs* by simply stating that Edward I was the second son of Henry III and married Marguerite.

le Beale sone of the said Phelip, and have made peas to gether. And that for the same peas the bettir to be holden the said King Phelip le Beale shuld geve in mariage to Edward of Carnarvan sone of the said Edward the First his secund doughtir named Isabel and shuld have bene cosins germaine. But that notwithstonding whan the said Edward the First was dede, the same King Edward the Secund shuld have refused to doo to the kinges of Ffraunce successoures of the said King Phelip le Beal the services which to them he ought to have doon by cause of the said duchie of Guyan and also of the said countie of Ponthieu.[289] Ffor which cause and for many great rebellions and disobeissances which were doon by the said Edward of |64r| Carnarvan and his officiers against the said king of Ffraunce and his, the most part of the said duche of Guyan and the countie of Ponthieu, and in especiall of the londes which shuld have ben geven to the king of Englond over the said III seneschalcies of Burdeulx, de Lannes and of Baxades shuld have ben seased in to kinges hondes.

And that the Englisshmen seyng that they shuld have lost all Guyan shuld have divised amonges them that King Edward of Carnarvan shuld transporte the said duchie of Guyan to his elder sone King Edward the III[de] sone of Dame Isabel of Ffraunce and nevew of the said III kinges brothern, and that he shuld goo to doo homage to King Charles le Beale his uncle, and to assaie to recover all the said londes. And in fournyssant of those thinges, he came to to [*sic*] the said King Charles his uncle and by the meane of the said Dame Isabel mother to the same Edward which was than with the said King Charles le Beal hir brother by cause of certain divisions that than were in Englond. The same King Charles for the love of the same Dame Isabel his suster, he shuld have rendred the duchie of Guyan and restored the same to the said Edward the III[de] with all his other londes.[290] And therfor the same Edward ded homage to the said King Charles for the said duchie of Guyan and thother londes in Ffraunce.[291]

|64v| It is sufficiently and pleynly declared afore at lengthe that ther was never cause doon, committed or geven by eny king of Englond or duke or erle of eny the said particuler londes of the heritage of Englond

---

[289] The Tudor writer omits the statement that Charles of Valois and his son Philippe were sent to Guyenne because of Edward II's refusal to pay homage (see p. 103). This marks the end of the translation of *Pour ce que plusieurs* in T, fo. 24v.

[290] This sentence is a summary of the longer speech attributed to Charles IV in the French treatise (see p. 104).

[291] The Tudor author omits the further statement in *Pour ce que plusieurs*, p. 104, that Isabella murdered Edward II and that their son became king by usurpation and also paid homage to Philippe VI of France at Amiens, as discussed on pp. 151–152.

in the parties of Ffraunce afore the said supposed treatie of Saint Loys or aftir wherfor to forfaite or confisque the said duchie of Guyan or eny other ther possessions or hereditamentes by eny maner, meane or cause, as is dampnably imagined. But that the kinges of Ffraunce of tirannie have made distructions and oppressed from diverse the kinges of Englond their hereditamentes by cautelous and false conspiracions and machinacions, not observyng or keping eny one longe treatie, promyse, apointement[292] nor ther solenne othes made to the kinges of Englond at eny tyme no longer till they might espie ther avauntage. For as sone as they cowde espie ther likelyhode of avauntage, they were no lenger keping ther appointementes the trew histories to witnesse and that aggreeth to an olde sentence, expressed of them in that behalf saying this, *Treugas astringent Galli vix dum modo invigent.*[293]

And it is also manifestly declared afore that the londes which ar supposed to be adjoinct by the surmysed treatie of Saint Loys, were and owe to be parcell of the said duche of Guyan and also is declared that there was no soche treatie for soche purpos betwix Saint Loys and the said King Henry the III[de] in maner as is surmitted and alledged.[294]

And it owe not to be denyed of right that the said king |**65r**| Edward the First was *primogenitus* elder sone and veray heir of the said King Henry the III[de] as may be clerely proved by trew and credible histories and matier of record in all the kinges recordes.[295] And the same King Edward the First espoused Dame Alianore doughtir of Ffernand king of Castel and of [. . .] his wief, doughtir and heir of [. . .] erle of the said countie of Ponthieu, and the said Quene Alianore wief of the said King Edward the First was onely doughtir and heir of the [. . .] wief of the said Ffernand and succeded aftir hir decesse to the said countie of Ponthieu.[296] Which King Edward the First and the same Alianore his wief heir of Ponthieu in the yere MCCIII[XX] IX ymmediately aftir the deth of hir said mother passed over the see to Amyens parcel of the said countie of Ponthieu and there were honorably receyved of the king of Ffraunce Phelip sone of Saint Loys his cosin germayn, which with his great lordes of Ffraunce were comen thether to receyve them. And than and there the same King Phelip rendred to the said

---

[292] The words 'made by them' are deleted.

[293] *Non inveni.* This maxim is repeated on p. 238. This paragraph does not appear in T.

[294] See pp. 198–202.

[295] For the legend that Edward I was, in fact, the younger brother of Edmund Crouchback, see p. 102, n. 255. The citation of histories and records does not appear in T, fo. 24v.

[296] The wife of Edward I was Eleanor of Castile, daughter of Fernando III of Castile. Eleanor's mother was Jeanne de Dammartin, heiress to Ponthieu through her mother, Marie, daughter of Guillaume IV, count of Ponthieu. Neither Jeanne nor William were identified by name in T, fo. 25r.

King Edward the First and to the said Dame Alianore his wief the same countie of Ponthieu and also Agenois, Lymosin, Perregourt and Xaintonge which cam by succession of heritage to the same Quene Alianore as heir to hir mothe lady in hir lief of all the same. And for the same the said King Phelip receyved homage of the said King Edward the First and of Quene Alianore his wief.[297]

And |65v| the same King Edward and Quene Alianore had issew together the said King Edward of Carnarvan, besides III elder sones which died enfantes whois names were Henry, John and Alphons. They had issue also V doughtres.[298] And the same Quene Alianore died *Idibus decembris* the yere MCCIIII^{XX} X.[299] And in the yere MCCIIII^{XX} XVIII the same King Edward the First espoused his secund wief Dame Margaret doughtir of the said King Phelip and suster of King Phelip le Beale.[300] But before this secund espousels in the yere MCCIIII^{XX} XIII discord happened upon the see betwix the marineres of Normandie and the marineres of Englond, where the Normans like wodemen toke the Englissh mariners and hyng them upon theyr seyle yardes and put them to crewell deth. Wherfor the Cink Poortes arrayed ther shippis and toke Normans and cast them into the see sparyng not one in lief of them they toke, the said King Henry [*sic*] not knowing therof afore it was doon. For which the Normans compleyned to the said King Phelip le Beale and therupon solenne ambassadeures went and passed from eyther king of Englond and Ffraunce to other for reformacion of that discord. But Charles counte de Valois brother by the father side of the same King Phelip le Beale of a wilde and proude mynde distourbed the reformacion of peas and excited and procured werre and distruction to be made upon the londes of the said King Edward the First, and upon that the same Charles countie de Valoys with a great power by the commaundement of the said King |66r|

---

[297] Jeanne de Dammartin died in 1279, and in that year Edward I and Eleanor travelled to Paris so that she might pay homage to Philippe III for Ponthieu. Negotiations were then held at Amiens, primarily to resolve differences over the Agenais. These events are conflated in the *Flores historiarum*, III, p. 52, which reported that Philippe gave up Sens, Limoges, Perigueux, Guyenne, and Pontigny. This account appears in T, fo. 25v.

[298] Edward I and Eleanor of Castile probably had fourteen children, though only one son (Edward of Caernarvon, the future Edward II) and five daughters (Eleanor, Joan, Margaret, Mary, and Elizabeth) reached adulthood.

[299] *Flores historiarum*, III, p. 71.

[300] *Flores historiarum*, III, p. 105. The date was not identified in T, which followed this with a statement that Edward I then married Marguerite, demonstrating that Ponthieu did not fall into his hands by that marriage. Before moving on to the story of the tensions between the English and Norman sailors, mistakenly set in 1299, this draft version reported that Edward I paid to homage to Philippe III in July 1274, that Eleanor did the same in 1279, and that Edward I came to Paris in 1295 (*recte* 1285) to do the same to Philippe IV: T, fos 25r–25v.

Phelip le Beale invaded and made werre and distructions upon the heretages of the said King Edward.[301]

And the same King Edward, not willing to doo eny thing against the forme of his homage and fealtie by hom doon to the said King Phelip le Beale in the yere MCCIIII^{XX} VI, immediately aftir the deth of the said King Phelip his father, for the duchie of Guyan and the countie of Ponthieu and for other londes,[302] treated with the same King Phelip le Beale in the yere MCCIIII^{XX} XIII. By which treatie he aggreed to take Dame Margaret sustir of the same King Phelip le Beale in mariage, and upon the appoinctementes of the same treatie he delivered to the same King Phelip Gascoign to hold for XL daies so that the same King Phelip shuld at the eend of those XL daies restore and delyver to the same King Edward the same cuntre of Gascoign again with all soche londes as he had taken from the same King Edward. But the same King Phelip le Beale, having Gascoign delivered to him as is aforesaid, ymmediatly he exiled from thens Edmond erle of Lancaster the King Edwardes brother, which held the same for his said brother, and exiled also from thens the quene of Navarre, wief of the said Edmond and mother to the wief of the same King Phelip, and all Englisshmen out of those parties.[303] Upon which and for that false and shameful demeanor of the same King Phelip wherof the report was in all christien regions to his reproche of vilanye, the said King Edward the III^{de} [sic] advertised by diverse cardenals |66v| that he was discharged of his othe and fealtie made to the said King Phelip in somoche as the same King Phelip had taken from him the londes wherby he ought suche service, disposed him to recover the same his hereditamentes by armed power, *quia injuriam armis irrogatam armorum propulsare remedia jura & leges permittunt.*[304] And maide therof all his lordes, barons & every other of every estate of Englond graunted to him great somes of mony with all their hertis coragiously and lovyngly. And in likewise the king of Scottes Alexander graunted also the same King Edward the revenus of all his londes in Englond for III yeres.[305] And the imperator of Almayne and also the king of Arragon sent their

---

[301] *Flores historiarum*, III, pp. 85–86, which did not identify the king of France, perhaps leading to the erroneous reference to a King Henry. On 15 May 1293, an Anglo-Bayonnaise fleet attacked Norman ships off the Breton coast. Philippe IV rejected Edward's proposal of a bipartite commission to investigate actions committed by both sides and cited the English king to appear before the Parlement of Paris.

[302] *Flores historiarum*, III, pp. 64–65. Edward I had paid homage to Philippe IV at Paris in July 1286.

[303] *Flores historiarum*, III, pp. 271–272. Edmund's second wife was Blanche of Artois (d. 1302), mother of Jeanne (d. 1305).

[304] This maxim also appears on pp. 190, 225, and 251–252.

[305] *Flores historiarum*, III, pp. 88 and 272. Alexander III died in 1286.

ambassades solennely to King Edward advertising him that if he wold entir his hereditamentes wherof he was in soche wise oppressed and wronged, they shuld ayde him to the best of ther power for the zeale of justice, and further shewed to him that it was lauful to the same King Edward to entir and possede his dew hereditamentes by armed power and those to possede by just and good title discharged for ever of almaner service due therfor afore to the corone of Ffraunce, and that he might laufully invade the londes of the same king of Ffraunce and to to [*sic*] him werre if it were in his power in example of his owne dedis to rewarde him with lyk mesured as he had used.[306]

Notwithstonding aftir |**67r**| by the procurement of the Pope Boniface to bothe said kinges of Englond and Fraunce the peas was formed at Rome in the vigil of the fest of the Appostles Peter and Paule in the yere MCCIIII^{XX} XVIII betwix the same kinges. By which was treated and aggreed that the said King Edward the First shuld have in mariage the said Margaret sustir of the said King Phelip le Beal, and that the said King Edward of Carnarvan shuld take in mariage the doughtir of the same Phelip, Dame Isabel, and that the duchie of Guyan, Gascogn and thother londes of the hereditamentes of the said King Edward except Normandie shuld be restored to the same King Edward.[307]

By which premisses is manifestly declared that the said King Edward the First had the said countie of Ponthieu with other londes by the right of his former wief the said Alianore doughtir of Castille as hir dew enheritaunce, and not in mariage with the said Margaret doughtir of Ffraunce as is surmytted. And did never eny disobeissaunce or other thing wherby to confisque eny thing to the king of Ffraunce, nor used himself to doo thing to his displeasur. But the tirannie and oppression of the said kinges of Ffraunce be apparent to ther reproche and infamie everlasting.[308]

And aftir that in the yere MCCCVI the said King Edward the First dubbed his sone the said King Edward of Carnarvan knight and gave and transported to him the duche of |**67v**| Guyan and Gascoyn,[309] and died in the yere MCCCVII, aftir whois deth the same King Edward of Carnarvan was coroned incytenant king of Englond,[310] and

---

[306] This is a liberal reworking of the account in the *Flores historiarum*, III, pp. 272–273.

[307] The treaty is cited, without detail, in the *Flores historiarum*, III, pp. 104 and 297. In T, fos 26r–26v, there was no mention of the events involving Edmund of Lancaster, and the marriage of Edward I to Marguerite was said to have taken place in 1299, securing a two-year truce and the restoration of Gascony and Guyenne in their original state.

[308] The arguments expressed in this paragraph appear at the end of this section in T, fo. 27r.

[309] *Flores historiarum*, III, p. 132.

[310] *Flores historiarum*, III, pp. 137 and 327–328.

incontinently the same yere he passed the see and presented hymself to the said King Phelip le Beal and the XXX day of Januarie he espoused the said Dame Isabel doughtir of the same King Phelip at Boloyn, there than beyng present the same King Phelip and Loys Hutin his elder sone than king of Navarre, Charles counte de Valoys, with many other great lordes of Ffraunce.[311] And at that tyme the same King Phelip le Beal receyved of the same Edward of Carnarvan homage for the duche of Guyan and thother his hereditamentes in those parties.

And aftir in the yere MCCCXX the same King Edward of Carnarvan with Quene Isabel his wief passed the see and than the same King Edward made homage for the premisses to Phelip le Long than king of Ffraunce and of Navarre which succeeded to the same aftir the deth of the said Loys Hutin his elder brother which was than dede without eny issue of his body.[312]

And aftir that Charles le Beale yonger sone of the said King Phelip le Beale beyng king of Ffraunce and of Navarre by succession aftir the deth of the said Phelip le Long than beyng also dede without issue of his body, caused the said King Edward of Carnarvan to be somoned to goo to make his homage to the same King Charles for the premisses, which to same King Edward was in his will redy to doo, but he was than busied with warres aswel for defend the rebellion of the Scottes as of other rebelles of |**68r**| Englond as is manifestly declared in histories. And for his excuse he first sent Sir Almery of Valence erle of Penbroke in ambassade for him to the said King Charles to shew the lette of his comyng for his excuse and to require and sewe for him to have respight of tyme to doo his said homage.[313] But the same King Charles, by exortacion of the said Charles de Valois and other of his affinite, and for that he was enformed that the said King Edward shuld not have entreated his suster the said Quene Isabel in the best manere, wold not in eny wise graunte eny soche respight. But ymmediatly sent the said Charles de Valois with a great power in to Guyan to oppresse from the said King Edward the duche of Guyan, by which power he oppressed from the same King Edward many castelles and townes in Guyan and Gascoign contrarie to justice and good order of eny lawe of God or man, for King Edward denyed not his services but sewed for respect upon reasonable consideracions.[314] And aftir that for the rather favor to have soche respect his sent his Quene and wief the said Dame Isabel suster of the said King Charles into Ffraunce to the

---

[311] *Flores historiarum*, III, pp. 141 and 330–331, though these two accounts suggested that the marriage took place on 28 January and 7 February, and did not name the individuals present at the service, except for the king of Navarre, Louis Hutin.

[312] *Flores historiarum*, III, p. 193.

[313] *Flores historiarum*, III, pp. 221 and 223.

[314] A liberal rendering of the *Flores historiarum*, III, p. 225.

same King Charles to sewe also for soche respect of doyng his homage hough so ever she sewed he sed not to have eny ressort. And than King Edward perceyvyng he coude not opteyne eny respect, by the advice of his counseill he gave and transported to his sone aftir King Edward the III^de the duchie of Guyan and the other his hereditamentes in the parties of beyond the |68v| see and commaunded thim that he shuld hast him to go to the said King Charles his uncle to doo to him homage dewe for the premisses. And so the same Edward the III^de duke of Guyan passed the see in the yere MCCCXXVI and went to the court of the king of Ffraunce and there was restored to the duchie of Guyan and so was admitted, avowed and taken by the said King Charles, which King Charles than receyved of the same homage aftir the usage therof.³¹⁵

And so appirath clerely that the said King Edward the Secund called of Carnarvan made never eny disobeissance rebellion to eny of the kinges of Ffraunce nor refused the doyng of his dewe services for his londes dewe, but suffred many ingratitudes and oppressions doon unto him and upon his londes by the kinges of Ffraunce. Of which kinges of Ffraunce the condicions be to use crueltie to soche as to them by humylite and love notte to suffre eny neighbor but wold oppresse all the histories of ther original and ther oppression in all ther contenewance, and ther usage at this day to witnesse wherof experience faileth not. And if the said King Edward the First and King Edward the Secund which were oppressed from ther heritage by the said kinges of Ffraunce had made werre upon them for the same and by like mesure have taken from the coroune and reame of Ffraunce and to have subdued them, they had good cause and title so to doo and to subdue tirantes, and ought not to be charged for the same. *Quia injuriam armis irrogatam, armoribus propulsare remedia leges et jura permittunt.*³¹⁶

|69r| *Capitulum XXII*³¹⁷

And where it is objected and submitted also in the said secund partie that Englisshmen shuld avaunte them that aftir all the said thinges by the treatie of Bretigny all the questiones, rancures and

---

³¹⁵ Prince Edward performed homage to Charles IV at Vincennes on 24 September 1325. See p. 104, n. 264.

³¹⁶ This maxim also appears on pp. 190, 222, and 251–252. The quotation does not appear in the equivalent section in T, fo. 27r, but was cited on three occasions in that manuscript, fos 15r, 39r, and 44r.

³¹⁷ This chapter translates and responds to *Pour ce que plusieurs*, pp. 105–108, and builds upon the material in T, fos 27v–38r.

debates were appointed and that by the treatie of peas final aswel
for the delyveraunce of John than king of Ffraunce, as to pacifie
all the quarelles which the said King Edward the III^{de} pretended
aswel to the corone of Ffraunce as to the singuler partes which
he quarelled within the said reame. The duche of Guyan which
shuld have extended by the treatie of Saint Loys and also the
counties of Poytow, Ponthieu, Agenois, Bigorre with the resortes
of Armynak and of other seignories of Gascoign, the cuntrees also
of Xaintonge and other more pleynly conteyned in the said treatie
shuld be purely and absolutly delivered without eny resorte or
sovereynte.[318] And that of wrong and without cause they shuld be
put out and forclosed.

And that for thanswer therof is alledged that the said treatie
of Bretigny shuld be often debated in somany places and in
presence of somany princes and preleates and namely of the pope
and his legates and otherwise, that every man might knowe that
the Englisshmen shuld have eny thyng by eny lawful meanes to
demaunde nothing by vertue therof, and that they shuld not have
accomplisshed nor |**69v**| nor [*sic*] holden of ther partie the same
treatie.[319]

But for the first partie, where they shuld have renounsed to the
corone of Ffraunce which shuld be the first & principal point, that
they shuld have willed to doo it. Secundly they shuld have doon
to be voided the companies owt of Ffraunce and every part of the
ream, wherof likewise they shuld have doo nothing.[320] Thirdly, the
prince of Wales and his officers aftir the said treatie shuld have
doon so many illes and excesses to them of Guyan that they shuld
have ben constrained to appelle to King Charles the Vth as to
ther sovereyn lord, the which King Charles nor yet King John
his father shuld not have renounsed to the resort of Guyan for
that the said King Edward shuld not in lykewise have renounsed
to the coroune of Ffraunce as he had sworne and promysed to
doo, which renonciacions they bothe shuld have made thoon aftir
thother. And that the king of Ffraunce shuld have sent at the day
therfor assigned notable persones of power sufficient to make the
renonciacions for his parte. And that for the parte of the king of
Englond none shuld have appiered, although that duly the same

---

[318] The Tudor author does not translate the full list of territories cited in the French
treatise (p. 105).

[319] This paragraph was omitted from T, fo. 27v.

[320] The Tudor writer does not translate the summary of the damage caused by the
Companies in the 1360s (p. 106).

king of Englond and his commissaries were duly appelled and attended for.[321]

And that by gret & mure deliberacion of counseill where the preres of Ffraunce and all the princes and prelates of the reame and other people of great estate shuld be called unto aftir the compleynt made to the said King Charles the Vth by his subgettes of Guyan of the wronges, griefes and excesses which the |**70r**| Englisshmen shuld have doon to them, shuld be saide and shewed to the king by many great reasons that with out charge of consciens or pretermission of his honour, he shuld not refuse the apell of the said lords of Guyan as a denegatour of justice. Wherupon the same King Charles the Vth shuld have receyved ther said appellacions.[322] And that the prince of Wales than duke of Guyan shuld have taken the commissaries of the said King Charles which shuld have ben sent to the said prince for the same matier and put them in prison.[323] And that the same prince not therwith content shuld have made werre against the said King Charles in augmentyng daily excesses, takinges and oppressions against the said King Charles and his subgettes of the londes and seignories whiche the said King Edward and the prince shuld have holden in ther possessions, obeissants to the reame of Ffraunce. Ffor which cause the said King Charles the Vth shuld have made declaration against the said King Edward and the prince of Wales aswel of the duchie of Guyan soche as the case apperteyned, and secretly in litil tyme almost all the subgettes of the said King Edward and the prince of Wales aswel of the duche of Guyan as of the counties of Poytow, Ponthieu, Xaintonge and elleswhere shuld have torned and put them in the hond and obeissance of the said King Charles the Vth.

And that there shuld have ben diverse other thinges within the said treatie of Bretigny which ought to have ben accomplisshed and doon by the said King Edward and |**70v**| the prince of Wales which they shuld not have accomplisshed, although that for the part of the said King John and the said duke of Normandie which aftir was called King Charles the Vth all the thinges which they ought to doo by the said treatie were accomplisshed, except that which touched the renonciacion of the resort of Guyan and other londes abovesaid. Which things shuld have comen by the defalt not

---

[321] Guillaume Cousinot had claimed that authentic letters proved this point (p. 107).

[322] This is a brief summary of the account of the purported efforts of Charles V to follow correct procedures in response to the appeal against the Black Prince (p. 107).

[323] The French treatise also noted that these emissaries were murdered and that Charles V subsequently sent other agents who were also imprisoned by the Black Prince (p. 107).

of the said King John and duke of Normandie, but by the defalt of the Englisshmen as is aforesaid.[324]

Trewly Englisshmen may saye and meyntene that they were put out and forclosed and desherited of the duche of Guyan and other londes afore lymyted without eny cause. But it is to my great merveill that the Ffrenshmen have no more shame than to write or make report of matier so direct false as they have doon in ther manyfold surmyses and objections recited afore this article, in this article and in tharticles folowing alledged for ther partie. And in this especially, for the said treatie and also the renonciacions ar to be shewed in writing under ther sealles, I doubt not undir the seale of the said King John, in the receipt at Westminster and the tenour therof be conteyned in diverse histories, and in especiall in the croniques of Maistre John Ffroisart.[325] And in this partie for the declaracion of the trouth to manifest knowledge to the reders herof it is necessarie |71r| and for that cause to recite ant to make mencion of the contentes of the same treatie, wherof theffect ensuyth.

Ffirst by the said treatie of Bretigny,[326] the said John than king of Ffraunce and the Charles the Vth his sone than duke of Normandie were bounde and made promyse to delyver and transport to the said King Edward the III[de] and his heires and successoures for ever the counties, citees, townes, castelles, forteresses, londes, isles, rentes, revenus and other londes and thinges heraftir rehersed, with all that the said King Edward the III[de] than helde in Guyan and Gascoign, to possede perpetuelly to the same King Edward his heirs and successoures, that was in demeane and that which was in fee before the tyme and in maner heraftir declared. That is to saye, the cite, castell and countie of Poitiers and all the londes and cuntre of Poytow to gether with the see of Thouars and the lond of Belleville;

[324] The Tudor author does not translate the report that both Emperor Charles IV and Pope Clement VI expressed their support for the French position on Brétigny (pp. 108–109).

[325] The following discussion of the treaty of Brétigny combines material from the treaty of Brétigny (8 May 1360), a letter patent issued by Edward III (probably on 15 May 1360), and the treaty of Calais (24 October 1360), and is extremely similar to the translation of Froissart by John Bourchier, first published in two volumes in 1522 and 1525, and itself based upon one of the earliest printed editions: Berners, *Froissart*, II, pp. 59–67. In T, fo. 27v, the author stated that 'it is necessarie to declare the hole contents of the said treatie of Bretigny, and therof Maister John Ffroissart in his first volume of his croniks hath made rehersall of this effect'.

[326] For the first part of the account of the treaty, the Tudor author is drawing upon Froissart's transcription of one of the letters that Edward III issued on 25 May 1360 (or, more likely, ten days earlier), which differs in some regards from the authentic copies of the treaty of Brétigny agreed on 8 May: Berners, *Froissart*, II, pp. 59–63, and Lettenhove, *Froissart*, VI, pp. 282–286, together with *Foedera*, VI, pp. 178–196.

the towne and castell of Xaintes and all the londes and counte of Xantonge on this side and beyond Charente, with the townes and the fortresses of the Rochel and Saint Wallery and their appurtenaunces and appendacies;[327] the cite and towne and castell of Agene & the cuntre of Agenoys; the cite, the towne, the castel and all the lond of Perregort and all the cuntre of Perregins; the cite and castell of Lymoges and the londes and cuntre of Lymosin; the cite and castell of Caours; the castel and cuntre of Tarbe; the londes, the cuntre and countie of Bigourre; the cuntre, the counte and the londes of Gourre; the cite and castel of Engolesme and all the cuntre of Engulmois; the cite, the towne and castell of Rodaix and the countie and cuntre |**71v**| of Rouergue. And if there were in the duche of Guyan eny seignouries as the countie de Ffoix, the counte of Armynak, the counte de Lisle, the vicomt of Garmayne, the counte of Perregourt, the viscount of Lymoges or other,[328] which helde eny londes within the metes of the said places they shuld doo therfor homage to the said King Edward and to his heires and successoures and all other services dewe by cause of their londes and places in maner and forme as they had doon in tymes passed although that the said King Edward the III^{de} nor other kinges of Englond had never eny thing therof.

And the viscounte of Monterel by the see in maner as in tyme passed and all that which the same King Edward or other kinges of Englond have holden and that which in the said londes in Monterell have be eny debates in parting of the lond, the said Ffrenssh King John promysed by the said treatie to make declaracion therof as hastely as he shuld may aftir his retorn into Ffraunce.

Item the countie of Ponthieu all intierly sauf & except that if eny things had ben aliened by the kinges of Englond which had regned in tymes passed to other persones than to kinges of Ffraunce, than those the same King John shuld not be bounde to delyver to the said King Edward. And if the same alienations were made to the kinges of Ffraunce which were for the tyme, without meane and if the said King John helde them tyme of that treatie, than the same King John shuld be bounde to delyver them to the said King Edward holy except that if the kinges of Ffraunce had them by exchaunge for other londes, the

---

[327] The letters patent of 25 May 1360 referred to 'la ville, chastiel et forterèce de le Rocelle', but this was not mentioned in the treaty of Brétigny and the concession was made conditional upon the release of King Jean II in article 14 of the treaty of Calais: Lettenhove, *Froissart*, VI, p. 283, and *GTGCA*, pp. 40 and 48. None of these documents referred to Saint-Valéry, which was also omitted by Berners, *Froissart*, II, p. 60.

[328] The 'visconte de Quarmaing' or Caraman was cited in the letters patent of 25 May 1360, but not in the treaty of Brétigny; he was mentioned in Berners, *Froissart*, II, p. 60. Neither this viscount nor the count of Périgord were cited in T, fo. 29r.

said King Edward |**72r**| shuld delyver to the said King John the same londes so exchanged for them. And if the kinges of Englond which had for the tyme aliened or transported eny thing to other persones than to the kinges of Ffraunce, and so were comen to the handes of the said King John, he shuld not be bounde to yelde the same. And if the same thinges owe eny homage unto the said King Edward or his successores. And if those thinges owe none homage to the said King Edward, he shuld geve a tenure to be doon to the said King Edward and to his heires and successoures within oon yere aftir his departing from Calais.

Item the towne and castell of Calais; the castel, towne and seignorie of Marke; the townes, castelles and seignories of Sangates, Coulongne, Hammes, Wales and Oye, with the londes, wodes, mersshes, riviers, rentes, revenus, seignories, advousons and adutements of chirches and all other appurtenaunces and places lieng adjoynyng betwix the metes ensrewyng, that is to saye from Calais unto the brynk of the rivier before Gravelines, and from that rivier unto Ffretin, and from thens by the valey beyond the mounteyne of Karlouly [Cauquelle], inclosing the same mounteyn and also unto the see with Sangates and all thappurtenunces; the castel, the towne and all holy the countie of Guynes with all the townes, castelles, forteresses, londes, places, homages, men, seignories, wodes, forestes and rightes of the same as holy as the erles of Guynes, of Calais, of Marke and of other places above named and as they |**72v**| obeyed to the king of Ffraunce and to the erles of Guynes which were for the tyme. All the thinges conteyned in this article of Calais and Marke the said king of Englond to holde in demeane, except the possessions & heritages of chirches which exceptions shal abide to the same chirches, and except the heritages of other people of Meke and Calais to the value of C li[vres] lond by yere, mony currant of that cuntre. But the habitacions and heritages sett in the towne of Calais and ther appurtenunces to abide to the dwellers and habitantes, to all the habitantes of Calais, Merke and other londes conteyned in this said article of Calais and all isles extending to the londes, cuntrees and places afore named with all other isles which the said king of Englond had or shuld have by this said treatie or recited in the same.

The said King John and his sone the said Charles the Vth shuld renounce all the said resortes and sovereintees, and to all the right that they had or might have in the premysses. And that the kinges of Englond shuld holde the same promysses as a voisin or neighbow without eny resort or sovereyntie of the kinges or reame of Ffraunce. And that all the right which the said King John had in the premisses, he gave, granted & transported to the kinges of England for ever perpetuelly.

And in the same treatie is conteyned that lykewise the said King Edward and his eldest sone Edward prince of Wales shuld renonce expressely to all thinges which ought not to be delyvered to him by the said treatie and in especial to the name and right of the corone of Ffraunce, and the homage, sovereynte and demeane of the duche of Normandie and of the counte of Torayne and of the counties of Angeo and Maine, and to |73r| the sovereynte and homage of the duche of Bretayn, except that the right of the erle of Mountfort which he had or ought to have in the same duche and cuntre of Bretayne were reserved and put by expresse woordes owt of the said treatie, sauf that the said II kinges of Englond [and Ffraunce],[329] Edward and John at ther comyng to Calais by the advyse of ther baronage shuld there treate of peax betwene the same erle of Montfort and Charles le Bloys contendantes for the same. And the said king of Englond [renounced]^T to all the demaundes that he made or might make for eny thing except the thinges which shuld be delivered or assigned to him and his heires by the said treatie. And that he shuld transporte and cesse all the right that he had in all the thinges which were not assigned to him by the said treatie.

Upon which aftir many alteracions had therupon and in especial for that the said renonciacions, transportes, cessiones and dimyses of the premisses as sone as the said King John shuld have delyvered to the said King Edward and his people and in especial to his deputies the cite and castell of Poitiers and all the lond & cuntre of Poytow; the fee of Thouars and of Belleville; the cite & castel of Agen and all the londes and cuntre of Agenois; the cite & castel, the londes & cuntre of Perregort & Perregins; the cite, castel and londes of Caours and Caoursin; the cite, castel and cuntre of Rodaix and Rouergue; the cite, castel and londe of Xaintes and Xaintonge, with the townes and forteresses of the Rochel and Saint Wallery;[330] the cite, castel and cuntre of Lymoges and Lymosin;[331] ant that which the said King Edward or other kinges of Englond of old tyme had in the towne of Monterell by the see with |73v| thappurtenunces. And also countre entierly of Ponthieu except and sauf as is in the tenor of that article in the said treatie making mencion of the same countie. *Item* the castel and towne of Calais, the castel, towne and seignorie of Sangates, Coulogne, Hammes, Wales and Oye, with the

---

[329] The words 'and of' are crossed out. T, fo. 30v, prefers 'the said II kinges of Englond and Ffraunce'.

[330] Lettenhove, *Froissart*, VI, p. 286, and see p. 229, n. 327 above.

[331] From this point onwards, the Tudor author departs from the text of the letter patent of 15 May 1360, as printed by Kervyn de Lettenhove in his edition of Froissart, and instead draws upon an amalgamation of the treaties of Brétigny and Calais, just as in Berners, *Froissart*, II, pp. 63–67.

londes, riviers, mersshes, wodes, rentes, seignories and other thinges conteyned in the article afore rehersed making mencion therof. *Item* the castel, the towne and entierly the counte of Guynes with all the londes, castelles, townes, forteresses, places, men, homages, seignories, wodes, forestes and rightes according to the tenor of the article therof more pleinly aperith and with all the isles and adjacent londes, cuntrees and places afore rehersed with thother isles which the said King Edward held that tyme.

The said II kings ought and promysed by faith and othes the oon to thother the same peas and treatie to holde, kepe and accomplissh without doyng eny thing to the contrarie, ffor and upon the accomplisshement and more ferme entirtenur of the said treatie, aftir that the said II kinges mette at Calais and there were bounde by obligacion and promyse and by faith and othes the same II kinges and ther elder sones the said Edward prince of Wales and the said Charles the Vth the oon partie to thother afor the tenur of the said treatie and accorded further as the tenour therof folowith.

Item,[332] it is accorded that the said King John and the said Charles his elder sone for them and ther heires for ever and as sone as they may without male engyne and at the furthest before the fest of Saint Michel than next comyng aftir oon yere, shuld yelde and delyver to the said King Edward and to his heires and successoures |74r| kinges of Englond and transpor in them the honoures, regalies, obeissances, homages, fealties, men, fees, services, recognisances, knowleges, oothes, rightes, manumyses and [impirriter?],[333] almaner jurisdictions high and lowe, ressortes, saufgardes, seignories and soverenities which aperteyned or ought to have apperteyned or might in eny wise apperteyne to the kinges and to the corone of Ffraunce or to eny other persone by cause of king or of the corone of Ffraunce what tyme so ever is, were or shuld be in citees, townes, castelles and forteresses, londes, isles, cuntrees and places aforenamed or eny of them or ther appurtenunces and appendacies what so ever they were, were they prince, duke, counte, visconte, archebisshop or other prelate of the churche, barons, noble or other what so ever, without eny thing to them ther heires or successoures the corone of Ffraunce or other what so ever to be holden nor reteyned nor reserved in the

---

[332] This corresponds with article 11 of the treaty agreed at Brétigny on 8 May 1360, which was suppressed in the treaty of Calais: *Foedera*, VI, pp. 183–184, and Berners, *Froissart*, II, pp. 63–64. Also see *GTGCA*, pp. 36–37; Pierre Chaplais (ed.), 'Some documents regarding the fulfillment and interpretation of the treaty of Brétigny, 1361–1369', *Camden Miscellany*, 19 (1952), pp. 1–84; and John Le Patourel, 'The treaty of Brétigny, 1360', in *idem*, *Feudal Empires: Norman and Plantagenet* (London, 1984), chapter 13.

[333] This is a translation of the phrase '*merum & mixtum imperium*', in *Foedera*, VI, p. 183.

same. Ffor which they, ther heires nor successoures, or eny kinges of Ffraunce or other what so ever he were or shuld be by cause of king or of the corone of Ffraunce ony thing might challenge or demaunde in tyme to come of the king of Englond, his heires or successoures or of eny his vassailes and subgettes aforesaid by cause of the said cuntrees and places above named. So that all the said personnes and ther heires & successores, all the persones, citees, townes, counties, londes, cuntrees, isles, castelles and places afore named and all thappertenunces and appendanncies shuld have and holde and to them shuld abide plenarily and perpetuelly, paisibly and frely |74v| in ther seignourie, sovereanite and obeissance, loialte and subjection as the predecessoures of the said King Edward kinges of Ffraunce those had or helde in tymes passed. And that the said kinges of Englond, ther heires and successoures shuld have and holde peasibly and perpetuelly all the cuntrees aforenamed in all fraunchise and libertie perpetuell as lord soverayn and liege and voisin of the king of Ffraunce and to the reame of Ffraunce without to knowlege soverynte or to doo obeissance, homage, ressort and subjection, and without doyng in tyme to come eny service or recognisaunce to the king or to the corone of Ffraunce of citees, counties, castelles, townes, cuntries, londes, isles, places and persones afore specified or for eny of them.

Item,[334] it was accorded that the said King John and his elder sone the said Charles the Vth shuld renounce expressely to the said ressortes and sovereynties and to all the right which they had or might have to all the thynges which by the said treatie ought to apperteyne to the said king of Englond. And semblably the same King Edward and his elder sone shuld renounce to all the thynges which by the said treatie ought not to be delyvered nor geven to the said King Edward and to all the demaundes that he made to the said King John. And in especial to the name and right and to the challenge of the corone and of the reame of Ffraunce, to the homage, sovereinte and demeane of the duchie of Normandie and of the duche of Torayne and of the counties of Angeo and of Maine, and to the sovereyntie and homage of the countie and cuntre of Fflaundres,[335] and to all |75r| other demaundes which the king of Englond made at the tyme of the said challenge or might make in tyme than to come to the said reame of Ffraunce by eny cause over and except that which by the said treatie ought to be delyvered and

---

[334] This corresponds with article 12 of the treaty agreed at Brétigny on 8 May 1360, which was also suppressed in the treaty of Calais: *Foedera*, VI, pp. 184–185, and Berners, *Froissart*, II, pp. 64–65.

[335] Like Bourchier, the anonymous Tudor author omits mention of 'la souvereineté & hommage du duchié de Bretaigne': see *Foedera*, VI, p. 184, and Berners, *Froissart*, II, p. 65.

abide to the king of Englond and his heires. And shuld transporte, cesse and leve thoon king to thother perpetuelly all the right and eny of them might have in all the thinges which by the said treatie owed to abide or be delyverd to thother, the tyme, place and whan the said renounciacions shuld be made.

And therupon the said King John and his elder sone Charles the Vth at Calais for the holding and accomplisshing the articles of the said treatie, renounced expressely the resortes and sovereynties comprised in the said articles and to all the right which they had or might have in all the thinges abovesaid, which the said King John had than delyvered to the said King Edward and to thother theraftir shuld be delyvered and apperteyne to the said King Edward by the said treatie, as by the lettres patentes therof may appere.[336] And in likewise the same King Edward and the said prince of Wales his elder sone also renounced expressely to all the thinges which by the said treatie and peax shuld not be delyvered to him for him and his heires and to all the demaundes which he might make against the said King John. And especiall to the name and to the right of the corone of Ffraunce and of the reame, and to the homage, sovereynte and demeane of the duche of Normandie, of the the [*sic*] duche or counte of Torayn, of the |75v| counties of Maine and of Angeo and to the soverainte & homage of the countie and cuntre of Fflaundres and all other demaundes which the same King Edward made or might make to the said King John for what cause so ever, over and excepted that which by the said treatie belonged or ought to apperteyne to the same King Edward and his heires.[337]

And also every of the same II kinges with ther said elder sones transported, cessed and left to thother to ther best they might all the right that every of them had or might have in all the thinges which by the said treatie ought to apperteyne and abide to thother of them, reserved to the chirches and to men of the churche that which apperteyned to them. And that the townes and fortereresses and all the habitacions and the dwellers in the same shalbe and abide in soche liberties and franchises as they were afore in the handes of the said King Edward and seignorie and to them shalbe confermed by the

---

[336] John Bourchier's translation did not include a reference to any letters patent, presumably the documents stipulating that the renunciations and cessions would take place at Bruges in 1361: Berners, *Froissart*, II, p. 65, and *GTGCA*, pp. 37–38, 46–47, and 175–179.

[337] T, fo. 32v, continued: 'as by the lettres patentes of the said King Edward and III^{de}, also rehersing the said treatie whereof the copie is conteyned in the first volume of cronikes of Maister John Ffroissart more pleynley doth appere.'

said King John if they were not contrarie to the said treatie or to the subjection othe same.[338]

And every of the said II kinges and ther said older sones by the said treatie committed them, ther heires and successoures for ther severall partes to the jurisdiction and cohercion of the chirche of Rome. And every of them willed and graunted that the pope shuld conferme the premisses in gyving monicions and maundementes generall for thaccomplisshement of the same against the said kinges, ther heirs and successoures against the comones, collieges, universities and singuler persones what so ever. And in gyving sentences generall of excommenqement of suspencion of entirdict to be cast upon them by violating of the said treatie as sone as eny of them shuld doo or attempte |**76r**| in occupieng towne, cite, castel or forteresse or doyng eny other thyng or greving or geving counseill, consort, favour or aide pryvely or openly against the said treatie or peax. Of the which sentences they shuld not be absolved until they had made pleyne satisfaction to all them which by suche dede or attempte shuld susteyne or might susteyne domage.[339]

And for the more sure holdyng, keping and observyng of the said treatie and peax perpetuelly was furthermore graunted by the said treatie for bothe parties that the pope shuld cause to be dissolved and shuld dissolve all pactions, confederacions, alliances and couvenantes what so ever they wer or might be prejudiciall or object against the said treatie, although they were that tyme or might be in tyme theraftir affermed and gevyn by peynes and by serements confermed by the pope or eny other, and to be eassed, cancelled and put to nought as thynges contrarie to the comon weale and to the said treatie, improufitable to all christianite and to the high displeasur of God. And that it shuld be by the pope ratified that none shuld be bounde to soche oothes, aliaunces and couvenantes and in especial the said King John and his said elder sone Charles the Vth for them, their heires & successoures graunted and promysed by the said treatie that they shuld departe from the confederacions which they had with the Scottes, and that from thensforth they shuld not geve to the Scottes eny aide, confort or assistence against the kinges of Englond. And in lykewise the said King Edward and his said elder sone the prince of Wales departed from their confederacion which they had with the

---

[338] The two issues were rehearsed in both the treaty of Brétigny and the treaty of Calais: *Foedera*, VI, pp. 189 and 191, and *GTGCA*, pp. 55 and 59. Also see Berners, *Froissart*, II, pp. 65–66. The liberties and franchises of the towns were not mentioned in T, fo. 32v.

[339] This account is similar to that in Berners, *Froissart*, II, p. 66, and follows the terms of the treaties of Brétigny and Calais, in *Foedera*, VI, pp. 192–194, and *GTGCA*, pp. 61–63.

Fflemynges.[340] And was aggreed by bothe the said kinges that the pope shuld |76v| prohibite that none suche confederacions, othes, alliaunces or couvenantes shuld be theraftir made, and if eny soche shuld be made, forthwith to be voide, eassed and irrited. And besides that the said II kinges and ther said elder sones decreed all the violatoures of the said traitie and peax to be adjuged traitours and proditoures.

And for further suretie for the observaunce of the same treatie and peax, every of the same II kinges and ther said elder sones, leyeng or puttyng ther right handes upon the patene with the consecrat body of our redemer Crist,[341] aftir the thrid *Agnus Dei* and *Dona nobis pacem* saide and ther lift handes upon the messeboke, sware to kepe and observe the said treatie and peas in every point therof inviolated. And promyssed for further sure observaunce of the premisses that all the sones of bothe kinges and XX^{ti} of the most noble blood of eyther of the said reames of Englond and of Ffraunce shuld also sware to hold and accomplissh the premisses and cause those to be holden and accomplisshed.[342]

According to which promyse[343] for the partie of the said King Edward, the secund Sonday of Lentyn, kalend Ffebruary in the yere MCCCLXI, solenne messe songe of the Trinite by Maister Simon Isleph archebisshop of Caunterbury and the third *Agnus dei* with *Dona nobis pacem* ended, the said King Edward stonding by with his sones and with the sones of the said King John with many other nobles many lightes and the crosses rered, XX^{ti} noble men, that is to saie Monsieur Phelip de Navare, Duc Henry of Lancastr, the duc of Bretayn, the erle of Stafford, the erle of Saresbury, the lord Mauny, the Captal de Beufs, the lord Mountford, Sir James Daudely, |77r| Roger Beauchamp, John Chandos, Raoul de Fferearys, Edward le Despensier, Thomas Ffelleton, Eustace Dembrechicourt, Ffrancque de Halle, John Mowbray, Barthilmew de Briennes and Henry Percy

---

[340] The end of the alliances with the Scots and Flemings was an important issue in the treaties of Brétigny and Calais, in *Foedera*, VI, p. 192, and *GTGCA*, pp. 60–61, though they were not mentioned in Berners, *Froissart*, II, pp. 66–67, and there was only a brief marginal note in T, fo. 33r, regarding the alliances.

[341] The eucharistic vessel known as the paten (*patène* in French) is a small shallow plate or disc of precious metal upon which the element of bread is offered to God at the Offertory of the Mass, and upon which the consecrated Host is again placed after the Fraction.

[342] Neither T, fo. 33r, nor Bourchier's translation of Froissart, provided such detailed information about the ceremony of oathtaking, suggesting that this was an authorial addition: Berners, *Froissart*, II, p. 67, and, for the requirements for the oath, see *Foedera*, VI, p. 193, and *GTGCA*, pp. 61–62.

[343] The words: 'XX^{ti} noble men' are crossed out.

sware for the performaunce of the said treatie and peas for the partie of the said King Edward.[344]

Aftir the stablisshement of the said treatie of Bretigny and concluded at Calais the yere MCCCLX, the said King John required of the said King Edward to comaund his comissaries and officiers to comaunde them to see all his subgettes shuld observe the premisses, to be aiding to conveye out of the parties of Ffraunce all voide and idell persones. Upon which the said King Edward by the name of Edward by the grace of God king of Englond and lord of Irelond and of Acquitaine directed his comission generall to all his capitaines of citees, townes, castelles, adherentes and allies in the parties of Ffraunce aswel in Picardie as in all other places, reciting a gret part of the said treatie and comaunding them that none of his subgettes or allies shuld doo or attempt eny thing contrarie to the said treatie. And if they shuld doo, without eny processe to be banysshed out of his reame, dominion and power and also comaunded that as case required, punicion shuld be doon to the violatoures of the said treatie as of proditours and traitours.[345] By which all companies were discharged out and from the retenue of the said King Edward and were put owt of fortresses and other places out of the dominion of the said King Edward, and out of suche forteresses and places soche as the said King Edward transported by the said treatie to the said King John. Albeit many of the sowdioures |77v| whiche duryng the werre betwix the said II kinges were reteyned somme of the partie of the Ffrenssh king and some of the partie of the king of Englond, aftir the conclusion of the said treatie assembled them to gether aswel of the Frensshmen, Picardes, Almaynes, Scottes, Fflemynges, Brabancoys and Englisshmen, Bretons, persons used to lyve of rapine chase, captaines of themself, calling themself enemyes to all the world, and made werre aswel upon the pope and the londes of the chirche as of every other prince for the tyme, and so were out of rule and governaunce and also the jurisdiction and power of the said king of Englond.

[344] This account does not appear in T, fo. 33r. A ceremony did take place at Westminster Abbey in early 1361, but it is unlikely that Henry of Lancaster attended given that he was seriously ill at the time and died on 23 March, while Sir John Chandos was involved in the systematic clearance of garrisons from Normandy in February, and others, including Sir James Audley, were still in France. Of the list of nineteen nobles identified here, fourteen took an oath to uphold the treaty of Calais upon its completion on 24 October 1360 and, more significantly, all nineteen were cited at the end of the transcription of the treaty in Berners, *Froissart*, II, p. 244.

[345] The letters patent of Edward III were recorded by Froissart, in Berners, *Froissart*, II, pp. 68–70, and Lettenhove, *Froissart*, VI, pp. 314–316.

And so apperith clerely that of wrong and of untrew cautell the Frensshmen have falsely imagined the said surmyse to excuse their owne myschief. Ffor that the said King John and his elder sone the said Charles the Vth as is afore declared in this answer had upon the conclusion of the said treatie of Bretigny expressely renounsed and transported the resort for his partie to be doon as was aggreed by the said treatie, if it were not by dissymylacion, and had put the said King Edward in possession of that which was assigned to the same King Edward by the same treatie. And that in lykewise the said King Edward and his elder sone the said prince of Wales renounsed to the name of the king of the reame of Ffraunce and to every other thing on his part to be doon according to the said treatie. And every of the same parties were according to the same treatie in peasible possession of his part assigned to him by the same and so contenued from the conclusion of the same which |78r| was as aforesaid in the yere MCCCLX until the yere MCCCLVIII, that the said Charles the said elder sone of the said King John called Charles the Vth beyng aftir the deth of the said King John his father king of Ffraunce according and by force of the said treatie and not otherwise of right, without jurisdiction, title of right, reasonable cause or colour, violating the said treatie against his solenne othes made as is afore rehersed upon the holy consecrat body of Crist and upon the holy evaungelies, and against his said boondes and promyses, dampnably under false pretense called again the resort of Guyan and Gascoign and of thother dominions which he had with his said father renounced afore. And caused the prince of Wales, the said elder sone of the said King Edward the III^{de}, than duke of Guyan by the transport of the same his father, to appere in the Parlement of the said Charles the Vth at Parys to answere to an appell of the erle of Armynak and certain other lordes, which than aswel of right as by the tenur of the said treatie were subgettes of the said King Edward, made for certain causes imagined by the said King Charles the Vth, the duke of Angeo his brother and by his counseill, contrarie to the said treatie and the trew menyng of the same.

And here it is to be noted what trust is and may be founde in Ffrensshmen in insuyng the steppes and usage of ther predecessoures and progenitores, never keping promyse, couvenaunte or eny thing that they graunte lenger than they may see their evident proufit, according as is made mencion by an olde proverbe, *Treugas astringent Galli vix dummodo invigent.*[346]

---

[346] *Non inveni.* This maxim was cited above, p. 220. This paragraph does not appear in T.

|78v| Ffor notwithstonding the great oothes solennely made upon the consecrat body of Crist and upon the missale by the said Charles the Vth as is aforesaid, the promyses and bondes and censures of the churche of Rome decreed in as ample and strait wise and by so great advise and deliberacion as never soche was had but onely for the sure observaunce of the said treatie and peas, the said Charles the Vth with the duke of Angeo his brother and thother his brothern, of a subtile, false and dampnable imaginacion, the breche of the said treatie by oon hole yere and more, with as gret cautelous myendes violated. The case beyng so that the duke of Berry, oon of the brothern of the said Charles the Vth with many other of the great lordes of the parties of Ffraunce were than in hostage in the custodie in Englond for the redempcion of the said King John than beyng unpaied, the said Charles the Vth prively and cautelously gave secret notice to the said hostagers of his entent to make werre upon the said Edward and the prince his sone, exciting the same hostagers to feyne causes to provide for themself to retorne into Ffraunce if it were possible. Wherupon they fayned crafty weyes and meanes to opteyne licence of the said King Edward for a certain tyme to visite ther cuntrie, promysyng ther retornes at the lymyted terme. And King Edward not thinking eny deceyt nor suspected ther such imaginacions & purposes of the partie of the said Charles the Vth nor for his partie for that til than the said treatie was perfitely kept and that therfor was so many boondes made aswel spirituel as temporell, at ther requestes licensed them to visite |79r| ther cuntrees upon ther faithfull promyses and othes to retorne in to Englond in lyke forme at the certain tymes to them lymyted, *Qui cito credit, levis est corde et minorabitur*.[347] Sauf and except diverse of them, as Sir Guy of Ligny and other, which without licence or notice of the said King Edward stole and conveyed themself out of Englond by cautelous meanes.[348]

And on and besides that in the tyme of the said yere of ther said imaginacions the said Charles the Vth in secret wise cautelously purchased and allied him freendes aswel by reteynyng of many or the most part of the afore rehersed companies which called themself enemyes to all the world, as of diverse other princes. And therupon aftir

---

[347] Ecclesiasticus 19: 4: '*Qui credit cito, levis corde est et minorabitur; et, qui delinquit in animam suam, quis innoxium faciet?*' This quotation does not appear in T.

[348] In T, fos 34r–35v, there is a longer account of the mounting opposition to the Black Prince in Gascony and of Gui de Ligny, drawn from Froissart: see Berners, *Froissart*, II, pp. 240–241 and 251, and Lettenhove, *Froissart*, VII, pp. 273–276, 284, and 295. In both Froissart and T, the report of Berry's supposed escape from England follows the account of the two messengers sent to the Black Prince's court; in reality, the French hostages were released following the payment of the majority of their ransoms in 1367.

that also allied him with the erle of Armynak and diverse other lordes of Gascoign, subgettes and in this behalf traytours and proditoures to the said King Edward. And than the said Charles the Vth and his proper counseill by great deliberation, imagined and devised the afore specified appell in writing to be put into the court of the said Charles the Vth in the names of the said erle of Armynak and of thother lordes of Gascoign, claymyng ressort to the court of the same court of Charles the Vth.[349] And the same appel so devised, II massengers, oon of them a clerk, thother a knight named Capounel, were sent to somone the said Prince Edward than duke of Guyan to appiere in the court of the said Charles the Vth at Parys to answere to the said |79v| appel.[350] Which II massengers came to the court of the said prince at Burdeulx namyng themself massengers of the said Charles the Vth and for that had great chiere. The same prince not doubting nor knowing of suche cause of ther comyng called them in to his presence where they delyvered to the same prince lettres of credence directed from the said Charles the Vth. And for his credence they publisshed the cause of ther comyng and so somoned the prince &c. And for that the same massengers shewed them self in uttraunce of ther credence and extencion of thermassage to be rather massengers for the said erle of Armynak and thother lordes of Gascoign, traitors to the said prince, than massengers for the said Charles the Vth, and were comen into the presence of the said prince and in to his dominion and power in so his dispight and displesure without his licence or sauf conduct, he committed them to prison in the cite of Agen as laufull was to doo.[351] And without eny other cause or ground, the said Charles the Vth by oon his varlet of smal reputation, defied the said King Edward and the prince his sone and was in soche ridinesse that the same day he, though the said King Edward was defied, with his power invaded the londes of the said prince and made open werre. *Dolosi semper querunt occasionem nocendi.*[352] And than the Frensshnmen used this parol, *Dieu*

---

[349] Froissart painted Charles V as a reluctant convert to the necessity of war: Berners, *Froissart*, II, pp. 230–231 and 240–246, and Lettenhove, *Froissart*, VII, pp. 253–255 and 274–287.

[350] Froissart identified the knight as Chaponnet de Chaponval: Lettenhove, *Froissart*, VII, p. 288 and Berners, *Froissart*, II, p. 247.

[351] This account echoes Berners, *Froissart*, II, pp. 247–250, and Lettenhove, *Froissart*, VII, pp. 288–295. In T, fo. 36r, the Tudor author followed Froissart in adding the fictional account of the escape of Berry and the French hostages from captivity in England, and the report that Charles V retained many of the captains of the Companies: Berners, *Froissart*, II, pp. 251 and 255–257, and Lettenhove, *Froissart*, VII, pp. 295 and 301–304.

[352] *Non inveni* (see p. 191).

doit Saint George est morte, le roy veillard est disconfort, le roy ne veult le prince ne poet or chansons, chansons cy averons bon deduit.[353]

|8or| Ffor which causes the said King Charles the Vth ought by the content of the said treatie to be reputed false, malvais and perjured and in soche blame and defame as a king sacred owith to be insoche case, and was digne to be disabled and to lose name and fame to his dampnable and shameful reproche for ever. And for that cause the said King Edward the III[de] and the said prince his sone and ther heires and successoures aftir them have had and now have good cause to make werre upon the heires of the said Charles the Vth and to reclayme and possede with the sufferaunce of God not oonly ther former hereditamentes of the corone and totalite of the reame of Ffraunce and thother duchies, counties and seignories afore rehersed, but also all that which that the Ffrensshmen and ther adherentes have and possede what so ever they be.

Capitulum XXIII[354]

And where in the said secund partie is also objected that the kinges of Englond, Henry the Vth and Henry the VIth, and ther adherentes, fautours and complices shuld have made werre against the kinges of Ffraunce, Charles the VIth and Charles the VIIth, for which cause |8ov| the now Frenssh king shuld have cause to take and applye all the londes and seignouries which the kinges of Englond and thers had in the reame of Ffraunce, and not onely in the reame of Ffraunce, but also in Englond and elleswhere where he might recover them, until that they of Englond shuld have repared the wronges, injuries and domages which they shuld have doon in the reame of Ffraunce.

And that by lettres auctentiques, croniques, histories and other knowleges,[355] it shuld be clere notairly and manifest without eny difficultie that the king of Ffraunce shuld by good and just title holde and possede the duchies of Normandie and of Guyan, the counties of Poytow, Angeo, Maine, Torain and Ponthieu and the other londes which that Englisshmen were wont to occupie in

---

[353] These quotations do not appear in T.

[354] This chapter translates and responds to *Pour ce que plusieurs*, pp. 111–113, though it omits the previous statement that Henry V and his son had committed three particular faults, in continuing to be disobedient, causing huge amounts of damage, and waging an unjust war (see pp. 110–111). This chapter builds upon T, fos 38v–40r.

[355] *Pour ce que plusieurs* also justified this argument by reference to canon and civil law as well as French custom (see p. 111).

the reame of Ffraunce. And also might lawfully recover the residew whan his pleasur shuld be to attende therunto. And that he might wele doo it without eny charge of dishonnor or of conscience and to make to them werre in Englond whan it shuld seme to him best.

And that to the contrarie of wrong and without cause with torcious quarell and without eny reasonable title or at the lest vaillable the Englisshmen shuld pretende eny right in the said londes and seignories, and that the Englisshmen might not of reason alledge or meyntene eny thing to the contrarie for that of reason they shuld suffre soche lawes, customes and usages of the cuntries where |81r| the thinges be situed or sette, and in lykewise soche as themself use in the reame of Englond. And that the Englisshmen shuld have had no right nor succession nor transport of the cuntrie of Wales nor other londes but for defalt of homages, by disobediences and by werre that the Walshmen made to the Englisshmen. By which title and none other the king of Englond shuld have posseded the said cuntre of Wales which Prince Leolyn was wont to holde, whom the Englisshmen shuld have caused to dye petously.[356] And for that they shuld not use in lyke cause in soche thinges, it shuld be clere that they shuld suffre lyke themself and that they shuld not be receyved to alledge to the contrarie.

It is sufficiently declared afore that the kinges of Englond by dew succession of enheritaunce over and besides the corone of Ffraunce have good and just title to the duchies of Normandie, Guyan and Gascoign, and to the counties of Poytow, Angeo, Maine, Torayn, Ponthieu and Champaine and to diverse other particuler londes in the parties of Ffraunce.[357] And that they therof except Champaine have ben in possession and |81v| season peasibly by soche succession of heritage and they were so taken, used and reputed aswel by than kinges of Ffraunce as by every other persone. And that they have dewly doon ther dew services for the same without contradiction, disclayme or denyer or refusell until they were wrongfully deforced and oppressed therfro in violent wise as is declared afore.

[356] The Tudor author omits the details of the territory of Llywelyn in Wales, the claim that the dukes of Brittany had inherited these lands by right of succession, and the argument that the kings of Scotland were unjustly deprived of Huntingdon, Northumberland, Tynedale, and many other lands in England (see pp. 112–113). He had earlier failed to translate the same argument that Cousinot had made regarding confiscation on p. 90, and here also omitted the brief response to these points that he had offered in T. See p. 244, n. 362.

[357] Champagne was not mentioned in this list in T, fo. 39r.

And also it is manifestly declared that the said King Edward the III[de] had good title by trew course of heritage to the corone and reame of Ffraunce, and that the aforenamed Phelip de Valois, the said King John his sone, the said Charles the Vth, Charles the VI, Charles the VIIth and ther successoures and the Ffrenssh king which now is, have of wrong without title, have intended and usurped the corone and reame of Ffraunce.[358]

And the said King Henry the Vth wele knowing his right in that behalf, with power entred first into Normandie and opteyned the possession therof and by processe also of the corone and reame of Ffraunce and of the other his hereditamentes by the agrement, assent and consent of the said Charles the VIth and auctorite of his Parlement and counseill generall of the III Estats of the reame of Ffraunce as is declared afore.[359] And by the same assent, consent and auctorite, the said Charles the VIIth than dolphin, was disabled for ever to clayme or to have eny succession to the corone or reame of Ffraunce or eny other londes in the same reame for the shameful murdre of his |82r| cosin John than duke of Burgoyne,[360] and for that he made open werre within the reame of Ffraunce against his said father and sovereyn lord the said King Charles the VIth and toke castelles, townes and forteresses, and robbed, murdred and toke prisoners the subgettes of the corone of Ffraunce and them redemed and raunsomed and many other violences and horrible malefices ded as ennemye to the corone and reame of Ffraunce and to the comon weale of the same. And by reason therof the said King Henry the Vth was possessed of the corone and reame of Ffraunce and of thother premisses and so possessed died seased therof. And all the same descended by dew course of enheritaunce to the said King Henry the VIth as son and heir of the said King Henry the Vth,[361] and was accordingly coroned, sacred and enoynted king of Ffraunce and in possession therof by a long tyme. By reason wherof the said King Henry the Vth and King Henry the VIth by good and just title made ther armees to have

---

[358] In T, fo. 39r, the author argued that the French kings had violently seized the lands of the ancestors of Henry V and had broken treaties, invoking the maxim *injuriam irrogatam armorum propulsare remedia leges et jura permittunt*.

[359] See pp. 165–170. The Tudor author conflates Henry V's invasions of France in 1415 and 1417 with the events following the murder of the duke of Burgundy by the Dauphin Charles in September 1419.

[360] The story of the murder of the duke of Burgundy, cited above on pp. 167–168, was repeated at this point in T, fo. 39v.

[361] In T, fo. 40r, Henry VI was identified as the heir of both Henry V and his wife, Katherine of Valois.

subdewed the said Charles the VIIth as traitor and proditor to the corone and reame of Ffraunce.[362]

|82v| *Capitulum XXIIII* [363]

And where in the said secund partie is surmytted that croniques and histories shuld speke that there was a certain treatie had betwix King Henry the III[de] of Englond sone of King John on the oon part and King Loys of Ffraunce ffather of Saint Loys on the other partie. And that by reason of a croisee which shuld have ben geven by the pope against the said King John and Henry the III[de] his sone and of the conquest of the same reame to gether with certain mony geven and delyvered to the said Loys of Ffraunce, by occasion wherof the same Loys for that cause shuld have passed into Englond and have had the possession of London, Lincoln and many other citees, townes and castelles of the same reame, and fealties and homages of the moost part of all the prelates, lordes & barons of the same reame which shuld have made to him oothes of fealtie as to ther sovereyn lord.

And by meane therof over and beyond the rever of Humbre entring towardes Scotlond. And that the mater of confisquacion and forfaiture shuld have ben so clere against the said King John aswel by cause of treason as of felonie and otherwise, and also shuld have ben so solennely declared by them to whom of right shuld apperteyne to doo. And for that cause shuld have ben geven III jorneyes solennely holden in the reame of Ffraunce, the oon at Estampes, the secund at Chartres at which II jornyes the said King John shuld have appiered in persone. And the III[de] jorney shuld |83r| have ben at Vendosme where he wold not appiere, but shuld have forfaited every wey to him possible against the said King Phelip than king of Ffraunce. At which place of Vendosme,

---

[362] In place of this final sentence, T, fo. 40r, addressed the French arguments relating to Wales: 'By the which it is evident that the kings of Englond hath good title aswel to the corone and totalite of the reame of Ffraunce as to all the particuler londs by succession of trewe enheritaunce, and that with good and true quarell and title may extende and clayme and with the suffraunce and enheritaunce, and that he may wele doo it without charge of consciens, insomoche as non of his predecessours in tymes passed have not disclaymed ay eny time nor refused in due maner and at convenient tyme to doo the due service to the true kings of Ffraunce, for the same as the said Prince Leolyn and also the kings of Scotts have refused to doo to the kings of Englond ther dew service dewe for ther londs.'

[363] This chapter partially translates and responds to *Pour ce que plusieurs*, pp. 113–115, building upon the material in T, fos 40r–44v.

declaracion shuld have ben solennely made against the said King John.[364]

And that the said Loys amonges other thinges by that title named hymself and bare the name of rightfull lord of the said reame of Englond by the said treatie. And that for to appese the said discorde, the parties shuld have appointed to gether that the prisonners of thoon part and of thother shuld be delyvered, peax final made betwix them and great somes of mony shuld have ben paied to the said Loys of Ffraunce for to retorne from those parties unto the parties of Ffraunce. And that the historie shuld further saye that the said king of Englond shuld have submytted him as subget to the king of Ffraunce II tymes in the yere. And in case that he shuld have resonable essonie or excuse that he might not come, that he shuld be bounde to sende notable men garnisshed with sufficient auctorite on his behalf in token of recognisaunce that he shuld holde him for subget of the king of Ffraunce. And on that shuld be bounde and submitted hym to serve the king of Ffraunce in his werres with certain nombre of men whan so ever the king of Ffraunce shuld geve to him knowlege therof.[365]

By which shuld be supposed shuld appiere that the werre which Englisshmen have made against the kinges of Ffraunce shuld be unjust & unresonable, and that by the meane therof it shuld be evident that the kinges of Englond shuld not onely have confisqued |83v| and forfaited all that they had in Ffraunce, but also the reame of Englond. And that by just and good quarell the king of Ffraunce shuld may demaunde that, and to make to them werre and to put him to peyne to invade and conquerre the same.

And that though the said submission shuld have no place, it shuld be clere and evident by the other meanes afore towched that wrongfully and against reason, the Englisshmen shuld make demaunde of the londes and seignouries particuler which they quarell in the reame of Ffraunce, wherof afore is made mencion. And that they shuld not have right nor title vailable, and if eny tyme they shuld have had by title of succession or otherwise, they

---

[364] This discussion of John's failure to attend three assemblies in 1202 is an incongruous insertion in this account of Prince Louis's invasions of England, especially as the paragraph had appeared earlier in *Pour ce que plusieurs*. The Tudor author repeats it here because it was accidentally duplicated in the printed editions of the French treatise. See pp. 29, 90–91, and p. 113, n. 298 above. The Tudor author had already dealt with King John's relations with Philippe Augustus in detail in chapter eleven, and therefore chose not to dwell on this point here. See p. 246, n. 367 and p. 251, n. 388.

[365] The Tudor author omits the discussion of Henry III's supposed promise to pay homage to the French crown after Prince Louis's invasion of England, which Cousinot admitted was not mentioned in 'la cronicque d'Angleterre': see p. 114.

shuld have lost, forfaited & confisqued them, and by good and just title the king of Ffraunce shuld have taken them in to his handes and reunyed them to the corone, and that justly, holily and laufully he might have doon and to him shuld apperteyne of right without eny reproof.

If there were no mater elles but the same whiche is conteyned in this latter surmyse, it is ynough to make apparent the false conjecture and imaginacions of the false myendes of the Frensshmen towardes the reame of Englond, and in especiall of the compiler of the aforesaid articles objected, alledged and surmytted. Who wold think that the pope would graunte eny croise against the partie or king whome |**84r**| he the same pope aided and for his defence excommenqed by censures of the chirche his adverse parties which invaded the reame of the same partie. The said King Phelip of Ffraunce and the said Loys his sone invaded with ther power the londes of the said King John aswel in the reame of Englond as in the duche of Normandie and other londes in the parties of Ffraunce, for which the same King Phelip and Loys were by the pope excommunicat.[366]

And hough eny jugement made or geven in the court of the king of Ffraunce shuld be in force or take effect against eny king of Englond for eny londes in Englond which never was nor is in eny point apperteynyng to the jurisdiction of the corone of Fraunce.[367] The reame of Englond at eny tyme from the first king or lord therof was never nor owght to be in subjection to the corone of Ffraunce nor other erthely prince but oonly undir the proper corone and king of Englond and under God. The reame and cuntre of Ffraunce whan it was called Gaule and also Ffraunce have ben at diverse tymes in subjection to diverse kinges of the reame of Englond whan it was called Bretain. Ffor Belyn somtyme king of this lond than called as is saide Bretain conquerred and held in subjection all Gaule which is in IIII principall partes as Gallia Belgica, Gallia Lugdonensis, Gallia Acquitanica and Gallia Narbonensis.[368] In likewise Maximian some tyme also king of this lond conquerred and put in his subjection all Gaule.[369] And so also ded king Arthur somtyme also king of this lond

---

[366] In fact, Pope Innocent III did excommunicate King John in 1209, and then formally deposed him in 1212, encouraging Philippe II to invade England, as reported in the *Flores historiarum*, II, pp. 138 and 144–145. This paragraph does not appear in T. For the excommunication of Philippe and Louis, see p. 250, n. 383.

[367] *Pour ce que plusieurs* did not argue that the judgement against King John in 1202 justified the invasion of England in 1216, though this case was actually made by Prince Louis himself, as suggested in the *Flores historiarum*, II, p. 159.

[368] See, for example, *Flores historiarum*, I, p. 61.

[369] See, for example, *Flores historiarum*, I, pp. 193–194, and also p. 259 below.

as is apparent in histories.[370] |84v| Ffor which causes the kings of Englond if they were not kinges of Ffraunce in right as they truly be as is declared afore, may laufully and without charge of consciens clayme sovereyntie of the kinges and reame of Ffraunce and to put them in dewe subjection to the corone of Englond as his subgettes.[371]

Neverthelesse in declaracion of the trouth in the premisses, so it was that duryng that the barones of Englond rebelled and made werre against the said King John of Englond ther sovereyn lord at the false conspiring of the said King Phelip and aftir the deth of Hubert somtyme archebisshop of Cantirbury,[372] the monks of Cauntirbury without licence of the said King John in derogacion of his right of the corone of Englond, about mydnight aftir ther matines songe, elected oon Mastir Reynold ther subprior to be archebisshop of Canturbury and sang *Te deum* and bare him and sett him first on the high alter, and aftir in the chaier of the archebisshop see.[373] And the same monkes, doubting for that they had made that ther ellecion without the kinges licence, if it shuld come to the kinges knowlege might be lett of ther purpose caused ther said ellect the supprior to make solenne othe afore them that without the assent of the said convent of monkes or licence by ther especial lettres, he shuld not shewe the lettres which they had made to him of that ellection nor shuld not in eny point disclose the election afore his comyng to the court of Rome for his consecracion. |85r| Wherupon the same ellect toke with him certain of those monkes and went his voiage towardes the court of Rome to have ben consecrat archebisshop of Cauntirbury afore eny knowlege of that ellection shuld have comen to the said King John. And the same ellect notwithstonding his said othe made to his monkes, as sone as he was come into Fflaundres, he disclosed openly that he was ellect of archebisshop of Cauntirbury and that was in his voiage towardes the court of Rome to be consecrat. And at his comyng to Rome he presented the said election to the pope and cardinales shewing his lettres of the same and required consecracion. But the pope delayed his consecracion until he shuld be bettir certefied of the trouth.[374]

And in the meane tyme the covent of monkes at Cauntirbury havyng enformacion that ther said elect had violated his othe made unto them and had disclosed ther secretes, sent certain of the convent to the said King John to purchase licence to procede to election

---

[370] See, for example, *Flores historiarum*, I, p. 266.

[371] This paragraph did not appear in T.

[372] Hubert Walter died on 13 July 1205.

[373] *Flores historiarum*, II, p. 130. In 1205, a number of the younger monks of Christ Church assembled secretly at night and elected their sub-prior, Reginald, as archbishop.

[374] *Flores historiarum*, II, p. 130.

and wold not that it shuld be knowen to the king of ther former election. And the same King John gave to them his lettres of licence to procede to election, enstauncing the monkes to elect Maistir John Grey than bisshop of Norwiche to be archebisshop of Cauntirbury. Wherupon the said convent of Cauntirbury in ther chapitre hous of oon assent elected the said Maistir John Grey to be archebisshop of Cauntirbury and that election solennely and openly denounsed, and set him on the high alter with singing *Te deum*, and aftir sett him in the archebisshops |**85v**| chaire.[375] Upon whiche King John put the said Maistir John Grey in possession of all the temporalities which than apperteyned to the archebisshop and directed his elegant epistle to the pope for the confirmacion and consecracion of the same Maistir John Grey to be archebisshop of Cauntirbury. Upon which double election grew moche errour, *pejor priori*, which was cause of many troubles in Englond and of asclaundres which hetherto be not in all pointes extinct touching the said King John and in especial in the mowthes of the Frensshmen.[376]

And every of the said electes, that is to saie the said Maistir John Grey for his partie and the said Maistir Reynold the subprior for his partie, contending in the court of Rome upon the said dowble election by the tyme of II yeres and more, and wold not agree but contenued the debate therof.[377] The pope perceyving the same exorted the same contendantes that they shuld cease ther quarelles persuading them with great affection to elect Maistir Stephen Langton, an Englisshman borne, to be archebisshop of Caunterbury. And the monkes beyng at Rome alledged that they might not soo doo without the kinges consent and also election to be made by ther entier convent, wherunto the pope saide that the said electes had than more power in the churche of Cauntirbury than the convent, and that the court of Rome used not to tarie the assent of temporell princes, sayeng further to them: 'You which be as ye ar sufficient to this election, we |**86r**| commaunde you in vertue of obedience and upon peyne of excommunicacion that you electe Maistir Stephen Langton to be archebisshop of Cauntirbury whom we institude into pastor of your sowles.' And the monkes feryng sentence of excommunicacion with murmure gave ther assent, except onely Maistir Elias of Branfeld which was there for the partie of the said Maistir Grey wold not geve his assent therto. All the other bare

---

[375] *Flores historiarum*, II, pp. 130–131. John de Gray was chosen as archbishop of Canterbury on 11 December 1205.

[376] *Flores historiarum*, II, p. 131, which concludes with the statement that '*in hac duplici electione factus est novissimus error pejor priore, quod fuit seminarium multarum in Anglia tribulationum et scandalorum, quae nunquam postea sedabantur penitus exstirpata.*'

[377] *Flores historiarum*, II, p. 134. Pope Innocent III annulled the election of John de Gray, bishop of Norwich, in March 1206.

the said election to the altere with *Te deum*. And therupon the said Maistir Stephen Langton the XV kalendes July in the yere MCCVII was consecrat archebisshop of Cauntirbury at Viterbe.[378]

And the pope aftir directed his elegant epistles to the said King John, desiring him to receyve the same archebisshop according. And whan King John had pleyn undirstonding of the premisses commaunded to avoide the monkes out of Cauntirbury as gilty of crime leze majestates.[379] For which aftir in the vigil of the fest of the Annunciacion of our lady Saint Marie, the reame of Englond was in interdict and aftir that suspended, notwithstonding the pope aftir that sent his subdiacon Pandulph into Englond with his grace and forme of peas if the said King John wold require it.[380] Wherfor the same King John was pacified with the pope by the legacie of the said Pandulph and, upon his othe and the othes of certain his barons that he shuld obeye the jugement |86v| of the chirche and that he shuld receyve the said Maistir Stephen as archebisshop of Cauntirbury, he opteyned the popes grace and the peax formed betwix the pope and the said King John the said entirdict was released, being present for the pope Nicholas bisshop of Tusculan, the Pandulph, the said Maister Stephen Langton, with many other bisshoppes, erles and barones of Englond, all that tyme contenewing the rebellion of many barones against the said King John by thehortement of the said Phelip king of Ffraunce.[381]

And the same king of Ffraunce in that tyme of entirdict and rebellion with armed power oppressed from the same King John the duche of Normandie with Bretayn and other londes adjoynant against the tenour of his writing and treatie of peax afore made betwix the said King Phelip and King John upon and for the mariage of the said Loys sone of the same King Phelip to the aforenamed Blanche doughtir of Spaine, nece of the said King John, and against his othes solennely therupon made.[382] And of his further dampnable myende procured and exorted diverse of the great lordes of Englond to conspire and pursiew

---

[378] *Flores historiarum*, II, pp. 134–135. Stephen Langton was consecrated by Pope Innocent III at Viterbo on 17 June 1207.

[379] *Flores historiarum*, II, p. 135.

[380] *Flores historiarum*, II, pp. 136, 140, and 143. King John expelled the monks from Christ Church on 11 July 1207 and the interdict was laid on his kingdom on 24 March 1208. In T, fo. 42r, the pope was said to have commanded all Christian princes to break off contact with John in 1211, on pain of excommunication.

[381] *Flores historiarum*, II, pp. 145–146 and 148. On 13 May 1213, John swore before the papal envoy, Pandulf, to obey the pope and to allow Langton to act as archbishop of Canterbury. Moreover, he went further in surrendering the English kingdom into the hands of the pope, to be returned to him as a fief, promising that English kings would rule as vassals of the pope, paying an annual tribute of 1,000 marks. The interdict was formally lifted from England on 29 June 1214.

[382] See pp. 185–186.

the total destruction of the said King John and to make the said Loys for ther king of Englond and for the same purpose the same Loys with his complices invaded the reame of Englond and made werre against the said King John for which the same Loys, his fautores and complices in the day of the fest of Saint Andrew theapostle the yere [. . .] were excommunicat |**87r**| by the popes auctorite.[383]

And the same Loys contenewed making werre in Englond against the said King John until the deth of the same King John, aftir whois deth the said King Henry the III^{de} sone of the same King John was coroned king of Englond beyng but IX yeres of age, which drave and chased the said Loys out of Englond as is declared afore.[384] Albe it the same Loys assembled a great power in Ffraunce and invaded again Englond and in the vigil of the fest of the Holy Trinite was veniquisshed by the said King Henry the III^{de} and moche of his people slayne.[385] And the same Loys was in soche distresse that he pursiewed and required Gualo the popes legat to be meane for him to be suffred to depart peasibly owt of Englond and to be absolved of the excommunicacion which was fulminat in him. And upon his long humble pursiewte in that behalf, in the vigil of the fest of the exaltation of the holy crosse,[386] he was pacified with the said King Henry the III^{de} and absolved by the said Gualo the popes legat, upon his solenne othes and promyses made openly that the same Loys with his retenue shuld stond and obeye to the jugement of the chirche, and that he shuld depart owt of Englond never to retorne into it again to doo therunto domage. And that he shuld to the best of his power and science indewce the said King Phelip his father without dissymelacion to restore and transporte to the said King Henry the III^{de} all the |**87v**| duchie of Normandie with all other hereditamentes which the said King Phelip or eny for him had taken and helde from the said King John or the same King Henry the III^{de}. And that whan the said Loys shuld be king of Ffraunce aftir the death of the said King Phelip or otherwise, he the same Loys without dificultie shuld resigne and restore to the said King Henry the

---

[383] *Flores historiarum*, II, p. 154, where this was said to have taken place on '*die sancti Andreae Apostoli*' without identifying the year, which was given as 1215 some two hundred and fifty words before. The Tudor author failed to give the year in the earlier account of these events on pp. 195–196, and in T, fol. 42v. He also conspicuously avoided mentioning that Prince Louis and the English rebels were excommunicated because they were acting against the king of England, '*Romanae ecclesiae vassallum*', following John's surrender of the kingdom into the hands of the papacy in 1213.

[384] *Flores historiarum*, II, pp. 162–164, and pp. 195–196 above.

[385] *Flores historiarum*, II, pp. 164–165, and p. 195 above. Henry III defeated Prince Louis at the battle of Lincoln on 20 May 1217. The reference to the vigil of the feast of the Holy Trinity was not given in T, fo. 43r.

[386] T, fo. 43r, added 'in the yere of our lord MCCXVII'.

said duche of Normandie and tother premisses without eny delaye.[387] Upon which treatie, peax, othes & promyses the said Loys was suffred to depart at his libertie out of Englond into the parties of Ffraunce, without that eny treatie were made betwix the said King Henry the III[de] & the said Loys other than is declared in this answer and not as is afore surmitted in the said secund partie.[388] And without that eny mony were delyvered to the said Loys by the said King Henry or eny persone for him for his departure out of Englond or for eny other cause, but in dede as the said Loys was in his jorney to depart out of Englond and passed by London the citesines of London which were the grosse aiders and conforters of the same Loys in his said werres, gave to him the same Loys VM markes towardes his charges, for which they were the more in the high displeasur of the said King Henry and so contenewed until they redemed his grace by ther gift to the same King Henry of other VM mark.[389] And without that the pope graunted eny croise against the said King John as is surmytted or against the said King Henry the III[de] for the conquest of Englond or for eny other cause.

And the reame of Englond was never geven to the said Loys |**88r**| wherby of right he shuld have taken upon him the name of king or lord of Englond nor toke fealties or homages of eny prelate, lord or baron there except but of certain traitours and rebelles ther unto reteyned by the said King Phelip of Ffraunce and the said Loys. And there was not eny maner confisquacion or forfaiture doon or committed by the said King John or the said King Henry the III[de] as is surmitted. Nor the said King Henry the III[de] never submytted him to be subget to the king of Ffraunce for the reame of Englond. But it apperith by evident declaracion that the said King Phelip and Loys were ever imaginatif to oppresse from the kinges of Englond ther hereditamentes in the parties beyond the see, and so they wold the reame of Englond if they might, *Nunquam Gallorum cessabit fraus patruorum.*[390]

And the werres which the kinges of Englond have made in the parties of Ffraunce have ben upon and for ther owne londes for the recover and defence of the same, by good and just title with reasonable cause to undoe the deforciones therof, *quia injuriam armis*

---

[387] *Flores historiarum*, II, pp. 165–166, and p. 196 above.

[388] T, fo. 43v, added a brief response to the claim that King John had been deprived of his lands in France after failing to attend Philippe II's court on three occasions. See p. 245, n. 364.

[389] *Flores historiarum*, II, p. 166.

[390] *Non inveni*. This quotation does not appear in the equivalent account in T, fo. 44r. See p. 191, n. 183.

irrogatam armorum propulsare remedia leges & jura permittunt.[391] And shuld nothing confique or forfaite for the same therby to geve eny title to the Frenssh king to holde eny parte of the hereditamentes of the kinges of Englond or eny cause to invade the reame of Englond. And if he wolde and were of myende to invade Englond, I trust that God wold geve to Englisshmen soche coragious hertes not oonly to defende ther paternell cuntre of Englond, thir heritage |88v| and ther wiefes and children against the Frensshmen that they shuld be confused of his presumpcion, but also to reclayme, entir and recover ther dewe hereditamentes aswel of the corone and totalite of the reame of Ffraunce as the particler londes and seignories of Normandie, Guyan, Gascogn, Angeo, Maine, Torayne, Poytow, Ponthieu, Champaigne, the Province with other diverse which the Ffrensshmen without colour of right or reasonable cause oppresse and holde from the high excellent and most vertuous my most dred sovereyn lord Henry the VIIIth of that name, king of Englond and of Ffraunce and lord of Ireland. And never aftir to geve trust and confidens to the Ffrensshmen which never were nor wol be trewe.

Gallorum ficta gens subdola gens maledicta.[392]

|89r| *Capitulum XXV*[393]

And where for and in the thrid part of the contentes of the false objectures, surmyses and imaginacions of the said Frenssh pamplet or codicil is surmytted that Englisshmen shuld compleyne them towching the breche or rumpure of the trewce which was made in the yere MIIII[C] XLIX under confiance of which trewce the Englisshmen shuld saye the lost the duche of Normandie and Guyan and therof they shuld have prayed to have restitution. And that the said trewce shuld begyn first in the yere MIIII[C] XLIIII in the monyth of May and that onely for the tyme of XXII monythes.[394] And that in that trewce the bothe kinges of Ffraunce and Englond shuld have comprised for eyther partie their allies and subgettes, and that for the partie of the king of Ffraunce shuld

---

[391] This maxim also appears on pp. 190, 222, and 225.

[392] *Non inveni.* This Latin quotation does not appear at the end of the equivalent section in T, fo. 44v. See p. 191, n. 182.

[393] This chapter offers an extremely abbreviated translation of the third section of *Pour ce que plusieurs*, pp. 116–134, and substantially redrafts T, fos 44v–49v. The final pages of T, fos 51v–52v, are extremely difficult to read but appear to represent an intermediate stage between the two versions.

[394] In *Pour ce que plusieurs*, the truce was said to have started in June 1444, though in fact the truce of Troyes was agreed on 28 May 1444 and ratified by Henry VI the following month (see p. 116). The date was given as June 1444 in T, fo. 44v.

have ben comprised amonges other princes and subgettes the duc
of Bretain which than was in his cuntre of Bretaine. And that in
likewise the king of Englond in his trewce shuld have recited the
allies & subgettes of the king of Ffraunce namely declared the
said duc of Bretaine and his cuntre as subget to the said king of
Ffraunce to be comprised in the said trewce of the partie of the
same king of Ffraunce, without that the said king of Englond shuld
have reclaymed or made mencion to the contrarie of the dede of
the duc of Bretaine or of his cuntre.

And that the said trewce of XXII monythes shuld theraftir be
prolonged for VII monythes and aftir that for V monythes and aftir
for |89v| VII monythes and also aftir for other XXII monythes.[395]
And that the same latter prorogation for XXII monythes shuld be
condicionel, that is to saye that if the king of Englond shuld delyver
Mans and thother places which he helde in the countie of Maine
before the fest of All Saints MIIII^C XLVII. And that for that the
said king of Englond shuld not have done it nor they which helde
the said places wold not obeye, it shuld behove to procede with
armed power.

And that whan the same appointement of Mans shuld have
ben made to put awey doubte that might happe for lett of the
prerogatives of the said trewce by cause of the said condicion not
accomplisshed, the commissaries of bothe kinges of Englond and
of Ffraunce shuld have condescended to make new trewce to have
dured II yeres, that is to saie until the first day of Aprill which was
abowt the holy wike afore Estir MIIII^C XLIX aftir the usage of
Ffraunce, and aftir the usage of Englond MIIII^C L. And that in
the same trewce the king of Ffraunce shuld have comprised on
his partie the said duc of Bretaine and his cuntre and duche as his
subgettes as he shuld have ben accustumed to have done afore. And
that whan the writinges shuld have ben shewed wretin accordingly,
without that of the partie of thenglisshmen the said duc shuld have
ben comprised in eny maner. But that the Englisshmen shuld in
using of cautelles have wrought a mervelous deceyt, that is to saye
that they shuld saye that they might not put the men of werre
of the reame of Ffraunce within the place |90r| of Mans but by
night tyme, and that they wold not delyver the place until they
shuld have had their appointementes. And that the matier shuld
have required scelerite for to eschewe many inconvenientes. And
that the commissaries of bothe princes shuld have appointed that
the said appointementes of the one part and of the other shuld
be delyvered at the said place. And that whan for that cause the

---

[395] In fact, the truce was prorogued for twelve months, as correctly noted in *Pour ce que
plusieurs*, p. 117. The same mistake appears in T, fo. 44v.

Patriarch of Poitiers and the other commissaries of the partie of Ffraunce shuld come about mydnight to the brinkes of the dikes of the cite of Mans at which place they shuld fynde than in lykewise the commissaries for the partie of the Englisshmen and shuld delyver ther appointementes of the one and of the other partie without light of candell or loking what was within, the Frensshmen trusting that the grosse of the said appointementes shuld have ben lyke at mydnight and incontinent the men of armes entred the said place. And that the said commissaries of the part of the Englisshmen in the trewce which they shuld have delyvered of ther parte in desceyt without consent of the commissaries of the partie for Ffraunce shuld have comprised the said duc of Bretaine on their partie aswel as the king of Ffraunce shuld have done for his partie.[396]

And that sone aftir those thinges done, the duc of Somerset which had the governaunce for the king of Englond in those cuntries under his obeissaunce as Normandie and other londes adjacentes, during the governaunce of which duc of Somerset many extorciones, excesses, entirprises & attemptees |90v| shuld have ben doon aswel by his commaundement as otherwise on his partie against the tenur of the said trewce.[397] And that Sir Ffrauncois de Surienne the Aragonois, beyng of the knightes of the Gartier and in service of the king of Englond, having charge of men of armes and of places for the king of Englond in Normandie, by the assent, knowlege and advowe of the kyng of Englond and of the duc of Suffolk and of the duc of Somerset and of many other principalles of Englond, shuld have taken by stelthe the castel and towne of Ffoulgiers and shuld have pilled and killed the people of those which were within the towne and take prisoners and shuld have made open werre in Bretaine as enemyes were accustomed to doo.[398] Ffor the which the king of Ffraunce required by Duc Ffrauncois of Bretaine to geve to hym provision, aide and socours in that matier shuld have sent of his counseill to the duc of Somerset to have knowen his entent and will touching the prise of Ffoulgiers, and if he wolde make eny reparacion. And besides that to the king

---

[396] The Tudor author omits the statement in *Pour ce que plusieurs* that this trick was the only justification for the subsequent capture of Fougères (see p. 118).

[397] Cousinot also reported that Charles VII sent a number of embassies to the duke of Somerset and to Henry VI, seeking an end to English infractions against the truce, and that he was drawing upon the deposition of François de Surienne himself for information on the capture of Fougères (see pp. 118–119).

[398] This ignores the repeated claims in the French treatise that Henry VI, his council, and Somerset all knew about Surienne's action, and that the duke supplied the mercenary with artillery and reinforcements after Fougères was taken (see p. 120).

of Englond for lyk cause.[399] And that there shuld not have ben had eny reparacion of the one part nor of thother.[400]

And that it shuld be shewed that from the tyme of King Clotaire the First sone of Clovys unto this present tyme, the duche of Bretaine shuld be of the reame of Ffraunce and subget of the kinges of Ffraunce. And that namely Saint Judicul king of Bretaine for that he shuld have disobeyed to the commissaries of King Dagobert, he shuld have moved his hoost against the said Saint Judicul, and the same Saint Juducul shuld have comen |**911**| to King Dagobert and have required mercy and have knowleged hym for him and his successoures to be his sovereyn lord by cause of his duchie of Bretaine, and all the kinges of Ffraunce which shuld be aftir him. And that in declaryng further for the new tyme, that is to saye from the tyme of King Phelip le Conquerant until this tyme, it shuld be clere and manifest that all the erles and dukes which shuld have ben in Bretaine shuld be men of the king of Ffraunce and to him shuld have done homage.[401]

And that the king of Englond might not pretende ignorance that the said Duc Ffrauncois of Bretaine in sewing his predecessoures shuld have done homage to the said King Charles the VIIth.[402] And that the same Duc Ffrauncois, doubting certain thinges which shuld have ben made with the Englisshmen aswel by Duc Giles his ffather as by Sir Giles his brother and other subgettes of the said duche in prejudice of the said King Charles, that eny thing might be demaunded of him or his subgettes therafter, shuld have taken obolicion of the said King Charles as of his sovereyn lord aswel for hymself as for the said Sir Giles his brother and all his duche, for all thinges which by his father Duc Giles and them all of his duche might have be done in the said matier. Which

---

[399] In *Pour ce que plusieurs*, these men were identified as Guillaume Cousinot, Pierre de Fontenil, and Jean Havart (see p. 120).

[400] The Tudor writer omits the French account of the English justification for the attack upon Fougères, namely that they were responding to infractions of the truce, including the imprisonment of Gilles de Bretagne, a vassal of Henry VI. *Pour ce que plusieurs* had also argued that the real reason for the English action was to persuade the duke of Brittany to abandon the side of Charles VII, and that the English were guilty of breaching the truce through various infractions, including the seizure of Fougères. See pp. 120–122.

[401] This paragraph did not appear in T. *Pour ce que plusieurs* had supported this argument by reference to authentic letters and also actions before the Parlement of Paris: see pp. 122–123.

[402] Again, the Tudor author omits the claims that the Parlement of Paris acted as court of last resort for cases from Brittany and that the duke had been listed as a subject of the king of France in the first truces, and could not have changed his status since then (see p. 123). This section begins on fo. 49r of T.

shuld be clere demonstraunce that he and his duche reputed them subgettes to the king of Ffraunce and not to the king of Englond.[403]

And that to the regarde of the said Sir Giles his brother, it shuld be clere that he shuld not have bene subget to the king of Englond |91v| for III reasons. The one by cause of his nativite for that he was borne in Bretanie which shuld be of the obeissance of Ffraunce.[404] The secund for that at the tyme whan he was taken, he shuld dwelle in the said duchie and there was maried and made there his residence. The III^de for that he possessed londes and seignories in the parties of Bretaine which should be of the foy and homage of the duc in pleyn fee and in arriere fee and dernier fee, resort to the corone of Ffraunce. And that therfor it should be evident that he shuld be man, subget and of thobeissance of the king of Ffraunce. And that whan he wold be man and subget of the king of Englond he shuld have forfaited. And that for doubte that he shuld have had to be repreved theraftir for the favour which had geven to the king of Englond and them of his partie, he wold be comprised in the abolicion wherof afore is made mention.[405]

And that considered, that the king of Englond and they of his partie shuld not have eny cause reasonable undir the coloures above precedent to take the said place of Ffoulgiers. And that shuld be clere infraction and breche of the trewce, entending namely the place wherof it shuld procede and by what commaundement, advowe and consentement it shuld be done. And yet more infractions of trewce in somoche that the said king of Englond and the said duc of Somerset wold have enforced against the tenore of the said trewce to attribute to them the subgection and obeissance of the said duc and duche of Bretaine.[406]

|92r| Trewe[407] it is that Englisshmen compleyned them and saide and yet saye that undir confidence of the said trewce they have hetherto lost Normandie & Guyan and many other londes of ther hereditamentes

---

[403] The French treatise concluded this point with a paragraph restating the position that the duke of Brittany was a vassal of Charles VII and had not given permission for the English to include his name amongst their allies on the truce (see p. 124).

[404] T, fo. 49r, merely stated 'thoon shuld be by cause of the obeissans of Ffraunce'.

[405] Cousinot also argued that Giles was not at liberty to switch his allegiance to another lord, especially an enemy of his sovereign and natural lord (see pp. 124–125).

[406] This paragraph does not appear in T. The Tudor author omits the remainder of the discussion in *Pour ce que plusieurs*, which provided a narrative of the unsuccessful French attempts to rescue the truce, recapitulating the previous arguments and also emphasizing that the responsibility for the eventual breach fell upon the instransigent English, together with a brief summary of the treatise as a whole (see pp. 125–134).

[407] Just as at the beginning of the response to the second section of *Pour ce que plusieurs* (p. 171), the scribe has left space for a two-line initial.

in the parties of beyond the see. And they may saye further that the cautelous and false breking of the Frensshmen of the said treatie and of all other treaties afore that tyme may be example and a president warnyng aswel for Englisshmen as for all other naciones to make or take any treatie or peas with Frensshmen and to trust therunto eny tyme heraftir for the Frensshmen never helde hetherto eny treatie or peax hough fermely so ever it were made by othes upon the consecrat body of Crist, the holy evangelies, by censures of the churche, by hostages or otherwise, lenger than they may espie ther singuler avauntage. And ther principall stodie is by cautelles, histories and recordes to witnesse.[408]

And trewe it is that in the yere MIIII^C XLIIII the said trewce was taken betwen the said King Henry the VIth king of Englond and of Ffraunce and the Frenssh king, the said Charles the VIIth, which called himself king of Ffraunce and usurped the same. And the same trewce was proroged at several tymes until the first day of Aprill in the year MIIII^C XLIX aftir the computation of Ffraunce and from that first day of Aprill until the first day of Junij than next folowing. But not upon soche condicion or in soche wise as is surmitted for the delyver of the cite of Mans or eny other, the tenores of the same treatie to witnes which be expressed in the croniques of Enguaran.[409] |92v| In whiche treatie oon point is conteyned of a marvelous cawtell for the Frensshmen to deceyve the Englishmen, that is to saye, it was agreed by the same treatie expressely that if any attemptates shuld be had against the said trewce, the same trewce shuld not therfor be broken, nor for that there shuld not be made eny werre on the one partie nor the other. But the same trewce shuld abide in the former force in like maner and forme as if nothing were done to the contrarie. But that the same attemptees shuld be repaired by the committors therof and punysshed by the conservatours and commissaries which therfor were commised and ordeyned by the said King Charles the VIIth for his partie and the said King Henry the VIth for his partie.[410]

The Frensshmen abiding in ther owne cuntre perceyved wele that Englishmen were of a desirous meende to resort home into ther natif cuntre Englond and therfor were often committing deputies for them in their offices in the parties of beyond the see, and perceyved also that there were in Englond gret divisions, grodges and rebelliones

[408] This paragraph does not appear in T.

[409] *Chronique de Monstrelet*, VI, pp. 96–107, and *Chronicles of Monstrelet*, II, pp. 136–138. Also see *GTGCA*, pp. 152–171.

[410] This is a close translation of article 12 of the truce of Tours: *GTGCA*, pp. 169–170. See *Chronique de Monstrelet*, VI, p. 105, and *Chronicles of Monstrelet*, II, p. 138. This article is not discussed in T.

amonges the lordes of Englond, that it was necessarie to the chief officiers of the king of Englond in the parties beyond the see to resorte in to Englond. And imagynyng that upon color of the said article of trews they might attempte som oon thing against the tenor of the said treatie without to be empeched for the same, but onely to make repaire and that by direction of ther owne commissaries which shuld be occasion that Englisshmen shuld also attempte som |**93r**| thing for ther partie to the contrarionste of the said trewce. And therupon duryng the same tyme of the said trewce, the said Charles the VIIth falsely and dampnably exorted and moved the said Ffrauncois duc of Bretain, than beyng subget and liegeman of the said king of Englond for his duche of Bretaine which than was and of right oweth to be subget onely to the duche of Normandie as is evidently declared afore and shal prove by the subsequentes,[411] which duche of Normandie was than in the possession of the said king of Englond, to forsake his said sovereyn lord the king of Englond, King Henry the VIth, and to be man of the said Charles the VIIth contrarie to right upon whiche and for the yerely pencion by the same Charles the VIIth graunted to the said Duc Ffrauncois.[412] The same Duc Ffrauncois in the yere MIIII[C] XLVI made first homage to the said Charles the VIIth and refused his said sovereyn lord King Henry the VIth.[413]

And of further cawtell the said Charles the VIIth ymmediatly aftir comaunded Sir Perrigent de Coitivy admirall for the said Charles, Sir Reynold de Drosnot bailif of Sens, and Sir Piers de Bresy seneschal for the said Charles in Poytow, to lye in awaite and take the said Sir Giles of Bretayn brother of the said Duc Ffrauncois and knight of the Gartier, liegeman and servunt of the said King Henry the VIth. Which toke the said Sir Giles of Bretaine and delyvered him by the commaundment of the said Charles the VIIth |**93v**| unto the said Duc Ffrauncois his brother, which duc by the exortation and procurement of the said Charles the VIIth, put the said Sir Giles in strait and peyneful prison to have compelled hym to have refused the said King Henry the VIth his dew sovereyn lord and to become man and homagier and servunt of the said Charles. And for that the same Sir Giles wold not refuse

---

[411] See p. 259.

[412] The Tudor author conveniently ignores the fact that the duke of Brittany was included on the French side in the truce of Tours in 1444, as Monstrelet himself had recorded: *Chronique de Monstrelet*, VI, p. 99, and *Chronicles of Monstrelet*, II, p. 137, together with *GTGCA*, pp. 163 and 187.

[413] *Chronicles of Monstrelet*, II, p. 142. Duke François I paid homage to King Charles VII on 16 March 1446. This paragraph is an extended version of material in T, fos 45v–46r.

the said King Henry for his sovereyn and dew sovereyn lord, he was murdred in prison.[414]

Which matiers were notarily infraction of the said trewce and contrarie to the tonne of the same by the said Charles the VIIth long afore the supposed taking of the said Ffoulgiers and in dispight of the said King Henry the VIth. And for to declare and prove that the rumpure and infraction of the said trewce was made, doon and executed by the said Charles the VIIth and on his partie, and not by eny meane of the partie of the said Henry the VIth nor the Englisshmen, and for that the Frensshmen alledge that the taking of Ffoulgiers shuld be first and principal cause of the breche of the said trewce which Ffoulgiers is parcel of the duchie of Bretayn, which duche they also alledge shuld be subget to the reame of Ffraunce, the trouth is that the duche and cuntre of Bretain of very right than was and owith to be subget to the said King Henry the VIth for diverse causes. The former cause was by reason that |91r| Maximian somtyme king of this reame of Englond conquerred the same cuntre of Bretayn whan it was called Armorik, and caused it to be habited with his subgettes Brettons and named it the Lesse Bretain, and aftir gave the same cuntrie to Conan Meriadok to hold of him and his successores kinges of this reame for ever.[415] The secund reason is that Rollo first duc of Normandie, subdued the same cuntrie of Bretain and Alain and Berengier, lordes of the cuntrie of Bretain, put them and ther heires and successoures in his subjection to be his men of fee and of foy and homage for ever.[416] And if eny right were due therof to the corone of Ffraunce, the same right was extinct for ever by II meanes. Thoon is for that Charles Simplex somtyme king of Ffraunce remitted and transported into the possession of the said Rollo all the right and demaunde which he had aswel in Bretain as in Normandie as is said afore.[417] The second men was by the graunt of the said Phelip called the Conquerant somtyme also king of Ffraunce made to Richard Cuer de Leon than king of Englond and duc of Normandie, as is made mencion in the [...] chapitre afore.[418]

---

[414] *Chronicles of Monstrelet*, II, pp. 143–144. The individuals charged with the action were Prégent de Coëtivy, Renaud de Dresnay, and Pierre de Brézé. This material also appears in T, fo. 46r.

[415] For one such account, see *Flores historiarum*, I, p. 196, and also p. 246 above.

[416] See p. 203.

[417] See p. 203.

[418] See chapter eleven, p. 179. This material appeared later in the equivalent section in T, fos 47v–48r, where there is no mention of Maximinianus, and the stories of Rollo and Richard I are reinforced by the stories that Arthur, duke of Brittany, paid homage to his uncle, King John, and Jean de Montfort did the same to King Edward III.

And the said Duc Ffrauncois of Bretaine was subget and in dede liegeman of the said King Henry the VIth and so had avowed, taken and served him and as soche |**94v**| ded homage to hym and sware foye and fealtie to hym in succeding his father and other his progenitores which successively had doon homage to the kinges of Englond havyng possession of the duche of Normandie.[419] And it is manyfest that the said King Henry the VI was coroned, accepted and taken and advowed as the trewe king of Ffraunce by all the pieres and III Estates of the reame of Ffraunce and by the said Duc Ffrauncois of Bretain. And for that the said King Henry the VIth was king of Ffraunce, sacred, enoyned and coroned as is declared afore and in laufull possession therof, if the case were soche, as it was not nor owith to be, that the duche of Bretain were ymmediatly holden of the corone of Ffraunce as is alledged afore, it provyth wele that the said Duc Ffrauncois was the tyme of the said treatie and afore dewe subget to the said King Henry the VIth king of Ffraunce.[420] And although the said Duc Ffrauncois of Bretain were of so dampnable myende and ill will that he wold disavowe his dew sovereyn lord the said King Henry the VIth king of Englond and of Ffraunce with the duche of Normandie, whom he had so taken, avowed, served and accepted, and to advowe an other prince to be his sovereyn lord, enemye and adversarie to his dewe and naturell sovereyn lord, it is not nor owith to be in his libertie nor in his power so to doo in prejudice of his naturell sovereyn lord without his consent, nor for that his dew sovereign lord is not to lose the cognisance of the wronges done to him.[421] But alwey to the dewe sovereyn lord is dewe all right of seignorie |**95r**| and subjection. By which premisses is manifest that aswel the said Duc Ffrauncois as Sir Giles his brother were subgettes and liegemen of the said King Henry the VIth by ther naturell birthe and by every other meane.

And in the yere MIIII[C] XLIIII the said trewce begon and made, the said King Henry the VIth comprised on his partie the said Duc Ffrauncois of Bretein in the same trewce with his cuntre of Bretaine as his subget and allye amonges other, and than was not claymed nor comprised in the said trewce for the partie of the said Charles the VIIth as allye or subjet to the same Charles.[422] And in likewise the said King Henry the VIth in every other of the prorogacion of the same trewce comprised the said Duc Ffrauncois of Bretaine and his cuntrie

---

[419] Duke François I had not paid homage to Henry VI upon inheriting the duchy of Brittany in 1442.
[420] See T, fos 49r–49v.
[421] This argument appeared in T, fo. 48v.
[422] See p. 258, n. 412.

on his partie as his subget of dutie.[423] And so is manifest that the taking, imprisonying and murdrying of the said Sir Giles de Bretain knight of the Garter and subget and liegeman to the said King Henry the VIth by the imaginacion, advowe, knowlege and assent of the said Charles the VIIth and compulcion to have caused him by peyne to have refused his said dewe sovereyn and naturell sovereyn lord the said King Henry the VIth, was clere infraction of the said trewce by and on the partie of the said Charles the VIIth, which was long afore the said supposing taking of Ffoulgiers upon and for the takyng of the said Sir Giles de Bretaine. By the content of the said cawtelous point of article conteyned in the said treatie, making mencion that if eny attemptates shuld be had against the said trewce, the same trewce shuld not be therfor broken &c.

The said |95v| King Henry the VIth not entending to violate or doo eny point against the tenore of the said trewce nor supposing eny soche cautell by the Frensshmen, sent his embassade to the said Charles the VIth by the bisshop of Excester and the Lord Audeley which made ther legacion in that behalf to the said Charles in a place in Torayn called Rassile nere to Chinon and on the behalf of ther maistir the said King Henry the VIth required of the said Charles the VIIth redresse to have the said Sir Giles de Bretaine delivered out of prison.[424] But ther was no redresse made, but uttirly denyed the delyver of him. And in more infraction of the said trewce the said Charles the VIIth sent the counte de Dunoys and in his conduct VIIM men of werre to beseige the said cite of Mans. And by his said commaundement the same counte de Dunoys with his arme assieged the same cite of Mans by a long tyme with soche force, the chief capteyn therof for the king of Englond than beyng in Englond, and the same cite being not garnisshed for defence therof in trust of the said trewce, that the citesines & habitantes therof were not of power to resiste the said assiegeantes but had with the cite be taken by force if the bisshop of Excester had not taken apoyntement with the said Charles for the delyver of the same cite of Mans.[425]

In the contentes of the said trewce, wherof the tenore is conteyned in the croniques of Enguereyn Monstrelet, natif and soget of Ffraunce,

---

[423] For the inclusion of Brittany as both a French and an English ally in the two versions of the prorogation of the truce in March 1448, see *Foedera*, XI, pp. 200 and 206.

[424] *Chronicles of Monstrelet*, II, p. 144. On 20 July 1446, Adam Moleyns, bishop of Chichester, and John, lord Dudley, travelled with other envoys to France to arrange the surrender of the county of Maine. This story appears in T, fo. 46v.

[425] *Chronicles of Monstrelet*, II, p. 146, and also see T fo. 46v. On 31 January 1448, Moleyns and Sir Robert Roos were commissioned to complete the cession of Maine, and a final agreement was signed on 15 March.

is made no mencion for the delyver of the cite of Mans nor eny londes in the countie of Maine to the said Charles the VIIth by the said King Henry the VIth in eny maner or by eny condicion.[426] |**96r**| And it is manifest in the same croniques of Enguereyn that the cite of Mans was delyvered by the apointement of the said bisshop of Excester in forme here declared by pleyn dailight and not by night. And the said Sir Ffrauncois de Surienne the Aragonoys which was felow and brother in armes to the said Sir Giles de Bretaine of his owne meende without knowlege or advowe of the said King Henry the VIth or the said duc of Somerset, made entirprise and toke Ffoulgiers aforeseid without brennyng, taking of prisoners or puttyng eny of the inhabitantes therof to redempcion for that the said Duc Ffrauncoys of Bretaine had than murdred the said Sir Giles de Bretayne his brother, and brother and felow in armes of the said Sir Frauncois de Surienne, so that he coude not have repaire or redresse of nor for him according to the said trewce nor the commissaries of the said Charles the VIIth wold in nowise order soche redresse. Neverthelesse the same Sir Ffrauncois de Surienne at all tymes offred to make repaire for the taking of Ffoulgiers if so were repaire shuld have ben made for the said Sir Giles.[427] But the said Charles the VIIth had theffect of the original of his purpos entending by the said article made in the said trewce and undirstode the devision and insurrections and also the rebelliones which were in Englond wherby Englisshmen shuld be in soche occupacion that they shuld have no tyme to passe in to the parties of Ffraunce for defence of ther londes there, incontinent without other pursuite made werre and invaded the londes of the said King Henry the VIth, and toke first by cawtell the town of Pont de l'Arche and therin toke the lord Ffacombregge prisonner with many other. And toke & pilled |**96v**| Bergeney and murdred all the Englisshemen therof.[428] And never after cessed not of werre until the said King Charles the VIIth had oppressed from the said King Henry the VIth all his hereditamentes beyond the see.

By which premisses is notorily declared that the said trewce was nowise condicionel for the delyver of the cite of Mans or eny londes in Maine as is afore surmytted, but that the cite of Mans was delyvered

---

[426] There was no mention of Maine in the truce of Tours, as demonstrated by the transcription in Monstrelet, but Henry VI had agreed to cede Maine on 22 December 1445: *L&P*, II, ii, pp. [639]–[642]. Also see T, fo. 46v.

[427] *Chronicles of Monstrelet*, II, pp. 148–149, though this account did not suggest that the action was carried out in order to secure the release of Gilles de Bretagne. Also see T, fo. 47r.

[428] *Chronicles of Monstrelet*, II, pp. 150–152, though this account did not include the claim that all the Englishmen in Gerberoy were murdered. Also see T, fo. 47v.

by dailyght upon soche apointement as in this answer is declared and not at mydnight nor in soche maner as is by the Frensshmen afore alledged. And it is apparent that the Englisshmen used not the surmytted cawtell in that behalf nor in the grosse of the said trewce as is surmytted nor in other maner than was by the commissaries of bothe parties agreed. And appirith also that the said Sir Giles of Bretaine was in nothing of his consent or agrement partie to the obolition afore rehersed made to the said Charles the VIIth nor in his myende or will to be comprised in the same as is surmytted.

And by the declaracions hertofore in this werke made, it is manifestly shewed that the Ffrenshmen without title, right or eny cause reasonable have deforsed the kinges of Englond, progenitoures to the high, excellent and most vertuous prince my most dred sovereyn lord Henry by the grace of God king of Englond and of Ffraunce and lord of Irelond, of the possession of the corone and reame of Ffraunce, and of the duchies of Normandie, Guyan and Gascoyn with the dominion and superiorite of |97r| Bretayn, and of the counties of Angeo, Maine, Torayn, Poytow, Ponthieu, Champaine and the Province with diverse other particuler londes and seignouries in the parties of beyond the see, the dewe and laufull heritage of my said sovereyn lord, by ther crafty and cautellous imaginacions and oppressions, as may be proved by famous and notable histories and croniques out of which I have framed this werk. Beseching the reders and herers therof to holde me excused of my rude Englissh for that I have no connyng in elequence. And if eny thing be herin superfluous or not agreable to ther meendes, to correct it and dowbt not to shew the said histories and croniques upon which I was induced for the grosse of the matier conteyned in the said declaracions.[429]

---

[429] At the bottom of the final folio of the treatise is a Victorine stanza on the Virgin Mary, similar to the verses in John of Garland, *The Stella Maris of John of Garland*, ed. E.F. Wilson (Cambridge, MA, 1946): '*Qui tonat in celis, dit prospera flamina, velis / Alma maris stella, fer nunc vexilla puella, / Mater virgo pia, regis memor esto Maria.*' These three lines have been neatly crossed out, and had not appeared in T.

APPENDIX I: COLLEGE OF ARMS MS ARUNDEL 39 (MS T)

This appendix presents the introduction and conclusion of the draft of the Tudor treatise.

|1r| Jhesus Maria[1]

Ffor that I remembred that every man is bounde by the commaundement of God principally and by the counsaill of the prudent to eschiew slouthe & idelnesse, mother and norices of all vices, and owe to put him unto vertuous occupacion and businesse. Thenne I havyng no great charge of occupacion but the charge of an office for to levye, gather and answer unto the right high, excellent and most vertuous, my most dredde soverayn lord Henry the VIIIth of that name king of Englond and of Ffraunce and lord of Irelond, the customes and subsidies of merchaundises of oon of his poortes of Englond and the businesse therof but at certain times and by reason of the same office sequestred from byeng & selling and the use of merchaundises and boound to attende in proper persone to the same to awaite the casueltie therof, so that many tymes I had litil to doo. Remembring that my said most drad soveraign lord had the name of king of Ffraunce and perceyved litil or nothing of the proufit therof nor yet of the duchees of Normandie and Acquitaine or Guyan or Gascoyn, the counties of Poytew, Angeo, Torayn and Mayne and also the countie of Ponthieu which as I have herd shuld belonge to his grace of right of enheritaunce by descent from his most noble pregenitoures. And knew not the direct cause of the lette therof why, but by common report that William de la Pole first duke of Suffolk, ayel to Edmond de la Pole now prisoner, havyng the governaunce of the most part of the premisses under and for the most vertuous prince of famous memorie King Henry the VIth, shuld have bargained and sold and so delivered the same to the Frenssh king for certain mony which the said duke shuld have taken to his owne use, which comon report gave not perfite knowlege to me therof, nor is not but seldom to be beleved. And for that me thought a right necessarie thing to make serche to come to the perfite knowlege in that behalf.

---

[1] Next to it, in a late-sixteenth-century hand, is written 'Roberti Hare 1563'.

And forsomoche as I had a book of cronikes in Frenssh compiled by the bisshop of Burges, and translated into |ɪᴠ| Frenssh tonge by oon Ffrere John Golein of the order of Carmelites at the commaundement of Charles le Beale somtyme king of Ffraunce yonger sone of King Phelip le Beale and yongest brother to Isabel somtyme quene of Englond wief of that noble prince King Edward the Secund, and endith the tyme of lief of the said Charles le Beale. After the deth of which said Charles the Beale the title of the corounes of Ffraunce and Navarre and the countie of Champaine in right descended and ought to have come to the most worthy prince King Edward the Thrid as cosin and heir to the said King Charles, that is to saye sone of the said Isabel, insomoche as the same Charles died without issue. And also had in my keping diverse other bookes of cronikes aswel in Ffrenssh and Latyn as in Englissh and Duche. I therfor gave me to stodie of the premisses, the rather for that than I had than my lyving of my soveraign lord by reason of the said office and to ny other persone I was most bounde to the kinges grace.

And the tyme of the same my stodie cam unto my hondes a litil boke or pamphlet imprinted conteynyng false, untrew and dampnable matier, divided into III principall partes. Whereof in the first partie is matier imagined to adnichil & destroye the title of enheritaunce which the kinges of Englond have pretende & clayme to the coroune and totalite of the reame of Ffraunce. In the secund partie is conteyned in likewise to adnichillate the title which the kinges of Englond hath to particuler londes within the reame of Ffraunce as Normandie with Bretayn, Acquitaune or Guyan, Gascoyn, Poytew, Angeo, Torayn, Mayne and Pontieu with their appertenances. In the thrid partie is conteyned the breking of the trewes betwene the than kinges of Englond and the Frenssh king in the yere of our lord Mᶜ IIIIᶜ XLIX which is ther surmitted shuld be broken on the partie |2ʀ| of the Englisshmen. And for that in the same thre principall partes is matier spoken at large and dispightfull reherse against the noble progenitoures of my said soveraign lord, kinges of Englond, entending by the same not oonly as is noted to adnichillat the true title of my said soveraign lord to all the premisses and every part therof,[2] but also by wey of a pedegre wold conveye other to be nere to the coroune of Englond therby to cause Englisshmen if he cowde to make werre amonges themself. And besides that wold and gevith falsly to the Ffrensh king title to the coroune of Englond. For the which causes I have put the more diligent studie to fynde the trouth out of the said cronikes and to impugne all the said phamphlet or

---

[2] Marginal note: 'thanyng holy the possession of the premisses percyvyng that Englisshmen used ther feates'.

litil boke emprinted, and to denounce and expresse the trouth to the confoundement and falsying of the same pamphlet or litil boke emprinted.[3]

And for the first partie of my said labor, I have noted a pedegre in a rolle aswel of the lyne or descent of the kinges of Englond as of the regions of Ffraunce, Castell & Leons, Arragon and Navarre, and also of the dukes of Normandie and Guyan, and of Angeo, Toreyn and Mayne, and of other seignories, by which may appere clerly that besides the said corounes of Englond and Ffrance, the duchies and counties of Normandie, Acquitaine, Gascoyn, Angeo, Mayne, Torayn, Poytow and Pontieu with thomage and fee of Bretain and other seignouries, the said most excellent prince my said soveraign lord King Henry the VIIIth hath good title to the coroune and reame of Navarre and to the countie of Champaine, as by the said rolle may appere.

And for the secund part of my said labor, I have wretin |2v| this litil boke to impugne the allegacions and fals surmyses made, the premisses rehersing the same their surmyses and in that directly as nere as my symple witte wol serve me. By which shal appere clerely that the matiers conteyned in the said pamplet emprinted be falsly and dampnably be forged of fals imaginacion, craftly entriked to begile the reders and herers therof.

|3r| The office of speking is wonderfull and a subtil thing geven by God to man to be knowen therby from all other bestes. And thoffice therof is so geven to man that the trouth which he conceyveth in mynde, he may manifest to another wherby men may help themself in knowlege of the trouth aswel as in other thinges necessarie to mannes lief. *Cum sit homo naturaliter animal sociale.*[4] And the contrarie therof is forboden by God and is wretin Exodus ca. XX[e], *Non loqueris contra proximum tuum falsum testimonium.*[5] And he that spekth falsly or by dissimulacion, he abusith thoffice of his tonge and in that he dooth injurie to God his creator and former of the same office of speking.

And than he the same persone what so ever he be which that hath taken upon him to imagine so false matier as is conteyned in a litle

---

[3] Marginal note: 'in whiche my stodie I have also be enformed that Loys the XIth king of Ffraunce, ffather to Charles which last died king of Ffraunce, wele percyvyng the Englisshmen were in division amonges themself as in parties betwix King Henry the VIth and the duke of York for the title of the corone'.

[4] This famous principle was derived from Aristotle's *Politics*, I, 2, 1253a2, and was frequently cited by Thomas Aquinas and other writers.

[5] Exodus 20: 16.

book or pamplet emprinted not without great and subtile and crafty fals conspiracion, divided into III principal partes, treating by the first part therof against the title of right which the noble kinges of Englond have and clayme to have to the coroune and totalite of the reame of Ffraunce, and by the secund part against the title and right which the said kinges of Englond to the particuler londes in Ffraunce as Normandie, Acquitaine and other, and by the III^{de} objecting and sayeng that the trewes had betwix the kinges of Ffraunce was broken by the Englisshmen in the yere of our lord God M^c IIII^C XLIX, may be sory if he be in lief or els he hath peyne elleswhere if it be to juge in abusing thoffice of his speche, and not observying the said commaundement insomoch as the matier by him fayned is so expressely against the trouth as is manifest expressed |3v| in diverse bookes of cronikes aswel compiled aswel by Ffrensshmen as diverse other regions. And for the trouth herof I shal principally grounde me a great part by the cronikes compiled by the somtyme bisshop of Burges in Latyn tonge and translated out of Latyn in to the Frenssh tonge by oon Maister John Golyn by the commaundement of Charles somtyme king of Ffraunce and Navarre, yonger sone of King Philip le Beale and brother to Quene Isabel wief of King Edward of Carnarvan, father and she mother to Edward the Thrid king of Englond and of Ffraunce. To which Edward the Third the right of the coroune and reame of Ffraunce and Navarre descended to the said king Edward the Thrid aftir the deth of the said King Charles, for that the same Charles decessed without issue. Which cronikes of the said bisshop of Burges maketh eend in the lief of the said Charles and afore the title of outher the corones of Ffraunce or Navarre descended to the said King Edward the Thridde.

|49v| By all which declaracions by wey of impugnementes or contradiction against the false, dampnable and diabolik fayned surmyses, objectures, alleggementes and demonstrances conteyned in the said Frenssh pamplet or booke compiled in to III principal partes sufficaently and truly notified and rehersed in this booke, it is sufficiently and notoirely shewed that the Ffrensshmen without right, title or cause reasonable have deforced the kinges of Englond, progenitoures to my said most dredde soverayn lord Henry by the grace of God now king of Englond and of Ffraunce and lord of Irelond, and yet hold, kepe and deforce from the same my soverayn lord |50r| not oonly the duchies of Normandie and Guyan & Gascoyn, and the counties of Ponthieu, Poytow, Angeo, Maine, Toreyn and ther appertenances and many other landes and seignories in the parties of beyond the see, but also the coroune and reame of Ffraunce with the

countie of Champaine, the dew and rightful enheritaunce of my said soverayn lord, bysides other seignories not rehersed nor touched in all this processe or demonstraunces which by wey of memores I purpose to write aftir the dend of this said matier.

And by this said declaration may appere the great, crafty, subtil and mischevous cautelles & entendementes of the Ffrensshmen contenewing the former use of the Ffrensshmen ever imaginyng, purposying and entending to oppresse, disturb and deforce their voisins and disherite them of their londes and seignories with so inordinat, covetise and arrogant myndes, not content with ther proper, but to be lordes and to have the soverainte of all the world if they might attayne therunto. And to color that their arrogant and covetous myndes and to come to atteyne to such soverainte they calle ther king the most christen prince and besides that use eloquent and dissimeled demonstraunce of wordes to fals purpose, hiding their fowle poison and intoxicat myndes wunder glose by the same, under color of trust to deceyve every other region. Ffor those Ffrensshmen never make or agree to leage, treatie or peas with eny prince but they wul have a subtil and a crafty and deceyvable sterting hole to take and leve at the pleasur, & that so craftely conveyed that they alwey have coloures of justification though it be never for false, as is notoirly declared in all histories and cronikes. Albe it as I am duly enformed by credible persones that Loys the Ffrenssh king, sone of the said Charles the VIIth, ded to be brought afore him all bookes of cronikes which were |50v|within his regalie and dominion and for that they were somoche declaring against him to defeat his title aswel of the coroune and reame of Ffraunce as of the duches of Normandie and Guyan and of the particuler seignories & londes aforerehersed and diverse other, afore the passage of King Edward the IIIIth, late king of Englond, into the parties of Ffraunce to have recovered his right of the premisses, the said Loys the Ffrenssh king caused all the said bookes of cronikes to be brent through out his dominions and caused the said boke conteynyng the fals imaginacions as is aforesaid divided into III principall partes and from thens hetherto cause in effect every yere to have new bookes to be made of cronikes of the reame of Ffraunce as by severall auctores to have ther fals and fayned imaginacions by processe of tyme to be of the more auctorite. Which newly compiled bookes of cronikes be emprinted by them and conveyed in to this reame of Englond and undir so fals pretence that the reders therof not have knowlege to the contrary may lightly be seducted and geve credens therunto, which in theffect of the causes conteyned in this boke be falsly imagined.

And concluding this werk which is not made to move or stere the king my soverayn lord to invade the reame of Ffraunce therin to move or mak werre for the premisses which if he ded shuld not be other but

therby shuld be moche confusion of humayn blode and theend therof
at the first begynnyng not knowen. But is writen oonly to enduce
his grace to take knowlege not oonly of his right to the contentes
in this same but also of the subtil and cautellous imaginacions of
his ennemyes the Ffrenshmen and also to consider the losses which
his noble progenitoures have susteyned by reason of the dyvysions
amonges the noble persones of this regne and to eschue lyk dangeres.
Quia omne regnum in se ipsum divisum desolabitur & domus supra &c.[6]

---

[6] Luke 11: 17: '*omne regnum in se ipsum divisum desolatur et domus supra domum cadet*'
(see p. 191).

APPENDIX II: MANUSCRIPT DESCRIPTIONS

A Paris, BNF MS français 5056

The manuscript contains *Pour ce que plusieurs* (fos 1r–30r),[1] together with *Audite celi* by Jean Juvénal des Ursins (fos 30v–51r)[2] and *L'instruction d'un jeune prince* by Ghillebert de Lannoy (fos 51v–67v).[3] For *Pour ce que plusieurs*, there is a heading, offering a four-line verse: 'A Treshault prince dessus tous renommé / Tres excellent de haulteur et puissance / Loys Onziesme de ce nom denommé / Trescrestien et noble roy de France'. The incipit is 'Pour ce que pleseurs a la relacion', and the explicit is 'feront au plaisir de Dieu, jusques a la fin. Amen'.

There are 73 vellum folios, measuring 315 mm by 245 mm, and the manuscript is ruled in a grid of 220 mm by 175 mm (37 lines) in red ink, with some light variations. The text appears to have been written by a single copyist in a neat gothic bastarda in brown ink. The capitals are presented in yellow and the chapter headings in the third text are in red; there is no rubrication and the citations are not marked. There is a six-line-high initial in brown and red, decorated in red and blue, at the start of the first text on folio 1r; four-line-high initials in the same style appear at the start of the texts on folios 30v and 51v, and a similar four-line-high initial at the start of the first chapter of the third treatise on folio 54r. A three-line-high initial in the same style marks the start of the third part of the first treatise on folio 22r. Two-line-high initials in red on brown and in blue on red appear throughout the text of the first treatise and in less copious quantities in that of the third. Folios B, C, 68, and 69 are blank, but folio 70r bears the inscription '*Sol[la] juvat virtus, cetera morte cadunt*' in a different early hand.

On folio 67v, there is a contemporary colophon: 'Ce livre est a Jehanne fille et seur de roy de France, duchesse de Bourbonnois et

---

[1] The transcription contained in this manuscript shares a number of distinctive elements with manuscripts CDMO.

[2] Jean Juvénal, I, pp. 94–281.

[3] Ghillebert de Lannoy, *Oeuvres de Ghillebert de Lannoy, voyageur, diplomate et moraliste*, ed. Charles Potvin (Louvain, 1878), pp. 327–431.

d'Auvergne, contesse de Clermont, de Forez et de l'Isle en Jordan et dame de Beaujeu, escript et perachevé en la ville d'Amboise le septiesme jour de fevrier l'an de grace mil CCCC soixante et neuf' and below the text is the signature 'Gontart'. Jeanne was the wife of Jean II, duke of Bourbon.

B   Paris, BNF MS français 5058

The manuscript contains *Pour ce que plusieurs* (fos 1r–64r).[4] The incipit is 'Pour ce que pluiseurs, a la relation' and the explicit reads 'lui et ses successeurs le feront pareillement jusquez a la fin. Amen.'

There are 73 vellum folios, measuring 310 mm by 220 mm. The text occupies an area of approximately 185 mm by 130 mm (28 lines) and the script is a neat gothic bastarda in dark brown ink, with rubrics in red. There are four- and two-line initials in gold together with red and blue, with white penwork, marking the major textual divisions; elsewhere there are one-line blue or gold letters with pen decoration in red and black. Folios B–D and 65–8 are blank. On fo. Av appears the Blois shelf mark, 'Des hystoires et livres n françoys Pul^to 3° / contre la muraille de vers la court / bloys'; there is also an early inscription, 'Justification de France contre l'Angleterre du temps du roy ['Charl. VIIe' crossed out] Loys XI', inserted in possibly a seventeenth-century hand. Folio 1r bears only the words, at the bottom of the recto, on the left, 'Priere Vaille'.

Folio 1r is adorned with a minature (figure 1) depicting two officials debating, while courtiers look on; the margins are filled with foliage and flowers, and also the shield of France directly below the picture. The minature almost certainly comes from the workshop of Guillaume Vrelant (1451–1481) in Bruges, and may be dated approximately to the 1460s. It is very similar to the minature in BR MSS 9469–9470 (K), which was also prepared by the workshop of Vrelant between 1460 and 1470.[5] A similar miniature may have appeared in Paris BNF MS nouvelle acquisition 6214 (F).

The manuscript originally belonged to Louis de Bruges, lord of Gruthuyse (d. 1492), and was incorporated by Louis XII into the library of Blois. It is not clear how the books came into the hands of Louis XII, though van Praet suggests that Jean de Bruges, son

---

[4] The transcription contained in this manuscript shares a number of distinctive features with manuscript F.

[5] See p. 282, n. 27.

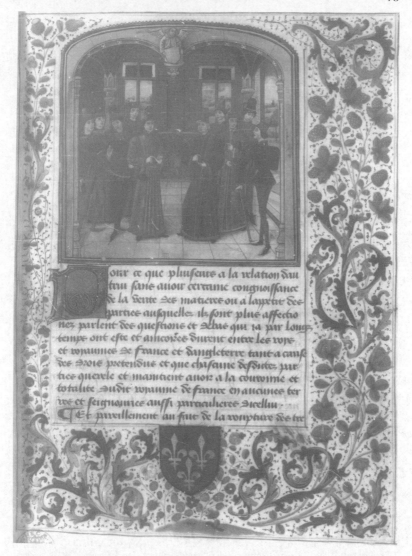

Figure 1 Paris, BNF MS français 5058, folio 1r

of Louis, might have paid homage to Louis XII by giving him the books.[6]

[6] Léopold Delisle, *Le Cabinet des manuscrits de la Bibliothèque Impériale* (4 vols, Paris, 1868–1891), I, pp. 140–144, and Joseph B.B. van Praet, *Recherches sur Louis de Bruges, seigneur de la Gruthuyse* (Paris, 1831), p. 82.

C   Paris, BNF MS français 12788

This manuscript contains *Pour ce que plusieurs* (fos 1r–42v),[7] along with
a continuation of the *Chroniques de Normandie* concerning the conquest
of Normandy by Henry V, 1414–1421 (fos 46r–92v);[8] *La Danse aux
aveugles*, a poem by Pierre Michaud (fos 93r–119v);[9] *L'Exclamation et regret
lamentable fait par le departement d'Estiennette de Paris, faicte a Tours, en l'annee
1468* by Jean Robertet, secretary of Jean II of Bourbon, comprising the
Response faicte par Guillaume Cosinot (fos 120v–124r) and a reply to this by
Robertet (fos 124v–126r);[10] an anonymous verse celebrating the glory
of wine (fos 127v–128r); an epitaph in verse for Philippe le Bon, duke
of Burgundy, attributed to Jean Molinet (fo. 128v);[11] the *Ballade sur la
révolte de Liége en 1467* by Jean Molinet, identified as the *Ballade faicte par
Maistre George Chastellain, serviteur de Monseiur de Bourgogne*, together with
the reply offered by Petit Dare of Rouen (fos 129r–129v).[12]

The incipit for *Pour ce que plusieurs* echoes the heading and incipit of
manuscript A: 'A treshault et excellent prince dessus tous renommé
tresexcellent de haulteur et puissance, Loys XIe de ce nom denomé,
tresnoble et tres crestien roy de France. Pour ce que plusieurs
a la relacion'. The explicit is 'Et comme ses predecesseurs l'ont
bien et justement conduicte jusques icy luy et ses sucesseurs feront
pareillement jusques en la fin. Amen. Explicit.'

There are 129 paper folios with watermarks, measuring 305 mm by
215 mm. There is a contemporary foliation which runs in the lower
left corner of versos: the first visible 'i' on modern pencil foliation 1,
and the last 'xli' on pencil foliation 39. Folio 'xii' is missing (between
folios 11v and 12r in the modern foliation),[13] so that the first quire now
contains just eleven folios, unlike the second, third, and fourth, which
all have twelve folios. The modern ink foliation does not recognise
this missing folio, and so is one behind at folio 'xli' (fo. 40); moreover
in the modern pencil foliation there are also two folios 20, and so it
is, in fact, two folios behind the contemporary foliation at folio 'xli'
(fo. 39). There are also two unfoliated leaves inserted between folios

---

[7] The transcription contained in this manuscript shares a number of distinctive
elements with manuscripts ADMO.

[8] Amédée Hellot (ed.), *Les Cronicques de Normandie (1223–1453)* (Rouen, 1881), pp. 15–70,
together with Peter S. Lewis, 'Note on the fifteenth-century *Grande Chronique de Normandie*',
Nottingham Medieval Studies, 46 (2002), pp. 185–198.

[9] Incomplete, missing the last eleven verses.

[10] Jean Robertet, *Oeuvres*, ed. Margaret Zsuppán (Geneva, 1970), pp. 33 and 148–158.

[11] Lewis Thorpe, 'Two epitaphs by Jean Molinet', *Scriptorium*, 8 (1954), pp. 284–286.

[12] Jean Molinet, *Les Faictz et dictz de Jean Molinet*, ed. Noël Dupire (3 vols, Paris, 1937–
1939), II, pp. 851–852. This work was a response to Chastellain's *Lyon rampant* (1467), as
discussed in Graeme Small, *George Chastellain and the Shaping of Valois Burgundy: political and
historical culture at court in the fifteenth century* (Woodbridge, 1997), p. 124.

[13] See p. 74, n. 119.

43 and 44, which we will identify as folios 43bis and 43ter. There is no ruling either for a text frame or lineation, and there is no sign of any pricking or of folding for the edges of the text, which occupies an area of around 220 mm by 140 mm and around 37–38 lines per folio. There are two or three scribes, the first from folios 1 to 43 (cursive bastarda), the second from folios 45 to 91 (bastarda), and the third, who is perhaps the same as the first (cursive bastarda), from folio 93 to the end. The ink is brown, the initials are in red over guide letters, and capitals are indicated in red. There is no decoration of the text, and note that there are more modern pen-trial doodles on the blank leaves. On folio 42v, the words 'fait l'an de grasse mil IIII^C LXXI le mois de juillet XVIIe' are written in red ink alongside and below the explicit to *Pour ce que plusieurs*; there are also two citations from *De officiis* of Cicero in a rather later hand on folio 16r in the margin above the text: '*Virtutis enin* [sic] *laus omnis in accione consistit*' (1, 6, § 19) and folio 43r, which, apart from pen trials, is blank except for the following citation: '*Nulla enin* [sic] *vite pars neque publicii neque privati neque forencibus ne que domesticis in rebus neque sy tecon agas quid, neque sy con altero contra has, vacare officio potest*' (I, 2, § 5). The watermark for the section containing *Pour ce que plusieurs* is of 'lettres soudées', as seen for example on fo. 43, and this reappears at the end of the manuscript.[14] In addition, there is a 'tête de boeuf', clearly visible on the blank half of fo. 44.[15]

The provenance of the manuscript is unknown, though the materials included in this collection suggest that it was composed for Guillaume Cousinot: each of the texts relates to his military, diplomatic, and literary activities. One of the pen trials on folio 91v reads: 'Robert le Grand demeurant a Rouen je vous'.

D   Paris, BNF MS français 15490

This manuscript contains *Pour ce que plusieurs* (fos 2r–3r),[16] *Pour vraye congnoissance avoir* (fos 4r–14v),[17] the *Memoire abregée grossement* (fos

---

[14] Charles-Moïse Briquet, *Les Filigranes* (2nd edn, Leipzig, 1923), no. 9749, and there are similar but not identical examples in Martin Wittek, *Inventaire des manuscrits de papier du XVe siècle conservés à la Bibliothèque Royale de Belgique et de leurs filigranes. III, manuscrits datés (1440–60)* (Brussels, 2004), nos 846 and 847.

[15] Briquet, *Les Filigranes*, no. 14239 and Wittek, *Inventaire des manuscrits de papier*, III, nos 1114–1140.

[16] The treatise ends abruptly at the equivalent of p. 55 above. This short transcription appears to share some distinctive elements with the version in manuscripts ACMO.

[17] This text also appears in BNF MS français 25159. See Kathleen Daly, '*Pour vraye congnoissance avoir*: historical culture and polemic in the French royal *Chambre des comptes* in Paris in the fifteenth century', *Nottingham Medieval Studies*, 49 (2005), pp. 142–189.

15r–38r),[18] and various treaties and diplomatic documents relating to negotiations between France and England between 1359 and 1369 (fos 43r–135v).[19] With regard to *Pour ce que plusieurs*, the incipit is '[P]ource que plusieurs ala relacion' and the explicit of the text, which ends abruptly in mid-column, is 'Philippe le Bel lequel fut roy, et l'autre Charles qui fut'.

There are 137 parchment folios, measuring 400 mm by 295 mm. The text is presented in two lined columns of 37 lines, covering an area approximately 255 mm by 72 mm each. The text would appear to be written in a number of different hands, all in a neat upright bastarda in dark brown ink. Rubrics are normally undistinguished, except in the table for the treaties where some red has been inserted to indicate chapters, though this is incomplete, and occasionally in the body of this section itself. Initials are not inserted, though space has been left for them: seven lines at the start of *Pour ce que plusieurs*; four lines for the beginning of *Pour vraye congnoissance avoir*; three lines at the start of the *Memoire abregée grossement* and two lines for the start of sections of *Pour ce que plusieurs* and *Pour vraye congnoissance avoir*. Space is left in fos 2r, 4r, and 45v for a miniature. From fo. 123v onwards, there are marginal notes in red ink, summarizing the sections of the treaties. The binding may be contemporary. 'Ancienne histoire contenant les querelles d'entres les Roys de France et d'Angleterre' is inscribed on folio 1r.

The provenance of the manuscript is unknown, though the treatise *Pour vraye congnoissance avoir* was composed in 1471 by an officer of the *Chambre des Comptes*, almost certainly Louis le Blanc, and so provides a *terminus antequam*. Indeed, this incomplete manuscript may well have served as Le Blanc's working manuscript.[20]

F   Paris, BNF MS nouvelle acquisition française 6214

This manuscript contains *Pour ce que plusieurs* (fos 1r–49v) and the *Vraie cronicque d'Escoce* (fos 50r–62r). With regard to *Pour ce que plusieurs*, the heading reads 'Cy commence le traittié des droits que le Roi Charles VIIe du nom a a la couronne et a la totalité du royaume de France et de la complainte que les Anglois font touchant la roupture des treves'.

---

[18] This dossier also appears in BR MS 10306–10307, BNF MS nouvelle acquisition française 6215, BNF MS Dupuy 306, and Bibliothèque de l'Arsenal MS 2450. See Montreuil, III, pp. 52–110.
[19] These documents are presented out of order and should be read as 43–66, 123–135, 109–122, and 67–108 (some leaves missing).
[20] Kathleen Daly, '*Pour vraye congnoissance avoir*', pp. 142–189.

The incipit reads 'Pour entrer esdictes matieres, affin que mieulx et clerement elles puissent estre entenduez, semble estre neccessaire declarier...',[21] and the explicit is 'feront pareillement jusquez a la fin. Amen.'

There are 64 vellum folios, measuring 300 mm by 225 mm. The first folio is missing, though this has been disguised by the addition of a rubric to the second folio, now fo. 1r. The folios are ruled in a grid of red ink, covering an area of 190 mm by 134 mm (31 lines). The script is a neat upright bastarda in dark brown ink; rubrics for the titles of the texts are red, in the same style. Two-, four- and five-line initials in gold, red, and blue, with white penwork mark the major textual divisions, and elsewhere there are one-line blue or gold letters with pen decoration in red and black. The script and the initials are almost identical to Paris, BNF MS français 5058 (B) and Brussels, BR MSS 9469–9470 (K), which adds strength to the view that the first folio was removed because it contained a minature.

The original owner of this manuscript, dating from the second half of the fifteenth century, is unknown. The coat of arms on fo. 62r seems to be that of the Gilliers family, but this is in fact a forgery according to Léopold Delisle and François Avril.[22]

H Paris, BNF MS nouvelle acquisition française 20962

This manuscript contains *Pour ce que plusieurs* (fos 4r–53v) and the *Vraie cronicque d'Escoce* (fos 53v–65v).

For *Pour ce que plusieurs*, the heading reads 'Cy ensuit le livre fait et compose de la querelle que de long temps a esté et est entre France et Angleterre. Et premier traicte de la demande que les Anglois font a la couronne et totalité du royaulme de France disans a tiltre heredital a eulx competer et apartenir comme cy aprés sera declairé en trois parties. *Item* aprés parle des croniques du royaulme d'Escoce'. The incipit is 'Pour respondre a pluseurs questions et demandes que les Anglois font tant au fait de la couronne de France et de la totalité du royaulme, comme de pluseurs terres et seignouries particulieres dudit royaulme. Et aussi de ce qu'ilz se complaingnent de la roupture des treves l'an mil IIII^C XLIX soubs confiance desquelles ilz dient avoir perdu et leur avoir esté osté par le feu roy Charles que Dieu pardonist les duchez de Normandye et de Guienne et aultres terres et seignouries qu'ilz tenoient es contez de Maine de Ponthieu et du

---

[21] See p. 54, n. 10.

[22] Kathleen Daly, 'The *Vraie cronicque d'Escoce* and Franco-Scottish diplomacy: an historical work by John Ireland?', *Nottingham Medieval Studies*, 35 (1991), p. 133.

Perche et es pays de France et [Beaumoisni] requerant prealablment et avant entendre a aultre appointement estre restituez en leur possession dont a tort et sans cause et contre les promesses et convenences faites entre les parties ilz dient avoir est despouilliez. Semble avant pouvoir peurement respondre aux choses dessusdites qu'il est de necessité de premierment entrendre les drois tiltres'.[23] The explicit is 'Fin de la tierce et derniere partie de ce present traictié'.

There are 70 vellum folios, measuring 285 mm by 200 mm. Folios 62 and 64 have been misplaced and should be read in reverse order. Each folio is ruled in a grid approximately 180 mm by 125 mm (36 lines). The script is neat and the ink is dark brown, with rubrics in blue and red/mauve. The initials are alternating gold and blue, with a six-line initial and a minature at the start of the manuscript, five-line initials marking major textual divisions in the first text, and a five-line initial introducing the *Vraie cronicque*; minor textual divisions in both texts are marked by two-line initials. The stamped leather binding may be contemporary with the manuscript. Marginalia are not contemporary.

The minature (figure 2), occupying twenty-one lines, shows two officials debating before an audience of five courtiers and the kings of France and England. This minature is much finer than those in BR MSS 9469–9470 (K) and Bibliothèque Nationale MS Français 5058 (B), and is from the Loire valley, almost certainly produced during the 1460s by Jean Roland III. The arms of Jacques d'Armagnac, duke of Nemours, are painted on the wall of the chamber above the two kings in the minature. He was judged by an arrêt on 10 July 1477, and lost all his personal possessions. His signature, 'JAQUES', together with the words 'pour Carlat' have been erased on fo. 66r; the volume was thus destined for the library of the château of Carlat.[24] Thus the manuscript dates to between 1464 and 1477.

J   Paris, Bibliothèque de l'Arsenal MS 3434

This manuscript contains an anonymous poem beginning '*De deux grans Roys le triumphe et puissance / C'est ferme accord, qui donne congnoissance*'

---

[23] See p. 54, n. 11.
[24] The artist is said to follow the style of the Master of the Harley Froissart (BL MS Harley 4379–4380) in Susan A. Blackman, 'The manuscripts and patronage of Jacques d'Armagnac, duke of Nemours (1433–1477)' (2 vols, PhD thesis, University of Pittsburgh, PA, 1993), II, pp. 271 and 418–420. Nemours's library is also discussed in Delisle, *Le Cabinet des manuscrits de la Bibliothèque Impériale*, I, pp. 86–91, though this manuscript is not mentioned.

Figure 2 Paris, BNF MS nouvelle acquisition française 20962, folio 4r

(fo. 2r), a list of the seven servants of Louis, duke of Orléans, who fought against seven Englishmen in 1401 (fo. 2v),[25] and *Pour ce que*

[25] The combat was reported in Louis Bellaguet (ed.), *Chronique du Religieux de Saint-Denis concernant le règne de Charles VI, de 1380 à 1422* (6 vols, Paris, 1839–1852), III, pp. 30–34.

plusieurs (fos 3r–79r). For *Pour ce que plusieurs*, the incipit reads 'Pour ce que plusieurs a la relacion' and the explicit is '..ledit roy d'Angleterre n'eust pas gardé sa promesse'.[26]

There are 78 parchment folios, plus two modern folios at the beginning and end, both included within the modern foliation; the folios measure 245 mm by 175 mm. A page has been removed between folios 68 and 69, and the text stops abruptly on fo. 79r, omitting a section equivalent to between eight and ten folios. The folios containing the text are ruled in a grid measuring 165 mm by 120 mm (26 lines). On a number of folios, an area of around 40 mm in depth has been removed; these extracts rarely reach to the inside margin, suggesting that the pieces were removed after binding, perhaps to remove some of the unrelated marginalia written in a later, childish hand. The script is a neat bastarda, in brown ink, and each paragraph begins with a two-line initial, alternating in red and white, with tiny holes cut out on the outside edges; the first initial of the treatise occupies eight lines. At the top of the first (modern) folio, are the words '79 feuillets Mai 1884', and in the same hand on the verso, 'histoire N°. 3591 (from the library of M. de Paulmy). *Traité sur les differends entres les rois de France et d'Angleterre et sur le fait de la rupture de 1449.*' Throughout the text there are marginalia, most of which do not relate to the text and are not contemporary.

The original owner of this manuscript, dating from the second half of the fifteenth century, is unknown.

K   Brussels, BR MS 9469–9470

This manuscript contains *Pour ce que plusieurs* (fos 1r–63r) and the *Vraie cronicque d'Escoce* (fos 64r–78r). For *Pour ce que plusieurs*, the incipit is 'Pource que pluiseurs a la relation' and the explicit is 'feront pareillement jusques a la fin. Amen.'

There are 78 vellum folios with three unfoliated leaves at the beginning and four at the end. The folios measure 310 mm by 220 mm. The script is a regular gothic bastarda, with occasional decorative pen cadeaux; brown ink with red initials. Additional rubrics introduce the second and third parts of *Pour ce que plusieurs*, the Quitclaim of Canterbury, and other important textual breaks. Three-line initials accompany a minature on fo. 1r and introduce the *Vraie cronicque*, while four-line initials mark the major divisions in *Pour ce que plusieurs*,

---

[26] The treatise ends abruptly at the equivalent of p. 126 above, thereby omitting the final section on the responsibility for the breach of the truce in 1449.

Figure 3 Brussels, BR MS 9469–9470, folio 1r

and two-line initials mark minor divisions in both texts. There is gold edging.

On the first folio, there is a miniature (figure 3) surrounded by acanthus. It depicts two officials debating while courtiers look on, and is clearly by the same artist as that in BNF MS français 5058 (B), from the workshops of Guillaume Vrelant (1451–1481) in Bruges. Dogaer has argued that the work of the artist and his workshop cannot be clearly distinguished, but Bousmanne states that it follows the style and technique of an individual that he calls the Master of the *Vraie cronicque d'Escoce*, to whom he also attributes twenty-seven other manuscripts continuing up until 1484–1486, ten years after the death of Vrelant. He also states that this was probably not ordered by the duke himself.[27] Neither Dogaer nor Bousmanne are aware of the parallel example in B.

The texts were copied together between 1464 and 1467 to form this manuscript. The Burgundian ducal inventory, compiled after the death of Philippe le Bon in 1467, gives the first words of the second and last folios of this manuscript, describing it as 'Ung autre volume couvert de cuyr noir a deux claons et cinq boutons de leton sur chascun coste histoire et intitulé Cronicque de France començant ou second feuillet conformé en raison naturelle et finissant au derrenier l'an M CCCC LX III environ la Toussains'. It was also cited in the inventory of the ducal library in 1487.[28] The manuscript was later owned by Louis XV, king of France, whose arms appear on the binding.

L   Brussels, BR MS 12192–12194

This manuscript contains the *Chronique du Pseudo-Turpin* (1206–1207) with an abridgement of the *Descriptio* interpolated and dedicated to Michel III de Harnes who died in 1231 (fos 1r–31r),[29] the *Chronique de la traïson et mort de Richart II* (fos 33r–78v)[30] and *Pour ce que plusieurs* (fos 80r–133r).

For *Pour ce que plusieurs*, the heading is almost the same as that in manuscript N: 'Cy sensieut la declaracion du droit que les Anglois pretendent ou royaume de France'. The incipit is 'Pour ce que pluseurs

[27] Georges Dogaer, *Flemish Miniature Painting in the Fifteenth and Sixteenth Centuries* (Amsterdam, 1987), pp. 99–105, and Bernard Bousmanne, *Item a Guillaume Wyelant aussi enlumineur: Willem Vrelant, un aspect de l'enluminure dans les Pays-Bas méridionaux sous le mécenat des ducs de Bourgogne Philippe le Bon et Charles le Téméraire* (Turnhout, 1997), pp. 57–58 and 230. Also see Bernard Bousmanne (ed.), *Guillaume Wielant ou Willem Vrelant, miniaturiste à la cour de Bourgogne au XVe siècle* (Brussels, 1997), pp. 20–21 and 56.

[28] Jean B.J. Barrois (ed.), *Bibliothèque protypographique, ou librairies des fils du roi Jean, Charles V, Jean de Berri, Philippe de Bourgogne et les siens* (Paris, 1830), pp. 208, 275, and 316.

[29] Brian Woledge and H.P. Clive (eds), *Repertoire des plus anciens textes en prose française depuis 842 jusqu'aux premières années du XIIIe siècle* (Geneva, 1964), pp. 101–102, and Brian Woledge (ed.), *Bibliographie des romans et nouvelles en prose française antérieurs à 1500. Supplément 1954–1973* (Geneva, 1975), pp. 86–87.

[30] Benjamin Williams (ed.), *Chronicque de la traïson et mort de Richart Deux roy dEngleterre* (London, 1846).

a la relacion' and the explicit is 'Explicit le traicté du droit que les Englois pretendent ou royaume de France en aucunes terres et segnouries & amen'.

There are 133 parchment folios measuring 290 mm by 200 mm, with two blank, unfoliated leaves at the beginning and two more at the end. The manuscript is ruled in an area averaging 180 mm by 140 mm (30 lines per page). The manuscript was written by one scribe in a gothic bastarda, in brown ink, with red for capitals, headings, and the underlining of Latin. There are decorated initials, with two-line capitals in red and there is a nine-line 'I' in the margin of fo. 108v and a seven-line 'I' in the margin of fo. 33. There are watermarks in seven of the quires, depicting a quartered shield with the arms of France (the fleurs-de-lis) in the first and fourth quadrants, and those of the Dauphin in the second and third; this watermark dates to between 1461 and 1473.[31]

The provenance of this manuscript is unknown.

M   Lille, Bibliothèque Municipale MS 322[32]

This manuscript contains the treaty of Bretigny (fos 1r–11r); the treaty of Troyes (fos 13r–18r); an incomplete copy of *Pour ce que plusieurs* (fos 19r–32r); a legal *casus* relating to primogeniture and the royal succession (fos 32v–42r); *Audite celi* by Jean Juvénal des Ursins (fos 43r–69v);[33] *Fluxo biennnale spacio* (fos 71r–82v);[34] *De quadam puella*, attributed to Jean Gerson (fos 82v–85v);[35] *De mirabili victoria*, attributed to Jean Gerson (fos 85v–87v);[36] an incomplete copy of the *Abregé des chroniques*,

[31] Alan Stevenson (ed.), *Les Filigranes: dictionnaire historique des marques de papier dès leur apparition vers 1282 jusqu'en 1600* (The New Briquet Jubilee edition, Amsterdam, 1968), no. 1654, which cites manuscripts from Sens (1479), Bellebranche (Sarthe, 1479), Bruges (1494), and Laon (1480–1484); Martin Wittek, *Inventaire des manuscrits de papier. III, manuscrits datés (1461–80)* (Brussels, 2005), nos 1340–1347, corresponding to Brussels BR MS 3533–3539, fos 1–10.

[32] Confusingly, this manuscript was identified as MS 539 in the *Catalogue général des manuscrits des Bibliothèques publiques de France* (55 vols, Paris, 1886–1933), XXVI.

[33] Jean Juvénal, I, pp. 94–281.

[34] Nicole Pons (ed.), *L'Honneur de la couronne de France: quatre libelles contre les Anglais (vers 1418–vers 1429)* (Paris, 1990), pp. 139–201.

[35] Jules-Etienne-Joseph Quicherat (ed.), *Procès de condamnation et de réhabilitation de Jeanne d'Arc dite la Pucelle* (5 vols, Paris, 1841–1849), III, pp. 411–421. See Georges Peyronnet, 'Gerson, Charles VII et Jeanne d'Arc: la propagande au service de la guerre', *Revue d'histoire ecclésiastique*, 84 (1989), pp. 334–370, and Dyan Elliott, 'Seeing double: Jean Gerson, the discernment of spirits, and Joan of Arc', *American Historical Review*, 107 (2001), pp. 26–54.

[36] Pierre Duparc (ed.), *Procès en nullité de la condamnation de Jeanne d'Arc* (5 vols, Paris 1977–1989), II, pp. 34–39, together with the secondary references in the previous note.

by Noël de Fribois (fos 89r–112r);[37] and a report of the battle of Nancy (fos 113r–115r).

With regard to *Pour ce que plusieurs*, the incipit reads 'Pour ce que plusieurs a la relacion' and the explicit is 'Et aprés la mort du Roy Charles VI^c son pere fut tenu'.[38]

There are 116 paper folios, measuring 270 mm by 200 mm. The folios are generally unruled (with the exceptions of the first quire, fos 1–12) and the number of lines varies between 36 and 39. The manuscript was written by a single copyist in an irregular hand, in brown ink; the capitals are marked by light lines in yellow ink, citations are underlined in brown, and the chapter titles, the explicits, the names of the protagonists in the *Fluxo biennale spacio*, and the marginal notes are underlined in red ink. There are no marginal decorations or illustrations, and the infrequent marginal annotations are post-medieval.

The manuscript was written after 1488. The provenance is unknown before the manuscript entered the possession of the cathedral chapter of St Pierre at Lille. It then passed to the Bibliothèque de Lille after the suppression of religious establishments during the Revolution.

N   Vienna, Österreichische Nationalbibliothek 3392[39]

This manuscript contains *L'État de la maison du duc Charles de Bourgogne dit le Hardy*, by Olivier de La Marche (fos 1r–63r);[40] *Sensieut ce qui est ordonne et conclud pour amener le corps de monseigneur le duc Philippe de Bourgogne et Madame Ysabeau sa femme* (fos 67r–76r); the *Controversie de noblesse*, translated by Jean Miélot from the *Declamatio de nobilitate inter Scipionem et Flaminium* by Buonaccorso de Montemagno (fos 77r–106r);[41] the *Débat de honneur*, translated by Jean Miélot from the Latin *Opusculum de presidencia* by Giovanni Aurispa (fos 106v–115r);[42] various tracts on chivalric, heraldic, and institutional matters, commencing with

[37] Noël de Fribois, *Abregé des croniques de France*, ed. Kathleen Daly (Paris, 2006).

[38] The treatise ends abruptly at the equivalent of p. 83 above. The transcription contained in this manuscript shares a number of distinctive elements with manuscripts ACDO.

[39] I have only consulted the microfilm of this manuscript.

[40] Olivier de La Marche, *Mémoires d'Olivier de La Marche, maître d'hôtel et capitaine des gardes de Charles le Téméraire*, ed. Henri Beaune and Jules d'Abraumont (4 vols, Paris, 1883–1888), IV, pp. 26–45.

[41] Arjo Vanderjagt (ed.), *Qui sa vertu anoblist: the concepts of 'noblesse' and 'chose publicque' in Burgundian political thought* (Groningen, 1981), pp. 181–224.

[42] *Ibid.*, pp. 151–180.

Comment on doibt faire ung nouvel empereur (fos 115r–126r);[43] the *Breviarium belli trojani* in verse (fos 126v–131r); *Pour ce que plusieurs* (fos 133r–212r); the *Chronique de la traïson et mort de Richart II* (fos 213r–282r);[44] and a fragment entitled *Quomodo processum sit in Philippo Pulchro baptizando* (fo. 282v).

For *Pour ce que plusieurs*, the heading echoes that in L, reading 'Cy sensieut la declaracion du droit que les Anglois pretendent a la couronne et au royaume de France'. The incipit is 'Pour ce que pluseurs a la relacion' and the explicit is 'Explicit le debat de France et d'Angleterre'.

The manuscript contains 282 paper folios, measuring 280 mm by 195 mm. The folios are unruled and the writing area varies in size but is usually 170 mm by 110 mm with around 26 lines of text. The manuscript was mainly written by one principal in a gothic bastarda, with two-line initials and a five-line initial at the start of *Pour ce que plusieurs*; a prayer at the beginning of the manuscript (fos IIv–IIIv) and the fragment at the end of the manuscript (fo. 282v) are written in different hands.

The provenance of the manuscript is unknown but it dates from the late-fifteenth or early sixteenth century.

O Città del Vaticano, Biblioteca Apostolica Vaticana MS Reginensi Latini 1933[45]

This manuscript contains *Pour ce que plusieurs* (fos 1r–88v).[46] The incipit is 'Pource que plusieurs ala relacion' and the explicit is 'Explicit le traictié d'entre les roys de France et d'Angleterre comme les filles ne pevent succeder ala couronne de France'.

The manuscript of 88 folios was written by a single scribe in a neat gothic bastarda. There is a three-line initial at the beginning of the treatise, on fo. 1r, and a two-line initial on fo. 33v, marking the beginning of the second section. There are marginal notes in the same hand on fos 34r, 34v, 40r, 41v, 42r, 43r, 49r, 49v, and 51r. On the first folio, there is a Greek inscription in a different hand, οἱς ἀλυχῶ, λίαν ἐυλυχῶ; at the bottom of the same folio is a coat of arms. On the final folio of the text, 88v, alongside the explicit, is written in a different hand, 'Ce livre est a Jehan Budé conseillier du roy et

[43] *Ibid.*, pp. 276–282.
[44] See L.
[45] I have only consulted the microfilm of this manuscript.
[46] The transcription contained in this manuscript shares a number of distinctive elements with manuscripts CDMO.

audencier de France, fait le XXIe de Decembre MCCCIIII^{XX} VI',
together with the signature of Jean Budé.[47]

Jean Budé (d. 1502) was a *notaire et secrétaire* to Louis XI and Charles
VIII, and became *audiencier* of France on the 16 August 1474, a post
that was confirmed in September 1483. He was a great bibliophile
and acquired an impressive library, of which fifty-two volumes are
conserved in French libraries.[48]

P   Paris, Bibliothèque Mazarine MS 2031

This manuscript contains *Pour ce que plusieurs* (fos 1r–53r). The incipit
is 'Pour ce que plusieurs a la relation' and the explicit reads 'feront
pareillement jusquez a la fin'.

There are 53 parchment folios and two additional folios at
the beginning and the end, measuring 300 mm by 220 mm. The
handwriting is very untidy and averages about 30 lines per page,
in an area of around 150 mm by 220 mm. The ink is brown, with
two-line initials in red at the start of each paragraph, starting from fo.
5r. On the first folio, the first initial is in blue ink, and has a caricature
in profile, facing to the right, as the curve of the letter P. The words
'La Loy Salicque' have been inscribed at the top of the first unfoliated
page.

The origin of this manuscript, dating from the second half of the
fifteenth century, is unknown.

Q   London, BL MS Additional 36541

This manuscript contains the *Chronique de la traïson et mort de Richart II* (fos
2r–59r)[49] and *Pour ce que plusieurs* (fos 60r–126v).[50] For *Pour ce que plusieurs*,
the heading reads 'Le traictié des questions et debatz qui ont esté et
font entre les roys et royaulmes de France et d'Engleterre, lequel livre
est devisé en III partie, dont la premiere parle des questions qui font
entre ledit deux rois, la seconde partie parle du droit et des quereles
que les Anglois font en aulcunes terres et seignories particulieres du
royaume de Franche, la tierce partie parle de la complaincte que les
Anglois font de la roupture des treves qui fit l'an de grace mil CCCC

---

[47] Budé's signature also appears in BNF MS 26431, p. 12, dated 20 January 1495.

[48] André Lapeyre and Rémy Scheurer, *Les Notaires et secrétaires du roi sous les règnes de Louis
XI, Charles VIII et Louis XII (1461–1515): notices personelles et généalogiques* (Paris, 1978), pp. 70–71.

[49] See L.

[50] Folio 85r is blank.

et quarante neuf par le fu roy Charle le VIIe'. The incipit is 'Pour ce que pluisseurs a la relacion' and the explicit is 'feront pareillement jusques a la fin'.

There are 126 foliated paper pages, measuring 265 mm by 195 mm. There are two unfoliated, blank pages at the beginning of the text (including the end paper attached to the binding), two unfoliated, ruled pages between the texts, and six unfoliated pages at the end, of which the first three are ruled, and the last is attached to the binding. The manuscript is ruled in an area averaging 170 mm by 120 mm, and is the work of a single copyist in a neat, uniform bastarda in brown ink. There is no underlining, but the rubrics introducing the two texts, and the second and third sections of *Pour ce que plusieurs*, are in red ink (fos 2r, 60r, 85v, and 110v). Capitals are in alternating red, green, and blue ink, and occupy two lines; the first capital of each text, and those at the beginning of the second and third sections of *Pour ce que plusieurs*, are in red ink and occupy five (fos 2r and 60r), four (fo. 110v), or three lines (fo. 85v). There are no marginalia or illuminations; at the top of the first endpaper is written 'from the library of Robert Steele // Wandsworth Common', and at the bottom of the second endpaper, 'purchased at Sothebys // Cat 1118 // 6 Dec. 1900'. After the last foliated page (126v), is inscribed '126ff, ROJ January 1900 // Examined by PB'.

The provenance of this fifteenth-century manuscript is unknown. It was purchased by Sir Thomas Phillipps at Sotheby's on 28 June 1861 and subsequently identified as Phillipps MS 15718. It was bought by the British Museum in 1900.

T London, College of Arms MS Arundel 39

This manuscript contains *A declaracion of the trew and dewe title of Henry VIII* (fos 1r–52v).

There are 52 paper folios, measuring 280 mm by 180 mm. The text appears in an unruled area of around 225 mm by 135 mm (34 lines). There are folios missing between fos 10v and 11r, 14v and 15r, and 25v and 26r, and a corner is missing from fo. 11. A large passage on fo. 14v has been crossed out and replaced by two inserted folios, 13 and 14, which are read in reverse order and are also severely damaged; another folio has been inserted between fos 27 and 29. There are also numerous marginal insertions, often relacing or extending material in the main text: see, for example, fos 10r, 12r, 14v, 15r, 18r, 19v, 22v, 23r, 27v, 39v, 45v, 46r, and 46v. The text appears to have been written by the author in a uniform fashion in brown ink, using the same secretary hand as manuscript W.[51] The watermarks depict a shield with the fleurs-de-lis, and above the shield is a cross with a small circle to the right, and stems of grass to the left. The extensive alterations made to the text suggest that this is a rough draft prepared by the author before writing manuscript W. On fo. 1r is an inscription, 'Roberti Hare, 1563'.[52]

W London, BL MS Additional 48005

This manuscript contains extracts from Roger of Howden's *Chronica*, partly in English translation (fos 1–4); *A declaracion of the trewe and dewe title of Henry VIII* (fos 6–97), a fragment of the pamphlet *Of the title of the house of York*, by Sir John Fortescue (fos 97a–97d);[53] a Latin paraphrase by Nicholas Upton (d. 1457) of Henry V's ordinances of Mantes, 1419 (fos 100–103b);[54] a writ issued on 14 July 1420 to the sheriffs to proclaim the treaty of Troyes, with the text of the treaty in English (fos 105–107b); a grant by King Stephen to Winchester Cathedral, dated Easter 1136 (fos 110–110b); names of magnates associated with the Constitutions of Clarendon, 1164, Magna Carta, 1215, and Magna Carta, 1225 (fos 111b, 112–113); Henry III's summons to the feudal host to assemble for the Welsh war on 1 August 1260 (fos 114–115b); Henry III's summons of the magnates to council at London on 13 December 1264 (fos 116–117); Edward I's summons to Edmund, Earl of Lancaster, to the war against Llewellyn, Prince of Wales, dated 12 December 1276 (fos 118–119); and summonses to Parliament, from 1295 to 1483 (fos 120–224).

There are 238 paper folios measuring 290 mm by 210 mm, together with five unfoliated pages at the beginning and additional pages inserted at folios 46*, 97(a)–97(d), 224*, and 224**. The six quires containing extracts from Roger of Howden and *A declaracion of the trewe and dewe title of Henry VIII* appear to form a discrete component in the

---

[51] The distinctive features of this hand are the shape of upper-case letters such as 'K', 'L', and 'R', the scythe-blade shape of 'T' or 'J', a 6-shaped final 's' with a curl at the top of the upsweeping finishing stroke, an 'e' with a hook upwards as a finish to the crossbar, an upper-case 'C' whose crossbar at the top does not always meet the curve of the left side of the letter, and a horned regular (not rounded secretary) form of 'e'.

[52] Andrew G. Watson, 'Robert Hare's books', in Anthony S.G. Edwards, Vincent Gillespie, and Ralph Hanna (eds), *The English Medieval Book: studies in memory of Jeremy Griffiths* (London, 2000), pp. 209–232, and Elisabeth Leedham-Green, 'Hare, Robert (c.1530–1611)', in *Oxford Dictionary of National Biography* (Oxford, 2004). See also p. 47 above.

[53] Margaret L. Kekewich, ' "Thou shalt be under the power of the man": Sir John Fortescue and the Yorkist succession', *Nottingham Medieval Studies*, 43 (1998), pp. 193–194 and 224–229.

[54] Francis P. Barnard (ed.), *The Essential Portions of Nicholas Upton's De Studio Militari before 1446. Translated by John Blount* (Oxford, 1931), pp. 49–58 and p. 60n.

manuscript. They have a writing area of 180 mm by 115 mm (30 lines) and are written in the same late-fifteenth-century secretary hand as manuscript T, with Latin quotations and the title page on fo. 6r written in a gothic script by the same scribe; the remainder of the manuscript generally has late-sixteenth- and seventeenth-century scripts, except for the fragments of a pamphlet written by Sir John Fortescue, inserted immediately after *A declaracion of the trewe and dewe title of Henry VIII*.[55] The quires containing extracts from Roger of Howden and *A declaracion of the trewe and dewe title of Henry VIII* also share the same watermark, a hand with the thumb to the right, pointing up towards a flower with five petals. In contrast, both the loose table of contents in a seventeenth-century hand and the eight unfoliated pages at the beginning have a watermark of a hunting dog wearing a collar above the word 'Feniwell', which also appears later in the manuscript, for example at fos 109, 119, 131, and 156. The binding is vellum with leather ties, and the spine has the number '6' and a very faint title in a seventeenth-century hand: '*Titulum ad Franciam*. Sumonitiones ad Parliamentum'.

This was originally manuscript 6 of the Yelverton collection of correspondence and papers of Robert Beale, Clerk of the Council (d. 1601). A seventeenth-century copy of *A declaracion of the trewe and dewe title of Henry VIII* and two other items from this manuscript appear in another Yelverton manuscript, 86, now BL MS Additional 48079, fos 30r–125v.[56]

Seventeenth-century manuscripts

Paris, BNF MS français 7144 contains *Pour ce que plusieurs*; *La vraie chronique d'Escoce*; a report on negotiations for the marriage of François I and the daughter of the king of England in 1525, written by Claude Dodieu, counsellor in the Parlement of Paris; a report of a conference between French and English diplomats regarding claims to the throne and the restitution of Boulogne; a treaty of alliance between Charles IX and Elizabeth I, dated 19 April 1572.

Paris, BNF MS français 17969 contains *Pour ce que plusieurs*.

Paris, BNF MS français 23364 contains *Pour ce que plusieurs* and a report of the commissioners negotiating in 1560 between François

---

[55] These are written in a late-fifteenth-century hand, different from the scribe of *A declaracion of the trewe and dewe title of Henry VIII*: see Kekewich, p. 193n.

[56] There are often extremely faint marks above words in W that may be the notational marks of the scribe of BL MS Additional 48079, highlighting words that he was unsure about.

II and Philip II regarding the abbey of Saint-Jean-au-Mont, near to Thérouanne.

Paris, BNF MS nouvelle acquisition française 7006 contains *Tres crestien, tres hault, tres puissant roy* by Jean Juvénal des Ursins and *Pour ce que plusieurs*.

Paris, Bibliothèque Sainte-Geneviève MS 794 contains *Tres crestien, tres hault, tres puissant roy* by Jean Juvénal des Ursins and *Pour ce que plusieurs*.

London, BL MS Additional 48079 (previously Yelverton MS 86) contains miscellaneous diplomatic and political papers, including an account of court expenses of the Sultan of Turkey written by William Harborne, ambassador at Constantinople, 1582; the *Declaracion upon certayn wrytinges* by Sir John Fortescue; *A declaracion of the trewe and dewe title of Henry VIII*; a writ issued on 14 July 1420 to the sheriffs to proclaim the treaty of Troyes, with the treaty in English; the Latin paraphrase by Nicholas Upton of Henry V's 1419 ordinances of Mantes; letters exchanged by Edward III and Pope Benedict XII in 1338 and 1339; a statement of Edward III's claim to the French throne, written in the sixteenth century.

APPENDIX III: A LOST MANUSCRIPT OF
POUR CE QUE PLUSIEURS

In 1465, Antoine de Castelnau, lord of Lau, was arrested following his involvement in the League of the Public Weal. Gaston IV de Foix-Béarn was the only great lord in the Midi to remain loyal to King Louis XI, and one of his rewards was Castelnau's Gascon fortress of Villandraut. Two chests full of treasure were taken from there to the castle of Nolibos at Mont-de-Marsan where, on 15 and 16 November 1467, a notarized inventory of their contents was drawn up by Bernard de La Chapelle, commissioner of Louis XI, along with Foix's representatives, Bernard de Béarn and Peyroton de Trescentz.[1]

This inventory listed forty-one books, all apparently in French, of which nineteen were illuminated. The collection included a Bible, French translations of works by Boethius and Boccaccio, the *Songe du vergier*, and the *Roman de la rose*. Many of the works were histories, including translations of Titus Livy, presumably by Pierre Bersuire, and of Valerius Maximus by Simon de Hesdin and Nicolas de Gonesse, as well as the *Chroniques* of Froissart and 'les ystoires de France', almost certainly the *Grandes chroniques*. The nineteenth item listed was: '*Item, ung autre livre couverture roge ferré escript en parchemin qui parle des debatz d'Angleterre et de France, commance Pour ce que plusieurs finist jusques à la fin.*' Tucoo-Chala speculated that this was *Le Débat des hérauts d'armes de France et d'Angleterre*, but there can be no doubt whatsoever that it was in fact Guillaume Cousinot's treatise, *Pour ce que plusieurs*.

There is no indication of where Castelnau obtained the books listed in the inventory. He presumably acquired *Pour ce que plusieurs* during his brief period of service at the court before his fall from grace. Castelnau had been a companion and close familiar of Louis in the Dauphiné

---

[1] The document survives in a later copy, alongside the transcription of an act dated 8 August 1587 and Louis XI's reinstatement of Castelnau on 27 February 1472: Pierre Tucoo-Chala, 'Un inventaire du trésor du château de Villandraut en 1467', *De Nérac à Condom. Fédération historique du Sud-Ouest. Actes du XXXVe congrès d'études régionales tenu à Condom, Flaran et Nérac, les 17, 18 et 19 juin 1983* (Agen, 1987), pp. 111–123. I am extremely grateful to Godfried Croenen for drawing this important information to my attention in time for it to be included in this volume.

and, after his friend became king in 1461, Castelnau was appointed seneschal of Guyenne, *grand chambellan* and *grand bouteiller*, and also served on the royal council.[2] His close involvement in administrative and diplomatic affairs at the time that Cousinot was writing, together with his access to Louis XI, would certainly have provided Castelnau with an opportunity to obtain a copy of *Pour ce que plusieurs*. This lost manuscript would seem to stand alongside surviving copies owned by Louis's sister, Jeanne de France (A), Jacques d'Armagnac, duke of Nemours (H), and administrators such as Cousinot (C) and Budé (O).[3]

---

[2] Pierre-Roger Gaussin, *Louis XI: un roi entre deux mondes* (Paris, 1976), pp. 127–128, and 'Les conseillers de Louis XI (1461–1483)', in Bernard Chevalier and Pierre Contamine (eds), *La France à la fin du XVe siècle: renouveau et apogée* (Paris, 1985), pp. 105–134, especially p. 114.

[3] See pp. 27–28 above.

INDEX